# Black Shoes and Blue Water

*CONTRIBUTIONS TO NAVAL HISTORY... NO. 6*

# Black Shoes and Blue Water

## Surface Warfare in the
## United States Navy, 1945–1975

*Malcolm Muir, Jr.*

Naval Historical Center
Department of the Navy
Washington, 1996

♾ The paper used in this publication meets the minimum
requirements of American National Standard for
Information Sciences—Permanence of Paper for Printed
Library Materials, ANSI Z39.48–1984.

**Library of Congress Cataloging-in-Publication Data**

Muir, Malcolm, 1943–
    Black shoes and blue water : surface warfare in the United Sates
Navy, 1945–1975 / Malcolm Muir, Jr.
      p.  cm. — (Contributions to naval history  ;  no. 6)
    Includes bibliographical references (p.   ) and index.
    ISBN 0–945274–31–9 (paper : alk. paper)
    1. United States.  Navy—History—20th century.  2. Warships—
United States—History—20th century.  3. Sea Power—History—20th
century.  4. United States—History, Naval—20th century.  I. Title.  II.
Series.
VA58.M85   1995
359'.00973—dc20                             95–2964

For sale by the U.S. Government Printing Office
Superintendent of Documents, Mail Stop: SSOP, Washington, DC 20402-9328

*To my wife, Carol*

# Contributions to Naval History Series

# The Author

Dr. Malcolm Muir, Jr., is professor of history and chair of the Department of History and Philosophy at Austin Peay State University. He is author of *The Iowa Class Battleships: Iowa, New Jersey, Missouri, and Wisconsin*, published by Blanford Press in 1987, and has written extensively for naval and military history journals. Dr. Muir earned his Ph.D. at Ohio State University in 1976. He resides in Clarksville, Tennessee, with his wife.

# Contents

# Illustrations

Photographs with NH and NHC numbers are held by the Naval Historical Center, Washington, DC 20374–5060; and those with 80–G, USA C, K, KN, and USN prefixes are held in the Still Pictures Branch, National Archives and Records Administration, College Park, MD 20740–6001.

# Foreword

Work on this study began in 1987–1988 when Professor Malcolm Muir, Jr., took leave from the Austin Peay State University in Clarksville, Tennessee, to become the first person to hold the Secretary of the Navy's Research Chair in Naval History. This appointment allowed Professor Muir to devote an uninterrupted year at the Naval Historical Center to writing a book on naval history.

Malcolm Muir's project now appears as the sixth volume in the Naval Historical Center's Contributions to Naval History series. The Contributions are concise studies addressing professional subjects of special interest to today's naval professionals. Professor Muir's account of the thirty-year development of surface warfare capabilities, especially within the Navy's cruiser and destroyer force, is a notable addition to that series. The author pays particular attention to the development of weapons, the evolution of sensors and command and control systems, and the institutional steps taken to professionalize the surface warfare community. This coverage allows us to understand the characteristics of a critical component of the United States Fleet that in the 1990s continues to be called upon by our nation's leaders to play multiple roles throughout the world.

Professor Muir faced a major challenge in addressing a subject that is large, complex, and sometimes controversial. For that reason, we are grateful to a number of surface warfare officers and historians who generously provided the author with their critical comments on earlier drafts of this history. Among these were Vice Admiral Henry C. Mustin, USN (Ret.), Captain Bernard D. Cole, USN, Rear Admiral Russell W. Gorman, USNR (Ret.), Norman Friedman, James R. Reckner, and Paul Stillwell. Reviewers from the Naval Historical Center's staff included former Director of Naval History Dean C. Allard, Edward J. Marolda, John C. Reilly, Jr., Commander Stephen R. Silverio, USN, and Captain Cletus F. Wise, USN. Despite the invaluable assistance provided by these experts, it should be understood that the views expressed in this history are solely those of Professor Muir and that the author's opinions do not necessarily reflect the position of the Departments of the Navy or Defense.

William S. Dudley
Director of Navy History

# Acknowledgments

A work of this nature is, by its essence, a collaborative project. I simply could not have written this study without the assistance of so many fellow historians and naval personnel, both civilian and in uniform. Friends and relatives gave invaluable moral and material backing.

First and foremost, let me thank those at the Naval Historical Center who helped me in so many different ways: Dr. Dean Allard, Dr. Ronald H. Spector, Captain Charles J. Smith, Dr. Edward J. Marolda, Dr. William S. Dudley, Bernard F. Cavalcante, John C. Reilly, Jr., Captain Rosario M. Rausa, Commander John Norton, Dr. Michael A. Palmer, Dr. Jeffrey Barlow, Charles R. Haberlein, Stanley Kalkus, Captain Ken Coskey, George W. Price III, Judith Short, Roy Grossnick, John Elliott, Regina Akers, Gordon Bowen-Hassel, Sandra Kay, Janice Bailey, Robert J. Cressman, Richard M. Walker, and Ella Nargele. For their painstaking work with the final manuscript, I am especially grateful to Sandy Doyle and Wendy Karppi.

At the Naval War College, I benefited from the aid of Captain Charles Chadbourne, Dr. Frank Uhlig, Jr., Dr. David Rosenberg, Captain Tim Somes, Captain Keith Stewart, Captain Jay Hurlbut, and Evelyn Cherpak.

Many officers and enlisted men gave their professional perspectives on various aspects of this study. Their memories supplemented archival sources, filled in gaps left by the destruction of documentary materials, added information that had never been written down, and gave a more personal flavor to the record. Although I have given credit in the bibliography and notes to all individuals who assisted in this way, I should, in fairness, highlight those who gave so generously of their time: Admirals James L. Holloway III, Stansfield Turner, and Elmo R. Zumwalt, Jr.; Vice Admirals Robert E. Adamson, Jr., James H. Doyle, David F. Emerson, Diego Hernandez, Gerald E. Miller, Henry C. Mustin, J. F. Parker, Frank W. Price, William Rowden, Frederick H. Schneider, Jr., Robert Walters, and Thomas R. Weschler; Rear Admirals Roland Guilbault and Mark W. Woods. Others whose aid was of special value included Captains William J. Manning, Robert C. Peniston, and Allan P. Slaff; Commanders James Stevens and Constantine Xefteris; Lieutenants Scott Hoffman, Frank Thorp, and W. Michael Tooker; FFCM (SW) Stephen Skelley; and FFCS (SW) James Schmitz.

Among fellow historians who inspired me in a variety of ways were Professors Carl Boyd, Preston J. Hubbard, Archer Jones, Allan R. Millet, and Spencer C. Tucker. I should also thank a number of colleagues at Austin Peay State University, my home institution in Clarksville, Tennessee, who helped me bring this project to fruition: Drs. John Butler, D'Ann Campbell, Richard P. Gildrie, James Nixon, and T. Howard Winn.

I would be remiss, too, were I not to mention the following individuals who rendered valuable assistance: Dorothy Goodis of the Center for Naval Analyses, Dr. Joseph Marchese of the David Taylor Research Center, Dr. Norman Polmar, Professor Jürgen Rohwer, William Seltzer, and Paul Stillwell of the U.S. Naval Institute. Naval Historical Center editors Sandra Doyle and Wendi Karppi deserve special recognition for their attention to editorial matters and photo selection.

And I am deeply grateful for the encouragement of my family, especially my father, Judge Malcolm Muir, and my mother-in-law, Helen W. Thornton. Most of all, I simply could not have finished this work without the unending support of my wife, Carol, who learned more about the recent U.S. Navy than she ever dreamed possible.

# Introduction

In the three decades following World War II, the surface warrior in the U.S. Navy was largely obscured by the brighter lights of the aviator and the submariner. Short of funds, saddled with obsolete equipment or with unreliable new technology, and facing a myriad of threats, the surface warrior was called upon to perform a bewildering variety of missions. The current slogan of surface warfare captures the challenge of the earlier Cold War period as well: "Up, Out, and Down."

An essential first task for this study was to define surface warfare. Were surface warriors all those who wore the black shoes that set certain officers apart from the aviators, who wore brown shoes? Is the term "surface warrior" broad enough then to embrace those in the amphibious, mine, and service forces?

Certainly the term does so today, and it has since 1975 when these formally separate entities were folded in with the cruiser and destroyer commands to make up the modern surface warfare community. However, this study concentrates on the thirty-year span after World War II, and the author will thus use the term "surface warfare" in the narrower sense to focus on the gun and missile ships, thereby regretfully cutting out the amphibious, mine, and service forces. They await their detailed treatment at other hands.*

This history will also touch only lightly on the operational performance of the surface navy during the era because that has been covered extensively in some fine monographs. Suffice it to say that the surface navy did its share to execute the foreign policy of the United States throughout the period, whether in cold war or hot. A highly visible emblem of America's power, the surface warship showed the flag, rescued American citizens and friendly foreign nationals from dangerous situations, enforced quarantines and blockades, and escorted merchantmen. In Korea and Vietnam, U.S. surface ships gave vital gunfire support to troops ashore and performed a host of other duties. Excellent detailed accounts of the operational side of the story are in print or in preparation; this study will examine operations insofar as they demonstrated the performance of the surface warrior and his equipment.

---

*For part of the mine warfare story, see Tamara Moser Melia, *"Damn the Torpedoes": A Short History of U.S. Naval Mine Countermeasures, 1777–1991* (Washington, 1991).

Similarly, the author will make no attempt to treat in exhaustive detail antisubmarine warfare. The "down"—the menace of the submarine—was a major problem for the entire Navy throughout these three decades. Indeed, surface line officers regarded the "down" at times as the most intractable of all their challenges, and this account will outline the dimensions of the problem and the principal countermeasures that the surface navy took. However, the complexities of the antisubmarine effort required a response across a broad naval spectrum to encompass patrol aircraft, specialized ASW carriers, attack submarines, and underwater barriers. The "down" deserves a specialized study of its own.

This work focuses most closely then on the "up and out"—that is, on the role played by the surface forces of the U.S. Navy in the maintenance of sea control against air and surface threats, as well as in the projection of power against strategic targets ashore. The study will follow a number of common threads through the three decades. One strand is the threat posed to the U.S. Navy's command of the sea by rival air and surface forces. From 1945 to 1975, the principal challenge came from the Soviet Union. That country followed a twisting path to sea power. At the end of World War II, the Soviet navy was composed of a poor assortment of worn-out surface ships—a negligible force in comparison with the all-conquering U.S. Navy. The Soviets quickly began construction of a large fleet of conservative ships better suited for conditions of the 1930s than of the 1950s. It was a force that American officers were confident they could handle with relative ease.

In mid-course, this ill-conceived Soviet program was abandoned for one which challenged Western sea control through technological innovation. Central to this strategy was the offsetting of the American asset of carrier aviation by the employment of the antiship missile. During the 1960s, the Soviets introduced a variety of these weapons and carried them on board a variety of platforms, including submarines and long-range aircraft. They also began the construction of innovative cruisers, destroyers, and patrol craft armed with these new weapons. Some of the smaller vessels they exported to satellite nations. Little noticed at first, the seriousness of these Soviet initiatives was dramatically highlighted when Egyptian patrol boats sank an Israeli destroyer with Soviet antiship missiles in 1967.

While the Soviet fleet was buying sea power on the cheap with these innovative new weapons, the U.S. surface forces were in serious decline. A common problem for top American naval planners during much of this period was the impending obsolescence of their huge fleet. Built during the later stages of World War II, American surface warships were all heading toward old age together. New construction could not begin to replace the war-built ships on a one-for-one basis. Modern ships, needing great volume for missiles and sensors, were much larger than their predecessors. A few were powered by nuclear engineering plants. These new surface warships were so expensive they were built only sporadically. A substantial number were begun in the late 1950s but a sad hiatus lasting eight years ensued from 1962 to 1970 when Congress ordered only two major surface vessels. By the beginning of the next decade, the U.S. Navy had so declined that some top surface warfare officers, such as Chief of Naval Operations Elmo R. Zumwalt, Jr., felt the United States would lose a conventional war with the Soviet navy. Fortunately, one of the finest destroyer designs of all time, the *Spruance* class, was coming to fruition. Ordered in large numbers, the *Spruance*s and their derivatives provided the platforms that helped maintain primacy in surface warfare for the U.S. Navy until the present.

A parallel thread running throughout the period is the serious difficulty the surface navy experienced in developing and deploying effective weapons on board its new warships. New Soviet jet aircraft and antiship missiles, especially those armed with nuclear devices, posed a severe challenge. The antiaircraft gun, already partially eclipsed in the closing stages of World War II by the kamikaze, was simply unable to destroy aerial intruders with certainty at adequate ranges. The surface navy turned to the guided missile for salvation but an ambitious program to develop three missiles of varying ranges ran well behind schedule and was hounded by grievous problems.

Moreover, the missile itself was only part of the solution to the aerial menace. Timely detection and classification of advanced aircraft presented an almost insoluble difficulty that only a true revolution in data processing could master. During this period, the surface navy led the way from grease pencil tracking aboard individual warships to the computer world, first with the Naval Tactical Data System and then with the Aegis combat system. The latter provided the single most important step in ensuring the survival of the surface vessel against complex aerial threats.

To the surprise of many, the gun survived during this period as a viable naval weapon. Dismissed by many observers as outdated, the gun would carve a niche for itself by providing terminal defense against missile attack. It would also remain the only economical means for surface ships to give continuous assistance to friendly forces ashore.

Supporting amphibious landings and carrier task forces were essential missions, but surface warriors also wanted to share in the Navy's offensive capabilities. To this end, they needed a long-range weapon that would enable them to strike effectively at enemy vessels and to project power far inland. Over the entire thirty-year period, they struggled to develop missiles to restore an offensive punch to their arm. Progress toward this goal was halting indeed. During the mid-1950s, the long-range cruise missile came tantalizingly close to realization, but just as this weapon was being deployed, it fell victim to budgetary stringencies. The expensive demands of the big carriers and the nuclear submarines took precedence and the funding. During the next two decades, the surface navy tried a variety of expedients to obtain a guided missile that could strike surface targets. The solution came only in the 1970s with two specialized missiles—Harpoon and Tomahawk—that restored to surface warriors their ability to hit hostile warships. In addition, the Tomahawk gave them a precision long-range strategic land-attack capability for the first time in history.

Surface sailors thought these weapons had arrived twenty years late and contrasted their lack of support with that accorded the aviators and the submariners. The shelving of the promising cruise missile technology in the 1950s simply confirmed for some in the surface line their feeling that surface warfare played third fiddle in the postwar Navy. An inevitable consequence of this perception was that many top graduates of the Naval Reserve Officer Training Corps and Annapolis elected the more glamorous and better paying warfare specialties. Even the top officers who chose surface warfare found their career paths constricted as most of the highest commands went to aviators and submariners. Conversely, failed aviators and submariners often built second careers in the surface line.

Another parallel thread common to this entire period is the drive by blackshoes for greater professionalization. In part, this ambition was expressed in a desire for pay and insignia equal to those accorded the other branches. The drive appeared elsewhere in surface warfare demands for tighter qualification standards and for more rigorous and formalized schooling in the surface warfare specialty. At the top levels of the Navy's administration, this goal expressed itself in the push by surface officers to gain equal representation with aviators and submariners in the Office of the Chief of Naval Operations. During the thirty years after World War II, headway toward all these goals proved halting, and reforms in personnel and organizational matters came in piecemeal fashion.

By 1975, surface warfare had made, by dint of painful effort, significant advances in specialized education, institutional voice, and professional reputation. These gains were paralleled by—and intertwined with—the blackshoe development of effective weapons, sensors, and ships against an ingenious foe. This then is the story of the decline and revival of the surface force—the oldest arm of the United States Navy.

# 1

# Sinking Fast:
# The Surface Navy, 1945–1950

World War II represented the great divide for the surface navy. Until that conflict, the lion's share of the U.S. Navy's budget went to the battleships, cruisers, and destroyers whose top officers made up the so-called Gun Club. These black-shoe officers dominated the Navy's principal decision-making body, the General Board, and such significant bureaus as the Bureau of Ships and the Bureau of Ordnance. But during the Pacific war, naval aviation seized the reins. The aircraft carrier with its longer reach supplanted the battleship as the arbiter of fleet actions; the aviators moved into dominant positions within the Navy's command structure.

This is not to say that the surface warrior did not play an important part in the victory at sea. U.S. battleships and cruisers engaged their counterparts on a number of significant occasions, especially during the Guadalcanal campaign and the Battle for Leyte Gulf. The destroyer enhanced its long-standing tradition as jack of all trades and master of many. And the larger gunnery ships gave valuable service in a number of roles: replenishing and repairing other ships in the fast carrier task forces, offering adequate flag space for fleet and force commanders, and turning their guns to support soldiers ashore and aircraft carriers against airborne attackers.

This last mission became increasingly difficult and important as enemy advances in technology and operating techniques bestowed increasing menace on aerial weapons in the later stages of the war. In the summer of 1943, the Germans began employing air-launched antiship missiles. Off Italy, these devices proved frighteningly effective when they badly damaged U.S. light cruiser *Savannah* (CL 42) and British battleship *Warspite* while sinking the new Italian battleship *Roma*. In the Pacific theater the following year, the Japanese introduced the kamikaze—essentially a big missile with human guidance. Although the kamikazes sank no large warships, they caused horrifying personnel casualties and sent to the bottom a great many smaller warships, especially unarmored destroyers. Too frequently, a kamikaze damaged by antiaircraft fire would continue on—"go ballistic"—into its target.

In response to the kamikaze, the U.S. Navy began work on two defenses particularly applicable to surface warships: better directed gunfire of larger caliber to smash up the attacking aircraft, and guided missiles that could intercept the enemy plane at a considerable distance from the task force.[1] Both initiatives were barely underway when the war ended. At V–J Day,

NH 95562

Light cruiser *Savannah* hit on No. 3 turret by a German FX–1400 glide-bomb off Salerno, Italy, 11 September 1943. Although the warhead exploded in the magazine, inrushing water saved the ship; 197 sailors died.

the Navy found itself in a most peculiar predicament. Its triumph in both oceans was so overwhelming that top budget cutters in the Truman administration began questioning the very existence of the service. In response, Navy spokesmen in September 1945 forecast for the service the broadest possible missions: protection of the homeland, maintenance of the Monroe Doctrine, and "commitments—not precise as to detail but clear in general form—of the US to preserve the peace of the world."[2] Naval leaders argued that these broad missions required a fleet of great size. In September 1945, Fleet Admiral Ernest J. King, in testimony before Congress, cited the Navy's experience at Okinawa as showing the variety of tasks and the numbers of ships and aircraft that the Navy would require in the future.[3]

Congressman Carl Vinson (D–Ga.), a longtime friend of the Navy, proposed that month to President Harry S. Truman a minimum postwar force of 37 fast aircraft carriers, 18 battleships, 82 cruisers, and 367 destroyers. The Army objected strenuously; the War Department noted that such a fleet would be five times larger than all the rest of the navies in the world combined, if the Royal Navy were discounted. A somewhat more realistic Navy proposal came from Secretary of the Navy James V. Forrestal, who suggested an active force of 15 fast carriers, 11 battleships, 49 cruisers, and 179

The Baker underwater detonation of Operation CROSSROADS on 25 July 1946.

destroyers. Whatever the differences in magnitude, both the Forrestal and Vinson proposals advanced a balanced navy with a very significant place for the traditional gun ships—the battleships, cruisers, and destroyers.[4]

The President would support neither plan. Determined to rein in deficit spending, Truman ordered defense funding slashed while relying increasingly on the U.S. nuclear monopoly to guarantee victory in the event of war. The Navy thus became involved in a savage contest for scarce funds with the Army, and after 1947, with its offspring, the Air Force. Following its successful employment of nuclear weapons, the Army Air Force claimed to have the answer to America's security needs. Spokesman for that service, General of the Army Henry H. Arnold, claimed in November 1945 that only heavy bombers would be able to lift the large nuclear weapons in the inventory.[5]

Nuclear weapons added major elements of uncertainty to the defense equation. Would the atomic bomb automatically give quick victory to the United States? Would it remain the sole possession of the strategic bombing forces, or would the Navy share in the nuclear strike mission? For how long would the weapon remain an American monopoly? All of these considerations were completely novel. Moreover, nuclear weapons represented not only an institutional challenge to the Navy. Some military analysts felt that they struck directly at the service's very existence. Airpower enthusi-

7

asts such as Alexander de Seversky pronounced the verdict that nuclear weapons had made navies obsolete.[6] Late in 1945 the House Committee on Naval Affairs dryly reported: "Some opinion has been expressed that the Navy is the principal casualty of the atomic bomb."[7]

Partly in response to such concerns, the Navy orchestrated tests at Bikini atoll in 1946.[8] Under the direction of ordnance expert Vice Admiral W. H. P. "Spike" Blandy, Operation CROSSROADS subjected over eighty warships loaded with over 10,000 pieces of equipment to two test shots, one an air burst and the other an underwater explosion. The results of this exercise, called "perhaps the most complicated laboratory set-up that has ever been undertaken," were reassuring to the Navy. True, the most heavily armored vessels succumbed to blast at very close range, but beyond three-quarters of a mile, even small craft escaped lethal damage. It appeared that, with open cruising formations, the U.S. Navy could operate in the nuclear age, especially if it were to develop effective long-range defenses.[9]

While nuclear weapons presented a distinctly new challenge, so did the nature of the emerging foreign threat. As World War II closed, Navy leaders, notably Secretary Forrestal and Admiral King, saw the Soviet Union as expansionist and antithetical to Western interests. With the Cold War intensifying, the Office of the Chief of Naval Operations (OPNAV) postulated that Soviet intentions were to dominate Europe and Asia, seize control of Great Britain, and then move against the United States. Soviet tactical air and ground forces were so powerful that one American scenario had the Soviet flag in the Pyrenees within seventy days of the outbreak of war.[10] Given these grim prospects, the U.S. Government forged increasingly firm bonds to friendly countries in Europe with the Truman Doctrine and a containment policy designed to prevent further Communist expansion. By late 1947, most observers saw the United States as linked permanently to the defense of western Europe, a commitment codified in 1949 through the formation of the North Atlantic Treaty Organization (NATO).

Some defense planners wondered whether the Navy would be of much value in a conflict with the Soviets. As one of the Navy's strongest congressional supporters, Senator David I. Walsh (D–Mass.), noted in July 1945, the USSR "will not be in a position to employ sea power effectively and is not particularly vulnerable to it."[11] Top Navy officers disagreed. They anticipated that the Soviet navy would play an essential role an offensive by safeguarding the coasts of the homeland, protecting the flanks of the advancing Red Army, and striking at Western seaborne communications.[12]

In response to such concerns, three top officers, Rear Admirals Arthur W. Radford and Blandy and Vice Admiral Harry W. Hill helped mold in October 1945 the Navy's Basic Post War Plan Number 1. Blandy and Hill proposed an offensive force built around twelve carriers, to be supported by five battleships and thirty-one cruisers. Radford, an aviator assigned to the

Bureau of Aeronautics at its inception in 1921, gave more weight to the aviation component and wrote separately to King, "I conclude that the battleship is obsolescent. Its usefulness, aside from amphibious support, does not justify its retention in numbers in the active postwar fleet where economy in men and money is a consideration."[13] Radford called for only one battleship on active duty as an experimental vessel. The fleet, he said, should be built around at least twenty fleet carriers.[14]

Admiral Chester W. Nimitz relieved King as Chief of Naval Operations in December 1945. In early 1946, the new CNO testified before Congress that the nation needed carriers "as the only means of providing a highly effective mobile tactical air force at sea or in coastal areas distant from our own prepared air bases...." Nimitz's statement went on to relegate surface warships to a secondary role: "Surface fighting ships [are needed] to support the amphibious forces and carrier forces and to furnish gunfire support for amphibious landings."[15]

This force structure, in which surface warships played a distinct second fiddle, represented the triumph of the aircraft carrier. With its versatility, long range, and striking power, the carrier was clearly the premier naval weapon; only the carrier had the reach to weaken a Soviet drive. In September 1945, Congressman Vinson proclaimed bluntly: "Let there be no mistake about the role of air power and carriers in the proposed postwar Navy. The fleet will be built around . . . the carrier."[16]

Aviators were gaining influence at all levels in the Navy. The war had almost doubled the proportion of officers who were aviators. In 1941, 16 percent of regular line officers and 12 percent of flag officers were aviators; by 1945, the figures were 23 percent and 27 percent respectively. This trend accelerated in the postwar period when, at Forrestal's initiative, Congress mandated a lower retirement age and enlarged the proportion of officers on the Navy's personnel rosters. The result was a marked increase in aviators reaching flag rank. By October 1949, of the twenty-two vice admirals on active duty, ten were aviators. Although only one of the five full admirals, Radford, wore wings, the Navy gained its first aviator CNO, the brilliant Admiral Forrest P. Sherman, in November of that year.[17]

Inevitably, more and more of the plum assignments went to aviators. Forrestal said forthrightly in December 1945, "The leading commands of the Navy will in time be occupied by men who deal with air in one form or another."[18] Within one year, both the Atlantic and Pacific Fleets were commanded by aviators, as were several key slots in OPNAV and even in the General Board and the Bureau of Ordnance, both bastions of the surface line.[19] Admittedly, these changes were evolutionary; blackshoes continued to hold important positions. Admiral Louis E. Denfeld, succeeding Nimitz as CNO in November 1945, was a surface warfare officer. Spike Blandy, the ordnance specialist, became Deputy Chief of Naval Operations (DCNO) for Special Weapons (OP–06) with responsibility for the Navy's nuclear research and certain guided missile programs. Blandy, in the words of one historian, "undoubtedly helped both his own image and that of the navy when he felicitously called Op–06 the 'Buck Rogers Division' of the navy." [20]

Within the Navy's administrative structure, aviation's influence was magnified by an anomaly in the composition of OPNAV. Under the CNO were five deputy chiefs. Four of these administered functional posts (Personnel, Administration, Naval Operations, and Logistics); the fifth was the Deputy Chief of Naval Operations for Air. Thus, aviation was the only one of the three platform communities, or "unions" (aviation, submarines, surface warfare), that held this type of special representation in the top counsels of the Navy. "A sort of little autonomous empire within the naval organization," [21] BUAER even controlled its own training—supposedly a function of Naval Personnel. Late in World War II, CNO King had apparently proposed giving equal voice to surface warfare and to submarines, but his reorganization efforts were blocked by Forrestal. Not until 1971 would King's change be implemented. [22]

Farther down the chain, aviation's attractions beckoned as carriers supplanted the battleship as the backbone of the fleet. By law since the 1920s, the commanding officers of carriers had to be aviators. Thus, because most of the big gunships were headed for retirement, surface line officers found less opportunity to command the type of ship necessary to move up to flag rank. [23]

With aviation seeming the fast track to the top, many ambitious junior officers elected to enroll in flight training at Pensacola, in sharp contrast to the prewar period when Annapolis graduates were advised to "get behind the big guns and stay there." [24] In 1939, the Navy had been so short on pilots that ensigns were forced to take the flight physical. Those who passed often went to great lengths to avoid aviation, and of the top ten graduates of the Naval Academy class that year, one chose aviation; one, submarines; and eight, the Postgraduate School leading to membership in the Gun Club. [25]

Symptomatic of the changes taking place over the next five years was the early career of a future CNO, James L. Holloway III. A graduate of the class of 1942, he was serving in the Pacific on board destroyers in 1944 when he received a letter from his father, the commanding officer of *Iowa* (BB 61), one of the Navy's newest battleships. The elder Holloway opined, "Carrier aviation is clearly the wave of the future. I urge you not to delay in putting in for flight training." Holloway earned his wings at Pensacola in 1946. [26]

The surface navy had no Pensacola. Training took place on board ship on an ad hoc basis—a system sometimes called "makee-learn." This method had worked well enough before World War II when it was relatively simple for an officer to become well indoctrinated in all branches of naval warfare. The state of the art remained essentially constant for many years; techniques, once learned, were applicable for a long time. It was not uncommon for an officer to serve in varied billets in aircraft carriers, battleships, cruisers, oilers, and supply ships, finding that, upon ultimately assuming command of a destroyer, everything he had learned during the preceding years was still current and useful. Nothing had changed.[27] The war reinforced the validity of the makee-learn method of training, because personnel transfers were infrequent, drill was constant, and the ship's company became thoroughly conversant with their jobs.[28]

In the postwar period, however, surface warships suffered from rapid personnel turnover, especially in leadership positions. Most surface line officers had a college degree, unlike the many aviators who had been accepted into wartime programs without even a high school diploma. The surface officers thus found themselves, as a rule, better educated but lower paid than their aviator counterparts who received a flight bonus. Experienced black-shoe officers left the service in large numbers.[29]

Inevitably, the rivalry between the branches, while usually good-natured, took on the occasional edge. In February 1950, Secretary of the Navy Francis P. Matthews tried to deemphasize the intramural competition among the unions within the Navy by forbidding the use of terms like "blackshoe" and "airedale." His lack of success is obvious given the continued prevalence of these nicknames within the Navy today.[30]

Inevitably, too, the changing trends in the fleet percolated down to the U.S. Naval Academy. The institution had offered aeronautics as early as 1920. In August 1945, the first aviator to be superintendent, Vice Admiral Aubrey W. Fitch, took the helm. In December of that year, naval aviation gained autonomous status as a separate academic department. All midshipmen after the war took basic work in aviation, submarine, and surface ship duties. Upon graduation, most newly commissioned officers chose one of these three career paths. As one observer pointed out, "Generally, these classmates do not meet again on grounds of common professional interest until the grade of Captain or flag rank, and sometimes never."[31]

Increasingly, the top half of the senior class opted for aviation or submarines.[32] The leading midshipman in the class of 1946, Stansfield Turner, did choose the surface warfare branch and explained in retrospect, "I looked on aviation more as an individual fighting thing. That's an oversimplification, but...an ensign [in surface warfare] leads a division, whereas an ensign in aviation, he goes out and does his thing."[33] Turner was an exception, however. By 1949, one prominent officer (a submariner) cautioned in the Naval Institute *Proceedings*: "The idea that the only roads to success are submarines and aviation is bad for the Navy and bad for the individual."[34]

At the top rung of the Navy's educational ladder, aviation was also taking on an increasingly important role. Assuming command of the Naval War College at Newport, Rhode Island, in 1946 was an officer with the perfect credentials to overhaul the curriculum: Admiral Raymond A. Spruance, the black-shoe victor at Midway. As his biographer has remarked, "Spruance knew that battleship-oriented officers had dominated the prewar college, that naval aviators had shunned the college, and that this separateness had generated a hostility between the two branches that had hurt the Navy during the war." [35] Spruance ordained a curriculum incorporating the latest in aviation, atomic energy, guided missiles, and electronics as well as a broader study of national security matters. [36]

As the Navy's budget shrank, the service was forced to make hard choices regarding its allocations of money. Complicating these internal deliberations over force structure were the challenges posed by such radical new weapons technologies as high-speed submarines, guided weapons, and jet aircraft. One class of officers at the Naval War College heard their July 1946 session prefaced: "During your course of instruction you will be given atomic bombs, guided missiles and super performance torpedoes to work with in your problems. In their use you will be unhampered by doctrine, because there isn't any." [37] In confronting these dangers, the Navy invested scarce dollars into research and development.

The meager funds available for new ship construction programs mirrored these technological uncertainties. Following Forrestal's elevation in 1947 as the first Secretary of Defense, Secretary of the Navy John L. Sullivan and his successor, Francis Matthews, put surface warfare on short rations. Submariners received substantial support for their guided missile efforts, and Captain Hyman G. Rickover won permission to begin development of nuclear propulsion for the undersea craft. The aviators also seemed to gain a major victory. Following early postwar initiatives by Forrestal and Nimitz, the brownshoes succeeded in obtaining permission in 1948 to formulate a strategic nuclear strike role for their aircraft and the promise of a giant new carrier, *United States* (CVA 58), to operate the requisite large bombers. Money came from the cancellation of several other projects, including surface ship conversions. [38]

Conventional naval vessels fared poorly in the last half of the decade. Officers watched their huge 1945 fleet evaporate as the budget cutters sent the majority of its warships to the reserve fleet, the scrapyards, or nuclear test sites. Over 2,000 ships were mothballed. One officer reflected, "the question mostly was what should we keep rather than what should we build." [39] Some new ships, such as heavy cruiser *Fall River* (CA 131), were laid up after a single tour of duty; in 1946 light cruiser *Galveston* (CL 93) went straight from the builder's yard to the reserve fleet without benefit of a commissioning ceremony. Of course if World War III were to be "an all-out nuclear blitz," [40] these cutbacks in conventional forces only made good sense.

Naturally, a shrinking fleet led to serious intramural fights as to its composition. Given the carrier's preeminence in the postwar Navy, major sur-

NH 93207

*Los Angeles* (CA 135), a *Baltimore*-class heavy cruiser, 21 March 1951.

face combatants were bound to suffer severely from the budget axe. With shore bombardment their sole surviving mission, all thirteen old battleships went to the breakers or into mothballs within a year following V–J Day. Surface warfare officers hoped to keep at least some of the fast battleships in commission. Not one of these was older than five years; their proponents argued their value for shore bombardment, antiaircraft defense, logistic support, and surface gunfire. But their advocates were bucking the tide, not only of hard financial reality, but of public perception. Spike Blandy admitted in a 1946 press interview that the very term "battleship admiral" was pejorative and a "generic term for all admirals who are too slow to recognize new developments."[41] In 1947, the four *South Dakota*s were mothballed, as were the two *North Carolina*s.[42]

By that year, only the four *Iowa*s flew their commissioning pennants. In many respects the finest battleships ever constructed, officers who served on board described them as "wonderful" and "superb."[43] The *Iowa*s had shown during the last stages of the Pacific war that they could render invaluable support for the fast carriers. They were tough ships; the Navy es-

13

timated that they could sustain up to one hundred heavy-caliber shell hits before sinking. And they had a certain "presence" that could be most valuable as a symbol of American might. For instance, the 1946 visit of *Missouri* (BB 63), reportedly at the suggestion of Forrest Sherman, to the Mediterranean was emblematic of the U.S. intent to make its presence felt in that tense region. Initially, Forrestal wanted to keep the *Iowa*s in the fleet, but by 1948, Navy planners strapped for funds projected the retirement of all four by 1950. Three did not last even that long; in 1949, *Missouri* remained the sole American battleship on active duty, sailing with a reduced complement as a training ship. In times of imploding budgets, the manning requirements of the battleships were a fatal drawback to keeping them in commission. With a full suite of 130 light antiaircraft guns, an *Iowa* required a total complement of nearly 2,800 men.[44]

The staffing differential alone gave cruisers a brighter future in the Navy's planning. A *Baltimore*-class heavy cruiser required only 1,100 sailors, and a *Cleveland*-class light cruiser, 1,000. With the battleship on its way out, planners saw significant missions for cruisers, especially if the Soviets developed atomic bombs. Nuclear weapons would force carrier task groups to disperse, leaving cruisers to screen against enemy surface raiders and to carry out long-range scouting in bad weather. By 1948, a typical fast carrier group was comprised of three carriers escorted by six cruisers and sixteen destroyers. With their ample spaces and communications equipment, certain heavy cruisers, such as *Saint Paul* (CA 73), frequently served as fleet flagships. Helping perform this function was the replacement of the catapult floatplanes with helicopters at the end of the decade. And with the battleship gun absent, the cruisers would also provide a "heavy" shore bombardment capability.[45]

The late war cruisers, whether heavy or light, shared certain virtues and defects. Their machinery plants of the tried-and-true 650-pound variety were reliable but labor intensive. With twin rudders and four screws, the cruisers handled exceptionally well, a reputation fondly remembered by many of their sailors in later years. For instance, Frederick H. Schneider, Jr., commanding officer of *Saint Paul* in 1960, took the *Baltimore*-class cruiser 45 miles up the difficult winding Saigon River using haystacks and outhouses as navigational aids. Shortly thereafter, *Saint Paul* "navigated the narrow, tricky Shimonoseki Strait at night and then ran the entire length of the Inland Sea, shooting the rapids off Takamatsu like we were a kayak. (God help us if we ever had a steering casualty). We could see the rocks close aboard the ship on both sides."[46] The war-built cruisers displayed a few defects, the most notable being their low and unflared bows. When steaming into rough head seas, the ships took great quantities of green water aboard, a trait shared with contemporary destroyers and even with the *Iowa*s.[47]

Practice firing the 5"/38 on board *Gainard* (DD 706), an *Allen M. Sumner*-class destroyer, off Newport, Rhode Island.

NHC L–File

The Navy in 1948 hoped to keep thirty cruisers in service with forty in reserve by 1950, but these figures proved too optimistic. A count for the President in March 1948 showed that the active cruiser force numbered only twenty-three fully operational ships (four heavy, fifteen light, and four antiaircraft cruisers) with four more ships immobilized or capable of only limited duty because of personnel shortages.[48]

Central to any balanced fleet was the destroyer. Nicknamed "tin cans" or "small boys," destroyers had carried out a myriad of missions during the war: plane guard duty, close support for amphibious forces, torpedo and gun attack against surface opponents, and radar picket patrol for the carrier task forces. Destroyers had shown their usefulness in countering two threats emerging late in the war: the kamikaze and the high-speed submarine. In 1948, the surface navy asked for 192 active-duty destroyers. Funding dictated a different picture: 82 ships fully operational with 52 more hobbling for lack of personnel.[49]

If the active destroyers were few in number, at least they were modern ships. Virtually all were less than five years old and became the *Fletcher*, *Allen M. Sumner*, and *Gearing* classes. Armed with 5"/38s, their split, 650-pound engineering plants gave both reliability and excellent damage control characteristics. On the debit side, they were small and very cramped. With air conditioning in only a few spaces, a tropical tour tested all on board. As more commodious ships entered the fleet in the 1950s, sailors regarded service in the older destroyers as a real hardship. One officer complained to the CNO in 1962, "In the World War II ships, creature comfort is positively non existent. The essential element of privacy, so important to human dignity, is almost wholly lacking."[50] The ships gave a rough ride; the heavy armament forward on the last two classes caused them to slam even in modest seas. Serious storms, such as the typhoon that hit *Agerholm* (DD 826) in 1970, caused sailors to fear for their lives. Despite their drawbacks, some of the World War II destroyers would serve over thirty years—well beyond their allotted span.[51] An officer who commanded them later characterized the ships as "like Model T Fords, very reliable for their age and simplicity."[52]

To conduct antisubmarine warfare (ASW), the destroyer force in World War II had been augmented by the smaller, slower destroyer escort. At V–J Day, the Navy counted 362 in commission, but they seemed too slow to cope with the fast submarines coming into the Soviet navy. By 1948, only six destroyer escorts remained operational, with six more capable of limited service.[53]

The active surface warships of all classes led busy lives in the postwar world. Cruisers and destroyers supported occupation forces in Japan by patrolling for contraband smugglers. Surface ships evacuated U.S. nationals from the Chinese mainland on the eve of the Communist takeover. The warships made goodwill tours to every ocean.[54]

And all this on a shoestring. So few large gunships remained in commission in the entire Navy that type commands were merged. With the permanent establishment of the Sixth Fleet in the Mediterranean in 1948 and the Seventh Fleet in the Pacific in 1949 came much longer deployments than before World War II. Sheer lack of personnel drove the efficiency of the warships well below wartime standards. The most experienced officers often went ashore after years of arduous wartime duty: one officer in 1947 received his first shore assignment since his graduation from the Naval Academy in 1939.[55] Given the lack of seasoned personnel, even a routine evolution could turn into "a watch standing ordeal."[56] Exercises were reduced in number or in difficulty in order to compensate.[57] One report sounded a plaintive note: "When . . . ammunition is available, it would be desirable to conduct actual firings as part of these exercises."[58]

If ships and men were scarce, so too was information about the most probable enemy—the Soviet Union. The Office of Naval Intelligence (ONI) was charged with briefing the CNO and his staff about the Soviet navy. Early in the Cold War era, ONI often had a difficult time peering behind the Iron Curtain. Officers at the Naval War College complained in 1948, "Information on the exact composition and location of the major units of PURPLE [Soviet] naval forces is meager." But by the early part of the

1950s, the picture ONI provided of Soviet operating forces, if not of construction programs, came into sharper focus.[59]

The most menacing Soviet maritime weapon was the submarine. ONI anticipated that the Soviets, having captured advanced German submarines, would build large numbers of such craft. One 1946 ONI estimate predicted the Soviets to have 300 of these submarines in service by 1950. Looking at this dire scenario, Admiral Nimitz wrote in a secret report in early 1946, "our present antisubmarine forces will be unable to cope with the submarine of the future with the same degree of effectiveness as attained in the past war."[60] In 1948, the Soviets announced publicly their intention to construct a submarine fleet of 1,200 vessels by 1965. A possible Soviet version of the German Type XXI was particularly worrisome; in 1950 ONI admitted that countering this high-speed boat exceeded U.S. Navy capabilities.

Exercises reinforced this gloomy outlook. U.S. surface officers found through experience just how difficult it was to combat modern, well-handled submarines. For example, during one 1948 exercise in the western Pacific, U.S. submarine *Segundo* (SS 398)

> experienced no difficulty in making and holding radar contact on the task force and made a number of excellent attacks, both day and night, in extremely limited visibility, including one against the task force while it was in ready formation with eccentric circular screen zigzagging out-of-phase with the cruisers.... On the anti-submarine side, on no occasion was sonar contact obtained by a destroyer before the *Segundo* released her firing signals, and in most cases destroyers were unable to make or hold contact even after the signals had accurately marked the submarine position.[61]

The commander of a destroyer task group in 1947 concluded after a similar experience that even fast naval forces would require continuous protection against submarines. Much slower merchant convoys would be even tougher to defend.[62]

Surface warfare specialists at sea and at Newport spent much of their time grappling with this threat to the oceanic lifelines. Strategists proposed taking the war to the source by attacking Soviet submarines in their lairs. On the technological side, new weapons and sensors, especially homing torpedoes and improved sound gear, held promise. An experimental projector dubbed Weapon A (Alfa or Able) which fired 12.75-inch ASW rockets was hurried into production. Even more ambitious was the Grebe, a small missile designed to carry a torpedo up to 20 miles from its launching ship.[63]

The standard ship sonar mounted on the hull, with a range of less than a mile, needed dramatic improvement. It suffered from serious interference if the destroyer was moving quickly or pitching badly. Varying temperature and salinity layers in the ocean could baffle the best sonar operator, whose job was made even more difficult by whales, wrecks, schools of fish and other such false targets. In 1946, the new destroyer *Witek* (DD 848) was committed to antisubmarine trials and reclassified EDD 848. The ship tested the sound gear from the surrendered German cruiser *Prinz Eugen*. Of even greater moment were the experiments conducted by the Naval Research Laboratory with a dunking sonar, wherein the transducer was lowered deep into the ocean. In 1947, this concept was tested on board ship and in the next year from a helicopter. Operational deployment of the promising new technology lay a decade away, however.[64]

The Navy needed better ASW ships as well as weaponry. Secretary Sullivan diverted scarce funds to build a specialized ASW cruiser, *Norfolk* (CLK 1), laid down in 1949 and entering service in 1953 (for details, see Chapter 2). A large vessel, she was far too expensive to duplicate, let alone produce in quantity. The Navy would have to make do with the ships left in its massive inventory from World War II. War with the Soviets might last eight or more years, according to some Navy projections, allowing for mobilization along the lines of the World War II experience. Accordingly, to counter large numbers of Soviet Type XXIs, the Navy converted eighteen *Fletcher*- and fifteen *Gearing*-class destroyers as prototypes (reclassified DDE) to carry advanced antisubmarine equipment, including Weapon A.[65] By 1950, naval intelligence concluded that the Soviets were not turning out advanced submarines in the great numbers originally feared. Consequently, the Navy initiated a program of continuous improvement to the destroyers in service rather than the large-scale conversion of mothballed ships. Development of the Grebe was also canceled.[66]

In contrast to the submarine threat, American naval planners were much more confident of the Navy's ability to readily defeat any Soviet surface force. Part of this assurance lay in the Navy's perception that the record of Soviet battleships, cruisers, and destroyers in World War II had been mediocre at best. ONI circulated an assessment by a group of German experts who found the record of the Soviets at sea in both world wars to be one of "striking failure."[67] In fact, American officers in the years immediately after World War II were almost dismissive of the Soviet surface force. The Soviet fleet of the period possessed only a small number of modern ships; a 1950 American estimate counted the Soviet strength at three battleships, nine heavy cruisers, three light cruisers, and fifty-one destroyers scattered among the four major Soviet fleets. There were no aircraft carriers.[68] The battleships in service were two czarist relics and an Italian prize of marginal utility. At best, these vessels might be of value for coastal bombardment purposes. Powerful Soviet battleships begun in the late 1930s had been wrecked on the ways by the retreating Wehrmacht. Wargamers at Newport postulating a Soviet attempt to seize Iceland noted in 1948, "no modern major [enemy] surface units are anticipated as PURPLE [the USSR] stopped all such construction in 1946 and concentrated on the building of submarines."[69]

U.S. naval officers briefly considered the possibility that the Soviets might build one or more battleships armed with missiles copied from the German V–1, and the Naval War College sometimes included such notional ships in its scenarios.[70] But by 1950, the Office of Naval Intelligence felt confident in saying: "Despite Soviet official pronouncements to the contrary, there is as yet little evidence of interest in capital ships. In fact since the Russo-Japanese war there has been an unmistakable trend away from the capital ship to the submarine."[71]

ONI was, in actuality, missing a major Soviet initiative. Soviet leaders began planning new big ships during the war and in 1949 laid down a "heavy cruiser" of 38,420 tons, the *Stalingrad*, at Nikolaev. The next year, a yard in Leningrad commenced a sister ship named *Moskva*. These ships were scheduled for completion by the end of the 1950s, but in 1954 the Soviet leadership stopped all large warship construction. At that time, *Stalingrad* was already in the water, and progress on *Moskva* was almost as advanced. Not until 1960 did ONI record in its publications the existence of these sizable Soviet vessels when the agency noted, "There is some evidence that two of a programmed four to six 'heavy cruisers' designated *Stalingrad* Class, had also been laid down, one at Nikolaev and one in Leningrad. Although called 'heavy cruisers' by the Soviets, these were to have been 44,000-ton ships armed with twelve 10- or 12-inch guns."[72]

In the immediate postwar period, ONI could paint a far clearer picture of those Soviet warships in commission. The best of these were the cruisers of the *Kirov* and *Chapaev* classes. Designed by the Italians prior to the war, the vessels stressed speed and, to a lesser extent, firepower at the expense of protection and range. Officers at the Naval War College in 1950 assessed the two classes as "modern and formidable."[73] ONI agreed:

> Soviet high-speed modern cruisers, some of them armed with 7.1-inch guns in three triple turrets, are the most formidable units of the fleet. These cruisers should be on paper at least, superior to any United States light cruisers but inferior to any United States heavy cruisers. They should, because of their speed (designed 37 knots), be capable of avoiding an engagement with any United States warship of greater fire power. Of low endurance these vessels were obviously designed for local defensive operations. This is apparent also from their absence from the Northern Fleet whose surface vessels are strategically located for offensive operations.[74]

On the broad oceans then, the Soviet surface forces posed little threat. In a 1948 forecast by the Naval War College concerning Soviet initiatives over the coming decade, officers concluded:

> The Russian naval effort will be predominantly, almost exclusively, subma-
> rine.... Emphasis on a well-rounded fleet will not occur until preparation
> for further operations against the Western Hemisphere after consolidation
> in Europe and the Middle East.... The pattern of warfare at sea will be
> similar to that of WWII with the exception that surface action will be rele-
> gated to a minor role, possibly only in the polar fringes or under conditions
> of reduced visibility.[75]

The Soviet weakness in surface ships meant that the U.S. Navy would
not need to escort convoys with anything larger than destroyers. In the
competition for defense monies, the other services took note of the slight
Soviet surface threat. For example, Army Chief of Staff Omar Bradley, in
testimony before the House Armed Services Committee, pointedly remarked that the Soviets and their satellites "have tremendous land forces
and tactical aviation, but their surface navy is negligible."[76]

Interestingly, the Royal Navy was not so sanguine about the danger
posed by Soviet cruisers acting as raiders. British naval aviators considered these fast ships as difficult targets, and the 1948 Fleet Air Arm
handbook suggested that two or three squadrons of carrier aircraft would
be required to cripple one cruiser. To combat these Soviet vessels, the
British began work on a number of specialized antiship weapons, including some ship-launched missiles. The Royal Navy also included 6-inch
guns on its new *Lion*-class cruisers largely to counter the armament of
their Soviet counterparts.[77]

Given the American perception that the Soviet surface threat was insignificant, the U.S. Navy abandoned more than its traditional reliance on
the big gunship. For decades, American planners had focused on the Pacific.
Now, wargamers at Newport postulated that the Atlantic Fleet would do
most of the fighting in a war with the Soviets. In one 1948 game at the
Naval War College, all large surface ships were deployed in the Atlantic, reflecting actual fleet dispositions. Beginning in 1946, partly at the urging of
Forrestal, the Navy had redeployed the bulk of its forces to the Atlantic,
and then in 1948 established the Sixth Fleet in the Mediterranean. The
western Pacific was almost abandoned. In 1948, the Soviet naval forces at
Vladivostok and Petropavlovsk were stronger on paper than the Far Eastern fleet headquartered in Japan. Each side had four cruisers, but the
twelve American destroyers were slightly outnumbered by their Soviet
counterparts. Neither side possessed an aircraft carrier. Early in 1950, only
one heavy cruiser and eight destroyers remained in that American Far
Eastern squadron, but it had been reinforced with one aircraft carrier.[78]

The American spotlight on the Atlantic lasted for almost two decades, intensifying after the formation of NATO in 1949. In consequence, the Atlantic
commands wielded significantly more influence on surface ship doctrine, design, and weapons development than did their Pacific counterparts. Until

1962, the principal surface warships operating in the Atlantic fell under one of two commands, Cruiser Force, U.S. Atlantic Fleet or Destroyer Force, U.S. Atlantic Fleet. In contrast, the Pacific Fleet in 1949 merged the two commands into the Cruiser Destroyer Force, Pacific Fleet (CRUDESPAC).[79]

With the Soviet submarine threat less intimidating than originally feared, Navy planners concentrated increasingly on the aerial menace. The Soviet air force was huge. One Navy Department estimate in 1948 placed 3,000 Soviet aircraft in the Far East—which at this time was a secondary theater. Many Soviet planes were, of course, fighters, but large numbers were attack planes armed with bombs. American officers feared that the Soviets might develop air-launched antiship missiles and frequently included these in war game scenarios and exercises. In fact, officers at the Naval War College thought it conceivable that Stalin's fliers might deliberately adopt suicide tactics, given the lethal record compiled by the kamikazes. Game rules referred to suicide aircraft as "guided missiles." Newport officers calculated their chances of hitting a large naval vessel at 45 percent and a destroyer at 30 percent—six times the success rate awarded a true guided missile, or "pilotless aircraft." Damage from a suicide aircraft hit equaled that from a 500-pound bomb.[80]

The Soviet readiness to use kamikazes might be questioned; most assuredly they were hard at work on producing antiship missiles. After all, they had captured the German Hs 293 and the FX 1400—two weapons which were frightening enough without further development. Secretary of Defense Forrestal worriedly admitted before Air Force Chief of Staff Hoyt S. Vandenberg in July 1948 to "serious misgivings about the capacity of the heavy ship to survive" in the face of such weapons.[81] Still, Forrestal added that he thought the perfection of guided missiles lay five to ten years in the future. If so, the Navy might have the necessary margin to develop the means to destroy enemy aircraft at long ranges.[82]

Obviously, the carrier's combat air patrol (CAP) would provide the first line of defense. Inner defenses were also essential to guard against "leakers" and in times of foul weather when CAP fighters would find operations difficult. To provide the close-in defenses, the *Worcester-* and *Des Moines-*class cruisers still under construction at V–J Day might prove of value against Soviet bombers. Although these ships had been designed largely to defeat threats that no longer existed, some officers thought they could be profitably employed against jet aircraft through imaginative use of their armament systems.[83]

Light cruisers *Worcester* (CL 144) and *Roanoke* (CL 145) had evolved from a pre-Pearl Harbor design intended to provide the battle fleet with a defense against heavy, high-altitude bombers. With twelve 6-inch guns elevating to 78 degrees, these ships could shoot 100-pound projectiles to a ceiling of 51,200 feet. Early tests with the weapons were so promising that designers contemplated a three-gun, 6-inch turret with a rate of fire of twenty-five rounds per minute. Existing light cruisers and the incomplete battleship *Kentucky* (BB 66) would be rebuilt to carry the piece. However, the 6-inch antiaircraft turret proved disappointingly unreliable in actual operation. *Worcester* and *Roanoke* themselves were handsome and maneuverable, but with their low freeboard, they were wet. The last of a long line of 6-inch gun cruisers, they remained in commission for hardly a decade before retiring in 1958.[84]

Oddly, the Navy got a much better return from the *Des Moines*-class heavy cruisers, meant with their rapid-fire 8-inch gun turrets to combat Japanese surface units. At almost 21,000 tons full load, *Des Moines* (CA 134), *Salem* (CA 139), and *Newport News* (CA 148) were the largest and most advanced heavy cruisers ever constructed by any power. Laid down in 1945, the class featured thick armored bulkheads for protection against antiship missiles. Their designated missions included "light cruiser destruction, commerce raiding, screening, reconnaissance, bombardment, and [serving] as a component of a task force subject to air and torpedo menace."[85]

Their main armament, although subject to some turret train roughness, offered greatly improved rapidity of fire over earlier heavy cruisers. Exercises demonstrated the potency of the new ships in surface actions. With automatic handling of the heavy projectiles allowing for the remarkable sustained rate of fire of ten rounds per minute (triple that of earlier 8-inch guns) and with a dedicated radar supplementing optical sights in the turret, the new gun seemed to hold great promise for antiaircraft purposes. As soon as the *Des Moines* cruisers were commissioned, they went to the Operational Development Force (OPDEVFOR). In 1949, *Newport News* did extensive firing against F6F drones, "using all promising methods of control" with "gratifying" results.[86] Unfortunately, a crushing disadvantage to the 8-inch as an antiaircraft weapon was its inability to elevate beyond 41 degrees. Against a low-level attack, the guns could do good work, but as one of their officers noted, "Just about the time that the aircraft was really getting to be within your range band, that's when you hit the stops in elevation."[87]

The three cruisers spent much of their careers as division flagships for which service they were particularly suited given their seaworthiness, commodious flag quarters, air conditioning, and high speed. When employed as fleet flagships, however, they were "stretched to the outside limit," in the words of one of their officers.[88] Crowding notwithstanding, *Salem* was to make seven deployments in the 1950s flying the flag of Sixth Fleet in the Mediterranean. *Des Moines* and *Salem* went into reserve at the end of the 1950s and were not stricken from the Navy's roster until 1991. *Newport News* stayed on active duty until 1975 as the last all-gun cruiser in the U.S. Navy. The ships are remembered with affection. One officer commented in retrospect, "The eight-inch [cruiser] was simply very rugged and dependable. The ship itself was magnificent. I think everyone loved those ships." [89]

The end of World War II caught two other big gunships in the late stages of construction: battleship *Kentucky* and large cruiser *Hawaii* (CB 3). With their big hulls and high speed, both seemed ideal for completion with advanced weapons suites. One plan in December 1945 anticipated that *Kentucky* would carry the 6-inch gun as an antiaircraft battleship, unofficially designated BB (AA). Other design studies showed them both being completed with guided missiles, including the Loon, the Navy's version of the German V–1. The Naval War College used both ships on the game board, in one instance "outfitting" *Kentucky* with two hundred Loons. At one point, *Hawaii* was to be converted to a command cruiser. But neither of the ships was ever finished. Technology was changing too fast, funds were too scarce, and the more urgent air and subsurface threats demanded the little money available. In late 1947, Secretary Sullivan halted their construction to foster antisubmarine projects, including ASW cruiser *Norfolk*.[90]

To bolster fleet air defense, the Navy initiated two other new warship designs which reached fruition in the 1950s. Beginning in 1948, incomplete heavy cruiser *Northampton* (CA 125) began to be converted into a fleet flagship. Commissioned in 1953, *Northampton*, redesignated CLC 1, would coordinate the air defense efforts of an entire fleet. And starting in 1949, the Navy laid down the four very large destroyers of the *Mitscher* class. These ships carried a significant antisubmarine armament, but their principal focus in sensors and in guns was on the antiaircraft capability. At almost 5,000 tons full load, these were the largest ships so far ordered under the destroyer designation by the U.S. Navy. As might be expected, they sported a number of innovative features, including the first 1,200-pound steam plant and the new 3-inch, 70-caliber rapid-fire antiaircraft gun. It is a measure of the Navy's preoccupation with the air menace that these ships were originally designed with the 3"/70 as their sole gun armament. Only the direct intervention of CNO Chester Nimitz placed two of the new 5"/54 guns on board. Nimitz felt that the smaller piece was too light to be effective against surface targets. The *Mitscher*s would not commission for four years; when they did, their many novel features caused serious headaches (for details, see Chapter 2).[91]

The new 3-inch, 70-caliber had evolved from the need to replace the Navy's standard light antiaircraft guns—the 40mm and the 20mm—which simply did not have the range, the weight of shell, nor the proximity fuze to combat high-speed aircraft. Some armaments specialists thought that guided missiles would provide the answer, but their operational debut lay in the dim future. As the Bureau of Ordnance (BUORD) remarked: "Due to the fact that guided missiles are in an embryonic state, the Navy would be

Practice firing the 3″/50 on a cruiser. Note the rear of the twin 5″/38 mount behind the 3-inch gun.

NH 79109

taking considerable risk during the next decade if it stopped other developments at this time and put major dependence on guided missiles."[92]

Guns would, of necessity, be made to offer the interim solution. The 3″/70 was, in some ways, decades ahead of its time. Largely automatic in its operation, with a trouble-shooting diagnostic system and an on-mount radar, the weapon could be fired in an emergency by one crewman. Its long barrel was designed to throw a shell to an altitude of 45,000 feet; early in its development, the gun demonstrated an ability to reach the remarkable rate of fire of ninety rounds per minute and to sustain sixty. The Bureau of Ordnance pushed the weapon hard, writing in late 1945, "this project is being prosecuted vigorously in the belief that such a weapon is necessary for future close-in machine gun defense against guided missiles and the larger, heavier, higher-speed bombers which will be developed."[93] The bureau projected fleet introduction to coincide with *Norfolk* and the *Mitscher*s. However, the complexity of both the gun and mount retarded development, and the weapon was not ready for fleet use until 1956. Consequently, the five ships went to sea with the less sophisticated 3"/50.[94]

The kamikaze had provided the initial impetus for this gun. With a sustained rate of fire of twenty rounds per minute and an altitude of 30,000 feet, the weapon was a marginal performer from the beginning against jet aircraft. Nonetheless, with the 3"/70 over budget and behind schedule, the Navy ordered 490 copies of the shorter weapon in 1946. First mounted on destroyer *Richard E. Kraus* (DD 849) in 1947, it remained the standard light gun on board surface warships well into the 1970s and served on certain auxiliary units through the 1980s, even though it had lost long before this time whatever antiaircraft capabilities it had originally possessed. The gun did see substantial operational service during the Vietnam conflict when it was employed as a shore bombardment weapon. Navy reports praised it for its high volume of fire and tightly grouped salvoes, although the small burst of the projectile proved difficult to spot in dense foliage.[95]

While some planners saw the 3"/70 as the gun of the future, others thought there was still a place for the heavier, albeit slower shooting, calibers. As noted earlier, CNO Nimitz pushed the development of a new 5-inch, in part because of its higher altitude and in part because he felt the 3-inch lacked sufficient punch against surface targets, whether afloat or ashore. Consequently, the Navy contracted with Northern Ordnance in 1946 to begin work on a new model (the Mk 42) of the long-barreled 5"/54, the "summit" in gun design according to some experts.[96] To provide a rate of fire double that of the classic 5"/38, the Mk 42 offered with its automatic ammunition handling system a theoretical forty rounds per minute, the redundancy of double ammunition hoists and twin control stations on top of the shield, and the ability to engage both surface and aerial targets (the latter to an altitude of 51,600 feet). Authorized for the four *Mitscher*-class ships of the 1948 program, the Mk 42 entered service in 1953. Like its companion piece, the 3"/50, it too would have a long and checkered career.[97]

But to many observers in the late 1940s, conventional guns were falling farther and farther behind the aircraft. Against high-altitude planes, the problem of aiming the shell became appallingly difficult. The flight time for the projectile could be as much as half a minute; the velocity and direction of the winds at high altitudes would have an unpredictable effect on the path of the shell; and the aircraft might well maneuver radically during the thirty seconds that the shell was in the air. One possible solution would be to slash the flight time of a projectile, and the Bureau of Ordnance briefly contemplated a 3-inch hypervelocity squeeze-bore gun, 147 calibers long with a designed muzzle velocity of 6,000 feet per second (as opposed to the 2,650 feet per second of the 3"/50). An alternative approach would be to put up many more projectiles, and to that end, the Bureau of Ordnance in

1949 toyed with liquid propellants. Neither visionary project got beyond the talking stage.[98]

Guiding the shell itself seemed a more attainable solution, although it too was fraught with obstacles. In 1947, the Bureau of Ordnance started work on a gun-launched guided missile—essentially a steerable projectile. For Project Zeus, the Naval Ordnance Laboratory experimented with two different types: one, a ramjet-powered shell; the other, a saboted high-velocity unpowered projectile. As funding tightened, the lab dropped the first and concentrated its testing on a saboted 4-inch projectile fired from an 8-inch smooth-bore gun. After spending slightly more than $2.5 million by 1949, the lab had shot seventy-six experimental rounds and had deflected some of the shells during flight with small rocket motors. As the chief of the Guided Missile Division in OPNAV, Rear Admiral Daniel Gallery, remarked before the Naval War College, "BuOrd are very hopeful and enthusiastic about it. What it really amounts to is pitching curves at them instead of straight fast balls."[99]

Having made this fine start, the Bureau of Ordnance proposed to apply the principle to other calibers with special attention to the 5-inch in light of the number of those guns in the fleet. Unhappily, the Zeus program received low priority and sparse funding despite the promising test results. For many, the day of the gun, even with radically improved projectiles, was over. As one ordnance expert who worked on weaponry at the Naval Proving Ground, Dahlgren, Virginia, later observed, "In fact, the current wisdom was that guns and ammunition were obsolescent. You could more or less just look forward a certain number of years and say there just wouldn't be any more guns. Ordnance would be all bombs, missiles, and rockets."[100] Shortly after World War II, the new head at the David W. Taylor Model Basin stopped all work at his facility on guns. Funds for gun range improvement dried up. At Dahlgren, most expenditures involved the proofing of munitions, not research and development. Money for the latter was going to the laboratories at China Lake, California, and White Sands, New Mexico. And what those desert laboratories were working on was the guided missile.[101]

Guided missiles offered a number of advantages over gun-fired projectiles: the missile did not have to withstand the high acceleration or rotational forces to which shells were subjected. For example, the 5"/38 projectile upon firing underwent an acceleration of 20,000 g's and was rotating at a speed of 30,000 rpm as it left the muzzle of the gun. Because missiles were subject to far less intense pressures, they could be designed with much greater latitude in terms of their aerodynamic or ballistic shape. Moreover, if the missile were large enough, its range could extend far beyond that of any conventional artillery projectile. And, of course, the prospect of guiding the missile in flight provided the most potent attraction.

Obstacles to the development of an operational antiaircraft missile were many, however. The Navy's choice of the name Bumblebee ("which just shouldn't be able to fly, but does")[102] for the program started in January 1944 was indicative of the difficulties lying ahead. Forrestal pushed missiles following the war for a number of missions. In July 1946, he ordered a "variety of guided missiles produced as a useful naval weapon of each type in the shortest practicable time" and the investigation of the practicability of nuclear warheads for the weapons. By August 1947, OPNAV had issued an immediate requirement for a ship-launched missile capable of intercepting and destroying, at the maximum range of its guidance, a large bomber flying at 750 mph at 60,000 feet and maneuvering at 3 g's. The Bureau of Ordnance summarized the fields in which research was essential to success: "aerodynamics, ballistics, thermodynamics, propulsion, radiation and electronics . . . high temperature metallurgy, ceramics, and magnetic materials." The bureau, which had cognizance over the Bumblebee program, was spurred on after the end of the war by the "considerable possibility that by major emphasis and mass scientific attack, some other country could develop radically advanced types of guided missiles in much less time than we now anticipate."[103]

This fear—the threat of a belligerent Soviet Union armed with advanced weapons—led the Navy to commit a major portion of its scarce funding to work in this area. The Navy was spending more than either the Army or Air Force. By 1947, a greater fraction of the bureau's resources was going into guided missiles than into any other of its research projects. In August of that year, BUORD had 1,835 people working on Bumblebee compared to 70 working on the gun-launched guided missile. Bright surface warfare officers were detailed to the missile projects. Many undertook study at elite civilian universities or at the Naval Postgraduate School where new courses focusing on guided missiles had been added to the curriculum. Some officers attended the Army's nine-month Anti-Aircraft Artillery School at Fort Bliss, Texas. Wherever they went, the pace was usually frenetic. Within a single year (August 1945–1946) one such officer studied fire control and guidance in the graduate school at MIT and then went to Johns Hopkins University, one of a handful of universities to continue defense work after V–J Day, for work at the Applied Physics Laboratory (APL). The contacts with APL, already famous in Navy circles for its major contributions to the proximity fuze, would prove especially fruitful to the Bureau of Ordnance in its attempts to field a family of antiaircraft missiles.[104]

The potential of the embryonic weapon exerted an immense attraction for officers. In the summer of 1946, missiles still in the planning stages figured prominently on the game board at the Naval War College; over the next several years, those under development were the subject of numerous lectures. Some experts were careful to caution against regarding the mis-

Admiral Arleigh Burke and Rear Admiral Daniel Gallery at Naval Air Station, Anacostia, 7 September 1956. By this point, Burke was Chief of Naval Operations and Gallery served as Chief of Naval Air Reserve Training.

NH 54908

sile as a panacea for all tactical challenges. For example, one overly ambitious 1947 Navy objective called for an antiaircraft missile capable of destroying any transsonic aircraft or guided missile within 300 miles of the launching ship. A missile expert, Dr. G. I. Welch, scotched such projections before a Newport audience:

> We are not now thinking in terms of building an anti-aircraft guided missile with a range of ninety miles. We don't have any idea of how to solve the required problems at that range at the present time. What we are doing is concentrating on ranges of about twenty miles where the complications introduced by evasion are relatively unimportant.... [T]he problems associated with guided missiles ... are plenty tough without trying to get guided missiles to do the impossible simply because there is an air of mystery about them.... It is not a question of getting guided missiles off the drawing board, but first a question of getting them on the drawing board." [105]

Rear Admiral Gallery cast the problem in a different light: "As in certain other processes which will readily come to mind, conception is an easy and often pleasant process, but giving birth is much more difficult." [106]

Delivering the Bumblebee series of missiles to the surface forces would require many midwives. The Bureau of Ordnance established or improved flight test stations at Inyokern, California, White Sands, and Point Mugu,

California; it built combustion laboratories and supersonic wind tunnels at MIT and Daingerfield, Texas. It also coordinated the efforts of organizations as disparate as Curtiss-Wright, Consolidated Vultee, Standard Oil, Bendix, Sylvania, and RCA; the bureau also tapped the expertise of such universities as Virginia, Texas, Princeton, Washington, and the New Mexico School of Mines.[107]

Bringing missiles to the fleet also involved turf battles in and outside the Navy. Throughout 1945–1947, the service had to struggle with the Army Air Force over a number of guided weapons. Much of the debate took place in the joint Aeronautical Board. Gallery analyzed these talks: "The Board meets—AAF and Navy tell each other what they propose to do—each views the other's proposal with scorn and skepticism, but neither can find any ironclad reason for blocking the other's proposal. After going through this procedure, it is customary for the services to say that their programs have been 'coordinated.'"[108] Of special interest to the surface navy was the Army Air Force's antiship missile with a "hydrobomb" warhead. By mid-1947, this particular issue was resolved with the transfer of project to the Bureau of Aeronautics.[109]

Within the Navy, both the Bureau of Aeronautics and the Bureau of Ordnance had initiated their own distinct programs during World War II. In 1947, Forrestal approved the establishment of the Guided Missile Division to coordinate the Navy's many efforts in the field. Its colorful chief, Rear Admiral Gallery, stated his main problem succinctly: "BuOrd and BuAer are very jealous of each other's efforts. BuAer feels that BuOrd is muscling in on their field and in my opinion they have invaded BuAer's field of cognizance...." He pointed to the heart of the matter: "BuOrd has the stronger motive to produce on guided missiles because if they don't... they become the Bureau of Obsolete Weapons, whereas BuAer's big interest is in aircraft which we know will be with us for some time."[110] Gallery attempted with some success to line off areas of responsibility, suggesting, for instance, that BUAER take over missiles carried by aircraft while BUORD work on those launched from ships.[111]

Both the Navy bureaus advanced a bewildering variety of missile projects during the immediate postwar period. Of greatest interest to the surface navy was the one that centered on the radical ramjet Bumblebee. The program confronted a host of technical unknowns. Key hurdles to be overcome included aerodynamic control and missile guidance at supersonic speeds. The program required the development of a novel engine; new solid-grain propellants for the booster rocket; specialized experimental vehicles, such as the Aerobee high-altitude sounding rocket; and a supersonic test missile, the STV–3. A major, although little heralded, advance involved the invention of telemetering equipment to allow detailed analysis of every function of the missile during flight. As one of the scientists associated with the project later remarked, "the Bumblebee program served to lay the technological foundations for much of the entire U.S. missile development, especially in the fields of supersonic aerodynamics and control, jet propulsion, radar guidance, solid rockets, and telemetry." [112]

In 1948, the Bumblebee family was renamed. The large ramjet Bumblebee I was dubbed Talos, after the Brass Man of Crete who pounced red hot upon his attackers, while the exotic, long-range Bumblebee II was called Triton, after a sea god. To some, the legendary Greek names seemed appropriate "because many felt that the surface-to-air missile was [itself] somewhat mythological." [113] In its initial version, Talos was supposed to carry a 300-pound warhead to a range of about 20 miles; for guidance, it would ride a radar beam focused on the target by the firing ship. Talos impressed all with its size and complexity. By the end of 1949, it had made only two test flights and, oddly, was lagging behind its STV–3 development vehicle, now being preened for service use as a weapon itself. [114] This STV–3 did so well in testing for Talos that the Bureau of Ordnance drafted it early in 1948 as a shorter-range missile to carry a 125-pound warhead out to 10 miles. Planners intended for it to destroy any airplanes (or even "guided bombs") that had leaked past Talos. In 1949, the militarized version of the STV–3 officially received the name Terrier. [115]

Much was expected of Terrier. BUORD hoped for high reliability through "ingenuity of design, carefully developed inspection procedures during production, and practically automatic checkout of the assembled missile." [116] And since Terrier was substantially smaller than its parent Talos, Gallery hoped that the Terrier launcher would fit on the same base ring as a 40mm quadruple mount. A heavy cruiser might then carry four or five mounts with perhaps three hundred Terriers in the magazines. Gallery added that "the expected probability of kill against the B–36 target [would be] between 50 and 70 percent per shot." [117]

Gallery's aiming in February 1950 at the Air Force's B–36 probably expressed more than the Navy's antipathy toward that giant bomber. The preceding year, the Soviets had exploded their first nuclear device, and OPNAV estimated in January 1950 that they had ten atomic bombs on hand and would add twenty more by the end of the year. With this development, it was utterly essential for the Navy to protect its carriers with an impenetrable defensive system, a Herculean task. The nuclear weapon problem was compounded by the fact that the bomber did not have to close its target to inflict lethal damage, whereas the principal threats to surface warships during World War II had been the aircraft—the dive bombers, torpedo planes, and kamikazes—that had pressed their attacks home. The high-altitude bomber in World War II had done virtually no damage to maneuvering warships. Now the new atomic weapons changed the equation radically. Physically large, they would require in turn a big aircraft for their delivery, but a single bomb exploding within a mile of a ship could be counted on to inflict fatal damage to any naval vessel, even one as tough as the new *Midway*-class carriers (designed to withstand up to twenty torpedo hits).[118]

Confronting the demand for a leak-proof roof over the carriers, the surface forces redoubled their efforts on antiaircraft missilery. In February 1950, Gallery reported at Newport that 21 percent of all the Defense Department's research and development budget was going for guided missiles, with the Navy receiving the lion's share. Gallery added that as head of the guided missile development branch of OPNAV, he was forced to spend much of his time defending his scarce funding from poachers within the Navy Department such as "the ASW boys."[119]

Gallery was anxious to put the new missiles to sea as quickly as possible. Even before the STV–3 became Terrier in the fall of 1949, the Navy asked Congress for the money to convert a heavy cruiser to a guided missile ship as part of its FY 50 program. Gallery told an audience at Newport that with shipborne fighter aircraft and antiaircraft missiles on surface ships, "we should be able to move in on any coast in the world and launch an attack without worrying too much about what is going to happen to our ships."[120]

The Navy also accelerated its efforts to perfect "soft-kill" defenses against an aerial threat. The Bureau of Ordnance had started work on electronic countermeasures (ECM) as early as 1942. In 1943, the resultant devices had performed successfully against German missiles. Off Anzio, Italy, American ECM gear decoyed the German Hs 293 glide bomb so well that only five of the seventy-five launched found their targets. By the end of the war, ECM technology, consisting mainly of chaff launchers and noise jammers, was being used to counter fire control radars. Naval officers continued work after the war on ECM measures designed to defeat radio, radar, and heat guidance systems in missiles.[121]

All areas of electronic warfare were becoming ever more critical. As planes flew faster, reaction times grew shorter, especially against low-flying aircraft. Airborne early warning radar usually picked up groups of low-flying aircraft, but it frequently missed solitary planes. For this reason alone, it was essential that surface warships carry elaborate radar installations. By the late 1940s, the naval architect found his hand increasingly directed by the weight and space requirements for the sensors in new ships like the *Mitscher*s. In short supply were the technicians to operate the ever more complicated equipment. One article in the Naval Institute *Proceedings* complained that the technicians, who required two years of training, left the service at the end of their first enlistment: "The Navy trains excellent technicians—for industry."[122] When the Navy attempted to entice 32,000 of its former electronics ratings from civilian life, only 400 replies came in.[123]

The surface navy was not stuck totally in a defensive crouch. In time-honored Navy tradition, surface warriors hoped to go on the offensive with weapons coming out of the new technology. In 1947, Admiral Spike Blandy forecast with a certain prescience that battleships "may be called on to fling these instruments of destruction, with atomic warheads, at coastal bases, ports and shipyards—or even to step entirely out of the Navy's traditional 'control-of-the-sea' role, and launch them at inland industrial cities."[124] During the latter part of World War II, some significant work had gone forward on missiles for attacking enemy ships or land targets. In pursuit of the latter mission, several projects were continued into the postwar period. Loon, the V–1 copy, was briefly considered. Work had started on Loon in September 1944; by 1949, surface ships shot sixty-one of the little missiles. Notably eccentric, Loons sometimes flew upside down for miles or went so far off course that they were eventually accompanied by armed chase planes. Admiral Gallery dismissed them as "a Chinese copy of the German buzz bomb."[125]

Loon might not work, but CNO Admiral Nimitz still saw power projection against land targets by means of missiles to be one of the principal missions of the future surface navy. In 1947, OPNAV issued a set of requirements for bombardment missiles. Surface warships would share in their development and deployment with aircraft carriers and submarines. One missile common to all three platforms was Regulus which was being designed to deliver a 3,000-pound payload up to 500 miles. Guidance posed serious problems early on, as did the missile's initial inability to carry the large nuclear warheads of the time. Regulus was thus first seen as very much an interim step to a precision long-range missile. Two such visionary projects were the whimsically named "Could Bee I" and the Triton with a proposed range of 2,000 miles. Ironically, the "interim" Regulus, which did not fly until 1951, would turn out to be the only designed-for-the-purpose bombardment missile carried operationally by U.S. surface warships until the 1980s.[126]

In light of the weak Soviet surface fleet, it is perhaps surprising that some of the Navy's antiship missile projects were continued after V–J Day. In this area, the surface warfare community had the support of the aviators. Wartime experience had shown that the best way to sink a large warship was by means of the torpedo. But delivering this weapon—whether by air or by surface ship—invariably involved a dangerously close approach to the well-armed target. And as radar-directed gunfire improved, torpedo attack became an increasingly chancy business. Similarly, dive bombing became more hazardous for the attacking aircraft.[127]

During the war, the Navy had developed a number of guided weapons designed to sink ships. One of these, the air-launched Bat, featured radar homing and was thus a "fire-and-forget" weapon. Bat appeared so promising that in January 1945, Admiral King ordered the acquisition of five thousand of the missiles and the conversion of three patrol plane squadrons to carry them. The weapon scored some successes in operations, but by that late stage of the war, it found targets scarce.[128]

Following V–J Day, the Navy looked at bombardment missiles for anti-ship purposes. In April 1946, the Office of Research and Development headed by Rear Admiral H. G. Bowen considered antishipping modifications for the Loon; the Naval War College added the Loon to some of its operations problems. However, the Newport officers concluded that the weapon's erratic performance and poor accuracy gave it little hope of success against ship targets. More promising was Regulus. The Navy's 1947 requirements listed ship in addition to shore targets as objectives for Regulus, although tactical use of this missile with its anticipated range of 500 miles would require a precision in guidance difficult to achieve.[129]

Two ship-launched missiles designed specifically to attack other warships were in varying stages of development at the end of the war. The Pilotless Aircraft Division of the Bureau of Aeronautics headed by the famous missile proponent Rear Admiral D. S. Fahrney was drawing preliminary plans for the P/A XIII missile with a plunging warhead designed to explode close to the hull of a warship. The Bureau of Ordnance was further along with Kingfisher, an ingenious winged torpedo which could be launched from either an aircraft or a ship. This weapon would ultimately be renamed Petrel and be operationally deployed by P–2 Neptune patrol squadrons (see Chapter 2). The ship-launched version of Kingfisher could be fired from its shipping crate—a measure which saved space and enhanced the missile's versatility in employment. This ingenious launcher, then, prefigured missile canisters in fleet use by over two decades.[130]

Except for Kingfisher/Petrel, none of these projects came to fruition, nor did OPNAV's ambitious 1947 objective to construct "a ship-to-ship guided missile of high precision" with ranges up to 500 miles.[131] Such a weapon proved difficult to perfect even more than a quarter of a century later. Nor did the Navy go ahead with its plans to convert old battleship *Colorado* (BB 45) to an antiship missile target. All these projects cost too much, and the threat seemed to lie elsewhere. As one officer in Fahrney's office wrote, "Surface ships are not expected to provide as many or as important targets for guided missiles . . . because of US naval supremacy. . . ." Also, carrier aviators were confident of their ability to sink any enemy surface ships.[132]

That is, if there were any carriers in the fleet—or even any fleet at all. Times were hard for the entire Navy in the last years of the 1940s. When Secretary of Defense Louis Johnson took office in March 1949, he was openly hostile to the service. His budget allocated it such slender operating funds that by early 1950, some ships were staffed with only two-thirds of their combat complements. As an index of the Navy's distress, even most of its hard-hitting carriers retired to pierside: by 1948, the Navy was asking the White House for a force of not thirty-seven fast carriers in commission, but rather of sixteen. The next year, only eight were on active duty.[133]

Worse, in April 1949, Johnson canceled the large carrier *United States* on the stocks, thereby ending, it seemed, any chance that the Navy would play a part in a nuclear war against the Soviets. Looking ahead, the Navy could envision a time when its sole mission would be defensive ASW. The ensuing furor, which pitted the Navy against the Army and Air Force in congressional hearings, came to be known as the "revolt of the admirals," and led to the resignation of CNO Denfeld and his replacement by Forrest Sherman.[134]

Some surface warfare officers feared the worst when aviator Sherman took office. He was, after all, the first full-fledged aviator to hold the Navy's top uniformed job (Fleet Admiral King had qualified for his wings only late in his career). In fact, Sherman obtained permission from the administration to upgrade two *Essex*-class carriers for the nuclear strike mission and even tentative backing for construction of a supercarrier (later named *Forrestal*, CVA 59). He also converted some additional billets to aviation.[135]

But Sherman also saved the career of one key surface officer: Captain Arleigh A. Burke. The veteran destroyerman had coordinated the Navy's campaign against the B–36, the mainstay of the Air Force's strategic bomber force. When Navy Secretary Matthews removed him from the flag officer selection list for his role in the "revolt," Burke seemed headed for retirement until Sherman interceded. In 1950, Burke made Rear Admiral; within five years, he would be CNO.[136]

In planning the Navy's force structure, Sherman wanted to maintain a balanced fleet. A litmus test for the new CNO came in late 1949 when Secretary Johnson attempted to mothball the Navy's last battleship, *Missouri*, by reducing the operating budget of the Atlantic Fleet. Sherman kept the ship in commission and employed her part of the time in training midshipmen. As one naval historian has noted, "This small victory did a great deal to restore confidence in Sherman within the Navy, especially among surface line officers, many of whom took it as a sign that Sherman sought a balanced fleet rather than one skewed toward carriers."[137]

Of greater significance, Sherman moved in November 1949 to retain thirteen cruisers slated for retirement. And in May 1950, at Sherman's behest, Congress voted funds for new surface ship construction and for the conversion of a heavy cruiser to a guided missile ship. The nadir for surface warfare had passed.

# 2

# The Surface Navy Enters the Missile Age, 1950–1955

The surface navy in the first five years of the 1950s benefited from several interlocking developments. First, the Korean War showed that limited war was still possible in an atomic age, and thus, that conventional weapons were still essential. Second, the Soviets unveiled a significant conventional navy featuring a large number of long-range gun cruisers. Third, the U.S. surface navy placed itself in the technological vanguard by sending to sea the world's first operational guided missiles, both offensive and defensive.

With the first Soviet A-bomb test of 1949, some American policymakers became concerned that the end of the U.S. nuclear monopoly meant a dramatic lessening of the deterrent capability of the U.S. nuclear arsenal. State Department planner Paul H. Nitze drew up a document called NSC–68 which advocated a quick buildup of conventional military forces to deter Soviet aggression by means other than nuclear war. President Truman reviewed this document in the spring of 1950 without taking action on it. The President's hand was forced on 25 June when Communist North Korean forces crossed the 38th parallel.[1]

American surface warships took part in the contest virtually from the beginning. Although only five U.S. vessels were in Japanese waters at the outbreak of the war, just four days after North Korean troops crossed the 38th parallel, the light cruiser *Juneau* (CL 119) and the destroyer *De Haven* (DD 727) opened the U.S. Navy's role in the struggle with a shore bombardment at Okkye on the east coast of the peninsula. On 2 July, *Juneau,* joined by British ships, fought the only naval engagement of the war—and a possibly decisive one. By sinking fifteen of the sixteen North Korean vessels headed for Pusan, the allied force deprived the Communists of the opportunity to seize that vital port by a coup de main.[2]

Reinforcements rushed to the scene. Heavy cruiser *Rochester* (CA 124), in the Philippines on the outbreak of hostilities, reached Korea in time to support the Army's landings at Pohang Dong on 18 July. *Rochester*'s sister *Helena* (CA 75) left Long Beach on 6 July, stopped at Pearl Harbor to take on ammunition, and by 7 August was shelling enemy installations in North Korea. Ten days later *Helena*, the destroyers of DESDIV 111, and four LSTs rescued almost 4,000 South Korean troops from the advancing enemy.[3]

Surface warships played a major role in the celebrated riposte at Inchon. With heavy cruiser *Toledo* (CA 133) as the task group flag, two U.S. cruisers and six destroyers, assisted by two British cruisers, entered Inchon harbor to beat down the North Korean defenses two days before the landings. The commanding officer of the cruiser division later reported, "It was most fortuitous that the ships went in to bombard when the water was just about at its low ebb because some of the shore batteries were located so low along the waterfront that the guns of the bombarding ships in some cases came down against their stops when depressed to fire at the lowest targets." [4]

The conventional nature of the Korean War largely validated the thinking behind NSC–68. Fears of a Soviet attack on western Europe also mandated an increased commitment in military strength to the NATO alliance. In July 1950, the Joint Chiefs of Staff (JCS) had recommended a navy of 911 vessels. Now in September, President Truman ordered the conventional buildup called for in NSC–68, which projected 1954 as the year of maximum danger when Soviet military power would reach its peak. Under the original NSC–68 proposal, the fleet was to number 324 major ships. By mid-1951, the target number had increased to 1,066 ships, including the 4 *Iowa*s, 2 guided missile and 12 conventional cruisers, and 194 destroyers. Much of this increase would be met, of course, by recommissioning ships from the mothball fleet; the rest would come from new construction. [5]

Thus, the Navy began reactivating many of the ships that it had just mothballed. Destroyer *Ault* (DD 698), decommissioned on 31 May 1950, was flying her pennant again on 15 November. Similarly, the slumber of heavy cruiser *Macon* (CA 132) in the mothball fleet lasted only from 12 April to 16 October 1950. Battleship *Missouri* was rejoined in the fleet by *Iowa*, *New Jersey* (BB 62), and *Wisconsin* (BB 64). Returning from mothballs were a total of 104 destroyers, 66 destroyer escorts, 5 heavy cruisers and 3 battleships. [6]

Problems abounded with the massive effort. Initial plans called for destroyers to be recommissioned in thirty days, a figure that one Navy evaluator called "entirely unrealistic." [7] Critical items of equipment, such as fire hoses and ordinary tools, were in short supply. Some ships were even unable to obtain essential publications, such as the BUSHIPS Manual; so many ships rejoined the Navy in such a short period that some were not on the mailing list for Navy Department Monthly Bulletins and received no response to their requests for inclusion. To provide the experienced personnel necessary to staff this armada, the Navy called reservists to active service, many of them veterans of World War II who came back hesitantly and at great personal sacrifice. The difficulties involved in this mobilization effort can perhaps be encapsulated by the experience of Lieutenant (j.g.) Richard G. Alexander who helped put the *Fletcher*-class destroyer *Rooks* (DD 804) back into commission.

Shortly after shakedown, *Rooks* came to the east coast, went into the Norfolk Navy Yard, and was "modernized" by replacing the 40mm battery with the 3-inch/50 rapid fire mounts, and the Mk 63 Fire Control System. I had two Fire Controlmen, and not more than three or four Gunners Mates. There were no schools ashore for these new guns or the fire control gear. The Navy had not filled a pipeline with trained people to go along with the equipment. It was makee learn. What a lousy situation![8]

Frustrating personnel shortages continued on board the surface warships throughout the Korean War. Ships on station frequently lost trained sailors, especially key petty officers, to ships working up.[9]

For the surface units patrolling off the coasts of Korea, gunfire support became their most significant task. The 8-inch artillery of the heavy cruisers garnered a fine score from Marine assessors with over half of the cruiser missions labeled "highly successful." The four battleships eventually fired many more 16-inch rounds than they had in World War II; the same Marine assessment team rated over two-thirds of their missions as "highly successful"—the top accolades given to any gun system. The biggest guns were especially impressive against hard targets, such as North Korean railroad tunnels.[10]

The sheer volume of surface fire support was phenomenal. From May 1951 to April 1952 alone, U.S. naval ships fired over 414,000 projectiles in 24,000 missions against shore targets. Very few problems arose. In twenty-one months, the big ships suffered seventeen premature detonations of 16-inch and 8-inch shells, a few very close to the gun muzzles. Not surprisingly, gun-bore erosion afflicted some of the vessels. An examination of *Missouri*'s guns after they had fired 1,600 rounds revealed scoring up to .85 inches deep inside the barrels. Destroyer *Lyman K. Swenson* (DD 729), on line virtually from the beginning of the war, reported in November 1950 that her repair crew was busy with the many cracks in welds and fittings appearing as a result of gun blast. The ship had expended 5,709 rounds of 5-inch ammunition in little over four months. Cruiser *Helena* fired so many missions that her entire main battery was replaced in December 1951. *Rochester*, in 198 days of Korean operations, steamed over 25,000 miles and fired over 5,000 8-inch and 5-inch shells. Overall, the performance of the gunships was most creditable, and the Naval War College, looking in 1954 at the record, assessed the gun as especially useful for "precision bombardment in support of troops."[11]

The achievement by the battleships and cruisers was all the more impressive given the lack of support by carrier aviation to gunfire spotting. Photo reconnaissance of gun strikes was infrequent, and the commanders of the Seventh Fleet never created a specialized unit dedicated to this work. Helicopters from the battleships and cruisers made up for some of the deficiency and showed their value in a number of other roles. *Rochester* used her helicopters to spot mines and for search and rescue missions. *Worcester* employed hers for plane guard and for ASW screening.[12]

The surface warships themselves performed a myriad of duties, including covering the evacuation at Wonsan. They interdicted North Korean barge traffic and controlled naval air operations. Operating as radar pickets, they scored notable successes in picking up Communist aircraft and vectoring combat air patrol against the enemy.[13]

Surface warships were not immune to enemy action. The radar picket destroyer *Southerland* (DDR 743), in dueling with seven Communist shore batteries for 23 minutes on 14 July 1952, suffered four direct hits. In another episode, shore batteries hit *Alfred A. Cunningham* (DD 752) with four shells, one of which burst a depth charge scattering flaming TNT down one side of the destroyer. *Saint Paul* suffered a direct hit on a 3-inch mount in the last days of the war. Even battleship *Wisconsin* was holed through a steel deck by a 155mm shell which wounded three sailors. In a most unusual occurrence early in the war, two Communist planes attacked cruiser *Rochester* with bombs, albeit without success. More threatening was the enemy use of mines, which damaged destroyers *Brush* (DD 745), *Mansfield* (DD 728), and most seriously, *Walke* (DD 723). The last hit a mine off Wonsan which killed twenty-six sailors and severely damaged the ship's hull. And a turret fire claimed the lives of thirty men on *Saint Paul* in April 1952.[14]

With the end of the Korean War came a change in direction in American defense policy. The new President, Dwight D. Eisenhower, initially proposed a strategy, dubbed the "New Look," to prepare both for a full-scale nuclear conflict and for limited wars, such as Korea. This approach abandoned the "critical year" postulated in NSC–68 and substituted a plan to build up Western strength for the "long haul." A perimeter was drawn around Communist holdings in Asia, and a policy of containment applied to that arena as well. Under the New Look, defense spending would reach a level almost triple that of the pre-Korean Truman years.[15]

On reflection President Eisenhower felt the sum so great as to threaten the nation with bankruptcy. In pursuit of a cheaper course of action, the administration adopted the policy often called Massive Retaliation.[16] In 1953 the President announced that henceforth, the United States "would place main but not sole reliance on nuclear weapons."[17] Such a strategy would permit economies in both manpower and financial resources in peacetime; in the event of war, liberal use of the weapons would bring quick victory. Because much of their deterrent value lay in the enemy's perception that they would be employed in armed conflict, public pronouncements by Western leaders were blunt. In a widely quoted statement, Field Marshall Bernard Montgomery declared in 1954, "With us [at NATO headquarters] it is no longer, 'They [tactical nuclear weapons] may possibly be used.' It is very definitely, 'They will be used if we are attacked.'"[18] Given this mindset, about half of all defense monies during the first Eisenhower administration went to the Air Force. The Navy took second place in the budget contest at 30 percent, with the Army coming in a poor third.[19] Admiral Radford, the naval aviation champion who was now chairman of the JCS, proclaimed at the end of 1953 that atomic weapons "have virtually achieved conventional status with our armed forces. Each service is capable of putting this weapon into combat use."[20]

And in fact, the Navy was hard at work developing its capabilities in nuclear warfare. In 1951, the A–2 Savage, a carrier aircraft capable of lifting the heavy atomic bombs, became operational. The next year, a carrier deployed to the Mediterranean with the planes and atomic weapons on board. The carrier navy had now taken its place alongside the Air Force's Strategic Air Command in the nuclear deterrent mission. Beginning in 1951, Congress funded a supercarrier annually for the next six years. And in the eyes of some, power projection ashore was really the only task that mattered. Noted military analyst Samuel P. Huntington remarked in 1954, "the fact that decisive actions will now take place on land means a drastic change in the mission of the Navy... a real revolution in naval thought and operations. For decades, the eyes of the Navy have been turned outward to the ocean and the blue water; now the Navy must . . . look inland where the new objectives lie."[21]

Some surface warfare officers objected to what they saw as an overemphasis on carrier-based nuclear armaments to solve all naval problems.

> [T]he aviators saw everything in terms of carrier strikes, with nukes, even. You have a submarine problem? Not to worry, we'll clean out the Kola Peninsula. This sort of thinking led to a denial of the need for "conventional" ASW forces—convoy protection, barriers, maritime aircraft etc. We had a very difficult time combating this thinking inside the Navy.... [22]

If the Navy were to land nuclear punches, it had best be prepared to take such blows. Some strategists postulated that the Soviets were more likely to use nuclear weapons at sea than they would be in a land war. The power of the new fusion bombs was awe-inspiring. By one estimate, the lethal blast wave from a typical Soviet hydrogen bomb, fuzed to explode at low altitude, would extend for 12 miles. Such a device bursting underwater would produce an immense shock wave capable of rupturing hulls, wrecking equipment, and throwing personnel against the overheads. Radioactive fallout could hazard ships over hundreds of square miles.[23]

Naval planners confronting such scenarios opened out task force formations at the cost of denying ships the mutual support that they had enjoyed during World War II. To escape radiation, personnel would retreat to "deep shelter" below the waterline for at least 24 hours. Sailors in certain critical spaces that could not be closed off from the atmosphere, such as the boiler rooms, would don protective gear and rotate with personnel in "deep shel-

80–G–669741

At the Naval Academy's Dahlgren Hall, outgoing CNO Admiral Robert B. Carney congratulates his successor, Admiral Burke, 17 August 1955. Between the two officers stands Secretary of the Navy Charles S. Thomas.

ter." To shed radioactive particles, Navy ships were increasingly fitted with wash-down systems to spray topside areas with seawater.[24]

While Navy leaders took the threat of nuclear Armageddon very seriously indeed, certain top officers were skeptical that the strategy of Massive Retaliation offered America a defense panacea. Chief of Naval Operations Robert B. Carney wrote openly in the Naval Institute *Proceedings* in May 1955, "If it is atomic war they want, we in the Navy are prepared to make our contribution, and we will also be ready to perform the one-thousand-and-one non-atomic tasks that are involved in this very complicated business of exercising sea power."[25] Privately, Carney disagreed with Admiral Radford's pronouncements before Congress that smaller atomic weapons had become "conventional weapons." Indeed, Carney doubted their use in any scenario short of a massive Soviet attack on western Europe.[26] Carney was one of the first important American strategists to discern that the growing Soviet nuclear arsenal might well lead to a nuclear stalemate—and to more limited wars like Korea. In his 1955 *Proceedings* piece, Carney trenchantly argued the case for balanced forces: "They [the Soviets] may devise nibbling methods in such a way that the use of atomic weapons would not be invoked. Should this happen and should we be caught without sufficient strength in the so-called field of conventional weapons and techniques, the futility of our position becomes readily apparent."[27] While forecasting Soviet advances in naval technology through atomic propulsion, jet aircraft, and guided missiles, Carney pointed specifically to the Soviet buildup of naval forces, both surface and submarine, as an indicator that they intended to seek "maritime preeminence."

In fact, the Soviets had embarked on a most ambitious warship building program. Beginning in 1951, the Soviets commissioned the first of a very large class of submarines that NATO called the *Whiskey* type. Although the earliest versions lacked snorkels and were slow underwater, they compensated for their lack of technical sophistication with sheer numbers. By 1957, 236 were in service. Entering the Soviet fleet starting in 1952 were the first high-speed submarines of the *Zulu* class, a clear derivative of the German Type XXI. Especially disturbing to U.S. planners were CIA reports as early as 1951 that certain Soviet submarines were fitted with guided missiles armed with nuclear warheads. In actuality, these reports were unduly alarmist, insofar as the first Soviet test of a submarine-launched missile occurred in 1955 when a modified *Zulu* fired a Scud from the surface.[28]

Rockets or no, the underwater threat was a serious one against both merchant ships and naval vessels. U.S. exercises repeatedly demonstrated the potency of the new streamlined submarine against fleet units. For instance, during one Pacific Fleet trial in August 1951, submarines tried on seven separate occasions to slip past the destroyers around cruiser *Rochester*. Not once were the attackers detected before making their torpedo runs. The commander of the cruiser division reported, "The inability of the destroyer sonar screen to prevent submarine penetration of the screen was of great concern to the Task Group Commander."[29] Two months later, the same officer noted of a subsequent exercise, "Both submarines penetrated the destroyer screen in all events. With one exception simulated and actual firing of torpedoes was accomplished such that good hits were or would have been obtained."[30] In a 1954 Pacific Fleet exercise, submarines broke through the destroyer screen on all but two of twenty-nine attempts. The commander of the defending destroyer flotilla commented, "The ineffectiveness of the convoy screen of destroyers was most bewildering and disheartening."[31]

Evaluators found ASW tactics, weapons, and sensors all faulty or inadequate. Zigzagging could not shake high-speed submarines; with short sonar ranges, typically of no more than 1,500 yards, picket destroyers ahead of the main body merely served "as a highway sign to the Task Group."[32] And the destroyers in the screen, usually stationed at intervals of 4,500 yards or more, were too often unable to pick up the submarines driving through gaps in the sonar coverage. Even when a submarine was

*Dealey*, the lead ship of the Navy's first postwar class of destroyer escorts.

detected, existing weaponry proved inadequate to the challenge. The antisubmarine rocket projector, Weapon A, had a range of only about 900 yards. Moreover, the complex device broke down frequently.[33]

Fortunately, a variety of important developments in antisubmarine warfare stood in the wings. Hydrophones fixed to the ocean bottom promised the early detection of Soviet submarines as they sortied into the North Atlantic. First tested in 1954 and operational by the end of the decade, the hydrophone network known as SOSUS (Sound Surveillance System) allowed broad location of Soviet submarines. Hunter-killer units built around converted *Essex*-class carriers would then prosecute the SOSUS contacts. Starting in 1954, these specialized antisubmarine carriers flew, in addition to fixed-wing aircraft, helicopters which immediately showed their ASW potential. Essentially invulnerable to the submarine, the helicopter's relatively high rate of speed enabled it to follow up submarine contacts quickly and at a distance from the carrier. Also, the helicopter's dipping sonar avoided certain problems such as quenching wherein the effectiveness of a hull-mounted set was degraded by air bubbles trapped in the sonar dome.[34] But sound equipment for ships was being upgraded too.

An improved sonar, the SQS–4, with a range of up to 8,000 yards was under development. Experiments beginning in 1954 with ricocheting sound beams off the ocean bottom held out hope for much longer sonar ranges.[35]

ASW weaponry advanced to take advantage of these extended detection ranges. Specifications drawn up for the rocket-assisted torpedo (RAT) called for a range of about 5,000 yards, which nearly matched the capabilities of the SQS–4 sonar. Fired from a simple launcher affixed to the side of a destroyer's 5"/38 mount, RAT had reached the testing stage by 1955; most destroyermen hoped for rapid and widespread deployment of the new weapon. Even more promising in its lethality was the nuclear depth charge. Project Hartwell, a 1951 study by the Massachusetts Institute of Technology, envisioned that tactical nuclear explosives detonated below 1,000 feet would "sink a submarine in a radius of over a mile while leaving surface vessels at a radius of a half a mile unaffected."[36]

Antisubmarine warfare also required new ships to carry the new weapons and sensors. Commissioning in 1953 was the singular 8,300-ton "hunter-killer cruiser" *Norfolk*, the first new surface vessel started after World War II. She was reclassified during construction as a destroyer leader (DL) and later as a frigate. Her design, with enclosed bridgework and a water wash-down system, was tailored for operations in a radioactive fallout area. During her seventeen years in commission, *Norfolk* alternated service as a flagship and as a test bed for antisubmarine gear such as advanced sonars and weapons.[37]

But *Norfolk* cost far too much to produce in quantity. If war broke out in Europe, NATO plans called for the immediate institution of the convoy system, and the Navy would need large numbers of escorts to protect merchant ships. To use the Korean conflict as a gauge, 99 percent of all men and materiel dispatched to the Far East had gone by sea. Thus, the Navy sought an inexpensive escort that could be built quickly and cheaply. The result was the *Dealey* class, with the lead ship (DE 1006) being laid down in 1952. Ultimately, only thirteen entered service. Of 1,817 tons full load, they carried a light gun armament of four 3"/50s, the new SQS–4 sonar, and, except for the lead ship, Weapon A. So light was their hull plating that "one night in a nest with wind pressure setting on would leave fender dents in the hulls that were there forever. By the time these ships were five years old they looked twenty."[38] As a further—and very controversial—economy measure, they had only a single screw, albeit a large one. Sacrificed, of course, was the redundancy which backup turbines and shafts brought. The single screw also made them tricky to handle at slow speeds, especially coming alongside piers. With 20,000 horsepower, the small ships could reach 28 knots which, in the words of one commanding officer,

> was a major tactical strength but [their] operational and logistics Achilles heel. Because *Lester* (DE 1022) could make twenty-eight knots it was often

> substituted for destroyers in the carrier screen. The fact that it had to be on full power constantly in order to keep up didn't seem to worry anyone except [those] who served in them. As I repeatedly warned, with no at sea redundancy and with very limited upkeep time alongside, the ships' engineering plants were soon worn out.[39]

And in fact, all were stricken before they had reached their twentieth birthday.[40]

Nonetheless, in the Navy's judgment, the *Dealey*s demonstrated that the savings in machinery costs for the single screw outweighed the risks involved, and the later *Garcia*, *Knox*, and *Oliver Hazard Perry* classes followed this basic machinery layout. And the *Dealey*s also set new open-ocean performance standards in the U.S. Navy for ships of their size. Twin rudders "like barn doors"[41] positioned inside the blade tips gave them a remarkably tight turning circle. A high bow and stern contributed to fine seakeeping qualities. The first commanding officer of *Dealey* remembered: "Her seaworthiness was unsurpassed. I rode out one hurricane as well as numerous North Atlantic gales and tropical storms while in command. I speak from extensive destroyer experience. She was the best!"[42]

In their two decades of service, the little ships served with hunter-killer task units and the Antisubmarine Defense Group Alfa, trained sonarmen at Key West, and journeyed far afield. Shortly after completion, *Joseph K. Taussig* (DE 1030) supported U.S. landings during the Lebanon crisis. Her sister, *Lester*, steamed over 18,000 miles during a Unitas exercise in 1962. *John Willis* (DE 1027) visited Norway that same year; the Norwegians thought enough of her to build five ships of a very similar design—the *Oslo* class.[43]

Older destroyer escorts in the fleet took on a mission never envisioned by their World War II designers: to provide early warning for the continental United States against strategic bombers. Thirty of the ships, redesignated DER, were modified between 1951 and 1956 with updated radars, an excellent communications suite, and fighter direction equipment. Their diesel engines conferred long range, reliability, and freedom from black soot; sixteen ships at a time generally patrolled on "the barriers" in the North Atlantic and North Pacific for up to a month without refueling.[44]

Duty on board them was arduous; the Combat Information Center (CIC) and radio personnel in particular maintained the equivalent of a General Quarters watch during the entire deployment. Modern fittings made the DERs "most habitable,"[45] although they were somewhat cramped; indeed, the captain's cabin was so small that the standard bunk had to be shortened to fit. And they operated in some of the stormiest waters on the oceans, with frequent winds of 70–90 miles per hour and seas of 40–50 feet. At times, the ships had to shut down their search antennas to keep them from blowing over the side. With only 6,400 horsepower from the diesels, the DERs experienced difficulty in turning in very high seas.[46]

Those who sailed on them often remembered the high esprit de corps of the crews. Robert C. Peniston, later captain of two fine ships—battleship *New Jersey* and missile cruiser *Albany* (CG 10)—remembered, "I would say that pound for pound *Savage* [DER 386] was the best ship I ever commanded. The crew was tops and wanted to stay on board. The ship's schedule was a real factor because the crew could plan their personal lives on it. They were willing to accept the rigors of the barrier knowing when they would be in port."[47] These patrols continued until 1965; some of the DERs then went on to such disparate duties as supporting Operation DEEP FREEZE in Antarctica and assisting with Market Time patrols off South Vietnam.[48]

Soviet strategic bomber and submarine forces were not the only challenges for American naval planners in the early 1950s. In 1949, ONI had forecast that a large-scale Soviet surface ship building program was unlikely, but cautioned with some prescience: "Sometimes only one strong personality is needed for changing basic views and remedying fundamental mistakes in thinking. . . . " That "personality" was, of course, to be Joseph Stalin. When he elevated Admiral N. G. Kuznetsov, a "cruiser man," to command the Soviet navy in 1951, ONI discerned the first evidence of Stalin's decision to create a major surface fleet. ONI then realized that the Soviet press began to take a different tack in describing the country's navy. No longer was it just to guard the Red Army's flanks and to defend the coasts. It was now "the powerful, growing fleet of a major maritime power." In the summer of 1951, ONI noted an increased tempo of cruiser building in the yards, an event that the office evaluated as "the most important development in the U.S.S.R. Navy construction up to the present time."[49]

What ONI was seeing underway was the *Sverdlov* cruiser program which resulted in the last conventional big gunships built by any naval power. According to later analysts, twenty-four of these "light" cruisers (17,200 tons full load and with twelve 6-inch guns) were planned. Construction of the lead ship began in the summer of 1949. At Stalin's death in 1953, twenty had been laid down, although only fourteen would be finished. These cruisers were accompanied by an equally extensive program of destroyer construction.[50]

Like the *Sverdlov*s, the new *Skoryy*-class destroyers were obsolescent by U.S. Navy standards and inferior in almost all respects to the *Gearing* class, almost a decade old in design. Mounting a heavy battery of ten torpedo tubes, the Soviet destroyers featured a single-purpose main battery of four 5.1-inch guns and a weak antiaircraft defense. However, by their sheer numbers alone—seventy in service by 1954—they could pose a menace, especially in northern waters. And more modern designs appeared in the offing.[51]

Adding to the growing Soviet surface forces was the large number of motor torpedo boats and other smaller craft. OPNAV opined that some of these might be suicide attack boats. Whether suicide or not, these small craft could "heckle" American naval forces in coastal waters. One intelligence estimate in 1952 stated that the Soviets had in service 50 PT boats in the Baltic Sea and 152 in the Northern fleet.[52]

Of all the new Soviet vessels, the *Sverdlov* cruisers attracted the most attention from ONI. Details as to their characteristics were naturally sketchy at first, but the new ships figured in a Naval War College fleet problem in September 1952. In this exercise, three *Sverdlov*s, under cover of weather too bad for flight operations, participated in an "attack" on an American convoy to Bear Island in the Barents Sea.[53]

In fact, ONI now anticipated that the Soviets would use their increasingly powerful surface forces aggressively: "The Russians incline toward the 'balanced force' concept in developing their fleet. . . . The Soviets can be expected not to repeat the German mistake of limiting the principal assault against enemy sea lines of communications to an unsupported submarine force."[54] The hard-driving director of OPNAV's Strategic Plans Division, Rear Admiral Burke, argued in a 1953 top-secret study:

> These Soviet surface naval forces are an additional threat to our control of the seas. The forces are sufficient to dominate the Baltic and Black Seas. They are a definite threat to our land armies. They possess sufficient amphibious potential for limited-range amphibious operations and could transport and support amphibious forces for assault upon Denmark, Norway, Turkey, Sweden and the Chinese off-shore islands. In addition, the surface forces are capable of conducting operations in direct support of the land armies in northern Europe through their dominance of Baltic coastal routes. They further have a capability for shipping attacks as commerce raiders which is increasing as new cruisers of the *Sverdlov* class are completed.[55]

Some American analysts correctly surmised that the increased cruiser construction presaged the building of true capital ships: aircraft carriers and battleships. Drawing an analogy from the Soviet building program of the late 1930s, ONI concluded that

> the appearance and continuing construction of oversize cruisers (15,000-ton *Sverdlov* class) and larger destroyers . . . seems to parallel earlier stages of the Soviet pre-World War II battle fleet program. In those days capital ships followed after a good head start had been made in cruiser and destroyer construction. Hence, rounding out with other major combatant types, to give the USSR a postwar big ship fleet, may be in prospect.[56]

But ONI was unable to verify its line of reasoning with any concrete information and noted "no valid indicators of the construction of aircraft carriers or big gun ships in Soviet yards during 1952."[57] In fact, battlecruisers *Stalingrad* and *Moskva* had been building since 1950.[58]

Western observers got their initial close look at *Sverdlov* in June 1953 during the Coronation Review at Spithead, England, which marked the first visit to a foreign port by a Soviet warship since World War II. ONI was impressed: "Long shrouded in secrecy, the *Sverdlov*'s emergence before the world's eyes created a very favorable impression. The ship's appearance was smart, ship handling of the skipper and crew was irreproachable, and the propaganda value for Soviet naval prestige was immense."[59]

Spurred by the large Soviet building program and working from the detailed view of *Sverdlov* obtained at Spithead, ONI in the fall of 1953 completed an extensive, secret assessment of the new Soviet cruisers. It concluded that *Sverdlov* was a basically conservative design, but compared to its predecessors it possessed significantly better antiaircraft capability, range, and survivability. Regarding the Soviet weapons systems on board the new cruiser, ONI paid a backhanded compliment by remarking that they "compare favorably with those used by the United States during World War II."[60]

The Soviets seemed to lag especially in the quality of their sensors. ONI remarked on the quantity of electronic gear that *Sverdlov* carried at Spithead, much of which appeared devoted to electronic countermeasures. U.S. analysts inferred: "emphasis on ECM gear and optical fire control systems suggests a possible Russian attempt to neutralize superior Western fire control radar and to capitalize on the Western tendency to cut back in optical fire control systems." In summary, ONI characterized *Sverdlov* as indicating a Soviet preference for "a greater number of combatant ships of relatively simple and rugged construction, but with good or above average striking power . . . to a restricted number of technically complex 'super ships.'"[61]

Looking at the *Sverdlov*s in retrospect, a number of senior U.S. officers of the late 1980s remembered the Soviet surface ships with a certain respect and, at the same time, with a confidence that the U.S. Navy of the 1950s could have coped with them relatively easily. However, archival records show that there was more concern within the Navy at that time than these officers recall. ONI evaluators writing in 1956 anticipated that the *Sverdlov*s and accompanying destroyers would operate principally in the Barents and Norwegian Seas within range of Soviet aircraft. The cruisers could range farther afield to threaten allied shipping during the conditions of bad visibility common to the Arctic where severe icing frequently prohibited allied carrier operations for days at a time. Particularly worrisome to American planners was the possibility that the Soviet cruisers might be armed in the near future with surface-to-surface missiles and with atomic projectiles for their guns. ONI added that Soviet seizure of the

Danish and Turkish Straits would allow surface units from the Baltic and Black Sea fleets to operate in the Mediterranean and North Seas. In such areas, the high density of shipping might allow raiders "to blend into the crowd." The problem of sorting the Soviet ships from the neutral and from the friendly (called later the "red, white, and blue" problem) was to become more severe over time.[62]

The Naval War College also paid substantial attention to the Soviet raiders. Officers on the game board were instructed that when a surface threat against a convoy developed "it will be considered paramount."[63] As more *Sverdlov*s entered the Soviet fleet, Newport officers conducted an increasing number of exercises centering on the defense of convoys against them. Most of these war games were logically set in the North Atlantic, but they were also played out in the eastern Mediterranean and even, in one case, in the Indian Ocean against Soviet forces based in Burma. A typical scenario involved U.S. naval forces defending a convoy to Bear Island with old battleship *Tennessee* (BB 43), six cruisers, and twenty-eight destroyers. In weather too severe for flight operations, the Soviets attacked with eleven cruisers and twenty destroyers. Unfortunately, no student solution is on file.[64]

The week-long exercises at Newport focusing on the surface warfare problem frequently took a historical bent by examining World War II engagements. In the fall of 1954 students looked at four surface battles: River Plate, Savo Island, Empress Augusta Bay, and the sinking of battlecruiser *Scharnhorst* off Norway in 1943. These studies were generally very thorough and involved a great deal of work with ballistics tables, maneuvering data, and other details of Allied and Axis World War II ships. For example, the class of 1955 was handed a twenty-six-page report listing the characteristics of all American battleships and cruisers in commission or reserve. When some officers questioned the worth of this historical approach, an instructor rejoined that the study of such actions allowed students to deduce tactical principles from actual historical cases. A debate ensued over the matter, and a survey of the sixty-three officers in the November 1954 exercise showed that fifty-five thought this sort of surface warfare study was valuable in the "so-called atomic age." But the next year, the time allotted to it was sliced by half—a harbinger of the death of tactical studies at the Naval War College.[65]

Occasional fleet exercises seemed to validate the threat of the surface raider, and certain surface officers felt the need to brush up on rusty techniques. In one 1954 test, heavy cruiser *Toledo* was able to approach within 5 miles of enemy carriers at night without being detected. Because some important convoys were protected only by destroyers, an OPNAV tactical publication in 1954 cautioned, "It is realized that destroyer torpedo attacks against modern radar-controlled gun systems are hazardous at very best and stand little chance of success unless supported by gunfire from heavy ships."[66] Moreover, an enemy cruiser at large also made defense against submarines more difficult, because the escort formations to cope with the two were quite different.[67]

With carrier magazines containing few antiship torpedoes, officers recommended a strong role for American surface warships in countering raiders. Newport planners especially appreciated the battleships for their value in Arctic operations. With their speed, seakeeping ability, and heavy protection, they frequently proved the queen on the chessboard. In a November 1954 study, the Soviet forces attacking a convoy on the game board outnumbered the NATO vessels two to one. But when an *Iowa*-class battleship—"superior to all types in heavy weather"—was brought into play, its gunfire "outweighs the entire PURPLE [Soviet] force by 3:1. This broadside can be brought to bear at ranges 4000 yards in excess of PURPLE CL [light cruiser] ranges."[68]

While surface ships maneuvered against a raider, OPNAV stressed that they keep accurate station in the dispersed task groups because U.S. cruisers would probably use missiles against the enemy surface ships. "Since cruiser surface-to-surface missiles could be used against raiders now, and surface-to-air missiles will be adapted for use against surface targets in the future, accurate station-keeping even under conditions when celestial navigation is difficult becomes more important to avoid being destroyed by mistake by friendly forces using these long-range weapons."[69]

Surface officers keenly anticipated the deployment of advanced tactical missiles on board their ships. The Naval War College suggested the development of such weapons with ranges of up to 500 miles that could be used "without waiting to gain air superiority and that are independent of weather conditions."[70] Nearer realization was Regulus, the air-breathing cruise missile developed by the Bureau of Aeronautics. By the end of the Korean War, it was about to enter service with a nuclear warhead on certain heavy cruisers. Although the missile was intended principally for the strategic strike role, Navy publications began listing Regulus as having an antiship capability. However, continuing guidance problems made the use of this weapon against mobile targets problematic, and some officers gave consideration to the employment of Terrier and Talos in the antiship mode instead. Development of this application for the missiles received only low priority, however.[71]

In fact, the Navy's overall antiship capabilities were withering, a matter which reflected the higher priority top planners assigned to countering other threats. The aviators were concentrating on the land-attack mission—whether strategic or tactical. By 1954, the Bureau of Ordnance listed only one aircraft-launched torpedo as having the surface ship as a target. This torpedo was the Mk 13, introduced to the fleet in 1938. BUORD noted the service status of the venerable weapon as "Issued to fleet. However, fleet use is limited." [72] For attack against Soviet surface warships, carrier aviators were developing by the early 1950s only two other precision weapons: an infrared guided bomb named Dove and an antiradar successor to BAT called Corvus. Neither became operational. Aviators were much more intent on refining their arsenal for strikes against land targets. [73]

With Regulus, the surface navy was eager to share in this land-attack mission. About the size and shape of a small fighter plane, Regulus achieved high subsonic speeds in level flight and, in its vertical terminal dive, crossed the sonic barrier. Major assets of the weapon included its ability to fly at altitudes from near wave-top level up to 35,000 feet, to follow several flight profiles, and to take evasive action against defenses. [74] An unusual feature of the design was that the flight test vehicles had retractable landing gear so that the missiles could be reused. Because each copy cost $270,000, the savings to the Navy was substantial considering that surface vessels and submarines would fire over eleven hundred "red birds" (practice shots) during the missile's career.

Regulus was large, at least by the standards of later cruise missiles, in order to carry the 120-kiloton W–5 nuclear warhead, approximately thirty-five copies of which were manufactured. Initial plans for the missile provided no alternative warhead. Insofar as any war with the Soviet Union would certainly be a nuclear conflict, this matter seemed unimportant. [75] The Korean War forced a reassessment of the issue; the Navy might fight more of these "brushfire" conflicts. In 1952, the CNO's office ruled: "The missile we place in our arsenals for Korean type war for use against ground targets must be capable of more accurate terminal attacks than corresponding type missiles produced for atomic war with Russia." In response, the Guided Missile Division prepared Regulus for a variety of tactical situations by developing a biological/chemical warhead and a conventional high-explosive model. [76]

A major problem with these alternative warheads was the necessity for precise guidance. Early on, the Navy had found this area to be the Achilles' heel of its entire bombardment missile program. Dan Gallery, the head of the Guided Missile Division, had remarked in the spring of 1948: "It is possible to build a transoceanic missile right now, but we don't know whether it would land in Spain, Portugal, or France." [77]

Regulus technicians tried a number of systems. The theoretically superior inertial guidance which emitted no external electronic signals (and thus provided no warning of the approaching missile nor any chance for jamming) depended on quantum improvements in gyroscopic bearings. Television guidance, long the subject of Navy experimentation, could give terminal accuracies on the order of 25 feet, but such guidance required a properly equipped escort plane to accompany the missile—often an impossibility. Another alternative was the bipolar navigation system wherein two guidance warships formed an electronic baseline close to the enemy coast; the missile then flew between their antennas. Aside from the obvious drawbacks of this clumsy arrangement, bipolar guidance proved terribly vulnerable to jamming.[78]

Regulus finally received a system called Trounce which theoretically required only one guidance warship and was much less susceptible to detection and jamming. Trounce was designed to allow the launching cruiser to control Regulus out to 350 miles and then to "hand-off" to the second vessel, thereby taking full advantage of the missile's range. In actual practice, it demanded the incorporation into the guidance system of arbitrary correction factors derived from the flight of a Trounce-equipped aircraft shortly before the Regulus fired.[79]

Despite these drawbacks, Navy cruisers accepted Regulus enthusiastically. It gave them their first truly advanced offensive weapon system—and at a low cost. Outfitting proved a simple matter because the ships had been constructed with a hangar at the stern for four scouting aircraft. The space was easily converted to stowage for Regulus missiles; the $450,000 price tag was cheap compared to the $4.5 million required for a submarine conversion. In October 1954, heavy cruiser *Los Angeles* (CA 135) carried out the first surface ship evaluations of the missile. Four months later, the ship successfully tested the system through to nuclear detonation and later in the year made the first cruiser deployment overseas with three missiles, each with the W–5 warhead. Eventually four cruisers carried the weapon (for details, see Chapter 3). Targeting was directed principally at Soviet submarine bases.[80]

If Regulus offered a long-range strategic strike role to U.S. cruisers, some black-shoe officers in OPNAV gave attention to resurrecting a much older mission: raiding enemy commerce. One OPNAV publication devoted specifically to raiding complained that the Navy thought too little about its possibilities: "Properly used, a raider can be of inestimable value and can give returns out of proportion to the effort put forth." American cruisers with their good speed, powerful armament, and excellent seakeeping qualities were "eminently suited for use as raiders."[81]

The OPNAV staffers admitted that conditions had to be unusually favorable for American cruisers to enter an area that might contain profitable targets. Poor weather and prolonged darkness might enable the warships to approach Soviet shipping bottlenecks, such as the swept channels near naval and shipping centers. Tactical deception might provide opportunities. Among the suggestions OPNAV offered were measures still practiced by the U.S. Navy today: deceptive lighting to disguise the raider as a merchant ship, falling in with neutral shipping, spurious radio emissions, or complete electronic silence.[82]

Much more likely than independent raider missions were concerted operations conducted by groups of surface warships. OPNAV, in formulating doctrine for such contingencies, cast aside the outmoded term "battle line" and substituted instead "surface action striking group" or "strength group." These formations would be organized primarily to oppose Soviet surface forces, but they might also support a landing, escort a convoy, or conduct a shore bombardment. OPNAV saw the last as an especially profitable employment, noting that once enemy air opposition was suppressed, surface warships could, "with great accuracy and economy," destroy enemy bases and land communications—difficult and expensive targets for carrier aircraft. With a bow to the future, OPNAV added, "surface-launched rockets, guided missiles, and atomic weapons may be used to accomplish this." [83]

Because a "surface action striking group" had its own special tactical and operational requirements, OPNAV composed in 1953 a lengthy tactical manual entitled "Striking Force Operations," officially designated Naval Warfare Publication (NWP) 20. This document spelled out the various tasks that battleships, cruisers, and destroyers might perform from the familiar wartime roles of carrier support and shore bombardment to activities in less belligerent situations, such as furnishing landing forces for evacuating nationals or assisting the victims of catastrophes. [84]

However, much of the emphasis of NWP 20 lay in its "Surface Action Striking Force Fighting Instructions." Included were subsections on the maneuvers of a surface action force, its tactics during an engagement, surface gunnery considerations, destroyer torpedo attack, and surface action involving small forces. The document devoted substantial space to distribution of fire and included the classic gunnery movement of crossing the enemy's T as well as such Nelsonian exhortations as "Victory is not complete unless the enemy force is annihilated. The ultimate aim is to destroy every enemy vessel." [85]

These doctrinal dictates obscured the fact that surface units seldom practiced any of these independent operations. Only in rare circumstances did destroyer flotillas or squadrons operate as such in exercises. It was equally unusual for cruisers and battleships to practice as divisions. In 1954, Arleigh Burke found that he was unable to concentrate the ships of Cruiser Division Six, theoretically under his command, for battle practice. In addition, ammunition for gunnery drills was frequently in short supply. Consequently, these surface warfare capabilities, so impressive on paper, remained largely that—paper capabilities. And as an apt Navy saying would have it: "If you don't practice it, you can't do it." [86]

The simple fact was that surface ships continued to play second fiddle to the aviators, and the tactical publications admitted as much. For instance, NWP 20 pointed out bluntly, "Carrier-based aircraft are the primary offensive weapon of the attack carrier striking force, with ships other than carriers acting primarily to support and screen against air and submarine threats, and acting secondarily against surface threats." Radar and aircraft had stripped from cruisers the element of surprise essential to their fulfillment of the scouting and raiding missions which had once been in their province. The OPNAV planners cautioned that the formation of a surface action striking group would weaken the carrier's screen and should be resorted to only when the enemy surface threat was primary and even in that case, only "when other means [namely, carrier air] cannot accomplish the desired result effectively."[87]

But NWP 20 did see bright prospects for the surface navy in a number of areas. The very size of the battleships and cruisers conferred on them important advantages, not the least of which was their amenability to modernization by the addition of radically improved weapons and sensors. OPNAV staffers saw future employment for the ships as offensive missile platforms, antiaircraft escorts, radar pickets, and aircraft controllers. Surface units practiced all of these functions.[88]

Shore bombardment received some increased attention in the Navy as a result of the Korean experience. Cruisers on occasion served as amphibious force flagships in exercises and honed their use of helicopters in fire support missions. A new institution, the Fleet Gunnery School, was split off from the Fleet Training Center in San Diego and established as a separate command at the same base. This institutional acknowledgment of the importance of gunnery was partially negated when, in 1954, the full-time officer billet devoted to amphibious gunnery in OPNAV was abolished. In the materiel sphere, the specialized shore bombardment fire control system first carried on board heavy cruiser *Salem* was installed in only a few other ships. And the inshore fire support craft *Carronade* (IFS 1, later LSR 1), intended as the first of a series, turned out an orphan. Commissioned in 1955, she went into mothballs five years later. Only the Vietnam struggle brought her back into the fleet.[89]

The Korean War did give a modest new lease on life to the shore support facilities for gunships. Some money went to Dahlgren for instrumentation on the gun range and for an ordnance computer program called the Naval Ordnance Research Calculator (NORC). The facility did a tremendous amount of work in proofing barrels, propellants, and projectiles to restock the Navy's magazines. At Pocatello, Idaho, the Naval Ordnance Plant, down to caretaker status by 1949, was also revitalized.[90]

The Korean War also demonstrated the challenges posed to the fleet by ever faster aircraft. Because the Soviets were bringing large numbers of jet bombers into their service, the problem intensified. For carrier fighters to intercept a Tu–4 bomber flying at 350 mph, the aircraft had to be detected 80 miles out; against a MiG–15 at 500 mph, the figure increased to 150 miles. Analysts thought the standard of Soviet aerial proficiency low, but the sheer number of their aircraft and the variety of attacks they might mount—horizontal, dive, glide, torpedo, night—constituted a serious threat. Adding to these concerns was the possibility that the Soviet aircraft might carry advanced weaponry such as guided missiles or special torpedoes that could be launched from high altitudes by jet aircraft. In addition, the possibility of suicide tactics continued to worry naval planners. One post-Korean estimate held that Russian kamikazes would hit their carrier targets 45 percent of the time, while Soviet guided missiles would have a success rate of 35 percent—and these figures were after interception by CAP and after accounting for the losses inflicted by antiaircraft fire.[91]

With hindsight, these alarming figures seem dismayingly accurate and were not, as a skeptic might have assumed, a budgetary crowbar to pry more money from Congress. Certainly fleet exercises underlined the difficulties the Navy was experiencing in coping with the jet aircraft threat. As the commander of one cruiser division reported in 1951, "with the realization that much greater aircraft speeds will be encountered under future combat conditions, a vast degree of improvement is mandatory."[92] Low-flying planes time and again penetrated task groups without being spotted.[93] Worse, after the Korean War, Soviet aircraft began overflying carrier task forces with virtual impunity. U.S. Navy surface units were simply finding it impossible to process with conventional "grease pencil" techniques the volume of information that sensors delivered. Officers who tackled the challenge concluded, "The use of individual plots for radar, the human passing of volumes of tactical information one item at a time, and the lack of coordinated reactions were leading the surface Navy to obsolescence."[94]

With the problem distressingly evident, both the Bureau of Ships and the Naval Research Laboratory began work on automated data processing systems. The analog technology of the time permitted only the most imperfect results; nonetheless some ships did receive tracking equipment under a program called Electronic Data System (EDS). The heart of EDS was an automated analog data processor developed by the Naval Research Laboratory. Holding out the possibility of major advances in military computers was the transistor, invented in 1948 and fostered by the Navy since 1949. In 1954, the Office of Naval Research initiated a joint project with the Air Force called Lamplight to tackle the air defense problem and data management in its broadest sense. The final report, issued in 1955 and called "The Defense of North America," suggested hopefully that the solution might lie with the development of an entirely new, digitally oriented system. But such a system lay far in the future.[95]

The much-improved combat information centers that surface warfare officers wanted in place of the extremely cramped facilities in the World War II vintage ships were also a distant possibility. Following a frustrating air defense drill in 1951 the commander of one destroyer squadron argued, "This type of exercise more fully emphasizes the inefficient designs of our

CICs. Facilities of destroyer flagships are inadequate and seriously over-crowded. This problem requires extensive study. It is a basic weakness."[96]

In the meantime, surface warriors labored with all the tools immediately at their disposal to counter the air threat. Early detection of enemy aircraft assumed ever greater importance. To combat low fliers, surface officers pushed for the deployment of an effective airborne early warning aircraft. Against aircraft at higher altitudes, surface ships with suitable radars could play an important role in fleet defense. Heavy cruiser *Helena* proved as much on 2 November 1952 when she picked up a large number of bogies flying out of Vladivostok. Fighters from carrier *Oriskany* (CV 34) intercepted the MiGs and shot down five of the seven engaged. Reviving a World War II measure, the Navy in 1952 began the conversion of twelve *Gearing*-class destroyers to carry the large SPS–8 height finder radar, Tactical Air Navigation (TACAN) air control beacons, and better communications. Each ship, reclassified as a DDR, required about nine months of extensive work; the electronics gear alone cost more than an entire World War II destroyer.[97]

The Bureau of Ordnance and the operating forces continued to try for refinements in antiaircraft gunnery. Doctrine at the beginning of the Korean War dictated that the combat air patrol break off at 10 miles to allow the cruisers and destroyers to use their antiaircraft guns.[98] The new *Des Moines*-class heavy cruisers with their rapid-fire 8-inch mounts exercised hard to bring their guns "up to speed." The main battery fire control system using full radar direction could aim the guns against aircraft up to the maximum elevation of 41 degrees. In 1952, the commander of the big gunships in the Atlantic Fleet ordered the new cruisers to conduct antiaircraft practices with their 8-inch weapons whenever practicable. One officer wrote that this directive "was received with much speculation by the uninitiated as to which type of practice would be practical and as to how the tractor pilots [of the target towing planes] would react."[99] Despite this skepticism, initial results seemed promising. In the spring of 1953, *Newport News* conducted two shoots with results judged "fair" and "excellent." The elevation restrictions on the gun hampered its altitude, of course, but the 8-inch could reach out to 25,000 yards, thus doubling the range of the ship's lighter antiaircraft weapons against low- or medium-altitude targets. The cruiser reported that its 8-inch might also be employed to harass snoopers or to break up large aircraft formations. The ship recommended the provision of a proximity fuze for the high-capacity projectile and a "full time" antiaircraft fire control system for the big guns.[100]

Of course, the 8-inch had never been designed as an antiaircraft weapon. Coming on line were three guns that had been: the 3"/50, the long-barreled 3"/70, and the 5"/54 Mk 42. The last made its appearance with the surface fleet in 1953 with the *Mitscher*-class destroyer leaders. With two control

One of the aft 5″/54 Mk 42 mounts on *Hull* (DD 945).

USN 1166035

stations, one for aerial and the other for surface targets, the weapon with its rapid rate of fire of forty rounds per minute was intended to be the equivalent of a twin 5″/38. The newer gun also featured a significant range advantage—25,900 yards versus 17,300 for the 5″/38. Among the criticisms leveled at the new weapon was its marginal magazine capacity in view of its high rate of fire. Moreover, the complexity of the mount meant reliability problems for the first part of its career. One officer recalled, "the way to look at [it] would be forty rounds the first minute, and then zero or maybe twenty."[101] When the mount malfunctioned, crewmen had to check hundreds of electrical interlocks one by one. Other serious troubles, including accidental explosions during action off South Vietnam, plagued the mount well into the 1960s; a series of modifications and a restricted rate of fire in the 1970s eventually cured the problems. In the late 1980s, some Navy ordnance specialists preferred the Mk 42 to the newer Mk 45, especially for its flexible ammunition supply which enabled gunners to switch quickly from one type of projectile to another.[102]

Entering the fleet in larger numbers in the 1950s was the 3″/50. Its reliability was a sometime thing. Heavy cruiser *Los Angeles*, operating off the east coast of Korea in late 1952, experienced short circuits that put three of her eight mounts out of commission for much of that tour. Even more troubling, the weapon already lagged well behind the rapid strides in aircraft development. Against jet aircraft with nuclear weapons, the 3"/50 was utterly inadequate with its maximum range of 30,000 feet. Its rate of fire of about fifty rounds per minute was marginal at best, and even at that, the gun suffered from bore erosion with a consequent decrease in barrel life.[103]

As the long-awaited 3"/70 showed, a cure for the slow rate of fire problem exacerbated the wear problem. When it finally entered service almost six years behind schedule, the Bureau of Ordnance billed it as "the fastest and most efficient antiaircraft weapon ever built."[104] At ninety rounds per minute, fast it was. One officer who worked with it said in retrospect, "When it did shoot, it shot a lot of bullets in a hurry."[105] Tests in 1955 showed an average rate of fire of 92.5 rounds per gun per minute. But bore erosion was so severe that BUORD hastened the work already begun in 1951 on a new cooler-burning propellant called Navy Cool (NACO). This research would finally pay off over a decade later when surface warships firing shore bombardment missions in Vietnam used NACO for several different gun calibers.[106]

Carrying the new guns into the fleet were the two new types of experimental warships funded late in the 1940s. *Norfolk* took the 3"/70 to sea for the first time in August 1955. Introducing the 5"/54 Mk 42 to the surface navy were the four ships of the *Mitscher* class. Given the size (4,855 tons full load) and cost ($18 million) of the *Mitschers*, their destroyer designation seemed too modest. To highlight their capabilities (and that of CLK *Norfolk*), the Navy introduced in 1951 the classification of destroyer leader (or DL). The new designator DL reflected their frequent employment as destroyer squadron flagships. While keeping the DL designator, the Navy dropped the term "destroyer leader" in 1955 and recategorized the ships as "frigates." Although the term "frigate" resonated in the Navy with glorious associations of the *Constitution* and her kin, it was in some ways unfortunate. During World War II, navies had tagged oceangoing antisubmarine escorts as frigates, and most fleets except for the U.S. Navy continued to do so throughout the postwar period, to the confusion of defense commentators. Only in 1975 did the U.S. Navy hew to the general foreign practice.[107]

Entering service as the Korean War ended, the *Mitschers* featured numerous innovations. The large-scale use of aluminum above the main deck gave them a very favorable metacentric height. With their high clipper bow and long forecastle deck, they were outstandingly seaworthy—an important consideration given their mission of screening aircraft carriers in all weather conditions. Habitability items new to destroyers included air conditioning in many spaces, innerspring mattresses and individual bunk lights for sailors, and salad bars and beverage dispensers in the galleys.[108]

*Mitschers* introduced 1,200-pound, 950-degree steam to the Navy. First tested in the partially reboilered destroyer *Dahlgren* (DD 187) in May 1939, the development of the high-pressure plant was delayed by the war. In comparison to the conventional 600-pound plant, 1,200-pound steam offered a number of advantages: good power responses without "rocking" the engines, much better efficiency in converting fuel to energy, and a smaller, lighter machinery plant for a specific power output. With more energy in the steam, the turbines for the main engines, pumps, and generators could be downsized but run at much higher speeds, thus delivering greater power than their predecessors. Some enthusiasts anticipated that moving to 1,200-pound steam would bring as great a step forward as the shift from coal to oil.[109]

Naturally, 1,200-pound steam presented special challenges. For designers, the higher temperatures necessitated the employment of exotic ferritic steel alloys containing molybdenum and vanadium. For sailors, the new plants demanded meticulous maintenance and close attention during operation. Cleaning procedures had to be followed on a regular basis, which frequently conflicted with the often-changing operational schedule of a warship. Low water in a boiler, caused by the fluctuating demands for speed, could occur in a matter of seconds. If the boiler were not secured immediately, serious equipment damage would ensue. The worst accident involving a 1,200-pound plant, however, was caused by a ruptured oil burner lead on board frigate *King* (DLG 10) in 1969 which caused an explosion on the ship. Four crewmen died; fifteen others were injured; and the ship lay without power off the Vietnamese coast for ten hours.[110]

Early on, the hazards of 1,200-pound steam were recognized as serious; the price of inattention was so great that rigorous preparation for the engineering watch was essential. To this end, the surface navy moved ship engineering training ashore. Thus, the problems associated with 1,200-pound steam was a major factor in the establishment of the Destroyer Engineering School at Newport. Eventually the Navy imposed on 1,200-pound steam the same rigorous standards applied to nuclear plants, including the establishment of the Senior Officer's Maintenance Course under nuclear management at Idaho Falls as well as painstaking testing procedures in the fleet. One officer who had intimate experience with 1,200-pound steam at a number of levels over a long career commented, "I participated in the Navy efforts to get well including the imposition of strict standards. Unfortunately, in my judgment, the powers that be did not always appreciate the fact that the resources available to the surface Navy did not in any way match those committed to the nuclear Navy." [111] Nonetheless, the surface navy eventually came to terms with 1,200-pound steam. By the late 1950s, "The crews were not 'scared' of the plants anymore, and had begun to take great pride in their reliability and performance." [112] The first captain of destroyer *Semmes* (DDG 18) recalled, "The 1200 pound steam plant was a joy and delight. We concentrated on maintenance and operator training, and used to have tours through the machinery spaces by the rest of the crew to 'see where the real men work.'" [113]

But for the commissioning crews of the four *Mitscher*s, such a happy state lay well over the horizon. The ambitious ships were laid down, two by Bath Iron Works and two by Bethlehem's Quincy yard, from October 1949 to February 1950. The Navy originally hoped to take delivery of the first of them by 1951, but *Mitscher* (DL 2) hoisted her commissioning pennant in May 1953. Part of the delay lay in the unusual contracting procedures by which the Navy eschewed competitive bidding in favor of parceling the work out among a large number of subcontractors, hoping thereby to keep some key defense firms in business. As construction times dragged out, costs rose. When Frederick H. Schneider, Jr., the first commanding officer of *Willis A. Lee* (DL 4), arrived at Bath, he found that the ship's scheduled sea trials had been canceled as an economy measure. Only by dint of vigorous effort was Schneider able to get them reinstated.[114]

And what problems they revealed! Between August 1953 and September 1954, Schneider put the ship through fourteen sets of builder's trials, eight pierside and six underway. Virtually all of the machinery gave trouble—the low-pressure turbines to such a degree that they had to be cut out of the ship and returned to the manufacturer. The other three ships suffered similar difficulties. On *Mitscher*, "All four main ship service steam generators had to be replaced (four months in the yard) after one unit ran away during lighting off and the turbine exploded. . . . Fragments came within inches of rupturing a main steam line, which would have killed everyone in the space." [115] When the ship attempted a shakedown cruise to Guantanamo Bay, the reduction gears for the starboard engine failed utterly. One of her officers remembered, "I made my slowest ocean voyage (nine knots) in the Navy's fastest ship (thirty-five knots)." [116] Reportedly, all of the ships operated for a time under a speed restriction of 20 knots because of the gear problem.

In service, the four frigates certainly presented challenges to their crews. One officer remembered of his tour on board *John S. McCain* (DL 3), "Boiler casualties were a weekly, if not daily, experience. Nearly as unreliable were the ship's service generators. In *McCain*, we often went to sea utilizing the auxiliary diesel generators for power and lighting just to avoid remaining constantly dockside." [117] Another officer who served on board the lead frigate recalled, "The final humiliation for the *Mitscher* came . . . when her forced circulation boilers [which] had been a terrible headache since commissioning finally failed so badly that the ship could not produce enough feed water to make up for the leaks. She was taken under tow by one of her *Dealey*-class DE escorts, while another *Dealey* steamed along side pumping feed water to her."[118] *Mitscher* and *John S. McCain* had to be completely reboiled.[119]

In the end, the four *Mitscher*s did repay the Navy for some of the trouble by acting as test platforms for new equipment. Despite their design emphasis on the antiaircraft mission, they were among the first with such antisubmarine devices as rocket-boosted torpedoes, drone helicopters, and bow-mounted sonar domes.[120] Some veterans remembered their time on board the ships with a certain pride, but others were caustic in their criticism: "An engineering dud";[121] "A BuShips war crime";[122] "Too bad for the problems because these ships carried the names of gallant WWII heroes."[123] Late in their careers the two reboiled ships were deemed reliable enough to be worth extensive modification with guided missiles and up-to-date ASW gear. Reclassified in 1968 as DDGs, *Mitscher* and *John S. McCain* served until 1978; *Willis A. Lee* and *Wilkinson* (DL 5) were decommissioned in 1969.

Even more radical than the *Mitscher*s was the experimental *Timmerman* (DD 828, later AG 152). Never intended as a prototype, the destroyer was built as a seagoing test bed. Laid down in 1945 as one of the *Gearing* class, her conventional appearance belied her experimental engineering plant and many other advanced features, all designed to cut weight drastically. The ship tested two different types of boilers, the more extreme of which operated at the highest steam pressure and temperature (2,000 pounds and 1,050 degrees) ever used for ship propulsion. The electrical system ran at 400 cycles and 1,000 volts rather than the conventional 60 cycles and 440 volts. Design specifications called for *Timmerman*'s lighter machinery to produce 100,000 shp rather than the 60,000 of a standard *Gearing*. To shave pounds, aluminum substituted for steel in the superstructure. Even the ship's sanitary plumbing, laundry, anchor windlass and steering gear pared off weight.[124]

Commissioned with a picked crew in September 1952, *Timmerman* immediately ran into troubles. Not that these were unexpected. Her commanding officer wrote:

> [T]he vessel was designed and built on the premise that if an individual piece of equipment did not fail then that piece of equipment was not designed close enough. . . . Experience to date indicates the vessel has been 99% a success because 99% of the equipment has failed in one way or another. . . . In the early days after commissioning it was not unusual to step cautiously into the "head" and wonder whether or not this was the unpredictable hour in which the flushing system would be lacking in pressure; or to go to the wardroom for dinner only to see gold buttoned uniforms face the white linen tablecloth while flashlights in hip pockets clanked against the chairs in anticipation of a power failure.[125]

The machinery broke down constantly; on one occasion when her emergency generator went dead, *Timmerman* was moored at Newport with a storm blowing up and no power whatsoever. During her first eight months in commission, she spent twenty-three hours at sea; wits referred to the ship as "Building 828." When she did sail, a tug or another destroyer often went with her. Given her incessant troubles, *Timmerman* probably never was able to run full power trials. She was scrapped in 1958, and a historical study by her builder, Bath Iron Works, concluded, "The *Timmerman* experiment proved more than anything else that the sound way to progress is step by step. Or maybe she proved that reliability required margins in design." [126]

Entering service at about the same time as *Timmerman* was another—and more successful—unusual vessel, the command ship *Northampton*, converted from a heavy cruiser hull. Carrying a light armament of four 5"/54s and eight 3"/50s (later 3"/70s), she featured a massive SPS–2 radar, a 125-foot communications antenna forward, and smooth contours designed to facilitate radioactive wash-down. With ample space for a fleet commander's staff, the ship was intended to coordinate air defense and, in an emergency, to embark the President and his most important advisers. Commissioned in 1953, for seventeen years *Northampton* served as a flagship, frequently for the Sixth Fleet, and as a test ship for the Navy's newest electronic and data processing gear. [127]

Far more conventional than *Northampton* and much more successful than the *Mitscher*s was the *Forrest Sherman* class—the only new surface warships larger than a destroyer escort ordered in the first half of the 1950s. These 4,900-ton destroyers, eighteen of which were ultimately completed in the last half of the decade, were designed to screen fast carriers. For antisubmarine work, they were fitted with the new SQS–4 sonar, Hedgehog mortars, and six 12.75-inch ASW torpedo tubes. Being the first U.S. destroyers with no antiship torpedoes (except for the first two units of the class), they also featured an unusual gun layout with two of their three 5"/54 Mk 42 gun mounts aft. This distribution was advertised as better suited for antiaircraft and shore bombardment work, but it attracted numerous barbed comments as did the seemingly light main armament with half the number of 5-inch barrels carried by the last of the World War II destroyers of the *Gearing* class. [128]

Like their contemporaries (the *Dealey*s and the *Mitscher*s), the *Forrest Sherman*s were handsome ships with seakeeping and handling to match. "Remarkably agile," was the verdict of one officer. [129] Their high bows and sheer forward enabled them to keep up with carriers in all but the worst weather, although really rough seas challenged their crews. The first commanding officer of the lead ship recalled, "She had quite a roll component. I saw her roll 45 degrees one time in a transit from Seattle to San Diego, but she would right herself relatively quickly and not hang there which most sailors do not care for." [130] In 1957, destroyer *Manley* (DD 940) proved her toughness when, caught in an Atlantic storm with winds up to 80 mph, she hit a mountainous wave that killed two men and flooded the galley and radar rooms. [131]

The *Forrest Sherman*s were afflicted with relatively few shortcomings. One officer remembered his ship, *Hull* (DD 945), as plagued with inferior drinking fountains—a problem he ascribed to the "low-bid syndrome." [132] Major equipment failures were few despite the 1,200-pound steam plant, although some of the ships did experience boiler blower and turbine problems. Improvements in habitability matched those in the *Mitscher*s. [133] One officer remembered:

> Like the *Mitscher* we finally had air conditioned living spaces, but the engineering spaces were as punishing as ever. Little gimmicks like individual bunk lights, and improved lockers, and foam rubber mattresses went a long way towards making the ship more comfortable. But she was still a big machine inhabited by some 350 men, and was a roller and pitcher like all her predecessors. Destroyer life was much improved, but not transformed. [134]

And in another important way, the *Forrest Sherman*s were quite traditional—in their armament. As the last of the all-gun destroyers in the Navy, a second commanding officer of the lead ship assessed her capabilities with some acerbity:

> *Forrest Sherman* (DD 931) was a beautiful ship and a delight to command, but she was obsolescent when she was designed. Her 5-inch/54s doubled the gunpower of any previous dual purpose destroyer, but her fire control equipment and radars were only marginally better. . . . Her habitability improvements, especially the air conditioning, was [*sic*] greatly appreciated, but as a fighting unit, she . . . represented the first step in the modern trend to build big, comfortable targets instead of lean, mean, combatants. [135]

An officer who served on *Jonas Ingram* (DD 938) echoed these sentiments:

> [S]he still had depth charge racks and hedgehogs—1945's latest. But she ran like a new watch, and was a great ship for shore bombardment and surface gunfire. In the face of jet air attack she was almost helpless. CIC was still operated by grease pencil and elastic-band grids. There was no height finder in her air search radar. And her hull was too small for a really big sonar. In short, a joy to serve in, and a winner if WWII was to be restarted . . . but we had to admit she was probably a 1944 destroyer designer's dream that came true in 1957 because nothing better could be done. [136]

As these officers knew, the balance scales of the 1950s were tilting ever further against the gun in the antiaircraft mission. The Bureau of Ordnance experimented with a host of measures and spent a "huge" portion of its annual budget on advanced projects to reverse the trend. Among its ventures were: variable depth rifling to reduce erosion, molybdenum barrels, a squeeze-bore gun, a saboted projectile, and jet-assisted shells. Especially intriguing for close-in defense was the liquid propellant gun begun in 1949. By 1954, BUORD had developed a 30mm prototype with a rate of fire of one thousand rounds per minute.[137]

Yet not one of these imaginative projects came close to realization. BUORD was rowing against the tide; the gun was basically obsolete for long-range antiaircraft purposes. Close range, or point defense, was not really the issue, and to bring down aircraft at the requisite distances required a projectile with reliable guidance—something that was simply beyond the technology of the time. Tube electronics were relatively large and comparatively fragile under the extreme g-loads exerted by a gun upon firing.[138]

Making a bad situation worse, the proximity-fuzed shell, which had been the ace-in-the-hole for antiaircraft artillery for more than a decade, was losing its edge. To explode the projectile, the proximity fuze had to come within 100 feet of the target aircraft. Even so, the lethal radius against a modern aircraft of the 3-inch shell, which broke up into a small number of "chunky" fragments, was less than 20 feet; of the 5-inch, about 30 feet. Against a fast-moving jet aircraft, these figures left distressingly little margin for error. Moreover, at 8 miles, the proximity fuze would cause the projectile to self-destruct. This range was simply too short to enable gunfire to protect a carrier in widely dispersed formations. One 1952 Newport study concluded pessimistically that the range of antiaircraft artillery could not be significantly improved, and that against maneuvering aerial targets at long ranges, gunnery problems were virtually insoluble. To defeat an enemy armed with nuclear bombs, the defenses would need to score an attrition rate of 100 percent.[139]

The question of antiaircraft defense was so urgent that guided missiles were hurried to deployment before they were truly ready. Shortly after the outbreak of the Korean War, the Joint Chiefs of Staff decided to push the Terrier into the earliest possible production (along with Nike for the Army and Sparrow for the Air Force) despite "the calculated risk" involved. The high command judged the gamble worth taking. The early introduction of Terrier into the fleet would do more than fill the gap between gunfire and the combat air patrol. It would also allow the surface ships to work out the operating techniques, tactics, and doctrine they would need for even more capable missiles in the pipeline.[140]

The accelerated development and production of Terrier involved a major effort by a host of labs, testing facilities, and ordnance plants. The Applied Physics Lab at Johns Hopkins University continued to play a key role in research; the Naval Ordnance Test Station, Inyokern, California, carried out much of the experimentation. The Navy teams scheduled to operate the missile on board ship trained together first at APL and later at the White

Sands Missile Range. Convair received a contract to produce 1,000 missiles at the rate of 75 per month. The Bureau of Ordnance also sponsored the construction of a manufacturing facility, the Naval Industrial Reserve Ordnance Plant at Pomona, California. Completed in 1953 after two years of work, the Pomona facility produced only Terrier missiles. Two factories manufactured the propellant grains: the Allegheny Ballistics Laboratory of the Hercules Powder Company at Cumberland, Maryland, and the Naval Powder Factory at Indian Head, Maryland. An index of the scale of the Navy's investment in Terrier is that the two Maryland facilities combined could produce 275 sets of booster and sustainer grains monthly or 1,000 on an around-the-clock basis and to the exclusion of any other effort. Each booster grain weighed 740 pounds and had the texture of hardwood.[141]

The Terrier missile itself was extremely complex with close to 100 vacuum tubes and 1,000 resistors, all of which had to function under wildly varying conditions of shock, humidity, temperature, and pressure. The whole missile, weighing slightly over one ton, was propelled to supersonic speed by its booster which burned out in three seconds. The missile was then captured by a radar beam and handed off at about nine seconds into flight to its guidance beam which Terrier rode to the target. Beam-riding offered the advantage that several missiles could follow the beam simultaneously. Prospects for Terrier seemed high enough that the missile elicited interest from both the Army and the Marines.[142]

Testing, which started in 1953, looked promising. BUORD officers calculated a single missile ought to have a kill probability of about 33 percent against a 600-mph aircraft. In a series of trials in the first half of 1953, the success rate against slower propeller-driven drones ran encouragingly at slightly over 50 percent. However, this first version of Terrier was unacceptable for use in the fleet because of its expense of production, difficulties in servicing, short storage life, and slow warm-up time.[143]

Still, BUORD seemed to have made a good start. In August 1953, the first shipboard firing by test ship *Mississippi* (EAG 128) resulted in a direct hit on an F6F drone by a Terrier flying without a warhead. By mid-1954, the bureau reported that direct hits on such targets had become "alarmingly" frequent—alarming because the missiles generally destroyed the drones, which were in short supply. Especially sweet was a demonstration attended by Admiral CNO Carney, who watched a salvo of two Terriers knock two drones "down in flames" with direct hits during an Atlantic Fleet exercise in the fall of the year.[144]

In fact, this success was particularly welcome because the test record of Terrier to date had actually been quite spotty. BOURD noted that the missile seemed woefully susceptible to "brass poisoning, that is, it performed erratically whenever admirals came around!"[145] The bureau later admitted with a certain understatement, "Combing the burrs out of Terrier took a bit of doing." [146] Numbered lots of one to almost seventy missiles were fired to correct particular problems. For instance, lot four suffered a high number of failures until one analyst working with films of the shots noticed what seemed to be flutter in the control surfaces. An aircraft camera mounted on the booster fins showed his hunch to be correct; a redesign was required. Such problems became so vexing that BUORD established a special team, the Terrier Task Group, to track down the causes; the Naval Ordnance Test Station set up its own Terrier Evaluation Committee. These ad hoc groups of missile specialists would be the first in a distressingly long series devoted to straightening out Terrier. The bureau tried to cover over its frustrations with a brave face. It reported in June 1954 that the preceding year had seen almost two hundred Terriers fired with "progressively improved results" including the first kill of a drone by a production prototype missile. [147]

The Applied Physics Laboratory joined in the efforts to fix Terrier. Looking over the production line at Convair, two APL engineers, Richard Kershner and Alexander Kossiakoff, suggested a radical change in the assembly of the missiles. The engineers proposed that, rather than building them like aircraft—constructing the airframe and then fitting the components to it—the missiles be built in sections, each of which could be tested independently. APL constructed ten missiles, designated the Terrier IB, by this method. Of the nine tested, eight were completely successful, "an unheard-of reliability for that time." [148] Modular construction soon became the norm, not only for Terrier, but for many other missiles. [149]

Meanwhile, the larger Talos was running about three years behind Terrier in development despite the earlier start enjoyed by the larger weapon. In sheer size and appearance, Talos was the most impressive antiaircraft missile ever employed by the U.S. Navy. Nineteen feet long and weighing 3,100 pounds without its booster (which added 11 feet in length and 4,425 pounds), the missile dwarfed even the 16-inch battleship projectile and inspired one officer to remark, "I can imagine that the gunnery and supply officers of the U.S.S. *Missouri* would have very little hair left after a tour of duty with this weapon." [150] Talos also impressed naval personnel by its incorporation of a number of advanced features, including the first rocket-launched supersonic ramjet engine and the first interferometric homing guidance. The Talos guidance system differed from Terrier's in that the Talos missile was launched directly into the guidance beam which it followed until the missile was 5 miles from the target at which point the terminal guidance took over. At long range, the guidance beam was programmed so that the missile would fly at high altitude to conserve fuel. An unanticipated side benefit of this feature was that when the missile was fired operationally off North Vietnam in the late 1960s, it reportedly achieved tactical surprise against enemy fighters by attacking from overhead. [151]

USN 659358

A Terrier is launched from *Mississippi*, 28 March 1955. The *Gearing*-class destroyer *Richard E. Kraus* (DD 849) steams close astern.

With its many innovations, the Talos missile, like Terrier, suffered from numerous "bugs" during its development. Frequently, mechanical failures would cause electrical failures, making diagnosis quite difficult. Nonetheless, the flight of prototypes in 1952 exhibited sufficient promise that BUORD began planning a host of improvements, namely, antiship and shore bombardment capabilities, an exotic continuous-rod warhead (see Chapter 3), a nuclear warhead, extension of the missile's range to 100 miles by 1961, and an unjammable guidance system. The schedule called for Talos to be operational by 1956.[152]

However promising Talos might be, only a cruiser could carry the Goliath. Surface warfare officers considered even Terrier (at 27 feet long and 2,400 pounds) big for destroyers. A smaller missile was needed, and not just for reasons of fit. Low-flying aircraft, which were difficult to detect at any distance, demanded a very fast response—something the larger missiles could

The Navy's first guided missile cruisers, *Canberra* and *Boston*, at Norfolk during change of command ceremonies when Rear Admiral Charles B. Martell relieved Rear Admiral Charles L. Melson as Commander Cruiser Division Four, 14 April 1958.

not give. Talos, in fact, had a *minimum* horizontal range of 4 miles; the big missile's terminal guidance system would not be able to acquire an approaching threat at a shorter distance. In March 1952, the Navy issued an operational requirement for a missile tailored to meet the demands of size and quick reaction. Two technical breakthroughs led to the development of Tartar: a continuous-wave illuminator homing system, and a solid-fuel rocket motor combining both the booster and sustainer in one engine which permitted a major size reduction. APL cooperated on the project; by July 1954, the basic outlines of the compact missile were on paper.[153]

Of course, missiles were just one part of the recipe for correcting the air/sea equation. The Navy would need ships to carry and control these new weapons, and the provision of suitable vessels would prove to be an immensely difficult task in itself. In 1950, Congress had approved the conversion of heavy cruisers *Boston* (CA 69) and *Canberra* (CA 70) as the Navy's first missile ships. Both were World War II veterans; *Boston* sported ten battle stars. The ships in their new guise were important enough that they traded their old heavy cruiser designation of CA for CAG with the G indicating their guided missile armament. They wore proudly the hull numbers 1 and 2 of the new G series of missile cruisers. Although some optimists thought the ships would be ready for trials by the summer of 1954, it was a measure of the complexity of their conversions that *Boston* did not recommission until the fall of 1955. *Canberra* followed suit the next spring.

Although the cruisers kept their two forward 8-inch turrets, the appearance of the ships changed markedly from the bridge aft. One of the stacks was entirely removed; the massive array of electronic gear stood out topside. In fact, certain flag officers prized them during their first years of service as G ships more for their search radars and modern combat information centers than for their missiles. In place of the after 8-inch turret stood two Terrier launchers, each with twin launching rails. Under these were the two rotary magazines holding a total of 144 Terriers. The Bureau of Ordnance noted the dangers inherent in the missile stowage: "Developed to be as unsafe to the enemy as practicable, Terrier presents unique safety problems to the user." [154] Each fully loaded magazine contained 40 tons of high explosive and propellant grain. The missiles were stowed with the warheads and the booster and sustainer igniters in place.[155]

To avoid a disastrous magazine explosion, the bureau in October 1953 initiated the Terrier Rocket Safety Test Program carried out at Dahlgren under the supervision of the Applied Physics Laboratory. As part of their investigation, technicians placed a missile in a simulated magazine and then intentionally ignited its sustainer. Flames from the propellant kindled the magnesium elements of the missile and set off the booster. Analysts concluded that the warhead would probably have detonated also, leading to a chain reaction within the magazine.[156] Such a disaster would doubtless destroy the ship. BUORD therefore worked safety features into the magazines. The missiles were stowed with their firing leads shorted, and blow-out plugs locked in the open position made both booster and sustainer nonpropulsive in the magazine.[157]

The magazine itself was a complex piece of equipment, nicknamed the "Coke machine" by crewmen. When its mechanism was activated, its seventy-two missiles, which weighed altogether 85 tons, could be moved rapidly and precisely by remote control. "A mechanical marvel" was one officer's assessment of the magazine.[158] Before being loaded on the launcher, the missile was readied for firing by crewmen who attached wings and fins as well as arming the warhead with a special tool.[159]

Even on the launcher, the missile presented special challenges. For one thing, it was attached to the launcher rail by lugs only at the ends of the booster. The missile therefore acted as a cantilever beam attached to the booster. With the missile and booster weighing over 2,350 pounds, the stress on the attachment lugs was so great that several broke during the early stages of development. To avoid such a failure on board ship, the launchers were restricted in movement to 40 degrees per second in elevation and 60 degrees in train. Additionally, special measures were required to prevent the missile from firing into the ship's structure. Given all these difficulties, the Bureau of Ordnance was proud of the fact that *Boston* and *Canberra* could fire a double missile salvo from each launcher every 25 seconds. In service, the launcher was to show itself very reliable.[160]

While undergoing their reconstruction in the yards, the two cruisers were equipped with improved messing and berthing spaces. Their engineering and propulsion plants received overhauls, and their 40mm antiaircraft guns were replaced by twelve 3"/50s. The recommissioning of *Boston* as CAG 1 on 1 November 1955 was important enough that the new CNO, Arleigh Burke, gave the keynote address. He drew particular attention to the numeral one on the ship's bow—"a symbol of great significance." The admiral continued, "This ship is the first of literally dozens of fighting ships that will don new armaments within the next five years."[161]

Burke's forecast heartened the surface community, many of whom saw the missile ship as their salvation. At a 1955 Pentagon conference on the new missile cruisers, Vice Admiral Robert Briscoe compared the fleet introduction of the surface-to-air guided missile to the introduction of aircraft in naval operations. One Naval War College seer even predicted the eventual replacement of piloted airplanes by the guided missile as the principal naval weapon.[162]

Despite new missile developments, surface warriors felt that they were still losing ground within the Navy. Aviation's place was so central that when a new personnel designation system was introduced in 1952, a surface line officer was officially described as "an officer not a member of the aeronautic organization." One analyst noted later that surface officers generally acquiesced to this new order "as long as ships were plentiful and promotions were equitable. Consequently, the continual policy drift away from emphasizing the utility and vital necessity of the surface ships was not forcefully addressed."[163]

Beginning in 1954, surface warriors found themselves falling behind a second branch, the nuclear submariners. With the success of *Nautilus* (SSN 571), Hyman Rickover's monastic order attracted many of the ambitious younger officers, especially those skilled in engineering. For instance, Stansfield Turner, recently having returned from a Rhodes scholarship stint in England, seriously considered transferring from the surface branch into nuclear submarines. He reminisced, "I could see that a lot of my classmates who were the brighter ones were going into the nuclear program."[164] The power plant in the Navy's future seemed certain to be nuclear, and it

Vice Admiral Hyman G. Rickover on board *Nautilus* (SSN 571).

SDAN 1104996

was wedded to the submarine for the immediate time to come. The surface navy now placed third in the Navy's pecking order.[165]

One 1953 article in the *Proceedings* analyzed reasons for the Navy's changing complexion. A career in aviation or in submarines paid a sizable dividend in increased pay. An aviator or submariner with the rank of commander received a monthly increment of $180; for a captain, the sum was $210. Submariners received dive pay only when actually engaged in seagoing duty, whereas the airman invariably drew his flight pay bonus as long as he remained a qualified aviator. In either case, compared to the surface officer the monetary gap in pay was substantial, often making "the difference between just barely managing and living a life of reasonable comfort."[166]

Pay, while not the motivating factor for most officers of any branch, could hardly be dismissed as unimportant. The same applied to status—

and here too, it seemed to some surface officers that their situation was deteriorating. One writer in the *Proceedings* lamented the diminution of the prestige associated with the line officer's star when it was worn by restricted line officers "designated for Engineering Duty," "designated for Aeronautical Engineering Duty," and "designated for Special Duty" in such disparate fields as law, naval intelligence, public information, psychology, and photography.[167]

If the surface officer was not especially moved by considerations of pay or prestige, he almost certainly was motivated by prospects of promotion and command. Here too, shoal water lay ahead. The number of surface warships in commission, especially of the larger gunships, was in decline for the rest of the decade following the Korean War. Inevitably, the odds against a young officer ever commanding a cruiser or battleship were high. One heavy cruiser skipper noted in 1955 that the personnel rosters of his ship listed seventy-five officers; in the entire Navy, only about twenty officers commanded major surface combatants. Frustrating for those officers who then reached this pinnacle was the fact that their tours lasted just one year (increased to eighteen months in the mid-1950s). For the new commanding officer, "time speeds by and his one year tour is half gone before he knows his way around the ship. He has scarcely had a chance to put into practice some of his stored-up ideas, when he finds himself a 'short-timer.'"[168]

Increasingly, a career in submarines or aviation was the fast track to the top. In the decade following World War II, aviators with the rank of captain enjoyed approximately a 40 percent selection for promotion, a figure double that of nonaviators. At the level of fleet command, aviators increasingly took the helm: Sixth Fleet in the Mediterranean went to aviator Forrest Sherman in 1948; Seventh Fleet in the western Pacific, to Harold M. Marting in 1951. Although no airman commanded the Atlantic Fleet until Thomas Moorer in 1965, the Pacific Fleet slot went, almost without exception from the end of World War II, to an aviator. By 1953, of the four-star admirals on the active list, one was a submariner, two were aviators, and two were surface warriors.[169]

It is important, however, not to paint too gloomy a picture of the personnel situation for the surface branch. Fine young midshipmen and Naval Reserve Officer Training Corps (NROTC) cadets, including some at the very top of their classes, elected surface warfare. Able black-shoe officers found promising avenues within the service—and outside it on temporary assignment to related agencies such as the Atomic Energy Commission.[170]

And at the CNO's level, surface warfare was certainly well represented in the 1950s. Forrest Sherman, the first aviator to serve in the position, died suddenly in July 1951. The next three officers to hold that post wore black shoes. Admiral William Fechteler, Sherman's successor, had commanded battleship *Indiana* (BB 58) for part of World War II and the Battleship-Cruiser Force in 1946–1947. Fechteler's two years at the Navy's helm were relatively undistinguished; he proposed few innovative policies of consequence. However, during his tenure, the Navy was successful in obtaining funding for a "balanced fleet" which revolved around the *Forrestal* class of supercarriers.[171]

Fechteler's retirement in 1953 coincided with the inauguration of the "New Look" in strategy. The new CNO, Robert Carney, a surface warrior and also a friend of naval aviation, found it an uphill struggle to maintain a balance within the Navy in light of this national strategy. Adding to Carney's difficulties was the fact that the chairman of the Joint Chiefs of Staff, Admiral Radford, enthusiastically embraced strategic bombing. Radford converted the Secretary of the Navy, Charles S. Thomas, to this viewpoint and consequently wielded enormous influence within the Navy. Radford pushed fellow aviators forward. The opportunity to lead the Navy's largest and most prestigious formations, the carrier battle groups, was restricted to aviators. Even the extremely able Arleigh Burke found himself denied such a command because he was a surface warrior. Carney said later of Radford: "His position, quite frankly, was to get all the aviators in the top positions."[172] It must have been a surprise to Radford then when Burke was named CNO in 1955. Burke would hold the Navy's top job for an unprecedented six years.[173]

# 3

# The Burke Years: Prosperity and Problems for the Surface Navy, 1955–1961

Arleigh Burke served as CNO during one of the critical periods for the U.S. Navy. Although American forces were not engaged in open warfare, they faced sharp challenges from the Soviet Union under its dynamic new dictator, Nikita Khrushchev. Breaking out of Stalin's chrysalis, the Soviet navy emerged as a technologically innovative force which introduced the antiship missile as its great force equalizer and began the production of advanced surface ships that would, within a decade, threaten American sea control. For the U.S. Navy, the period was likewise one of rapid and far-reaching technological ferment. As the surface navy grappled with the problems of incorporating into its ships radical advancements in data processing, guided missiles, nuclear propulsion, and atomic warheads, it found itself coming in third in the race for funding with the aviators and submariners.

Following Stalin's death, the Soviet surface navy became an increasingly visible tool of Communist foreign policy. The smart new *Sverdlov*-class cruisers continued to make a strong impression abroad and with ONI. American intelligence officers also noted the transfer of *Sverdlov*s and new destroyers to the Far East, giving the Soviet Pacific Fleet for the first time "prestige type ships with which to maintain 'face' in the Orient vis-á-vis the U.S. Navy."[1]

By early 1956, ONI assessed in a top-secret study the place of the new Soviet cruisers in the Kremlin's ambitions of world domination. "The Soviet leaders' keen awareness of the influence of sea power has induced them to funnel a significant segment of the USSR's economy into naval construction; since World War II the USSR has built more cruisers, destroyers and submarines than the rest of the world combined."[2] ONI counted on Soviet rosters 28 cruisers and 220 destroyers, most of them of recent construction. New destroyers of the *Kotlin* class featured much improved antiaircraft capabilities. ONI also noted the long reach that these modern ships gave the Soviet leadership: "In the event of a Viet Minh attack against South Vietnam or Laos, the Soviets could deploy to the South China Sea, and even into the Gulf of Tonkin, a task force of cruisers, destroyers and submarines to influence SEATO reactions."[3] These concerns were not idle ones; by 1959, Soviet surface warships were appearing in Indonesian waters. In the Atlantic theater, ONI opined in early 1956, "The Free World need not expect a Soviet repetition of German shortcomings in the Battle of the Atlantic. On the contrary we may expect to find submarine and surface forces operating aggressively, with air reconnaissance and air support, fully ready to exploit tactical surprises."[4]

The newly emergent Soviet leadership, using one of the *Sverdlov*s as a stage, revealed its intentions that same year for its new cruiser force. In a dramatic publicity flourish, Nikita Khrushchev and Nikolai Bulganin chose *Ordzhonikidze* to transport them to England. Along for the four-day ride by invitation was Captain A. P. W. Northey, RN, the British naval attaché in Moscow. A guest at Khrushchev's birthday banquet, the British officer had an opportunity to talk to the brash Soviet dictator about his naval plans. Khrushchev bluntly informed Northey that the *Sverdlov*s would play only a bit part in the Soviet navy of the future; center stage would be occupied by submarines armed with guided missiles. Northey added, "Mr. Khrushchev appeared completely fascinated by the possibilities of guided missiles in any role."[5] In the guided missile navy that Khrushchev envisioned, the *Sverdlov*s were obsolete, although the dictator hinted that they might be rearmed with missiles. Later in 1956, a Soviet naval officer in Murmansk bluntly told the U.S. naval attaché, "Cruisers with conventional guns are useless for modern warfare."[6] As another sign that the Soviets would shift their naval emphasis, the "cruiser man" Admiral Kuznetsov lost his job at the top of the Soviet fleet to the innovative Sergei Gorshkov, only forty-five years old.[7]

ONI corroborated the declining fortunes of the *Sverdlov*s by looking at the Soviet building program. Three of the cruisers under construction at Leningrad in 1956 were proceeding at a leisurely pace. In 1957, work came to a standstill, and in the spring of 1958, ONI reported that of the four *Sverdlov*s still incomplete, one was being dismantled. ONI predicted that the Soviets would design any guided missile ships around the new weapons. Therefore, the *Sverdlov*s on the ways would either be scrapped or finished up as hybrids.[8]

ONI thinking proved accurate. All of the incomplete *Sverdlov* hulls were broken up. Only two of the completed *Sverdlov*s ever carried guided missiles; neither ship was operationally successful in that role. However, Khrushchev's prediction made in San Francisco in 1959 that 90 to 95 percent of all Soviet cruisers would be scrapped proved erroneous. The *Sverdlov*s long outlived their powerful detractor. Of the eleven completed, nine served late into the 1980s; two were converted to command ships and seven, essentially unchanged, continued as flagships.[9]

Also pruned were many of the other conventional warships embodied in Stalin's program. Of the 80 *Skoryy*-class destroyers ordered, 51 were completed. As for the massive diesel submarine program, about 300 boats were finished, out of the 1,200 envisioned. The Soviets instead shifted their emphasis to the nuclear-powered *November* class, much more capable and expensive vessels. The first of fourteen of these attack boats was rushed to sea in 1958.[10]

For the two years following Khrushchev's revelations in 1956, the Soviet navy seemed, to Western eyes, caught in a state of suspended animation. ONI analysts suspected that the Soviets had a large missile program underway, but no missile ships appeared. With Soviet warship construction programs moribund, ONI turned to Soviet literature for telltale signs. The Soviets were writing a great deal about missile-armed submarines but had little to say about missiles on board surface craft, except to note the difficulties that NATO countries were experiencing in this area. ONI predicted cautiously that the Soviets might find it to their interest to invest in the new missile and nuclear technologies for all classes of vessels, thereby starting over on a fairly even basis with the West.[11]

In reading the tea leaves, ONI in 1958 seized on comments in a Soviet article which analysts called the first major Soviet discussion of naval strategy in a decade. The author, a captain first rank, seemed particularly intrigued with the possibilities of combining nuclear-tipped guided missiles and light naval craft. Here was a combination that might strike telling blows at the backbone of Western naval strength—the large warships in the carrier task forces. Lending spice to these calculations was the appearance of the only new type of Soviet surface craft between 1956 and 1958: a hydrofoil torpedo boat propelled by gas turbine engines. Innovation stood in the wings.[12]

In 1959, ONI sighted for the first time the long-anticipated Soviet antiship missile. Dubbed later with the NATO designation the SS–N–1 Scrubber, the weapon resembled a MiG aircraft. ONI estimated that the 30-foot-long weapon had a warhead of 1,000 pounds, a speed of 600 knots, and a maximum range of 150 miles. At shorter distances of up to 30 miles, radar from the firing ship would provide guidance for the first part of the flight. When the missile neared its target, a terminal homer in the Scrubber's nose took over direction. Longer-range use required intermediate control by either a ship or an aircraft. The missile could attack land targets in addition to ships. Its basic characteristics—large size, relative simplicity, and hands-off guidance system—set the pattern that virtually all Soviet antiship missiles would follow.[13]

Naturally, the Soviets developed platforms to operate the new missile. In October 1958 Western intelligence sources sighted a modified *Kotlin*-class destroyer with much of her conventional armament replaced by a guided missile installation dominating the entire aft part of the vessel. Given the bulkiness of the launcher and magazine spaces, ONI hypothesized that the missile, which was under cover, had to be an antiship weapon as opposed to an antiaircraft missile requiring high-speed handling.[14]

The Soviets completed four of these converted destroyers, dubbed *Kildins*. They were quickly upstaged by the first purpose-built warship armed with antiship missiles, the *Krupnyy* class. ONI noted both the strengths and weaknesses of the new ship. With its large missiles and its mobility, the type could threaten major ship targets, especially aircraft carriers. Secondary missions might include strategic attack against land targets or support for ground forces. But the *Krupnyy* lacked an effective antiaircraft system and so would be vulnerable to carrier air power. Like the missile it carried, the *Krupnyy* set the mold both in its strengths and weaknesses for Soviet surface warships in the forthcoming decade and beyond. ONI forecast that the Soviets would build fifty guided missile destroyers within five years and cautioned that with a major effort, that figure could be increased to as many as two hundred.[15]

Compounding their capabilities in coastal waters, the Soviets deployed fast patrol craft armed with antiship missiles. The first of these were modified P–6 torpedo boats, the new variant being dubbed *Komar* (Russian for "mosquito") by NATO. One American officer compared the transformation to "turning a patrol boat into a battleship."[16] First sighted in 1959, the *Komar*s carried two missiles. The next year ONI recorded a larger version, the *Osa* ("wasp"). Designed from the outset for the purpose, the *Osa*s carried four missiles. Although hidden in their containers, these weapons clearly differed from the Scrubber in their smaller size and hence shorter range. Details about the mysterious rocket, later called Styx, remained hazy for several years. In analyzing the capabilities of the new missile boats, ONI saw their small size as restricting their movements to coastal waters and their role to repelling amphibious assaults or setting up ambushes against major warships along indented coastlines. ONI warned that these small vessels could inflict tremendous damage against major targets. The analysts predicted that the missile boats would put a premium on "early detection, classification, accuracy of target data, and reliability of weapons systems."[17]

Other types of Soviet antiship missiles also threatened American naval supremacy. In 1960, Khrushchev startled Vice President Richard M. Nixon: ridiculing aircraft carriers and cruisers, the dictator claimed that the Soviet navy would soon send to sea submarines armed with ballistic and antiship missiles with ranges up to 1,000 kilometers. ONI analysts editorialized, "These are very specific statements and deserve to be taken seriously, even allowing for Khrushchev's braggadocio and penchant for exaggeration."[18] At this time, the Soviet deployment of submarines armed with missiles had already begun. In 1956, modified *Zulu*s carrying two Scud ballistic missiles were the first boats to deploy operationally. The following year, Western intelligence sources photographed a *Whiskey* class with missile containers housing what proved to be the earliest land-attack versions of the Shaddock cruise missile. ONI was certain that this missile would be honed for antiship use, as indeed proved to be the case—the first operational variant going to sea in 1961.[19]

Complementing the submarine-launched missiles were similar Soviet air-launched weapons. ONI had anticipated Soviet initiatives in this area ever since Khrushchev backed down from a 1957 statement that manned aircraft were obsolete. ONI believed the replacement of light attack aircraft by medium bombers, especially the Tu–16 Badger, heralded the operational debut of air-launched antiship missiles. Entering the Soviet inventory in 1958 was the AS–1 Kennel. Looking like a small MiG–15, the missile carried a 900 kilogram warhead over a range beyond 50 miles at more than 600 mph. In 1960, ONI had identified another such a weapon (probably the AS–2 Kipper) and estimated that it armed several Badger regiments.[20]

While the Soviets were investing in radical new weaponry, the U.S. Navy was not standing idle. In fact, the Burke years were among the most innovative in its entire history. Nuclear-powered submarines underwent major improvements, especially with the design of new hull shapes for high underwater speeds. Moreover, the submariners coupled nuclear power with the strategic strike role by bringing the Polaris ballistic missile from conception to deployment during Burke's tenure—a remarkable feat. Added to these major initiatives were the investments in naval aviation with three large conventionally powered attack carriers funded; the design and construction of the first nuclear-powered carrier, *Enterprise* (CVAN 65); and the introduction of advanced aircraft. Additionally, nuclear weapons entered the Navy's arsenal in a wide variety of sizes and in great numbers.

The Navy's initiatives during the Burke years in the area of strategic attack were essential to its survival as a viable force. Throughout the late 1950s, the Eisenhower administration continued to espouse the New Look strategy. To top policymakers outside the Navy, and to some inside, the strategic strike mission executed by the carriers and the submarines was the task that truly mattered. Any war with the Soviets would be total; American forces would use nuclear weapons from the outset and in most conceivable military circumstances.

Admiral Burke took an increasingly skeptical view of the New Look. An officer of wide experience, Burke before World War II had earned a graduate degree in chemical engineering and was a member of the prestigious Gun Club. In 1937, he began his long association with destroyers which culminated during World War II in his famous victory over the vaunted Japanese at Empress Augusta Bay in 1943. The next year, "Thirty-One Knot" Burke on the staff of Task Force 58 learned carrier operations at the elbow of the master, Vice Admiral Marc A. Mitscher. After narrowly surviving the struggle with the Air Force in the 1949 "revolt of the admirals" affair, Rear Admiral Burke was commanding the Destroyer Force, Atlantic Fleet, when President Eisenhower reached ninety-two places down the flag officers' list to move him to Chief of Naval Operations. His ability was such that he was reappointed in 1957 and 1959.[21]

As CNO, Burke saw full-scale nuclear war as a lessening possibility because the Soviets were building their arsenal up to parity with that of the United States. In early 1957, Burke bluntly stated, "A limited war is the type of war most likely to occur in the thermonuclear age."[22] Echoing this view were widely read and persuasive volumes published months later by civilian strategists Henry Kissinger and Robert Osgood.

The next year, Burke pushed his point: a preoccupation with nuclear strategy "has caused us to generate excessive forces for retaliation and not give enough thought to those forces useable in more limited situations."[23] Burke accordingly proposed a long-range plan for the Navy's structure that gave significant provision for conventional forces. Three years in the making, the study, entitled "The Navy of the 1970 Era," included major building programs to rejuvenate the surface forces with seventy-two guided missile cruisers or frigates.[24]

These new ships would be very much needed. A major problem facing surface officers was the block obsolescence of their warships. At current building rates, almost half of the Navy's ships in 1963 would be overage. Not only were these vessels getting weary, but the large numbers of World War II-era destroyers could no longer counter the new threats posed by the Soviets. To replace all of these ships was far beyond the resources of the Navy. Consequently, a modernization program called Fleet Rehabilitation and Modernization (FRAM) starting in 1959 boosted the destroyers' antisubmarine performance.[25]

The menace of the nuclear-powered submarine demanded concerted attention. The new SQS–4 sonar and the rocket-boosted torpedo RAT seemed a match for the fast diesel-electric submarine, but the new nuclear boats upped the ante once again. The Navy's first nuclear submarines, *Nautilus* and *Seawolf* (SSN 575), dramatized in exercises the challenges that the surface navy confronted. The commander of *Seawolf*, R. B. Laning, later wrote:

> Whenever an ASW hunter-killer group commander would deny that his carrier had been sunk during an exercise, we would show him pictures of the carrier's screws and views of the hangar deck. Wilkinson [the CO of *Nautilus*] even fired green star clusters that landed on the carrier's deck....[26]

Laning suggested to the commander of the Atlantic Fleet destroyers that the surface navy establish a destroyer school and a technological development group, develop a specialized insignia to bolster esprit de corps, and build quiet destroyers capable of using a towed passive sonar. Surface warriors knew they needed greatly improved sensors and weapons, especially in terms of range.[27]

Showing real promise was the helicopter. Mating the rotary wing aircraft and the escort vessel had begun in 1947 with Royal Navy experiments. The Canadian navy, with its *St. Laurent* class, was the first to add permanent helicopter facilities. In 1957, *Mitscher*, the first of the U.S. frigates to fly a helicopter, used hers to excellent effect in a "dogfight" with *Seawolf*. Soon thereafter, *Mitscher* and destroyers *Manley* and *Hazelwood* (DD 531) tested a drone helicopter built by the Kaman Aircraft Company. Results were promising enough that the Navy went ahead with the concept, now named Drone Antisubmarine Helicopter (DASH).[28]

Another hopeful development was the variable depth sonar, installed first in destroyer escorts on board *John Willis* in 1959. Bow installations, to put the sonar ahead of the turbulence generated by the bow wave, appeared in the late 1950s, although they degraded shiphandling to a certain degree and made drydocking much more difficult. The SQS–4 sonar, which had represented such an advance in the early 1950s, was already outmoded by the new SQS–23, a lower frequency set with a range out to 12,000 yards. Beginning in 1958, the SQS–23 went on board the destroyers. Ultimately, the Navy produced 197 sets.[29]

But matériel could be just part of the answer to the newest Soviet submarines. Convoy and task force protection became much more difficult in the face of nuclear weapons which mandated very open formations. Persistent prosecution of submarine contacts might well denude a formation of essential protection, especially given the shrinking numbers of antisubmarine craft. And those Soviet submarines armed with land-attack missiles would demand special attention.[30]

To grapple with these problems, CINCLANT Admiral Jerauld Wright established in April 1958 Antisubmarine Defense Group Alfa, composed of a standard hunter-killer group (of an antisubmarine carrier and destroyers) reinforced by a shore-based patrol plane squadron and two submarines. Spending at least 50 percent of its time at sea, the force sharpened antisubmarine tactics and strategy. Within a year, Task Group Alfa's efforts showed that the defense of ship formations and the defense of the continental United States were of one cloth—both demanded area coverage on a very large scale. In 1959, a *Proceedings* article summed up the findings of Task Group Alfa by noting, "Antisubmarine defense is as big a problem as continental air defense and must be approached on as broad a basis. . . . Every existing equipment and technique must be exploited to the utmost." The article concluded with the sardonic comment, "A most encouraging feature is that there is so much room for progress."[31]

This pessimistic assessment was echoed within the Navy in various ways. After tours in all four numbered fleets, the commander of the Cruiser Force, Atlantic Fleet reported to the new CINCLANT Admiral Robert L. Dennison:

> ASW is considered to be unsatisfactory in all Fleets. It is obviously inadequate, especially at those times when an unfavorable layer effect is prevalent (practically all summer in the Mediterranean). For ASW, there has been no apparent resurgence of self-confidence such as AAW [antiair warfare] has received from the introduction of missilery. The same ships which participate in AAW are needed for the ASW effort, but there is insufficient coordinated tactical direction of the two efforts.[32]

As for specialized ASW ships, only convoy escorts were being constructed, and these in very small numbers—between 1952 and 1961, on the average of two per year. The last of the *Dealey* class, *Hooper* (DE 1026), was completed in April 1958, leaving only the four escorts of the *Claud Jones* class in the pipeline. Of about the same size (1,916 tons full load) as their predecessors, the new ships were cheaper—and even less capable. The sonar system (SQS–4) remained the same, but armament was reduced to two 3"/50, two Hedgehogs, depth charges, and lightweight antisubmarine torpedoes. Powered by diesels instead of a steam plant, *Claud Jones* (DE 1033) could make only 21.5 knots. One commanding officer of *McMorris* (DE 1036) later evaluated his little ship: "AAW—zero; ASW—excellent for convoy duty only. Anti-surface—zero. Handiness, seaworthiness, habitability, endurance, range—outstanding. It could get you there but you couldn't fight real well."[33] With such minimal capabilities, the four ships of the *Claud Jones* class lasted for less than fifteen years before their transfer to Indonesia in 1973–1974.

For ASW specialists, the skimpy building program was symptomatic of a Navy in which antisubmarine warfare took a back seat to more spectacular systems, such as guided missiles, attack carriers and nuclear submarines.[34] The ASW program was not entirely neglected, however. Despite the fact that most of the destroyers, frigates, and even the cruisers under construction or conversion were first and foremost antiaircraft ships, they would be fitted with the most modern sonar and ASW weapons. Major improvements in ASW systems beckoned with the SQS–26 sonar and the rocket-boosted homing torpedo called ASROC, although these would not be ready for operational deployment until the next decade. Also, the nuclear attack submarines just entering service became potent ASW craft in their own right.[35]

For the surface navy, a larger and more capable escort, *Bronstein* (DE 1037), was on the drawing board. The FRAM program also promised more immediate help. The consequence of a study initiated by Secretary of the Navy Thomas S. Gates, Jr., FRAM envisioned lengthening the service life

KN–1961

*Hooper*, a *Dealey*-class destroyer escort, closes *Kearsarge* (CVS 33) to take on fuel. Her forward 3″/50 mount is enclosed.

of destroyers for up to eight years. The modernization effort, to extend over a four-year period, was to have a priority "comparable to that of Polaris."[36]

The most extensive conversion, the FRAM I, involved the rehabilitation of all shipboard components and the provision of ASROC, DASH, and the SQS–23 sonar. By way of space and weight compensation, the destroyers lost one of the three 5-inch gun mounts, in some cases the stern mount leaving a blind spot aft of the ship. Berthing and messing spaces were modernized. This extensive work took, typically, nine to ten months per destroyer. Seventy-nine ships of the *Gearing* class ultimately received the FRAM I update. The FRAM II conversion fitted the ships with DASH, but not ASROC; their SQS–4 was modified and supplemented with a variable depth sonar.[37] Thirty-three *Allen M. Sumners*, three *Fletcher*-class DDEs, and sixteen *Gearings* received this lesser refit.

The FRAM I ships emerged from the yards greatly improved in ASW capability, although the FRAM II conversions were less successful. When DASH failed in actual service, the FRAM II ships, lacking ASROC, were left with no long-range ASW weapon. In any case, costs for the program were certainly attractive in relative terms: $11 million for a FRAM I con-

81

version ($7 million for FRAM II) compared to $27 million for a new escort or to $38 million for a guided missile destroyer. Later, when the Vietnam War cut into the Navy's funds for new construction, the FRAM ships soldiered on well past their allotted span, a few steaming into the 1980s with the U.S. Navy. Others went to friendly countries. Two remained on active duty with the Turkish navy into the 1990s.[38]

If the FRAM program gave destroyers a new lease on life in ASW, many analysts saw no future at all for the conventional battleship and cruiser with their voracious demands for personnel and with gun armaments which seemed so out of place in a missile age. Officially, the Navy still listed for the battleships and cruisers a number of missions: "To engage in combat operations against combatant surface ships, to bombard shore installations, and to provide defense against airborne threats." Many experts thought aviation was better able to do these jobs at cheaper cost.[39] Given the large Soviet investment in cruisers and destroyers, some U.S. surface officers hoped to keep three *Iowa* in commission. Plans for the active ships envisioned upgrading their antiaircraft armament with the 3"/50; however, these guns were never fitted. The Navy did provide the battleships with an atomic projectile, officially the Mk 23, nicknamed Katie. The shell possessed a yield of about 15 to 20 kilotons, roughly equivalent to the bomb dropped on Hiroshima. Each battleship was to carry nine of the nuclear shells; whether they ever did so remains uncertain. After Korea, the *Iowas* spent much of their time as training vessels, a role that cost them in reduced operational readiness. During exercises of the Battleship-Cruiser Force, Atlantic Fleet in the summer of 1956, heavy cruisers won the top four places with the *Iowa* battleships taking three of the last four slots. The following June, *Iowa* and *Wisconsin* made a major public appearance by heading the 14-mile-long line of ships from seventeen countries at the Hampton Roads International Naval Review, but that was the last hurrah for the battleships—or so it seemed. *New Jersey* was already headed for the mothball fleet, and she was joined by the other two within months. For the first time since 1895, the U.S. Navy listed no battleship on its active duty rosters.[40]

With the *Iowas* in reserve, the type command reverted to the name Cruiser Force. It too seemed doomed to extinction as its ships retired. When Burke had taken over as CNO in 1955, three battleships and seventeen cruisers—all gunships—had made up the type commands; by the time he stepped down in 1961, the Navy counted only four conventional heavy cruisers on its active rosters—*Saint Paul*, *Helena*, *Los Angeles*, and *Newport News*. Moreover, the reserve fleets were winnowed of many of their big gun vessels. Cutting torches dismantled eleven battleships and the two large cruisers *Alaska* (CB 1) and *Guam* (CB 2) by 1962. Eight heavy and eighteen light cruisers also went to the breakers.[41]

Guided missile cruiser *Little Rock*. Note the enlarged forward superstructure which provided flag spaces.

The four heavy cruisers remaining in commission were proud ships, despite the feeling among many that they were the lingering survivors of another era. They continued their frequent service as flagships; indeed, *Saint Paul* in 1959 became the permanent flagship of the Seventh Fleet and operated out of Yokosuka, the first U.S. Navy warship to be homeported in the Far East since the days before World War II. Her commanding officer in 1960–1961, Captain Frederick H. Schneider, Jr., remembered the high quality of her personnel: "The waiting list of requests for duty on board was about ten pages long and included virtually every rate. I can't recall even one request for transfer off the ship, nor do I remember a single court martial."[42] Three of the 5-inch mounts and one 8-inch turret sported Es; the cooks won the Ney Award, given for the best food on a large combatant across the entire Navy. A red engineering E adorned the stack, a distinction which the engineers showed they deserved when, in an emergency, they answered a backing bell in just over ten minutes, despite the plant being on two hours' notice.[43]

To offset his reductions in gunships, Burke proposed a major program of surface ship construction and conversion. He argued from the beginning of his tenure that one of the Navy's most serious deficiencies was its lack of guided missile ships to fend off the Soviet air threat. The conversion of existing ships offered the only economically attractive way to get missiles to sea quickly. By 1957, Burke had convinced Congress to fund nine missile cruisers to reinforce the first G ships, *Boston* and *Canberra*. Three heavy cruisers of the *Baltimore* class and six light cruisers of the *Cleveland* class went to the yards for extensive overhauls. The nine ships emerged in three distinct groups. *Galveston* (CLG 3, ex CL 93) and *Topeka* (CLG 8, ex CL 67) kept half of their gunnery armament. The other four light cruisers—*Little Rock* (CLG 4, ex CL 92), *Oklahoma City* (CLG 5, ex CL 91), *Providence* (CLG 6, ex CL 82), and *Springfield* (CLG 7, ex CL 66)—were more extensively altered with capacious command facilities so that they could serve as fleet flagships. They retained only one of their four original 6-inch gun turrets. Plans called for the three heavy cruisers to be changed beyond recognition. Stripped completely of their guns and superstructures, *Albany* (CG 10, ex CA 123), *Chicago* (CG 11, ex CA 136), and *Columbus* (CG 12, ex CA 74) were completely reconstructed with a modernistic appearance. "Macks," a combination of masts and stacks, dominated their look amidships; they bristled with sensors and missile launchers from stem to stern.[44]

The first of the conversions, *Galveston*, was hurried through to completion in less than two years; the five remaining light cruisers rejoined the

KN–11658

*Columbus* fires a Tartar, October 1965. Note the Talos on the launcher.

fleet in 1959 or 1960. The three *Albany*s, almost completely rebuilt, took significantly longer, returning to service from 1962–1964. These ships lost their earlier CA designation; with the guided missile virtually their only weapon, the *Albany*s became CGs. The less radical light cruiser conversions were listed as CLGs.[45]

*Galveston* was, despite her pedigree as a *Cleveland*-class light cruiser, virtually a brand-new ship. Completed in 1946, she had gone straight to the mothball fleet without commissioning. In the spring of 1958, she sailed for the first time, wearing her CLG number 3 on her bow. On 24 February 1959, she fired, successfully, the first Talos shot at sea. Over the next three years, *Galveston* gave the naval term "trials" a new twist. She was so frequently under alteration at the Philadelphia Navy Yard that most of the families of her crew moved from her ostensible homeport of Norfolk to the Philadelphia area. Her crew tested—and in some cases initiated—significant measures in making Talos workable. For instance, the ship evaluated improved versions of the missile itself, of its guidance equipment, and of its diagnostic and corrective maintenance setup. The system redesigns were then incorporated into the later Talos ships. One writer asserted that *Galveston*'s most significant contribution was "the nurturing of a cadre of Talos sailors, both officers and enlisted" who were to go on to staff the other Talos ships entering the fleet. *Galveston* herself finally joined Cruiser-Destroyer Flotilla Nine in the Pacific, 24 August 1962, over four years after her commissioning.[46]

Compared with *Boston* and *Canberra*, the light cruiser conversions were significantly cheaper, in large part because their missile stowage was above decks rather than in the deep "Coke machine" launchers. Half of these ships carried Terrier (*Topeka*, *Providence*, and *Springfield*); the others, Talos (*Galveston*, *Little Rock*, and *Oklahoma City*). The Terrier ships stowed 120 missiles; the Talos missile was so large that only 46 of the weapons, stowed horizontally without fins or tail surfaces, fit into the magazines. Blow-out panels and elaborate sprinkling systems were installed to preserve the ship in the event of the accidental ignition of a missile. As the "birds" moved to the launching rails, missile technicians attached the flight appendages, an operation taking about 10 seconds. The ships could fire two missiles every 45 seconds. Although the control system could track up to six targets, it could designate only two to the fire control channels. Here was a significant weak spot: even these modernized ships were vulnerable to mass coordinated attacks.[47] Exercises emphasized another problem endemic to the single-ender design. A 1965 assessment of *Galveston* read:

> Missiles aft and guns forward make life difficult. If the second missile shot at an incoming jet misses, it may be too late to turn around to unmask the guns. Or, unmasking the bow guns may mask the missiles on a second aircraft at greater range. The accompanying ASW destroyer must also consider

it his mission to fire [his] guns when Galveston's stern is exposed to close-in low flyers.[48]

Aside from the missile installations, the nine converted cruisers carried up-to-date sonar installations. An unusual piece of gear for a cruiser, the SQS–23 sonar was on board to permit more open fleet formations. In theory, the cruisers could assist with the sonar coverage of a task group and also help direct DASH, for which they were given control facilities. The ships carried no antisubmarine weapons themselves. One commander of *Topeka* tried without success to obtain MK 46 torpedo tubes. He recalled, "We spent little, if any, time on ASW training. Our view of sonar employment was to detect in order to avoid."[49]

The ships showed their World War II heritage in a number of ways, some beneficial, some not. Habitability was little improved over earlier standards with the important exception of air conditioning throughout the living spaces. The 600-pound engineering plant was prone to steam leaks, at least in *Topeka,* but it was extremely reliable. Aside from short upkeep periods, *Springfield* went from her recommissioning in 1960 to 1967 without a major machinery overhaul.[50]

Seagoing characteristics, too, reflected their ancestry. The ships handled superbly: according to a *Topeka* commanding officer, "as agile as a destroyer!"[51] That ship survived "a very severe typhoon with minimal damage."[52] Shortcomings were few. The additional topweight imposed by the radars, masts, and missile direction equipment required ballasting and gave them uncomfortable roll characteristics in heavy seas. One commanding officer of *Albany* recalled:

> [T]he ship was not the most pleasant ride. When folks wished us fair winds and following seas, I always said they were not welcome. With a following sea, the ship wanted to dive to starboard or port depending on the direction of the sea. If from dead astern, she wanted to bury her prow. I am sure the ship was more stable when a gun cruiser.[53]

As was typical of most U.S. designs of World War II vintage, the ships tended to take green water over the bow. This characteristic was especially pronounced in the four *Cleveland*s configured as flagships with the forward location of their large deckhouses.[54]

For the four ships so fitted (*Little Rock*, *Oklahoma City*, *Providence*, and *Springfield*), the command function frequently took precedence over combat readiness. For example, *Springfield* flew the flag of Sixth Fleet for almost seven years and was usually homeported at Villefranche-sur-Mer. One of her captains recalled that combat training simply was incompatible with flag duties much of the time. In his two years on board, the ship fired her Terriers only twice.[55] Another *Springfield* commanding officer viewed the flag mission with a jaundiced eye:

They . . . put on a hotel for an Admiral and a huge staff. The two six-pounders of her Saluting Battery became her "Main Battery." She carried twelve boats and as many motor vehicles, so her topsides amidships was cluttered. She was cursed with a helicopter, the care and operation of which occupied much of my time and was the source of continual friction with the Admiral. Our helicopter was a nice little HUP at first, but later it was replaced with a maddeningly unreliable jet powered UH–2. [*Springfield*] looked more like the Coney Island skyline than a well armed man-o-war, but it was sure great duty to be home-ported and operate in the Med![56]

The six *Cleveland*s steamed through the 1960s; the lack of flag facilities sent *Topeka* and *Galveston* to the scrapyard first. The other two Terrier ships were decommissioned in 1973, while *Little Rock* and *Oklahoma City*, with Talos and flag accommodations, lasted until 1976 and 1979, respectively.[57]

Compared to the *Cleveland* conversions, the *Albany*-class "double-enders" came with significant improvements. They boasted a significant ASW capability with ASROC complementing the SQS–23 sonar. Their two new magazines held 104 complete Talos, all ready for service, as opposed to only 16 ready weapons in *Galveston*, *Little Rock*, and *Oklahoma City*. On the *Albany*s, nuclear and conventional warheads could be intermixed in any combination. Additionally the Mk 12 launching system was fitted with a means to jettison dud missiles on the rail—a significant worry for the earlier systems. When they rejoined the fleet beginning in 1962, the *Albany*s also carried a secondary battery of eighty shorter-range Tartars for which two double launchers were fitted, one on each side of the bridge. Conspicuously absent in the first two conversions were any guns at all. Some surface warriors argued for a backup artillery battery, but as one reminisced, "Just the word 'missile' became very sexy."[58] Guns seemed antiquated. The type commander in the Pacific questioned the need to keep any 6-inch guns on the missile flagships, but Burke ordered their retention out of concern for the dwindling number of rifles available in the fleet to support amphibious operations. Surface warriors were proud of their high-tech vessels. The publication *Cruiser-Destroyerman* remarked, "The modern cruiser . . . armed with missiles . . . packs more firepower than any dreadnought of the war years."[59]

Unfortunately, these cruiser conversions were immensely expensive. *Albany* cost $170 million to rebuild. Three further ships were canceled. Many blackshoes were concerned that the Navy would never be able to afford an adequate number of missile cruisers. Some operational analysts wondered if several smaller missile ships spaced at the outer fringes of a task group might not be preferable to a single cruiser in the center of the formation. As a result of these considerations, the Navy tested the feasibility of converting destroyers for missile work. On hand were large numbers of *Gearing*s. In 1955, one of these ships, *Gyatt* (DD 712), began at Boston Naval

USN 1057769

*Gyatt* with Terriers on the rails aft at Corfu, Greece, in 1961. Anchored along-side is submarine *Diablo* (SS 479).

Shipyard an austere reconstruction to become the Navy's first missile de-stroyer, redesignated DDG 1. The two forward 5″/38 mounts stayed on board; the aft mount was replaced by a Terrier twin-arm missile launcher. In light of the small size of the ship, the magazine held only fourteen mis-siles. A modified gunfire control radar provided the missile guidance, and experimental fin stabilizers modeled on a British system reduced the rolling so typical of destroyers.[60]

From her reclassification in May 1957, *Gyatt* began three years of inten-sive evaluation work. Although publicly touted a success at the time, *Gyatt*, in fact, showed that the size of the Terrier and its ancillary equipment sim-ply were too large for a *Gearing* hull. In 1962, Terrier came off, and the ship's hull number reverted to DD 712. Nonetheless, the experience gained with *Gyatt* helped speed the development of the Tartar missile system.[61]

Even while *Gyatt* was fitting out, the Navy was finalizing drawings for new classes of missile escorts. A committee chaired by Rear Admiral W. G. Schindler had begun planning work on these ships in 1954; Congress funded the first of them in 1956. During Burke's six years as CNO, the Navy laid down over forty of these ships in four distinct classes. Smallest

USN 1173540

*Farragut* (DDG 37, ex-DLG 6) steaming off St. Croix in 1978. Note the ASROC "box" forward and the empty Terrier launcher aft.

and most numerous were the twenty-three destroyers (designated DDGs) of the *Charles F. Adams* class (of 4,526 tons full load). As an improved *Forrest Sherman* type, they carried one Tartar missile launcher, two 5"/54 Mk 42 guns, and ASROC—a significant armament for such a relatively small ship.[62] Larger were the ten ships of the *Farragut* class. Six thousand tons allowed for a Terrier launcher rather than Tartar, although the *Farragut*s carried only one 5-inch. Their size entitled them to the new appellation frigate (DLG), rather than destroyer (DDG). Disposing of the 5-inch altogether were the nine frigates of the *Leahy* class. In some ways diminutive versions of the *Albany*-class Talos cruisers, the *Leahy*s were also double-enders with two twin Terrier launchers. The 8,200-ton design supposedly met the requirement for "a limited defense against surface craft" with four 3"/50s.[63]

Few apologized for the slight gun armament. The Bureau of Ordnance, while admitting that their appearance might suggest weakness, bragged, "but to one who knows her she will be very different indeed: a destroyer type more powerful than any battleship ever built." With eighty Terriers, "each ship is capable of shooting down Mach 2 jet aircraft at twenty miles with conventional high-explosive warhead missiles; capable of destroying a formation of aircraft with a nuclear warhead missile; and capable of delivering a nuclear warhead against a surface target or a shore target."[64]

There were also no apologies for lack of armor worked into any of these designs. As one Naval War College study concluded, "The projectile, that is, the rocket, the torpedo, and the atomic bomb, seems to have won with some finality the age-old struggle of armor versus projectiles."[65] Because even the best-protected modern ships could be sunk with relative ease by these weapons, heavy armor simply was not worth the investment, especially insofar as its weight and expense might detract from more active measures. Designers went in the other direction emphasizing light construction materials, especially to cut down on topweight. With the large antennas carried high on the ships' superstructures, stability represented an increasing problem. Aluminum instead of steel became the metal of choice for higher areas; its rustproof nature added to its attractiveness.

Surface warriors might debate particulars, but all sailors looked forward to taking delivery of advanced missile ships. Schedules called for eleven ships equipped with Terrier to be in service by the end of 1960, with ten more coming on line in the next two years. The close of 1964 would see all such Terrier ships in commission, plus the twenty-three destroyers of the *Charles F. Adams* class armed with Tartar. Reinforcing this ambitious new construction program would be the addition of Terrier or Tartar batteries to all the earlier postwar frigates and destroyers. And Terrier would go into the latest supercarriers under construction. The rapid pace of missile deployment was a source of great pride for surface warfare officers and contrasted sharply with the situation in allied navies: the Royal Navy anticipated delivery of its first missile ship in 1962; for France, the projected date was 1965. Of all the warships in the "Arleigh Burke Navy" under construction, the most eagerly awaited by surface sailors was the world's first nuclear-propelled naval surface vessel, cruiser *Long Beach* (CGN 9, ex-CLGN/CGN 160).[66]

Burke had pushed for nuclear surface ships as soon as he entered office. Specifically, he directed the preparation of designs for a nuclear carrier, cruiser, and frigate—*Enterprise*, *Long Beach*, and *Bainbridge* (DLGN 25), respectively. The cruiser entered service in September 1961, one month after Burke departed and two months before the carrier. Novel in so many ways, her blocky silhouette and total absence of stacks advertised her nuclear power plant which gave *Long Beach* virtually unlimited range.[67] An observer could also note the special fixed-array radars, designated the SPS–32/33, on the sides of the superstructure. With their steerable beams, the distinctive flat-faced antennas could track automatically a large number of targets at once. From the standpoint of the naval architect, the new radars affixed to the superstructure also eased design problems. Unfortunately, the hard-wired computer on *Long Beach* was difficult to modify or update. The new radar technology on *Long Beach* was, in 1961, ahead of its time and suffered from a significant failure rate and very high costs. The SPS–32/33 system appeared on only one other ship, carrier *Enterprise*.[68]

Certainly new for a U.S. cruiser was her lack of armor and the total absence of guns. Both features attracted adverse comment from within the service. True, her missile armament was impressive: three launchers, two forward for Terrier with one aft for Talos. Her magazines held 120 Terriers and 46 Talos, but some officers noted that in any situation short of nuclear war, the ship would be defenseless against other surface vessels, even a mere torpedo boat. If tactical nuclear weapons could be used in an antiship mode, then *Long Beach* could resort to the Talos or, in the original ship design, to the Regulus. The winged Regulus was intended to lend a strategic strike capability to the ship, as was the later plan to place eight Polaris missiles on board the vessel. Burke thought that with improved guidance the ballistic missile might have tactical applications.[69]

At 17,000 tons, *Long Beach* was a large ship. Some would argue that she was the only true cruiser built by the Navy following World War II. Burke intended her to be capable of independent operations in classic cruiser fashion, but the cancellation of her Regulus II and Polaris missiles hampered her abilities in this area. Her cost was commensurate with her size: $333 million, a staggering figure given that the original estimate had been $80 million. Her elaborate equipment drove up the price tag; the missile outfit alone ran to $44 million. The ship was hurried forward in an ultimately losing effort to beat the Soviet nuclear-powered icebreaker *Lenin* to sea. When *Long Beach* commissioned in September 1961, her only fully operational weapons system was her ASROC launcher. She was not truly ready for combat until the end of the next year.[70]

While *Long Beach* was still on the drawing board, advocates of nuclear propulsion considered placing reactors in smaller warships. With the space and weight demands of a nuclear power plant, the most compact practicable design still required a vessel with a displacement of over 8,000 tons. In 1959, the first nuclear frigate, *Bainbridge*, was laid down. The ship duplicated the basic layout of the *Leahy*s with Terrier launchers at both ends and a meager gun armament of four 3″/50s. This ship was, from the beginning, the source of great contention within the destroyer force. Pushed by the destroyer type commander in the Atlantic Fleet for her great capabilities, *Bainbridge* was opposed by his opposite number in the Pacific who argued that for the cost of one nuclear frigate the Navy could obtain three or four conventional destroyers. Apparently a factor in proceeding with the ship was the support of Admiral Rickover whose office designed a lightweight reactor especially for *Bainbridge*.[71]

Admiral Burke saw many advantages to be reaped from the wholesale exploitation of nuclear propulsion for surface warships. In addition to unlimited cruising endurance at high speeds, nuclear propulsion gave tactical freedom from the refueling rendezvous and reduced the number of supporting ships in a task group. A nuclear plant offered ready power for the voracious electronics packages going into new ships and cut down on the corrosion of delicate antennas by stack gases. Burke saw these attributes as so valuable that his long-range plan for "The Navy of the 1970 Era" envisioned six all-nuclear carrier task groups. To reach this goal, the surface navy would need to construct during the 1960s twelve nuclear cruisers and eighteen nuclear frigates. However, the escalating costs of *Long Beach* and *Bainbridge* called these ambitious plans into question, and Burke established a special body, the Hubbard Committee, to look into the matter. It concluded that the Navy needed more surface ships than it could ever afford if it elected to buy a large number of nuclear-powered vessels. The committee advised against funding any more of the advanced ships until those still under construction had been thoroughly tested at sea. These findings were obviously unpalatable to the nuclear advocates. Not surprisingly, a second committee, made up of officers more favorable to the Rickover view, rendered a different verdict. Nuclear power for surface warships would remain a hot issue both inside the Navy and in the halls of Congress well into the 1970s.[72]

Out of the public eye was the surface navy's concerns for its wilting ability to fight surface warships and to project power ashore. Surface line officers held high hopes for improvements in both areas when Burke took the helm. These aspirations were based largely on the deployment and improvement of the Regulus. Three additional heavy cruiser conversions followed *Los Angeles* in 1955: *Helena*, *Macon*, and *Toledo*. Each ship carried three of the missiles in the capacious hangar aft. With ample space for test equipment and spare parts, ordnance technicians on board the cruisers could perform maintenance and repairs. They also could mate the missile with its warhead on board—an impossibility in the cramped hangars on the submarine conversions. Thus, the cruisermen could switch nuclear and conventional warheads as the tactical situation dictated.[73]

On board ship, the Regulus installation was the responsibility of the main battery officer. When the first Regulus missile was hoisted onto *Los Angeles* in 1955, Lieutenant Robert H. Wertheim held that job. He later recalled that the missile presented its share of headaches, such as securing the nuclear warheads and limiting access to the Regulus spaces. In enforcing the latter duty, Wertheim ran afoul of the cruiser's damage control officer who demanded access to all areas of the ship. Wertheim related that this officer "armed himself with a set of bolt cutters and as fast as I would add padlocks he would snip them off."[74]

Preparing the missile for launch was a laborious proposition that took six hours. To attach the 1,000-pound booster, the crew used block and tackle—"at best...a difficult and tedious operation."[75] Some of the ancillary equipment gave trouble early in the program: the crane, for instance, was "prone to run away" if the ship was rolling. The first Regulus launcher on the cruisers was a jury-rigged arrangement composed of a set of rails elevated by a hydraulic lift. Once sailors moved the missile out of the hangar and put it on the launcher, they started the missile's engine and activated the lift. Wertheim recalled the scene:

> Visualize . . . a small jet airplane up on rails that were elevated high into the air and pointing up on an angle of 35 or 40 degrees, supported by two arms extended vertically. . . . As the ship would roll this whole mechanism would sway back and forth, wave around in the breeze so to speak . . . with the jet engine whining and with the high explosive in a nuclear warhead and jato bottles ready to be ignited—the whole thing was a disaster waiting for a place to happen.[76]

Improved equipment soon replaced this risky arrangement; Regulus officers deemed launches possible at speeds up to 25 knots in smooth sea conditions.[77]

Guidance for the missile, characterized by one officer as "primitive," continued to present problems. Cruisermen sometimes simply used a chase plane to control the missile. Wertheim characterized this arrangement as "just another aircraft to carry the bomb,"[78] albeit giving greater ability to penetrate enemy defenses and more safety to the aviator of the manned aircraft. But even this type of guidance gave spotty results, although in wartime Regulus would compensate for its lack of accuracy with its large nuclear warhead. Carrying either the W–5 nuclear warhead or a W–27 thermonuclear warhead with a yield of 1.9 megatons, Regulus was mainly targeted against Soviet air and submarine bases.[79]

In June 1957, *Helena* put on the first public demonstration of a cruiser-launched Regulus when one of her missiles flew 280 miles over the East China Sea to score a direct hit on the target island, Okino Daito Shima. The ship's operations officer exulted, "The experimenting is over. This is our heavy punch!"[80] Not all the missiles shot so straight; one of *Helena*'s missed its mark by 10 miles. Notwithstanding this inconsistent performance, the cruisers had been making operational patrols since 1955. *Macon*, usually based at Norfolk, assisted with the evacuation of U.S. dependents during the Suez crisis of 1956. The other three Regulus-equipped cruisers operated in the Pacific. Both *Los Angeles* and *Helena* steamed with the Seventh Fleet during the Quemoy-Matsu crises of 1955 and 1958.[81]

Cruisermen worked hard to hone the missile's performance so that the weapon could be employed tactically against ships or small military targets ashore like radar installations. Some black-shoe officers foresaw Regulus preceding an air strike to suppress enemy antiaircraft sites and radar installations in order to allow carrier aircraft greater freedom to concentrate on their offensive objectives. To carry out such missions, Regulus needed to combine great accuracy with a "fire-and-forget" method of guidance. By 1958, the Navy was exploring two complicated tracks: inertial navigation and terrain recognition. Running into numerous roadblocks,

Submarine *Grayback* (SSG 574) fires the first Regulus II off the California coast, 17 September 1958. The missile's target was Edwards Air Force Base, 200 miles away.

these two techniques would ultimately yield extraordinary results in the 1970s. As promising first steps were made in these new guidance methods, surface warfare officers included Regulus in the new *Albany* and *Long Beach* cruiser designs. By 1957, supporters of the missile were calling for thirty-one cruisers to carry it.[82]

However, these ambitious plans faced a potentially lethal challenge on the horizon: the solid-fueled, ballistic missile Polaris with its two trumps of undersea launch and immunity to defensive measures. Against Polaris, Regulus supporters argued that their winged air-breather offered a number of significant advantages. The cruise missile, with its promise of greater accuracy, could hit a variety of objectives, whereas Polaris in its original versions was essentially a city-busting weapon. Ballistic missiles were useless against moving targets and could be backtracked by radar to give a good idea of the location of the launching vessel. Unlike a ballistic missile, Regulus could be redirected in flight. In fact, several top officers formally endorsed the position that the Navy should not give high priority to Polaris. They argued that the Regulus cruise missiles in the fleet and under development could undertake any strategic mission, thereby making the technologically risky Polaris redundant.[83]

Supporters of the cruise missile were banking heavily on the fruition of the Regulus II program which had started in May 1950. The logical continuation of the subsonic program into the supersonic realm, the swept-wing missile was designed for Mach 2 speed; a range of 500 miles at that velocity (or substantially longer with subsonic cruise and a Mach 2 dash at the end); an altitude of 60,000 feet; and the same warhead as the Regulus I. To reach such ambitious goals, the designers produced a very large missile, 56 feet long and weighing almost 12 tons.[84]

By 1958, the flight test program was underway and running remarkably smoothly; of its forty-eight flights in all, the missile failed completely in only four. In January 1958, the Navy signed a production contract. Some NATO governments also evinced interest, as did even the U.S. Air Force which briefly considered the missile as a standoff weapon for the new B–52.[85]

Despite the seemingly rosy future, the Regulus II program was, in fact, in deep trouble. Facing a tight Eisenhower budget, the Navy found itself funding too many advanced and expensive programs: *Forrestal*-class supercarriers at the rate of one a year, Polaris, and Rickover's atomic energy plants. The first two were in direct competition with Regulus II. And, when aviators saw funding for both Regulus II and manned aircraft coming "out of the same pocket," there was no doubt about which bill would not be paid.[86]

Cruisermen watched as the FY 58 budget reduced the number of their ships that would carry Regulus from thirty-one to eighteen, then to twelve. Suddenly in December 1958, the ax fell when Regulus II was cut altogether from the budget. Appearing before Lyndon B. Johnson's Senate committee, Secretary Gates laid the case against Regulus II: at almost $1.4 million per missile, the program was expensive, especially considering that virtually none of the requisite shore support facilities were yet in place. The latest number of projected Regulus II ships—twelve submarines and twelve cruisers for 1970—was too small to be cost effective. Gates added that carrier aviation, Regulus I, and Polaris could carry out virtually all of Regulus II's missions. These arguments proved convincing despite the fact that Admiral Burke carried the case for the missile all the way to President Eisenhower.[87]

The program was not a total loss, however. The Navy had made valuable progress in guidance; the inertial system was 90 percent complete at Regulus II's cancellation, and the testing of the radar map-matching technology was 50 percent complete. The research accomplished in both these areas was to be of great value to the Navy when it reactivated its cruise missile programs in the 1970s.[88]

For a time, plans called for *Long Beach* and the projected second batch of *Albany*s to carry Polaris. Some officers even hoped to put Polaris in destroyers, but in the end only submarines carried the ballistic missile. Many policymakers then and later considered the cancellation of Regulus II a serious error, especially when coupled with the ending of its more capable follow-on, the Triton. In protest, the project officer for the missiles requested retirement from the Navy. Retrospectively, one admiral assessed the Regulus II cancelation as "the biggest single weapons mistake the United States Navy ever made." [89] Another surface warfare officer, Elmo R. Zumwalt, Jr., later CNO, recalled that he was "absolutely horrified" when Regulus was canceled." [90] Many other officers were equally vehement. [91]

In retrospect, it can be argued that Burke wisely decided to give the limited funds at his disposal to Polaris and carrier aviation. But the surface warfare community bitterly regretted the decision, and many black-shoe officers felt that intraservice rivalry had dictated the verdict. Zumwalt suspected that "the reluctance of the aviators' union to give up any portion of its jurisdiction played a large part in the decision." [92] In fact, many aviators doubted whether the Navy needed a cruise missile at all. Rear Admiral Thomas H. Moorer, carrier advocate and later CNO, contrasted the weapon with the attack aircraft by pointing out that the airplane was always recallable, always redirectable, and always reusable. [93] The missile cost approximately as much as the airplane and was expended in one shot. As to the growing Soviet surface fleet, U.S. aviators were certain that their attack aircraft could easily deal with these vessels. The weakness of Soviet antiaircraft defenses on board their surface ships simply reinforced the cockiness of American brownshoes. Their confidence that the airplane could do it all lasted until 1967. [94]

The aviators were so assured during the late 1950s of their mastery over the surface warship that they abandoned two missiles specifically developed for this mission. One was Petrel, the winged torpedo. Carried by a P–2 Neptune patrol bomber, the device would be dropped well outside the range of a Soviet cruiser's antiaircraft battery. With its basic fuselage being a Mk 21 acoustic homing torpedo to which were attached wings, a turbojet engine, and a guidance and control system, the Petrel homed in on the enemy ship with its active radar. Its very low-altitude approach minimized both radar detection and proximity fuze effectiveness. Less than a mile from its target, the missile jettisoned its nose, wings, and tail, and the torpedo descended to the water by parachute. Tested in a variety of conditions from the Arctic to the tropics, this ingenious, if complex device, worked surprisingly well. One officer who tested Petrel noted that it would have been especially effective at night. In 1956, it was deployed in the Mediterranean. But given budgetary constraints, Petrel quickly left the fleet for Reserve squadrons and was then scrapped altogether by 1959. [95]

Also abandoned was development of the supersonic air-to-surface guided missile Corvus. Intended for precise delivery of a nuclear warhead against radar installations and ships, Corvus was slated for testing in 1960. Escalating costs halted the program. The cancellation of the more capable

Corvus worried its project development officer, who later recalled saying in defense of Corvus, "Look, you have done away with Petrel, and the *Sverdlov* cruiser is still there, and we are rapidly becoming a navy incapable of fighting in an engagement at sea." [96] Presumably, carriers would rely on tactical nuclear bombs dropped by F9F–8B Cougars, on board since 1956. By 1960, the only advanced conventional weapon available to carrier aviators for antiship use was Bullpup, a small missile with a 250-pound warhead intended for close support of troops and "for use against small tactical targets ashore and afloat." [97]

As American antiship capabilities diminished, Soviet warships began to operate more aggressively. In 1960, destroyer *Barry* (DD 933) transiting the Baltic was trailed by East German light craft and then harassed by a Soviet *Riga*-class escort ship which almost collided with the American warship. This episode would be only the first of a long string of such incidents over the next two decades. In narrow waters especially, the anemic surface power of U.S. warships worried their officers. Zumwalt later related his concern when he took the new frigate *Dewey* (DLG 14) into the Baltic. Dependent on air coverage for defense against Soviet surface vessels, Zumwalt related that he felt his ship, lacking any antiship torpedoes or missiles, was "castrated." [98]

To compensate, surface sailors pushed for modifications of their antisubmarine and antiaircraft weapons. In 1956, one study concluded that the rocket-boosted antisubmarine torpedo ASROC under development, if used with a nuclear warhead, might inflict crippling damage on a Soviet cruiser by its mining effect. That same year, the Applied Physics Lab began looking closely at Talos and Terrier as ship killers, particularly during bad weather when aircraft were stuck on the flight deck. APL wanted to obtain direct hits on enemy warships "in view of at least the possibility of a nonnuclear war." [99] Work went ahead on a low-priority basis, and by 1958, the Bureau of Ships listed a surface-to-surface capability as a secondary mission for Talos. The bureau credited the version armed with a small nuclear warhead as capable of inflicting severe damage to a battleship. APL pointed out that the principal limitation of the missile in this role was its beam-riding guidance system which gave it a very limited range against surface targets. [100]

Range aside, officers saw Talos as a potent weapon against enemy warships. The proposed nuclear version would yield a sure kill and also would give the missile a strong shore bombardment capability. Even with a conventional warhead, the missile, weighing 3,000 pounds minus the booster, promised to cripple any vessel. At shorter ranges, the large quantity of unexpended JP5 fuel still in the missile would add dramatically to the damage. When compared to Regulus, Talos was superior as an antiship weapon in its automated handling, ready availability, and much greater numbers on board the cruisers. Its major drawback was that only a few ships would ever carry it.[101]

But then, few except blackshoes thought that surface ships would ever need an antiship capability. Cruisers, frigates, and destroyers existed principally to back up the carriers. As one officer at Newport condescendingly put the matter, "Even the carrier striking force needs the support of surface ships."[102] Surface warriors in this universe could best serve by perfecting their skills at antisubmarine work and especially their antiair capabilities.

Pursuant to both those missions, the Navy made major gains in its quest for a better data processing system. Leaders at sea were being inundated by the flood of information coming from the multitude of sensors carried by and flown from a naval task force. The first exploratory steps taken early in the decade had led some officers to conclude that pursuit of a data processing solution with the existing analog technology was a waste of time. In 1955, two commanders, Edward Svendsen and Irvin McNally, wrote the specifications for a revolutionary system, the Naval Tactical Data System (NTDS). In an age when the computer industry was embryonic, the small team led by these two officers developed the most complex multicomputer system of their day.[103]

Despite the fact that the transistor was little more than a laboratory curiosity, Svendsen and McNally turned to solid state hardware to solve a variety of problems inherent in the existing vacuum tube technology. The solid state equipment was much more compact, required far less power, and, according to its adherents, would become significantly more reliable than analog equipment. The adoption of digital equipment also made possible the integration of various systems on board a warship. For instance, a significant problem plaguing surface warriors for some time had been the difficulty of "handing-off" an incoming airplane or missile from the search to the tracking radars. Now, the digital revolution held out the prospect of replacing a bewildering variety of analog panels with a few standardized modules. Helping Svendsen and McNally solve the problem of how these modules could "talk" to each other was Seymour Cray, considered by some experts as the world's most successful computer designer.[104]

NTDS coordinated the collection of data from a wide variety of sensors (such as the human eye, radar, sonar, ECM gear, and navigational equipment) and from a wide variety of sources (such as ships in a task group, surveillance aircraft, and submarines). The system then correlated all of this information to present a display of the situation in "real-time." As one officer noted enthusiastically, "A lookout's report might be compared to a radar report, and this could be compared to a communication report." Digital computers made this feat possible; data handling by tapes or cards simply could not provide the requisite speed. Equally important, NTDS permitted automatic interchange of information among a number of warships about air, surface, or subsurface threats and the location of friendly units. The net result was a system that provided a commander with an up-to-the-minute picture of the tactical situation facing his force. On the other side of the coin, NTDS could not ascertain the accuracy of the data fed to it; erroneous information would automatically be broadcast to all units on the net.[105]

Notwithstanding, NTDS proved an extraordinary boon. BUSHIPS set up in 1956 a special project office under the Assistant Chief of Electronics to develop and procure NTDS. OPNAV enthusiastically embraced the system and established Fleet Computer Programming Centers at Dam Neck, Virginia, and San Diego, California. The Bureau of Naval Personnel began listing new specialist classifications like computer programmer and systems analyst. Progress came quickly, in part because of generous funding, in part because of the rather loose, informal nature of the project which demanded little paperwork and depended largely on the informed judgment of the personnel involved. The first test of a completed system began in April 1959. CNO Burke took a personal interest in seeing NTDS in the fleet and ordered that it be included in five ships: carriers *Oriskany* and *Enterprise*, cruiser *Long Beach*, and frigates *King* and *Mahan* (DLG 11). The last two, commissioned in 1960, were the first new ships with the system. Early tests of NTDS were most promising, proving that a force of naval vessels could operate as if they were one ship. With the tight coordination of all sensors and weapons, the Navy gained a "jump in combat capability" and thus a major force multiplier.[106]

Less satisfactory, but more touted, was the service debut of the 3–Ts: Talos, Terrier, and Tartar. Rear Admiral William "Savvy" Sides, an ordnance officer who had headed the missile development section of OPNAV, became commanding officer of Cruiser Division Six composed of the Navy's first missile ships, *Boston* and *Canberra*. Their shakedown attracted interest from the most influential quarters. President Eisenhower himself was on board *Canberra* for twelve days in March 1957. In the late winter of 1956, *Boston* fired her Terriers in front of four groups of VIPs, including seventy-six senators and congressmen, the chief of the Bureau of Ordnance, the Guided Missile Committee from the office of the Secretary of Defense, and a bevy of reporters. These stage-managed shoots went well as *Boston* successfully fired four salvos of two missiles at F6F drones. The commander of the Operational Development Force gave Terrier his stamp of approval by judging the missile ready for fleet use, even though he tempered his enthusiasm by urging the missile's continual upgrading to meet future air threats.[107]

In fact, as Terrier entered service, it suffered from several serious deficiencies. The first versions of the missile had a range of only 10 miles. The vacuum tubes in the missiles mandated a 20-second warm-up period; pro-

The 3–Ts, clockwise from top left: Talos missiles in *Little Rock*, November 1960; two twin Terrier launchers on board *Mississippi* in 1954; a Tartar missile in guided missile destroyer *John King* (DDG 3) in 1969.

KN–1117

USN 644287

K–79884

longed warm-up would damage the tube electronics, so the weapons officer often faced a delicate judgment call. The SPQ–5 guidance radar was, in the words of one officer, "unbelievably complex and unreliable." [108] In view of the increasing speeds of the enemy jet aircraft, the Navy estimated that for a Terrier ship to shoot down a Mach 2 target, the cruiser needed to pick up the threat with search radar at no less than 150 miles and to begin tracking it by air intercept radar at 100 miles. Following one 1958 exercise, the commander of a cruiser division reported that 200 miles was the minimum acceptable distance for initial detection. Fortunately, the new SPS–29 air search set under development demonstrated its ability to spot aircraft at over 240 miles, given the right conditions. [109] On the debit side of the ledger, low-altitude planes remained tough to detect. Additionally, the Terrier's high-explosive warhead seemed insufficiently lethal against a high-speed target. A number of fixes were in the works, including a one-kiloton nuclear warhead and an improved missile with double the range of the original Terrier. The new weapon, dubbed the BT–3, featured tail control and a beam-riding guidance system. Both augured much upgraded performance; the BT–3 was rushed into the fleet in 1960—too precipitously, as events would prove. [110]

Terrier shared many of the same teething troubles with Talos, which itself had fallen even farther behind schedule. Originally slated for operational deployment by 1956, Talos was not fired at sea until 1959. During the initial trials by *Galveston* and then for as long as the weapon remained in the fleet, the huge missile with its 40,000-horsepower ramjet made quite an impression on naval personnel. One sailor summed up a Talos shot with the word "Thunderous." [111] The commanding officer of *Galveston* called it "Spectacular." [112] A *Long Beach* officer said simply of a Talos launch, "It shook the ship." [113] A *Little Rock* missile technician remembered that whenever a Talos was fired, any loose objects, including light fixtures, fell down from the overheads. [114] The departing missile scorched the deck paint, and the "seaman [had] his work cut out for him." [115]

Early comparisons between Terrier and Talos in the fleet gave the nod to the big missile. During a weapons test conducted by *Canberra* and *Galveston* in December 1959, the 10-mile Terrier system was overwhelmed by simultaneous aircraft attacks. Talos fared better: "The longer range Talos missile enables a ship to methodically select targets and shoot with relative leisure compared to the frantic activity of the Terrier ship engaging targets inside its short range envelope." [116] Burke publicly called Talos "the best antiaircraft missile in any arsenal in the world." [117] The Continental Air Defense Command considered it for duty as an antiballistic missile. [118]

Despite these optimistic assessments, the Navy's test firings and fleet exercises demonstrated that early versions of Talos lacked the range and low-altitude capabilities that the Navy wanted. Both problems were ad-

*Little Rock* fires a Talos, 4 May 1961.

USN 1057626

dressed, although success proved elusive until well into the 1960s. The tests of both Terrier and Talos also showed a need for improved capabilities against jamming, more automation in responding to threats, and digital processing computers for better accuracy and maintainability. The tracking, capture, and guidance radar beams needed more precise alignment (or columnation)—a problem unsolved with the long-range Talos until the fabrication of new optical measurement equipment. The Bureau of Ordnance also paid special attention to the development of a better warhead. Conventional types broke into fragments ranging in size from microscopic dust to 6-pound metal chunks. The smallest pieces were not lethal; the largest, inefficient. Ordnance considered a number of advanced designs including warheads delivering an air blast, metal cubes, or clusters of submunitions. Eventually the bureau settled on the continuous-rod warhead. This exotic piece of weaponry was made up of concentric layers of square rods welded at the ends. An explosive in the center of the rod bundle would throw the metal pieces outward at terrific velocity which would then cut through aircraft control surfaces. This warhead was first tested successfully in 1957.[119]

Aside from hardware problems, exercises at sea revealed both successes and difficulties in employing the both missiles. *Canberra* in 1960 undertook a round-the-world voyage in which she worked out with all four fleets. Following a particularly intense week of antiairwarfare drill with the First

Fleet, the commander of the cruiser division was pleased to note, "Results of these exercises were very heartening. A new spirit of confidence in the Fleet's ability to master the Anti-Air Warfare problem was clearly apparent." [120] On occasion, the missile cruisers showed such proficiency at keeping track of the aerial picture that they began taking responsibility from the carriers for coordinating the air defense of a task group. In 1960, Rear Admiral U. S. Grant Sharp, the head of the Pacific Fleet's Cruiser-Destroyer Force, recommended:

> The CRUDIV commander is more advantageously positioned to view and coordinate the AAW effort of a task group and, operating in a cruiser with a primary mission of air defense, is more free to concentrate on the command and control of overall AAW effort. At the same time, the carrier, free of ADC [air defense command] responsibilities is better able to concentrate on air operations. Under EMCON [emission control] conditions, the carrier location is made more secure by reason of AAW being controlled from the cruiser, with the necessary attendant radar and communication emissions. [121]

The early exercises revealed certain problems, as well. In tight formations, falling missile boosters endangered other ships. *Boston* reported that a shortage of specialized spare parts seriously degraded the readiness of her battery. And missiles were too expensive to shoot often: *Boston* fired three Terriers in one quarter of 1959; *Topeka* expended four from October 1960 to November 1961. [122]

USN 1044091

Cruiser *Boston* on carrier escort duties, 15 July 1959.

More disturbing, *Canberra*'s crew frequently found sorting friendly from enemy planes a terrible challenge. Her report following Seventh Fleet trials during which she "rode shotgun" for carrier *Oriskany* stated bluntly,

> With the carrier as the prime target for attack and also the base of operations for CAP, the 20 mile area is highly congested. At one time, *Canberra* reported 25 contacts on radar. . . . Under such circumstances the radar sorting problem becomes impossible with present radar and as a result, some friendlies will be destroyed.[123]

And time after time, low fliers continued to sneak through the radar coverage.[124] The commander of Cruiser Division One concluded after a Seventh Fleet exercise,

> Each low-flying raid was able to enter the carrier vital area undetected and unopposed. Conclusion: Inability to detect, and destroy low-flying raids is an unacceptable situation. To handle the low-flyers we must have effective AEW [airborne early warning] aircraft. . . . Tartar DDG's in vital area, when available, may improve the low-flyer kill situation.[125]

Tartar was in fact under accelerated development to give smaller surface warships the protection they needed against low-altitude, high-speed threats. Such targets had presented, to a beam-rider like Terrier, the special difficulties associated with multipath phenomenon wherein parts of the radar beam were reflected off the ocean's surface rather than the attacking aircraft or missile. Tartar featured a superior semiactive guidance system with the missile homing in on radar energy generated by the firing ship and then reflected by the target. Although studies for such a missile had begun in 1951, early design difficulties prevented the establishment of a hardware development program. Breakthroughs by 1955 in fire control, guidance, and aerodynamics allowed Tartar to go forward. At 1,000 pounds, the Tartar required simplicity. Its rocket motor contained both booster and sustainer in one package. Target intercepts very close to the water mandated special electronic fuzing to initiate the 100-pound continuous-rod warhead, which later went into Terrier as well. Although Tartar shared many other features with Terrier, it employed a novel glass radome with better rain-erosion resistance, a serious problem for high-speed missiles fired at low-altitude targets because hitting raindrops was like running into steel pellets.[126]

Tartar's first successful test came at China Lake in 1956. The missile received high priority; the Navy intended to send Tartar to sea in 1960 on *Charles F. Adams* (DDG 2). The Bureau of Ordnance devised a new launcher that occupied about the same space as a 5"/54 gun mount. Forty-two missiles were stowed in two concentric rings directly under the launcher and ready to be rammed onto the rail by remote control. As ever, the bureau worried that if one missile ignited accidentally, it would set fire to the propellant in the rest. BUORD added dryly, "This holocaust would cook off the warheads. The situation, although spectacular, would be highly undesirable."[127] To prevent such a disaster, the bureau developed a ducting system to vent the gases from an accidental ignition outside the magazine. *Charles F. Adams* took the Tartar to sea on schedule in 1960. Sadly, this missile too hobbled into the fleet.[128] One officer remembered, "its fire control radar, the SPG–51, set new records of unreliability!"[129]

All three new missile systems bedeviled surface line officers. Sea conditions caused problems, especially with electronics and circuits, that had been unanticipated in testing ashore. The missiles showed themselves to be too vulnerable to electronic countermeasures. Even the testing procedures proved inadequate to identify precise problem areas. Worst of all, the missiles were too slow in the face of evolving Soviet supersonic aircraft and antiship missiles. Requiring lengthy warm-up times, the missiles in flight demanded significant direction from the launching ship to achieve a successful intercept. The launching ship could thus control only a small number of missiles at one time, and its systems were vulnerable to being swamped by a large number of attackers. Facing these myriad problems, new G ships like *Galveston* frequently spent most or all of their first commissions working under the auspices of the Operational Development Force rather than joining carrier task groups.[130]

The afflictions of the 3–Ts became so widely known that Soviet commentators mocked them in professional publications. In 1959, the Navy began the Terrier/Tartar Reliability Improvement Program, another of the long series of efforts. Emphasizing interchangeability of components between Tartar and Terrier, the scheme also aimed to reduce production costs while improving reliability. At the same time, both Terrier and Tartar were the beneficiaries of redesigns intended to give them quicker reaction times, better guidance, and greater reach.[131]

In the long run, these redesigns could only be stopgap measures. Advanced systems were essential if surface warships were to function in the sort of threatening environment envisioned for the 1970s. Evincing considerable foresight in 1956, the Bureau of Ordnance began development of a new antiaircraft missile system called Typhon. In cooperation with the Applied Physics Lab and Westinghouse, BUORD by 1959 had sketched out the numerous advances requisite to Typhon's success. A phased-array radar using electronically steered beams of radar energy would replace clumsy separate systems by performing simultaneously the functions of search, tracking, target acquisition, and missile guidance. Vacuum tube technology would give way throughout the system to digital computers. The Typhon missile itself would come in two versions—medium and long range, with maximum commonality between the two. The latter would have a range of at least 200 miles; the former, 40 miles. A new vertical launch system would replace the conventional rotary launcher with its arms and rails. Early plans called for pressurized tubes capable of throwing the missiles several hundred feet into the air. Duds would simply fall into the water instead of hanging up on the launcher arm. Such a system could achieve a very rapid rate of fire. All the elements making up Typhon would be designed from the beginning as an integrated system, in contrast to the jury-rigged 3–Ts. By 1960, Typhon had reached the contract stage, with Westinghouse beginning work on the prototype AN/SPG–59 radar.[132]

The high profile of the missile in the surface fleet led the Atlantic destroyer command in 1957 to caution that gunnery was still to be taken seriously. In response to its rhetorical question "Why worry about guns when they will be replaced soon by missiles?" Commander Destroyers, Atlantic (COMDESLANT) noted the cost of missile ships and predicted that 90 percent of the surface ships would continue to rely on guns for their principal antiaircraft defense in the foreseeable future. Even when all surface ships were propelled by nuclear power plants and armed with guided missiles, COMDESLANT saw a future for guns to defend against aerial targets that had leaked past the minimum range of the defensive missiles, to provide shore bombardment, and to engage surface targets, including submarines brought to the surface. Accordingly, he called for continued work on such gunnery improvements as greater accuracy, higher muzzle velocities, and increased rates of fire.[133]

This call went largely unanswered. In the late 1950s, BUORD could afford only a pittance for gun development. For instance, in 1958 the Naval Powder Factory spent only 3 percent of its budget for work on gun propellants. In fact, the bureau converted a number of its ranges from the testing of guns to the testing of missile warheads. The Naval Ordnance Station at Indian Head, Maryland, did achieve a major advance during the period when it perfected NACO, the cooler-burning propellant. Tests showed that NACO extended the life of 3-inch gun barrels by a factor of eight. Indian Head registered only half that improvement with the NACO it was developing for the 5"/54 because the ordnance station ran out of gun money before it could complete its study. Ironically, NACO showed itself to be especially valuable on board missile ships by lessening muzzle blast pressures—an important consideration in light of the large number of fragile sensors carried topside by modern naval vessels. Despite all the advantages realized with NACO, BUORD funding was so tight that NACO was "placed on the shelf for possible future use" and did not reach the fleet until 1968.[134]

Similarly, BUORD suffered from a chronic shortage of funds to provide ammunition for the newest guns, especially the 5"/54. Stockpiles for older weapons dwindled. Many ships practiced their shooting only on rare occasions. New gun designs were conspicuously absent from the list of bureau projects during the later 1950s. With the 3″/70 suffering terminal problems, the Navy looked north for a quick fix when OPDEVFOR evaluated the Canadian 3″/70 fitted to RCN escort vessels. Summarizing the declining status of gunnery in the U.S. Navy was an illustration which appeared late in the decade in the *Bulletin of Ordnance Information*. Underneath the photograph of a worker cutting up 14-inch gun barrels was a caption reading: "The Naval Proving Ground, Dahlgren, is the site of this conclusive indication of the end of the era when the battleship ruled the seas." [135]

The converging developments in ordnance were reflected in the curriculum at the Naval War College. By the late 1950s, virtually all the student problems at Newport treated questions relating to air or submarine warfare. When the 1958 curriculum devoted one week to the study of surface warfare problems, the officer introducing the exercises sounded apologetic. Tactical studies atrophied; by 1959, the very word "tactics" did not appear in a single course description. The Navy's principal doctrinal publication at the end of the decade dealing with surface warfare, *Naval Weapons Selection—Ships*, was a slightly warmed-over version of the 1953 treatment, modified only by the addition of two appendixes. [136]

In the Navy's broader educational system, the surface branch received similar short shrift. Officers could study tactics at the Fleet Antisubmarine Warfare School, the Submarine School, or the Fleet Antiair Warfare School. There was no surface warfare school. Ensigns learned as best they could on the job; the results were personnel with marginal competence, poor esprit, and a low retention rate. The problem was so serious that Rear Admiral Charles E. Weakley, head of the Atlantic Fleet's destroyers, in 1959 asked the Bureau of Personnel to make radical changes. The fruition of Weakley's efforts would come early in the next decade. [137]

Nor did the increasingly complex equipment going on board surface warships receive the shore training support it needed. New sailors, whether officer or enlisted, learned to operate the gear at the control panels, a situation BUPERS found utterly unsatisfactory by the late 1950s: "We were barely maintaining our wartime equipment; this increasingly intricate gear promised to dump the Fleet right on its face. Something had to be done, and fast." [138] The Navy's immediate response was to commission technician petty officers who obtained a college degree with a curriculum focused in electronics. But some observers expressed concern that this road was turning the surface navy into a splintered community of narrowly educated specialists. [139]

Outlets for surface warriors to express their professional concerns were few. The only publication aimed specifically at the surface line was *Destroyerman*, put out by the Atlantic Fleet. Small in format, *Destroyerman* was more a newsletter than a journal of professional opinion. Admiral Burke himself complained that surface officers suffered from a constricted

NH 84168

President Ngo Dinh Diem reviewing heavy cruiser *Los Angeles* at Saigon, October 1956. Note the Regulus I missile.

outlook. Others leveled this criticism at all communities within the Navy. A 1958 report by the head of ONI identified parochialism as an endemic problem which tended "to encourage the formation of cliques and to discourage viewpoints and thinking oriented toward the best interests of the Navy as a whole." [140]

In fact, the Navy was on the brink of a major organizational reshuffling to speed the design of new warships. With sensors and missiles so complex and demanding of space, they could no longer be devised in a vacuum and then simply added onto hulls. Many officers felt that the bureau system was incapable of the coordination necessary to develop the complicated weapons systems that warships had become. Two bodies called the Libby and Franke boards considered these problems. The outcome of their reports was the abolition of some of the Navy's most hallowed institutions. In December 1959, the Bureau of Ordnance, which dated to 1842, merged with the Bureau of Aeronautics, begun in 1921, to become the short-lived and unwieldy Bureau of Naval Weapons (BUWEPS). Reflecting the Navy's emphasis on missiles was the change in title of certain of its facilities. The Naval Powder Factory became the Naval Propellant Plant, and Dahlgren, which had officially been called the Naval Proving Ground since 1918, became the Naval Weapons Laboratory.[141]

Also changing was the surface navy's Atlantic focus. In the Burke years, surface warships of the Atlantic and Mediterranean Fleets made headlines by deploying to the Baltic and Black Seas and screening the 1958 landings in Lebanon. But in the Far East, Seventh fleet cruisers and destroyers undertook increasingly visible deployments. In 1957, destroyers *Southerland* and *Henderson* (DD 785) gave assistance to flood victims in Ceylon. In 1958, Seventh Fleet cruisers and destroyers covered the landing of supplies at Quemoy and Matsu. Two years earlier, on 24 October 1956, heavy cruiser *Los Angeles* paid a highly publicized visit—the first by a U.S. warship—to the new Republic of Vietnam. The cruiser, with one of her Regulus missiles on proud display, hosted the South Vietnamese leader, Ngo Dinh Diem.[142] Closer to home, surface warships began their long association with America's space program by plucking Mercury astronauts from the Atlantic.

The pace of operations for the sailors was hard; the typical surface warship during the late 1950s spent more than half of each year underway. Two examples might suffice: *Hammerberg* (DE 1015) in eleven months participated in ASW operations with friendly navies from Norway to Chile. *Forrest Sherman* from July to November 1958 exercised off Puerto Rico, operated in the Mediterranean, joined the Seventh Fleet off Quemoy, and ended her odyssey in Norfolk, having circumnavigated the globe. Sailors worked as hard as their ships. One boatswain's mate who enlisted in 1950 made nine deployments over the next decade, with each tour in excess of six months.[143]

President Eisenhower had appointed Arleigh Burke CNO in 1955 to "speed up the Navy's assimilation of new technology, appoint younger, more vigorous officers to positions of responsibility, and provide inspiration to a somewhat demoralized fleet." As Burke's biographer has noted, all three expectations were realized. Late in his tenure as CNO, Admiral Burke himself looked at the Navy's future with a certain satisfaction:

> These wonderful innovations—nuclear power, nuclear weapons, supersonic aircraft, guided missiles—are the harbingers of the Navy of the future. They hold the promise of the new Navy of fantastic power, range and mobility—a Navy which will prove equal to the greatest challenge the maritime world has ever faced. The future is limited only by our imagination and our zeal![144]

In sum, during the six years of Burke's tutelage, the surface navy had made some significant steps: it began an ambitious program to acquire large numbers of guided missile cruisers and destroyers; it laid down its first nuclear-powered warships; it pushed ahead work on NTDS when that system seemed positively visionary. Counterbalancing these advances in surface warfare were the cancellation of the promising Regulus II missile and the rapidly decreasing numbers of heavy gunships. Both would be sorely missed in the next decade.

4

# Caught in the Doldrums:
# Surface Warfare, 1961–1965

Arleigh Burke's retirement coincided with a reorientation of national defense strategy by the incoming Kennedy administration emphasizing capabilities for conventional war. This strategy should logically have led to a buttressing of the surface navy, but in most areas, it did not despite an increasing threat by innovative Soviet ships and cruise missiles and despite sharp international crises in which cruisers and destroyers flexed American muscles. Progress in surface warfare during the period was stumbling at best.

John F. Kennedy came to the presidency intent on providing an alternative to the New Look nuclear strategy of the preceding administration. With the Soviet buildup in nuclear forces, a stalemate in strategic weapons was crystallizing. America's reliance on the hydrogen bomb as the panacea for its security needs—always a weak reed, in the Navy's view—was no longer a tenable policy.

In recasting America's defense posture, Kennedy gave major authority to Secretary of Defense Robert S. McNamara. A brilliant, if astringent individual, McNamara placed great weight on preparing America's strategic forces to ride out a surprise attack and on bolstering conventional forces in the NATO alliance—a strategy labeled Flexible Response. Assuming nuclear deadlock, McNamara saw Europe as the theater where a confrontation would most likely occur, a perception heightened by the Berlin crisis of 1961. This emphasis on Europe elicited enthusiastic support from the Army and even the Air Force, but it left the Navy playing a supporting role. Specifically, the focus on NATO relegated the Pacific to a secondary theater and also mandated that the Navy devote a great deal of attention to antisubmarine warfare. If central Europe was the most likely arena for a hot war, the principal task of the Navy would be to convoy reinforcements from North America to that front. Power projection could be left to the Air Force.[1]

Not surprisingly, Navy planners were uncomfortable with McNamara's overarching framework. They argued that war at sea would never be confined to one theater, but would inevitably take place worldwide. They also postulated a scenario in which a naval war might develop independently of a land war. Other naval studies indicated that Soviet provocations might best be countered by reprisals at sea, thereby lessening the risk of nuclear

Secretary of Defense Robert S. McNamara on board the guided missile destroyer *John King,* 13 July 1962.

USN 1071913

escalation. For instance, in November 1961, the Navy deployed an ASW task group to the North Atlantic "for possible employment in the harassing of Soviet naval operations as a counter to Soviet harassment in Berlin." [2] In any case, the Navy maintained that as the Soviet conventional land and air forces became more powerful, the naval strength of the United States should weigh as an important equalizer for NATO. [3]

Paying little attention to the Navy's brief, McNamara moved quickly to reorient defense spending to support his strategic conceptions. The budget estimates for 1962, amended three times between March and July 1961, provided additional funding for an invulnerable nuclear deterrent force and improved conventional capabilities. These and later reconfigurations of the budget brought joy to only a few in Navy circles. McNamara stated openly that he thought "NATO naval forces in some areas . . . already exceed our needs"; he proposed to shift funds to "more urgently needed" ground forces. [4]

On the block specifically was money for the Navy's big carriers whose principal mission was nuclear deterrence, a task increasingly filled, in McNamara's eyes, by Polaris and land-based missiles. In February 1962, he relieved the carriers of their responsibility for strategic nuclear attack. Very skeptical of the big ships, he ordered three consecutive studies to determine their utility. While grudgingly accepting a role for them in limited war, McNamara refused to request funds for additional carrier construction in FY 62, 64, or 65. For the surface navy, the stakes were high. The guided missile cruisers, frigates, and destroyers entering service were all tied in mission to the carrier. If the carrier was through, so presumably would be the surface navy's premier warships. On the other hand, the ASW escort forces would benefit from McNamara's analysis.[5]

Ironically, the most severe international crisis of the Kennedy presidency—the Cuban Missile Crisis—showed the Navy off to great advantage. Surface warships proved their utility once again. When the crisis began on 20 October 1962, the cruisers, frigates, and destroyers of the Atlantic Fleet were scattered from the Mediterranean to Chile. The ships of Destroyer Squadron 22 were preparing for yard work; some had machinery apart or magazines empty. Illustrating the furious efforts to put the ships to sea was the experience of one crewman on leave from *Maloy* (DE 791). Determined to make his ship's sailing, the sailor returned to base "with the help of the Connecticut State Police. A relay of three patrolmen, sometimes reaching speeds of 120 mph, deposited the man on the pier just one minute before the gangway was hauled up."[6]

Within three days, 52 surface warships were headed for Cuban waters; by mid-November, COMCRUDESLANT counted 2 cruisers and 115 destroyer types under his command enforcing the President's quarantine. *Newport News* flew the flag of Second Fleet. Some of the Navy's newest guided missile ships participated, including *Lawrence* (DDG 4), fresh from her shakedown cruise. Although sailors only boarded one ship headed toward Cuba (the Lebanese *Marucla* on 26 October), they intercepted and visually inspected many more and then monitored the Soviet withdrawal of the missiles from the island. ASW operations proved especially gratifying.[7]

By demonstrating the utility of sea power, the Cuban Missile Crisis spurred the Soviets to strengthen their fleet, leading to accelerated deployment of antiship missiles and construction of a number of innovative platforms for these potent weapons. Soviet surface forces received boosted priority. Leading this buildup was Admiral Gorshkov. He had at first echoed Khrushchev's denunciations of cruisers, but by 1963 Gorshkov was insisting on their usefulness. In a *Pravda* article, he ranked missile-armed surface warships on a par with submarines.[8]

The missile that would attract the most publicity over the long term was the least capable in the Soviet stable. The SS–N–2 Styx, first spotted under wraps in 1959 on board *Komar*-class missile boats, became fully operational by 1961. Over the next three decades, it would prove itself in combat to be a dangerous, albeit unsophisticated, weapon. Burke opined later that the Soviets "took a cheap Regulus II and made a very good missile out of it."[9] With a range of about 15 miles, the Styx followed a preset course for the first two-thirds of its flight; then its radar switched on as the weapon closed in on its target. At its speed of Mach 0.9, the missile at that point was only 30 seconds away from impact. The 1,100-pound shaped charge warhead was sited just ahead of the fuel tank so that the gas jet from the warhead would burn a hole deep into the target. Any unexpended fuel would multiply the damage. The Soviets calculated that two missiles hitting a destroyer would sink it.[10]

To carry Styx, the Soviets sped up construction of their *Komar-* and *Osa-* class missile boats in the early 1960s. About 100 of the small, wooden-hulled *Komar*s entered service; the larger, steel *Osa*s were produced in greater numbers, with 175 being finished. The *Osa*s and *Komar*s were particularly dangerous close to shore. Their detection by eye or even radar was quite difficult especially against a land background. An *Osa* or *Komar* with a larger ship to seaward was likely to spot the other ship's upper works and get its missiles away before itself being spotted. Even attack aviators rated such small vessels as hard targets at night. The tensions over Cuba moved the Soviets to transfer twelve *Komar*s to Fidel Castro's navy in 1962.[11]

Of less concern to American officers was the outwardly much more impressive *Kynda* class of missile cruisers, four of which were completed in the first half of the decade. Designed in the late 1950s, the lead ship, *Grozny*, entered service in June 1962. The "first truly modern Soviet sur-

USN 1111964

A Soviet *Osa*-class guided missile patrol boat.

A Soviet Styx missile is loaded on board an *Osa*-class boat. This photo was printed in the magazine *Soviet Warrior* in 1963.

face ships," [12] these impressive-looking cruisers were comparable in size to *Leahy*-class frigates and carried virtually all new sensors and weapons. Easily the most fearsome of the latter was the SS–N–3 Shaddock. An anti-ship missile weighing almost 6 tons, the Shaddock carried a one-ton conventional warhead or a 350-kiloton nuclear warhead to a distance of 250 miles; with the exception of certain strike aircraft, the Shaddock was the longest-ranged antiship weapon in the world. The missile suffered from certain drawbacks. Like the Talos, it required in-flight guidance, generally by having the firing vessel feed to the missile at mid-course inputs from a specially configured targeting aircraft, usually a turboprop Tu–20 Bear–D. Additionally, the missile's radar cross section was relatively large. [13]

American naval officers regarded the *Kynda*-Shaddock combination with interest and a certain respect, but they felt it would prove terribly vulnerable to carrier aviation. One surface sailor called it "very fragile system." [14] Although the *Kynda*s were equipped with antiaircraft missiles and were usually accompanied by the fast *Kashin*-class destroyers, carrier aviators were quite confident that they could deal with these Soviet surface vessels. Most American officers believed that the only way the Soviets could get in an effective blow with this system was by a surprise attack at the beginning of a war—truly a one-shot affair. [15]

But the *Kynda*s were just one of several threats looming on the horizon. At this time the Soviets also began the deployment of the Shaddock in several classes of submarines. About twelve submarines of the *Whiskey* type were modified in the late 1950s to carry from one to four Shaddocks. The hasty nature of their conversion was reflected in their clumsy appearance. The more capable, purpose-built *Juliett* class showed much finer lines while carrying four Shaddocks. Even more threatening was the service introduction in 1962 of the nuclear-powered *Echo II*-class submarines, each armed with eight Shaddocks. [16] Of course, these submarines put not only American naval forces at risk; versions of the new Soviet missiles could attack U.S. bases and cities directly. A land-attack version of Shaddock went to sea on board an *Echo* in 1960. In 1964, the Soviets began regular operational deployments off the Atlantic coast of the United States. [17]

Additionally, the Soviets introduced advanced air-launched antiship missiles. The AS–2 Kipper, entering service use in 1960 or 1961, was carried by the Badger bomber. With a standoff range of over 100 miles, the Kipper resembled the Shaddock in size and speed. The Soviets also began trailing U.S. aircraft carriers into the middle Atlantic and south of Midway with the long-range Bear beginning in early 1963. [18]

The first half of the 1960s brought challenges aplenty to the American surface navy, not all of which were generated by the Soviets. The feeling among surface warfare officers that they were poor cousins in the Navy intensified during this period. By this point, Rickover's program signed up with its lures of prestige and high pay many of the brightest young ensigns. Other junior officers were "drafted" into nuclear engineering; those ordered to nuclear training faced the options of compliance or resignation from the Navy. Most of the graduates of the program then went to submarines. Aviation continued to draw many with its attractive flight pay and long spells of duty ashore. It is only fair to emphasize that despite the blandishments of aviation and submarine duty, fine officers elected the surface branch or chose to remain in it. For instance, Robert P. Foreman, asked to join the prestigious Polaris team, refused on the grounds that Raborn's program had collected more than enough talent, whereas antiairwarfare needs were pressing and undersupported. [19]

Surface warfare officers reacted in varying ways to this continual drain on talent, potential or actual. One contributor to the *Proceedings* wrote:

[A]s the Force has watched with mixed feelings of pride and anguish some of its finest officers depart for duty in submarines, aviation, and other ship types, so too have these other programs come to count, year after year, on the input from the Force. Destroyer-trained junior officers have traditionally been categorized among those with the most fully developed sense of professionalism, a high degree of technical and operational skill; in short, the most ship-oriented junior officers in the service.[20]

Another contributor to the same journal felt bitter about the implied slight that his specialty was, in his words, the "last alternative short of a physical disqualification from active duty."[21]

Adding insult to injury was the "second career syndrome" in which a failed aviator or submariner could continue his naval career as a black-shoe. A surface officer remembered one of the selling points with the other communities: "If you don't quite make it with us, you can always go surface."[22] Of course, those who switched to surface warfare did so for a variety of reasons. The surface line benefited, for example, from diesel submariners and "front-enders" (weapons specialists) in nuclear attack submarines whose advancement was blocked because they were not trained in nuclear propulsion.[23]

Many surface line officers also believed that aviators had unfairly monopolized the top operating commands. Following Burke, the next three CNOs, Admirals George W. Anderson, Jr., David L. McDonald, and Thomas Moorer, all wore wings. During their years in office (1961–1970), the forward-deployed fleets (the Sixth and Seventh) were commanded only by aviators. Elmo Zumwalt later wrote: "This . . . provoked some hard feelings among surface officers, including me."[24] At the next level of command, no surface warfare officer commanded a carrier task group, the Navy's most prestigious battle formation, until 1960 when Arthur R. Gralla hoisted his flag in antisubmarine carrier *Intrepid* (CVS 11) of TG 60.2 in the Sixth Fleet. Such command opportunities remained rare.[25]

At the rank of commander or captain, surface warfare specialists found aviators and submariners monopolizing many of the most desirable seagoing assignments. To qualify for flag rank, an officer needed a major ship command. Thus, submariners chosen for captain who had never served a day in surface warships frequently received orders to a cruiser or a destroyer flotilla. One aviator detailed as skipper of the escort carrier *Thetis Bay* (CVE 90) asked a black-shoe friend, "How do I get a ship underway?"[26] The plum surface warship assignment at the turn of the decade was cruiser *Long Beach*, the world's first nuclear warship. Symptomatically, she went to submariner Eugene P. Wilkinson, the first commanding officer of *Nautilus*. Surface officers then pushed hard for the first nuclear frigate to go to a destroyer sailor, and Admiral Burke so directed.[27]

On the reverse of the coin, the surface officer would not, except in the most unusual circumstances, command units containing submarines or aircraft until he reached the level of fleet or amphibious group commander. Surface sailors discerned other oddities in the command picture. Early in the 1960s, a number of the most promising young ordnance officers, prime candidates for the troubled missile ships, found themselves "swanning around" in fleet tugs and minesweepers because their detailers in BU-PERS thought such early commands were good for their careers. In the acid words of one witness, "The Navy's needs seemed to be second fiddle."[28] More explicable, but still discouraging to some, was the slow ascension to destroyer command, coming at the thirteen- to fourteen-year service level, in contrast to five or six during World War II. And a captain headed for flag rank continued to have little chance to enjoy or master his next level of command—generally that of a guided missile cruiser. For instance, the first five COs of *Topeka* served tours truncated to one year to allow other upward-bound officers to "check that block."[29]

Surface warfare officers naturally resented being treated as second class—and their higher resignation rate reflected this disenchantment. Their job was a most difficult one with its multifaceted challenges. As the Bureau of Naval Weapons noted in 1963, "The spectrum of threats to which a surface unit must be responsive ranges from submarine-launched antiship ballistic missiles to attacks by small craft in restricted waters. The mission assigned to such a unit might vary from attack carrier task force air defense to the close support of an amphibious landing."[30]

Surface warfare officers increasingly took their message to the pages of the Naval Institute *Proceedings*. A spate of articles appeared in the first part of the decade. The author of one of the most farsighted was Elmo Zumwalt, the captain of guided missile frigate *Dewey*. Commander Zumwalt proposed a reorganization of OPNAV by creating the office of DCNO (Surface Warfare) as a direct counterpart to DCNO (Air). The new office, Zumwalt maintained, should exercise central control of surface ship matters and plan surface ship construction. The DCNO (Surface Warfare) remained a dream for a decade until Zumwalt became the CNO.[31]

Other surface officers promoted their own insignia to match the aviator's wings and the submariner's dolphins. One blackshoe advanced, unsuccessfully, such a device with a shield, ship's wheel, and long glass. In 1964, the matter came before the Alford Board, a special task force on officer retention. This body considered a number of measures to heighten the status and sharpen the abilities of surface officers. The board rejected the identifying device as well as special monetary compensation for the surface line along the lines of dive or flight pay. The panel based its conclusions partly on the lack of specific hazards confronting surface warriors similar to the dangers inherent in submarine and carrier operations. Besides, the Alford

Board noted with an accountant's eye that there were enough qualified surface officers to fill the billets. The committee did recommend expanded formal schooling for surface warfare officers and a career planning board within the Bureau of Naval Personnel. The Navy adopted only the last of the Alford recommendations.[32]

The surface navy shared at least one personnel problem with the other branches: at the enlisted level, the differential in pay for qualified enlisted men and their civilian counterparts drove some of the best bluejackets out of the fleet. A union shipyard employee on weekend overtime could earn ten times as much as the sailor beside him. The captain of *Long Beach* noted one case:

> The *Long Beach* had the misfortune to witness a classic example of morale mismanagement upon the occasion of the sub-contractor hiring on a Monday a *Long Beach* fire control technician discharged from the Navy on the preceding Friday. This technician (admittedly outstanding) resumed his old work, working alongside his former shipmates at a significantly higher pay rate and shorter hours. Such a practice is, to belabor the obvious, not conducive to a high reenlistment rate, particularly in a rating group already beset with critical shortages in reenlistment.[33]

Lengthening deployments also cut the reenlistment level. The commanding officer of destroyer *Davis* (DD 937) reported at the end of 1962, "*Davis* ... has spent 648 days out of the last 853 days out of her home port. Thus a man standing one duty day in three has been able to be with his family for a total of 136 days in 853."[34] Little wonder that only one fire control technician in seven was signing up for a second tour. And the Navy had invested at least thirty-eight weeks of specialized training in each of those ratings. In the average fleet destroyer, the leading electronics technician was a second class with less than four years of experience.[35]

On board the newest missile ships with their complex and troublesome equipment, the workload was frequently crushing. In vessels undergoing development or evaluation tests, "technicians must work night and day to perform the required tests, adjustments, and repairs necessary for the perfect functioning of the systems which is required. 'Night and day' is not a phrase; it is the simple truth. ... "[36]

Hard work was no stranger to any Navy branch, but differences in living standards rankled some surface sailors. "Sub bases are beautiful places," mused one officer.[37] Another reflected on the living conditions on board an older destroyer during a major overhaul—"so bad that we should not ask any sailor to endure them"—and contrasted them with a submarine commencing an overhaul. "In short order the ... living barge is alongside. This is a matter of routine, and submariners take it for granted."[38] More important than creature comforts were differentials between the warfare communities in the allocation of personnel and materiel. The same officer pointed to the "sub-safe" program and asked why there was "no similar organized and concerted effort to make quality assurance a vital factor for the surface ship." [39]

Surface sailors also wanted increased professional development through better schooling. In spite of the multifaceted challenges that they confronted, surface warfare officers traveled no formal educational path leading to qualification in their speciality, unlike the aviators and submariners who had their own professional schools. The surface line was the only one that took ensigns straight from the Naval Academy, Officer Candidate School (OCS), or Naval Reserve Officer Training Corps (NROTC) and put them in responsible billets at sea with no additional schooling. [40] Training for the surface navy remained very much a hit or miss proposition, similar to an apprenticeship. Admiral David E. Jeremiah recalled that very junior officers often served as department heads in destroyers. When he was an ensign, Jeremiah found himself certified as a qualified Officer of the Deck by the commanding officer of his ship after standing only three watches. [41] This approach was less and less satisfactory as more complex equipment came on board new ships. [42] The commanding officer of destroyer *Davis*, Commander Allan P. Slaff, felt strongly enough about disparities in manning policies and levels to write a twelve-page letter directly to CNO Admiral Anderson at the end of 1962. While the destroyer force went chronically short-handed, diesel submarines were putting to sea with 110 percent of their rated billets, the extra crewmen officially on board for training. In comparing his destroyer's engineering department with its 1,200-pound plant to that of carrier *Wasp* (CVS 18) (with 600-pound machinery), Slaff found that the carrier also had on board 110 percent of her allowance, in sharp contrast to his destroyer which was making do with 84 percent—on a much more demanding plant. Slaff bluntly told the CNO that many of his men were working more than 100 hours a week. To top off Slaff's problems, he lost 213 (or 92 percent) of his crew to transfers within fifteen months. Such chronic shortstaffing and churning of the ship's force badly affected his junior officers who greatly needed the advice of experienced enlisted men. Aside from the executive and supply officers, the highest-ranking officer on *Davis* was a j.g. The ship had no warrant officers on board. Thus the young, unseasoned officers ended by carrying much of the load—a recipe for frustration. Across the surface navy, ensigns were filling almost 10 percent of the department head slots. The personnel situation on *Davis* was sadly typical of the surface navy in the early 1960s. [43]

To rectify this situation, Chief of Naval Personnel Vice Admiral William R. Smedberg III recommended in 1961 the establishment of a school for fledgling destroyer officers. By using existing DESLANT and and Fleet Training Center facilities at Newport, start-up was quick and expenses negligible. Opened in January 1962, the U.S. Naval Destroyer School was charged with the mission of providing "the Destroyer Force, through a system of functional education and training, with officers professionally qualified and motivated to function as effective naval leaders on board ship."[44] The thirty-nine officers of the first class (all but two were j.g.s) took a 24-week course with the heaviest concentration on engineering (170 hours) followed closely by work in weapons (90 hours for gunnery, 50 for antisubmarine warfare, and 10 for missilery). Other areas of the curriculum included operations (60 hours of CIC [Combat Information Center], 30 hours of communications, 35 hours of navigation, and 25 hours of seamanship). "Executive" work occupied 65 hours (45 hours of organization and administration, 10 of leadership, and 10 of shipboard training). Visiting lecturers from the staff or student body of the Naval War College spoke on subjects as diverse as replenishment, oceanography, and ASW operations. Each class spent one-eighth of its time at sea on board the two school destroyers.[45]

The curriculum was demanding, and an attendee had to agree to extend his service commitment for two years, but as the reputation of the institution increased, class size grew to ninety in 1965. Students received their subsequent assignments depending on their class standing. The number of graduates by 1965 was sufficient to end "fleet-ups" of department heads in all but the oldest escort ships, and even those vessels had at least one graduate on board. The Destroyer School quickly became the shortest route to division command and to promotion.[46]

The Destroyer School represented an important advance for surface warriors; some wanted to go even farther with a mandatory branch training program similar to the Army's armor or infantry schools. A suggested name was the Surface Line School, but this proposition went nowhere.[47]

Surface warfare specialists achieved gains through other organizational reforms. In January 1962, Captain Isaac C. Kidd, Jr., activated the first all-guided missile unit in the Atlantic, Destroyer Division (DESDIV) 182, with five frigates (DLGs). Several months later, the destroyer/frigate and cruiser commands were folded together given that the basic distinction between the cruiser and the destroyer was blurring. Cruisers were fitting out with sonar; the *Farragut*-class destroyers carried guided missiles. The new organizations were called Cruiser-Destroyer Flotillas (CRUDESFLOT). The CRUDESFLOTs were amorphous in their composition as ships on their rosters went into overhaul or as cruisers rotated tours from the flotillas to duty as fleet flagships.[48]

A few surface officers argued that individual warships should be permanently assigned to the CRUDESFLOTs; they could then be wedded to specific carriers. Working with a carrier and its aircraft sometimes involved intricate station-keeping with specific aircraft engagement zones and elaborate procedures to ensure that the missile ships did not shoot down a friendly aircraft by accident. Were the carrier permanently grouped with its escorts, all the ships could polish their skills by working for long periods together as a unit.[49]

This viewpoint was a minority one in the surface line. Most felt that such an arrangement would deprive them of responsibility. Too often a destroyer or frigate assigned to a carrier would spend a great deal of time on the elementary task of plane guard duty. Battle practice for the surface ships tended to center on antiaircraft exercises to the exclusion of other missions. A cruiser or destroyer would thus be deprived of opportunities to practice shore bombardment, antisubmarine drill, or antisurface training. Missile ships stationed with the Sixth Fleet in the Mediterranean would sometimes go for a year without firing a gun or working against a live submarine. As the commanding officer of the new guided missile destroyer *Lawrence* wrote after his ship's first tour in the Mediterranean, "The major flaw in Sixth Fleet operations is that everything else is subordinated to the overriding objective of pilot training. The fallacy of this approach may one day be demonstrated when superbly trained pilots attempt to get their jets off a flight deck that has a 30 degree tilt because team effort was neglected."[50]

When the missile cruisers served as flagships, they found that their tours varied enormously depending entirely on the interests of the admiral embarked. Some flag officers wanted to see the ships exercise their weapons, especially the latest missiles. At the other end of the scale was the commander of the Sixth Fleet who ordered his flagship kept away from the rest of his warships so that he could plan operations without the distractions inherent in tactical drills. His cruiser became, in essence, "a communications yacht."[51] As such, *Springfield* reportedly went three years in the Mediterranean without making a single hit with her missile battery. Another extreme example of this removal of a flagship from the rest of the fleet was the homeporting arrangements of the Sixth Fleet once France left NATO. The cruiser flagship was based at Gaeta, Italy; all the other ships homeported in the Mediterranean operated out of Naples.[52]

Funds for training were scarce for surface warfare in the early 1960s. COMCRUDESLANT reported that some of his ships were "living off the shelf for lack of money";[53] that is, they were eating up their inventories of spare parts. Overhauls were deferred, as was much equipment repair. Aging ships—many of them now entering their third decade—worsened an already bad situation.[54]

Aggravating all these disturbing trends were the demands that the new G ships made on strained resources. A typical modern sonar system required twenty-one sonarmen, twelve of whom needed special schooling to operate the equipment properly. Certain of the sophisticated new systems, such as DASH, worked poorly, and spare parts for the new equipment were often in short supply. The parts list for a *Farragut*-class frigate contained 35,000 separate items stowed in twenty-five widely scattered spaces. Components prone to failure frequently took two or three weeks to reach a ship on distant station. In the interim, a critical system was "down"—a situation "entirely unacceptable in wartime."[55]

A seeming bright spot in this otherwise cloudy picture was the entry into service of the missile ships ordered in the Burke years, even though many of the vessels were six months or more behind schedule. By the start of 1964, fifty-six G ships were operational: twelve cruisers, twenty-one frigates, and twenty-three destroyers.

All of the last made up the *Charles F. Adams* class. The first combatants to carry Tartar (with an improved single-arm launcher in the later ships), their other advanced features included an all-aluminum superstructure to reduce topside weight, 1,200-pound steam, ASROC, and SQS–23 sonar. The one-level combat information center, placed just behind the pilot house, provided upgraded command facilities. The high clipper bow and sheer forward gave excellent seakeeping characteristics, as operations by *Richard E. Byrd* (DDG 23) in the Davis Strait between Greenland and Baffin Island demonstrated in the winter of 1966. Air conditioning in all living and operations spaces plus modern bunks and furniture made for "a quantum jump" in habitability over the World War II destroyers.[56] Given the state of the art, the *Charles F. Adams* class was capable in all areas of warfare—surface, ASW, and antiair. West Germany and Australia thought enough of the design that each purchased three of the destroyers from American yards.[57]

The first U.S. Navy ships of the class to commission suffered from a number of "bugs," especially those built by New York Shipbuilding Company, "the shipyard that enjoyed at that time the worst reputation of all the shipyards then building Navy combat ships."[58] The commissioning crew of *Lawrence* uncovered 400 major discrepancies in the ship's hull and engineering plant, which the yard fixed only after much footdragging. Exercises of DESRON 18—the first all-guided missile destroyer squadron formed in mid-1962 of *Dahlgren* (DLG 12), *Pratt* (DLG 13), *John King* (DDG 3), *Lawrence*, and *Sampson* (DDG 10)—showed that the SPS–39 search radar gave inadequate performance and often failed altogether. The SPG–51 fire control radars demanded "constant peaking and tweaking."[59]

Despite the problems endemic in the Tartar missile and its associated systems, hard work ultimately made for antiaircraft performances by the *Charles F. Adams* ships that were acceptable—or better. For instance, *Tattnall* (DDG 19), in a test shortly after her commissioning in 1963, shot forty of the missiles and scored twenty hits—a fine figure for the day, and "a proud moment for *Tattnall*," in the words of her commanding officer.[60] *Semmes* reportedly knocked down thirteen drones with thirteen missiles at about the same time.[61]

Some of the destroyers were involved in other trials. *Sampson* for instance successfully replenished her Tartar magazines by helicopter in

*Claude V. Ricketts* during the multinational crew experiments, 12 August 1964.

KN–9582–D

1964. *Claude V. Ricketts* (DDG 5), named for a champion of the multilateral force concept, operated in 1965 with a crew from several NATO nations. Over the long run, veterans of service in *Charles F. Adams*-class destroyers remembered them fondly: "well-designed ships for that era";[62] "most versatile and a welcome addition to the fast carrier task forces";[63] "excellent multi-purpose ships with a high order of reliability, seaworthiness and habitability";[64] "one of the best buys the U.S. Navy ever made";[65] "love of my life."[66]

Contemporaries of the *Charles F. Adams* destroyers were the guided missile frigates of the *Farragut* class. Resounding with names from the Navy's past like Mahan, King, MacDonough, Dewey, and Preble, the ten ships of the class were similar in most respects to their destroyer counterparts except for their main battery. The frigates were armed with Terrier rather than Tartar; the larger ships gave up one 5"/45 barrel to their ASROC mount positioned right in front of the bridge. The ships were pioneers in several areas. *Dewey* was the Navy's first purpose-built missile ship to be commissioned, on 7 December 1959 under Commander Zumwalt. Her machinery was controlled by an automatic combustion system which regulated feedwater, air supply, and firing rate for smokeless operation. *King* and *Mahan* introduced NTDS to the fleet.[67]

Naturally, the ships shared all the woes of the Terrier and thus frequented the practice ranges. *Mahan* spent the first eighteen months in commission proofing her weapons. Some officers felt the *Farragut*s, for their size, were short-legged (with a range of 5,000 miles at 20), but one commanding officer summed up his impressions of *Coontz* (DLG 9), built by the Puget Sound Naval Shipyard: "sleek, powerful, and nimble."[68]

Entering the Navy beginning in August 1962 were the nine later frigates of the *Leahy* class. Over 2,000 tons heavier than the *Farragut*s, the "double-enders" carried Terrier launchers fore and aft. Given the state of Terrier early in the ships' careers, one commanding officer of *Leahy* (DLG 16) noted of the missile control radars, "two of the four installed were usually 'spare parts lockers' for the two years I was aboard."[69] Gun armament was restricted to four 3-inchers. Officers commanding the frigates were irritated by their lack of gun power. Aside from these objects of controversy, one critic noted in the *Proceedings* that the ships cost $75 million each and were as large as World War II antiaircraft cruisers.[70]

But their size did give certain important advantages. The frigates possessed a markedly better range than their predecessors; after one trans-Atlantic run with a carrier task force, *Leahy* retained a higher percentage of fuel than did cruiser *Boston*. And their size, in conjunction with their knuckled hull designed to protect their forward missile launcher, made them excellent sea boats. The commissioning officer of *Reeves* (DLG 24) wrote: "I thought that I was riding the *Queen Mary* compared to the rough rides I had experienced over the years . . . in smaller destroyer types."[71] On the debit side, *Reeves* was slightly sluggish in docking and possessed a fairly large turning circle.[72]

Seizing the spotlight from the *Leahy*s was *Bainbridge*, the nuclear version of her oil-fired contemporaries in armament, sensors, and overall layout. Named for the Navy's first destroyer, *Bainbridge* proudly carried the bell of DD 1. In appearance, the new ship, breaking with the flush deck traditional since the *Fletcher*s of World War II, even looked a bit like the first. Her first commanding officer, Captain Raymond Peet, called DLGN 25 "an elegant ship"—a comment that could be applied even to her wardroom decor. From a donation, Peet's wife bought several fine paintings by modern artists, including one by Bernard Buffet which occasioned great comment in the French press when the frigate visited Toulon.[73]

Commissioning a year ahead of the 8,000-ton *Bainbridge* was the 16,602-ton nuclear cruiser *Long Beach*, armed with one Talos and two Terrier launchers, plus ASROC. Secretary McNamara rejected arming her with eight Polaris ballistic missiles on the grounds of cost. *Long Beach* boasted an 80,000-horsepower plant with all the virtues the Navy had come to expect from a Rickover product. Unhappily, the cruiser was plagued with missile and electronic problems. Surface officers attributed part of the trouble to the shipyard attention that Rickover commanded for his realm. The main battery officer of *Long Beach* remarked on the infinite care accorded the nuclear components as they were fitted into the ship. In contrast, his first Talos missile to be hoisted on board was damaged by careless shipyard handling. Some of the nonnuclear officers on this ship felt they were "stepchildren."[74]

Nuclear power did offer great advantages to the surface warships, if not to the enormous degree that it did to submarines. The most obvious gain lay in vastly increased range: *Bainbridge*, for instance, could travel 5,000 hours at full power; in actual service, this meant three to four years before refueling. Her first commanding officer "drove" the ship for 75,000 miles during his two-year tour; the frigate had traveled 180,000 miles when she refueled. Improvements soon led to cores that would last ten years.[75]

A host of important military advantages followed from this single attribute of astounding range. Loosed from dependence on tankers (which needed protection themselves), a nuclear task force could travel faster and was more likely to achieve surprise. Freedom from fuel restrictions allowed ships to skirt storms readily; low fuel state would not endanger a ship's stability. No stacks allowed for tighter sealing of the ship's interior against biological, chemical, and nuclear contaminants; it also meant no smoke corrosion and more room for antennas. Nuclear power was plentiful power, virtually inexhaustible for the voracious electrical demands of modern sensors, communications, and weaponry. Power came instantly upon demand: the level in a reactor could, in a fraction of a second, be raised from one watt to 1.5 million kilowatts. In addition to answering sudden power needs, the plant could provide steam for instantaneous acceleration or backing. Because extra personnel were not required to staff stations at full power, the nuclear plant needed fewer crew than did a corresponding 1,200-pound plant. The only inherent drawback to the nuclear plant was the length of time required to start it up from total shutdown or to cool it down for maintenance.[76]

The initial service of *Long Beach* and *Bainbridge* certainly showed off the advantages of their nuclear plants. In that area, at least, they met all expectations. On her commissioning in September 1961, *Long Beach* became the flagship for the Atlantic Fleet cruiser force and served also in the Alternate National Military Command role where her freedom from replenishment ships made a strong impression on top planners.[77] From her commissioning to her first refueling in 1964, she steamed 167,000 miles. The reliability of the two ships was another strong suit. *Bainbridge* never even had to return from trials to the Bethlehem Quincy building yard for repairs. In her first two years, *Bainbridge* suffered only one engineering casualty, albeit one of some seriousness. Peet, her commanding officer, who had quarreled earlier with Admiral Rickover, recalled the incident:

> He wasn't going to talk to me, and told his secretary to get the information. . . . I said, "You tell Admiral Rickover two words. If he doesn't want to talk to me, I'm going to hang up, but I think he will."
>
> And she said, "All right, what are the two words?"
>
> And I said, "Stuck rods." Now in reactor parlance if you have rods stuck, you have real trouble. You control the reactor with fuel rods; when you pull your rods out, the reactor goes critical and you generate heat and steam. When you push the rods in, the neutrons are absorbed, and the reactor is stable and shut down. He was on that phone immediately. . . . He knew I had a real problem. We agreed that I'd try to drive them in with the rod control drive motors. . . . If you drive something that's stuck, you tend to get shavings in the primary coolant system. These shavings can become radioactive and contaminate the system. Not a serious condition, but it could be a problem.[78]

Peet attributed much of the success of his ship to her fine crew. Not surprisingly, the nuclear ships acted as a talent magnet. In her first year, *Bainbridge* won an overall E for best cruiser or destroyer in the Atlantic Fleet. "All departments wanted to come up to the standards of the engineers," said Peet.[79] The ships showcased not only the reactor; improved habitability was very much a strong point. *Bainbridge* boasted a sizable library and ample stowage space for over 40,000 spare parts. These considerations were especially important given the extended range of the ships. Peet argued that the limiting factor in the employment of his ship was the endurance of the crew; he proposed that the Navy seriously consider staffing surface ships with two alternating crews, as was done with Polaris submarines.[80]

In 1964, the Navy's three nuclear surface ships, *Long Beach*, *Bainbridge*, and carrier *Enterprise*, demonstrated their reach in Operation SEA ORBIT, a circumnavigation of the world without refueling or replenishing. Commanded by Rear Admiral Bernard M. Strean, the three warships departed from Gibraltar on 31 July. Over the next fifty-eight steaming days, they traveled 30,500 miles at an average speed of 25 knots. Strean later assessed the performance of the two surface combatants.

Carrier *Enterprise*, cruiser *Long Beach,* and frigate *Bainbridge* operate in the Mediterranean, 18 June 1964, immediately prior to Operation SEA ORBIT.

The *Long Beach* and *Bainbridge* performed admirably and without incident concerning their power plants. . . . As to their seaworthiness the *Bainbridge* was near perfection. The *Long Beach* was designed with a large radar array topside and was somewhat top heavy. As an example, this cruiser rolled 45 degrees at Cape Horn in a freak roll at the area of the world's worst weather.[81]

This cruise seemed to vindicate the nuclear prophets, many of whom were influential figures, such as Vice Admiral William F. Raborn, Jr., the "father" of Polaris. Raborn had been forecasting a Navy in which conventionally powered ships would be phased out by the end of the 1970s. In April 1963, Secretary of the Navy Fred H. Korth and CNO Anderson had written to McNamara advocating that all future combatant ships over 8,000 tons be constructed with nuclear plants.[82]

The Secretary of Defense was deeply skeptical of nuclear power, as indeed were many naval officers. No one questioned its tactical or strategic advantages; money was the issue. Nuclear ships were markedly more expensive than their conventional counterparts. For instance, the initial price tag for *Leahy* totaled $75 million; for *Bainbridge*, $150 million. Cruiser *Long Beach*'s appalling cost of $333 million dollars was much more than that of a *Forrestal*-class carrier. Nuclear champions argued with some force that their ships achieved a variety of hidden savings by needing, for example, fewer support ships, fewer repairs, and no fuel for a long period. Even so, skeptics calculated that the nuclear ship would, over a twenty-year span, cost about 1.5 times more than her conventional peer. As one contributor to the *Proceedings* argued, "Two nuclear surface ships just cannot do the work of three of the others."[83] Pointing out that 75 percent of the Navy's destroyers dated to the World War II era, another officer added, "This senseless search for the perfect destroyer—the USS *Utopia*—could [because of exorbitant cost] emasculate the Navy's destroyer force."[84]

In fact, prospects for any additional large surface warships looked increasingly dim. Given the missions of surface vessels "to conduct anti-air, anti-ship, and anti-submarine warfare as well as precise shore bombardment,"[85] the price of complex equipment was escalating rapidly as was ship size, even in conventionally powered craft. The *Farragut*-class frigates displaced 5,648 tons full load; the *Leahy*s, 7,590. Less than two years separated the lead ships of the two classes. Despite this growth in size, competing missions made intense demands on space and weight allocations in even the newest warships. Building specialized antisubmarine and antiaircraft ships seemed at first glance uneconomical, but the antiaircraft weapons suites cost so much that the Navy had to cut Tartar out of most destroyer escorts in order to get the number of antisubmarine vessels that it needed.[86]

Projections from the Burke years had called for the construction in the mid-1960s of five new nuclear-powered cruisers equipped with the advanced Typhon missile system. However, these ships had swelled on the drawing board to 10,000 tons, and McNamara killed the vessels in the fall of 1961, leaving ten missile frigates slated to carry Typhon. But as the Typhon program ran into trouble, the frigates too were axed. The planned conversions of earlier destroyers and frigates to a Talos or Terrier capability were slashed; McNamara eliminated *Norfolk* and sixteen destroyers slated for significant missile upgrades.[87]

The first half of the 1960s then was a relatively dry period for the construction of new frigates and destroyers. Congress paid for nine *Belknap*s in FY 61 and 62; the lead frigate commissioned in November 1964. "Single-enders" with the aft missile launcher of their predecessors (the *Leahy*s) replaced by a 5-inch Mk 42, reportedly as a result of "lessons learned" from the Cuban Missile Crisis, these 8,000-ton ships were criticized as "regressive" for mounting two missile directors rather than four. Their new Mk 10 missile launcher did allow either ASROC or Terrier to be selected as necessary, and the ship's single magazine housed sixty missiles rather than the eighty in the *Leahy*s' two magazines. The gun also gave the *Belknap*s a shore bombardment capability lacking in the preceding class. The commander of the Operational Evaluation Force delivered his verdict on the trade of a missile launcher for a gun mount: "It is unfortunate that magazine space in the DLG 26 class was cut back . . . in order to provide space for what must at the time [have] appeared to be the only feasible means of regaining a surface-to-surface capability—5-inch guns."[88]

Congress mandated a different sort of swap when it directed in the 1962 budget that the tenth *Belknap* be completed with a nuclear power plant. When she emerged from the Camden, New Jersey, building yard in 1967, *Truxtun* (DLGN 35) at 8,800 tons was a slightly enlarged *Belknap* with the gun and missile positions reversed. She would be the last nuclear surface combatant to enter service for seven years. The budgets for FY 63 and 64 contained no funds for these advanced craft which Secretary McNamara opposed on the grounds of expense. Worse, the administration sought no conventional destroyers or frigates either during those two years—and this despite the authorization of carrier *John F. Kennedy* (CVA 67) in FY 63. Almost unbelievably, the budgets for FY 65 and 66 contained no money whatsoever for new destroyers, frigates, or cruisers. Indeed, when Congress in FY 66 voted $20 million to start a nuclear frigate, McNamara sequestered the funds. Four years went by without the authorization of a single major surface warship![89]

This four-year hiatus occurred in large part as a result of McNamara's emphasis on NATO, with his concomitant view that the surface navy's principal role should be convoy defense. In the event of a conventional war in Europe, supplying the needs of the NATO allies alone daunted planners. For instance, Britain in 1942 had brought in 35 million tons of cargo from abroad; in 1965, the NATO countries in northwestern Europe alone imported 400 million tons. The sparest projections called for 12 convoys monthly to Europe, each convoy needing 10 to 12 escorts. Thus, NATO navies required a minimum of 120 escorts; counts of available NATO ships found fewer than half that number available. These dreary calculations looked even more depressing when the Mediterranean was factored in. Antisubmarine warfare in that sea presented special challenges due to its shallow water and varying temperature layers. Given these realities, ASW in the early 1960s became, in the judgment of one black-shoe officer, "the single dominating structure in the Navy's strategy."[90] Admiral Jerauld Wright, CINCLANT from 1954 to 1960, stated: "The primary mission of every combat ship in the Atlantic Fleet is antisubmarine. Everything else is secondary."[91] Resources devoted to constructing an effective ASW defense would protect the convoys on which NATO so depended—and the continental United States. As Secretary of the Navy Paul Nitze, the author of NSC–68, remarked in March 1964, "every dollar we spend for nonstrategic nuclear war ASW forces is also a dollar spent to protect our homeland against the SLBM [submarine-launched ballistic missile]."[92]

Given these stakes, the Navy attacked the ASW problem from promising angles of strategy, operations, tactics, and weaponry. Navy planners hoped to cut down on the number of submarines reaching the convoys by establishing barriers across the choke points, especially the Greenland-Iceland-United Kingdom gap, which the Soviet submarines would transit. SOSUS arrays were, by this time, fully capable of supporting operational forces by locating submarines at distances of hundreds of miles and then fixing their positions to about 40 miles. Appearing early in the 1960s was a supplement to SOSUS: ship-towed passive sonar arrays (SURTASS) to locate submarines outside the areas observed by the fixed SOSUS net.[93]

All three of the Navy's combat branches would take part in ASW. Nuclear attack submarines, generously funded by the Kennedy administration, would operate close to Soviet bases. Big carriers would strike at the Soviet submarine lairs. From shore fields, long-range aircraft, in particular the new P–3 Orion, would patrol the choke points. Hunter-killer groups built around specialized antisubmarine carriers would prosecute contacts with their S–2 Tracker planes and helicopters.[94]

In this multilayered system, surface warships would play an essential role in the carrier task forces, the HUK groups, and the convoy escort units. To execute these missions, the commander of the Atlantic Fleet's Cruiser-Destroyer Force in 1964–1965 believed that what he needed most was a greatly increased number of ASW ships. Quality and new capabilities were important, but "the Atlantic battle would require substantial numbers of ASW ships and aircraft to be successful."[95]

These words found a receptive ear in Secretary McNamara. When he took office, only two ASW escorts, funded but not started, were in the pipeline. Substantially larger (at 2,723 tons full load) than the *Dealey* and *Claud Jones* classes, *Bronstein* (DE 1037) and *McCloy* (DE 1038) featured the new SQS–26 sonar, long antisubmarine torpedo tubes mounted in the stern, ASROC, and DASH. Offsetting these modern features were a 3"/50 gun armament and a speed of 26 knots, inadequate for steaming with an ASW carrier.

The two *Bronstein*s were quickly reinforced; McNamara channeled major resources to escort construction. The FY 62–67 budgets funded sixty surface warships designed principally for ASW, a fivefold increase over the previous decade. The first of McNamara's ships, *Garcia* (DE 1040), kept the ASW weaponry and sensors of the *Bronstein*s, but upgraded the guns to two 5"/38s and increased the speed through lightweight, pressure-fired boilers. *Garcia* was laid down in 1962, followed by nine like units over the next two years, plus one experimental ship, *Glover* (AGDE 1). To herd convoys in areas of higher air threat, the Navy began six similar ships of the *Brooke* class. These surrendered one 5-inch gun and the long torpedo tubes to gain a Tartar launcher and magazine for sixteen missiles.[96]

The seventeen ships of the *Garcia* and *Brooke* classes, with their "barndoor" rudder, all shared excellent seakeeping and good maneuverability in the open sea, despite their single screw. One commanding officer of *Bradley* (DE 1041) remembered, "When [the ship was] handled properly a submarine had a difficult time turning inside her."[97] Close inshore, the single rudder and the large bow sonar dome hampered them somewhat. More detrimental, the novel machinery installation, with the firebox under pressure by a gas turbine supercharger, proved the ships' Achilles' heel. When working, the system pleased sailors with its responsiveness. But the plant suffered a high failure rate because it was never adequately supported, according to *Bradley*'s CO. Also, the ships were twice the size of a World War II destroyer escort and, of course, more than twice as expensive—the *Brooke*-class DEG cost $31.5 million, not much less than a *Charles F. Adams* DDG at $38 million. Given the uncertainties of the pressure-fired boilers, the Navy went back to the "conventional" 1,200-pound plant for its next escorts, the *Knox* class, twenty-six of which were ordered in 1964 and 1965 alone. Work on the lead ship began in 1965; the Navy would not take delivery for another four years.[98]

To fill the gap until the new ASW ships arrived, McNamara expanded the FRAM program. Costs were certainly attractive: conversion of a de-

In drydock at Boston Naval Shipyard, *Willis A. Lee* shows her prototype SQS–26 sonar.

USN 1115109

stroyer to the most capable FRAM I standards was priced at $11 million compared to $27 million for a *Garcia*. Weapons and sensors, although not identical, were similar. Of course, the projected life of the former was only about a third that of the new escort, and habitability was marginal, at best. Nonetheless, the quick fix was attractive, and the first Kennedy budget supplement diverted ten additional destroyers to the yards for FRAM overhauls. Certain of the newer surface warships from the 1950s also underwent modernization: ten of the *Dealey*s were fitted with SQS–23 sonar and DASH. Some of the *Forrest Sherman*s received ASROC; all got the SQS–23 sonar.[99]

The new sound systems represented an enormous step forward by using the principles of bottom bounce and convergence zone (in which a sound pulse, transmitted to the ocean depths, is refracted toward the surface at a substantial distance where it can bounce off a target, returning an echo). Under the right conditions, the SQS–26 could reach out to 70,000 yards or 40 miles. First fitted in *Willis A. Lee* in 1961, the sonar was operational two years later. The bow mount of the SQS–26 made for clumsier ship handling, but it put the set far from the ship's own engine noise and out of bow wave turbulence.[100]

Teamed with the advanced sonars were much more capable ASW weapons. ASROC entered service in 1961; its 10-kilometer range represented a vast improvement over previous weapons. So did ASROC's one-kiloton nuclear depth charge, tested by destroyer *Agerholm* in Operation DOMINIC in May 1962. ASROC ships frequently carried the nuclear ASROC, although these became a distinct liability to destroyer types engaged in shore bombardment off the Vietnamese coast later in the decade. The alternative payload was a Mk 46 homing torpedo, one of the new anti-submarine torpedoes entering production at this time. The Mk 46, which remained the standard ASW torpedo for decades, could also be fired from an escort's lightweight shipboard tubes to track down submarines which had closed the range.[101]

More heralded but less successful than ASROC or the Mk 46 was DASH. Under development from 1958, the little helicopter officially passed ship qualification trials on destroyer *Buck* (DD 761) in 1963. For a time, the Navy gave serious consideration to replacing ASROC altogether with DASH. But serious problems dogged the program. Accidents were frequent; ultimately over half of the 746 drones built crashed. Crews sarcastically referred to DASH as the "Down At Sea Helicopter."[102] DASH would win a measure of redemption in Vietnam as a reconnaissance drone. The alternative, a light manned ASW helicopter suitable for destroyer types, came under investigation beginning in 1962, although its fruition as LAMPS (Light Airborne Multi-Purpose System) lay years in the future.

An ASROC is loaded on board *Norfolk* (DL 1) at Key West for trials, June 1960.

USN 710732

Another promising new technology was the hydrofoil. As submarines made dramatic gains in speed, surface ships were hardpressed to keep pace. One solution was to speed up the weapon delivery system (as in ASROC or the helicopter); a second option was to speed up the platform. Because conventional hull forms could not be driven much beyond 35 knots without incurring drastically increased power demands, the hydrofoil appeared worth investigation. In 1963, the Navy tested the world's first combatant hydrofoil, *High Point* (PCH 1). Powered by gas turbine engines, the craft could hit 45 knots when up on her foils. Adopting sprint and drift tactics, *High Point* seemed potentially valuable for ASW work in coastal waters.[103]

While these important avenues in technology were under investigation, the Navy also invested heavily in underwater research. The 1963 budget contained $124 million for probes into many aspects of the ocean environment, such as bottom characteristics, heat distribution, and salinity. The Navy also acquired a fine range for testing underwater ordnance and sound equipment in the Bahamas called the Atlantic Underwater Test and Evaluation Center (AUTEC).[104]

USN 1058529

A mock-up of the DASH helicopter with two homing torpedoes.

The Cuban Missile Crisis gave a great morale boost to the ASW community. Searching an area of 3.5 million square miles, American warships detected Soviet diesel submarines and hounded them until they surfaced. For instance, destroyer *Cony* (DDE 508), working with an S–2 Tracker on 27 October 1962, reported little difficulty in staying on top of a submarine until it came up for air. One torpedoman on destroyer *Conway* (DDE 507) remarked proudly: "Throughout our ASW patrolling, we often wondered if all our work was being done in vain, but, finding contacts with, and surfacing a Russian submarine, we finally got to see what our job really was. The surfacing of the Russian submarine was the highlight of all our ASW training and operations." [105] CNO Anderson proudly remarked, "Our aircraft and ships were . . . engaged in the most extensive, and I might add, the most productive, antisubmarine warfare operations since World War II." [106]

However, in U.S. fleet exercises the uneven performance of ASW units gave serious cause for concern. On occasion, ASW warships were shown to good advantage as in a January 1965 convoy exercise in the North Atlantic. The escorts foiled twelve of fourteen screen penetration attempts, and "killed" eleven subs for a loss of seven escorts and four merchantmen. Aircraft on station bagged an additional submarine. [107] In contrast, two other exercises in roughly the same time frame gave quite different results. A First Fleet carrier task force protected by seven destroyers and

*High Point* up on her foils.

two guided missile frigates with assistance from two patrol squadrons and the eastern Pacific SOSUS net managed only three submarine "kills," all by aircraft. The two opposing submarines frequently passed close to the task force, made twenty-six attacks, and simulated a Soviet *Echo* launching its missiles by running on the surface for an hour undetected. The report of the cruiser-destroyer flotilla involved concluded tersely, "The ASW performance by Task Force 13 during this exercise was unsatisfactory." [108] In a similar exercise two years later, submarines attacked "any and all surface ships at will without being detected." [109]

The reason for the widely varying results of these three exercises can probably be deduced from the forces involved in them. In the first—the 1965 defense of convoy—the ASW ships were escorts devoted to the purpose. In the second and third examples, the sub hunters were destroyer types which spent little time on ASW. This sort of mediocre performance by the Navy's new and expensive surface warships occasioned critical comment in the *Proceedings*. Articles in that journal blasted the lack of time devoted to antisubmarine training; one author pointed out that a destroyer went through refresher training for six weeks every three years. Of that six-week stint, only about 17 percent of the time went to ASW with even these minimal tests rigged by dictating the submarine's course, depth, and speed in advance to ensure contact "in the interest of maximum training."[110] Following refresher training, some destroyers headed for a deployment with a hunter-killer group where they in fact developed "an eye-opening ability to detect and to kill opposing submarines."[111] But most new ships joined a carrier group, and chances for their personnel to exercise their skills came rarely. During the average commander's two-year tour on the bridge of a destroyer or frigate, he would be fortunate to have 36 hours of "ping time" with a "live" submarine. In light of this fact, all the great advances—in the new sound systems, in oceanography, and in data processing—which promised an ASW solution if used properly, more frequently became part of the problem. As one ASW specialist wrote:

> Arrayed against the submarine is the most massive and expensive operation ever conceived by man to combat a single weapon system. . . . Each new system or technique is usually based on a newly discovered physical phenomenon, or on a new data processing system, or on a new electronic innovation. And the new systems are added to the older ones, increasing the total number available, thus creating new and more complicated combinations and permutations of equipments to be fitted together into a coherent pattern of tactics.[112]

These frustrations were commmon in the ASW community. One officer noted:

> The problems in the field are tremendous, and getting worse, not only because of the increasing capabilities of submarines, but also because of the increasing complexity and capability of the weapons devised to combat them. These combine to make ASW a masochist's paradise, bringing to mind the old story about the man who loved to hit himself on the head with a hammer because it felt so good when he stopped. Perhaps the simile does not apply, though, because in ASW you never get the chance to stop hitting yourself on the head.[113]

And in fairness to the overburdened commander of the new G ship, his problems in AAW were as serious as those in ASW. Funds were rarely adequate to keep both systems operating at peak efficiency. ASROC vied directly with the antiaircraft missiles for harried ordnance technicians. As an ASW officer noted, "Make no mistake about it—aboard these new destroyers the anti-air guided missiles are in competition with antisubmarine weapons from the standpoints of logistics and command attention. And in that arena the ASW battery usually comes out second best."[114]

Partly responsible for this ordering of priorities was the fact that the new frigates and destroyers continued to suffer terrible problems with their missile systems. In fact, the entire antiaircraft arena resembled the situation in ASW: promising technologies mired in operational realities. As for the most immediate danger, Styx and Shaddock were, in certain modes and certain scenarios, very much a threat; in others, they seemed well in hand. With ample warning on the high seas, officers felt that they could take the measure of either missile. Both flew at subsonic speeds; both were the size of small aircraft and gave large radar reflections. Early versions of Styx and Shaddock traveled high enough so that they could be spotted by radar with relative ease. As noted, the Shaddock, fired at long range, required targeting data for mid-course flight correction, and the large aircraft or the surface ships that would do this job looked to be vulnerable to U.S. countermeasures. Nonetheless, certain U.S. tactical exercises were showing that these missiles might present significant problems if they were launched at a short distance or if they flew just above the water. After one drill that tested surface ships against jet aircraft in May 1962, a destroyer squadron commander noted that "the success of the low flyer was a significant feature of this exercise."[115] Most of the low-altitude attackers went undetected; one plane was discovered only when it flew directly over the cruiser *Saint Paul*.[116]

Surface officers were depending on the maturation of the 3–Ts to provide a counter, but continuing problems with the missiles caused serious doubt as to their capability, despite all the work done on them. As before, they occasionally turned in an impressive performance. For example in a fall 1961 demonstration shoot, *Topeka* downed a drone with a Terrier in front of Naval War College officers, including some from foreign navies. But a pivotal incident occurred during a fleet review given for President Kennedy when the new missile frigate *Dewey* missed a propeller drone with three Terriers in a row. Kennedy was disappointed enough with this miserable show to raise the matter specifically with aviator Vice Admiral Moorer, who was paying a courtesy call at the White House before taking command of the Seventh Fleet in October 1962.[117]

The continued erratic performance of the missiles in fleet exercises over the next years did nothing to dispel the feeling that something was terribly wrong. For instance, in one 1964 drill, the First Fleet ships *Providence*, *Dale* (DLG 19), and *Halsey* (DLG 23)—the latter two brand-new "double-enders"—were subjected to multiple air attacks by high and low fliers, plus planes simulating Soviet AS–1 and AS–2 antiship missiles. Chaff drops and jamming made the defenders' problems more difficult, as did the failure of firecontrol equipment. A launcher casualty for which *Providence* had no spare part took the cruiser out of the game altogether. Of the 178 raiders that evaded carrier fighters, the ships' missiles downed, aside from "numerous friendly and non-exercise aircraft," only twelve of the enemy. Antiaircraft gunfire accounted for three more.[118] Writing from the Atlantic Fleet earlier that same year, Allan Slaff commanding *Luce* (DLG 7) commented acidly on "the extremely poor results that Terrier missile ships have attained in firing BT/BTN missiles during recent months with a success rate of only seven percent. That this deplorable rate is unacceptable from both the readiness as well as possible funding support point of view is well recognized. . . . "[119]

In fact, shortly after the debacle witnessed by President Kennedy, the Navy began serious efforts to get to the bottom of the matter. Milton Shaw, a top member of Rickover's staff who had become conversant with 3–T difficulties during the fitting out of *Long Beach* and *Bainbridge*, wrote a systematic report for the Assistant Secretary of the Navy for Research and Development. The study concluded in January 1962 that the guided missile systems on board twenty-eight ships in commission and thirty-eight more under construction could not be called operational. Of the six Talos cruisers ostensibly in the fleet by the end of that year, only *Galveston* was truly operational. Six billion dollars, worth of vessels were in service with defective systems! In the words of one missile officer, "So there sat the SMS [surface missile systems] fleet—the Navy's best and newest ships— pierside and casrept'd." [120] The whole business was intensely frustrating to the surface navy. [121]

Top policymakers took a hand in setting matters right. Secretary of the Navy Korth "wanted action and wanted it now." [122] Korth created the Special Navy Task Force in July 1962 under Rear Admiral Eli Reich. A submarine hero from World War II and a former commanding officer of *Canberra*, Reich was "one tough cookie." [123] Responsible directly to the Secretary himself, Reich had orders to make the 3–Ts (by this point frequently called the "Terrible Ts") plus Typhon, also troubled, perform to specifications by "the earliest practicable time." [124] Although officially called the Special Navy Task Force for Surface Missile Systems, Reich's rehabilitative effort was known informally as the "Get Well" program. The office lasted until 1974— an index of the difficult task it faced. As one officer said, "the 'Get Well Program' is one of those deceptively mild phrases by which a ministering physician softens a family's realization of the unpleasant and serious facts of a situation. For the 'getting well' period is long, the convalescence painful, and relapses frequent." [125] It was to be followed closely by a modernization program ("3–T Improvement"). Reich brought both the Applied Physics Lab and industry into the effort. [126]

Close scrutiny by Reich's team revealed a host of problems. In Terrier, poor workmanship and sloppy inspection at the factory simply prefaced materiel deficiencies which ran the gamut from inadequate shock insulators to unsatisfactory snap rings on the booster fins to low rod velocity in the warhead. Talos suffered from combuster burn-through problems and other ailments. [127]

In the end, the 3–T investigators revealed three major problem areas and proposed solutions in each. First, the missile systems, containing complex chains of components, were frequently rendered inoperative by the failure of one element before the missile was even fired. The Reich team said that the solution lay in the redesign of components to improve their reliability and in the provision of ample spare parts. Second, the lack of uniformity in system operating procedures, especially in the complex and ever-changing fleet environment, caused delays and errors in the long series of pre-firing events. The answer here was also complex, keying on accumulating data from the fleet and training missilemen thoroughly to deal with these complications. Third, far too many missiles that got airborne simply missed their targets. Evaluators assigned failures about evenly to the missiles themselves and to the shipboard equipment, such as the computers, the launcher, and the tracking or illuminating radars. For instance, evaluators found that battery alignment and transmission checks were often perfunctory, on the mistaken assumption that the missile would guide itself to the target. The Get Well team pointed out that significant improvement was possible by dint of unremitting attention to detail on the part of well-trained crews performing extra inspections on the missiles and the ancillary equipment.[128]

The Reich panel concluded that the delivery of an entirely new missile system was required. Efforts in this direction led ultimately to the Standard missile system, but the Navy in 1962 could not wait for Standard to materialize. It had to bring the 3–Ts "up to speed." Admiral Reich reported, "The conflict between meeting ship completion schedules and delivering ships with operable missile systems has been the subject of Navy-wide conferences."[129] Now, missile reliability won out; Talos cruisers were held up until the missile problems were fixed. Reich's team pushed through a host of changes: the Naval Surface Missile System Engineering Station at Port Hueneme was established to provide system integration; special teams to assist ships in missile qualification were formed; ordnance officers were assigned to the missile plants; a logistics support program was initiated; an analysis group was created to examine all missile firings; and closed loop detailing was imposed on certain officer and enlisted missile billets, both ashore and afloat.[130]

By the end of the year, Talos was in shape to go to sea; four hundred of the reworked missiles went to the depots ready for loading on board the cruisers. In January 1963, *Albany* made headlines by firing three missiles simultaneously. By 1966, the Navy could report real progress in missile readiness: slightly over half the Tartars and Terriers shot in FY 66 hit their targets; the longer-ranged Talos scored a success rate of 35 percent. These figures represented a significant improvement, especially when compared with the 7 percent success rate for Terrier in early 1964. Moreover, advances in missilery were benefiting all three of the weapons. Denser fuels with higher energy content gave significantly extended ranges; for instance, Terrier in 1963 flew out to 40 miles as opposed to 20 in earlier versions. Talos by this point was passing the 100-mile mark, a figure at the outer limits of its guidance equipment. Besides extended range, technicians worked into Talos a home-on-jam feature so effective that a jammer acted as a magnet for the missile. In tests, the missile's performance against jamming targets was superior to nonjamming ones.[131]

Counterbalancing these successes was McNamara's cancellation of Typhon, a program begun by the Applied Physics Laboratory in 1957 to develop a missile system impervious to saturation. Typhon was designed to mount a defense-in-depth with medium- and long-range missiles against high-performance airplanes and antiship missiles whether launched by surface ships, submarines, or aircraft. The architects of Typhon took special pains to ensure the system's operability in a heavy ECM environment. Major components of Typhon included a missile with a range of 200 miles for use especially against standoff jamming aircraft and airplanes carrying antiship missiles; a medium-range (40 miles) quick reaction missile to destroy closer targets; and a new radar with electronic scanning and weapon control. The Typhon program also included the development of more lethal warheads to meet advanced enemy threats. Planners anticipated, for instance, that Soviet rockets might confront an American antiaircraft missile with a closing speed of Mach 8. By 1963, Typhon was well along. Nine prototype missiles had flown at White Sands, and the radar was being installed in the trials ship *Norton Sound* (AVM 1).[132]

The Typhon radar was the most radically advanced piece of the system. Casting aside the conventional rotating search and guidance antennas, Typhon's radar steered its beams electronically. It performed both search and guidance with a capability to track hundreds of targets at once and to guide up to thirty missiles against thirty different targets simultaneously. Nevertheless, this radar proved to be the downfall of Typhon. It was complex, heavy, and extremely expensive. In November 1963, the program took a major hit when Secretary Korth asked Congress to transfer prospective funding from ships designed to carry Typhon to the Get Well program. In 1964, McNamara terminated Typhon altogether, although the radar was tested into 1966. It was not a total loss, however, because the Navy realized significant technical advances in missile guidance. The basic concepts behind the Typhon radar would reemerge later as Aegis; in fact, the most influential figure connected with that later successful effort, Rear Admiral Wayne E. Meyer, has said that "without Typhon, there would be no Aegis."[133]

Typhon led to another important gain. When combined with the 3–T Get Well program, it ultimately resulted in the Standard missile system: a weapon that could, by varying only the propulsion, serve the fleet as both a medium- and long-range missile in Tartar and Terrier ships. In 1963, with Typhon clearly on the ropes, the CNO formally asked for an Advanced Surface Missile System (ASMS) to enable new cruisers and destroyers to defeat massive, sophisticated air attacks in a heavy ECM environment. Heading the study team was Rear Admiral Frederic S. Withington, called back from retirement. Withington, in a break with tradition, brought representatives from the defense industry into the very early stages of the design process, a practice that would become commonplace over the next two decades. In pursuing the advanced missiles, Withington's team worked under the enjoinder that the new weapons were to be compatible with existing launching and guidance systems. The designers took from Typhon a number of missile improvements, including an adaptive autopilot, electric tail actuators, and a battery-operated power supply. By April 1964, Withington's group had made such progress that the Secretary of the Navy formally approved the development of the Standard; the Navy let a contract with General Dynamics, Pomona, at the end of the year.[134]

The digital revolution in electronics continued to sweep through the surface navy. The first steps had been taken with the Naval Tactical Data System; its development and deployment continued apace. For instance, in the newest frigates, the integration of the search and fire control radars was advanced to such a degree that the firing key for the missiles was relocated to the NTDS consoles allowing a faster reaction to hostile aircraft. NTDS could be programmed to test itself frequently; in consequence it proved much more reliable than the analog systems it was replacing.[135]

Early exercises showed how vastly superior NTDS ships were at processing data compared to their non-NTDS counterparts. In operations, the system proved a key element in allowing a task group to spread out, yet act in a coordinated fashion, in the face of an air threat. Naturally, it took time to get NTDS to all the units in the fleet. The *Leahy* missile frigates received the system during refits from 1967 to 1972; *Albany* got hers during a major overhaul, 1967–1969; even nuclear *Bainbridge* was lacking certain elements in her NTDS suite in 1968. Some of the guided missile ships never received the system, including twenty *Charles F. Adams*-class ships which were still keeping a manual plot in the mid-1980s.[136]

Developments in electronics were having an increasing impact on costs and ship design itself. Some new radar antennas were so big that their sail area adversely affected ship stability even more than their weight, which was considerable and carried high in the ship. In the relentless search for suitable masthead space for the proliferating and sensitive antennas, designers copied the solution pioneered by the *Albany*-class CG conversion and placed them on the stacks, which then became "macks." Less obvious to the eye but quite as real were the mushrooming demands by the electronics equipment for space, maintenance, cooling, and electrical power. In monetary costs alone, a ship's electronics suite by 1963 accounted for 40 percent of the price of the vessel. The equipment demanded more servants: a destroyer with the SQS–4 needed ten sonarmen; the allowance for ships with the SQS–26 was nineteen. And of course, the larger crews dictated additional space; bigger ships were the inevitable consequence. Increasingly, the Bureau of Ships brought together the naval architect and the electronics engineer at the earliest stages of ship design.[137]

If the computer revolution challenged naval architects, it brought a host of benefits to the surface navy. Officers working on missile development could begin to predict much more accurately the behavior of missiles before they were fired on the test ranges. The number of test shots necessary to verify a missile's performance dropped dramatically. In another vein, the Bureau of Naval Weapons was experimenting successfully by 1962 with digital fire control for Terrier. Digital technology also allowed improvements in ship design, especially in regard to the placement of missile systems in relation to delicate electronics—a touchy and complex matter. As the revolution in data processing progressed, smaller ships could carry much more capable equipment.[138]

In the electronics sphere, the Navy of the early 1960s began to pay increased attention to the often overlooked areas of electronic countermeasures and counter-countermeasures (ECCM). One widely circulated paper from Commander Operational Test and Evaluation Force (COMOPTEV-FOR) in early 1963 lamented, "The Navy has sadly neglected electronic countermeasures and counter-countermeasures, and only recently has taken positive steps to better the situation."[139] The paper demanded studies of the effects of heavy jamming on search and fire control radars and asked for an evaluation of missile "home-on-jam" modes.

Soon after, APL organized a jamming test using a specially configured B–47 against one of the Navy's newest frigates, *Harry E. Yarnell* (DLG 17). Held off the Virginia capes at 0200 to avoid massive interference with civilian television reception, the "sobering success of that educational endeavor"[140] persuaded the Navy to set up the Fleet Electronic Warfare Support Evaluation Group. Fleet exercises began to include much more work with ECM. For instance, in a First Fleet test in 1964, the ULQ–6 deception repeater, when properly used, proved effective in causing simulated missiles to break lock on their targets. And new sensors, such as the AN/SPG–59 radar being developed for Typhon, were incorporating significant ECCM features. The result was a race rather similar to the earlier contest between armor and projectile.[141]

The Navy also began paying more attention to a weapon given up by many for dead—the gun. Part of the reason for the renewed interest lay in the incapacity of the 3–Ts. After watching the *Dewey* fiasco, Kennedy had personally ordered the new missile cruisers equipped with guns. The 5″/38 guns in single mountings looked quite antiquated on such ships as *Albany* and *Long Beach*, but the old weapons did give some capability against small craft and slow-moving airplanes.[142]

In fact, many surface officers worried about the decreasing number of guns in the fleet. With heavy cruisers *Helena* and *Los Angeles* joining the mothball fleet in 1963, CINCPAC Admiral John H. Sides reported that only eighteen 8-inch and eighteen 6-inch guns remained on active service ships. By 1964, just two conventional heavy cruisers, *Newport News* and *Saint Paul*, continued in commission. Accompanying the falling number of big rifles in service, officers noted a distressing decline in gunnery skills throughout the surface navy as the warships concentrated on other missions. The most ambitious fire controlmen wanted to work with missiles, not guns. Ships held gunnery practice rarely; some destroyers went six months without firing a single round. Even so, fleet ammunition stockpiles were dwindling as money went elsewhere. Following one of the rare exercises, "unusual in that ships were required to conduct live shore bombardment firing on short notice," the commander of the cruiser division involved recommended, "Schedule more shore bombardment for cruisers and destroyers in recognition of the fact that our most likely war will be a limited one and shore bombardment will be required."[143]

His words fell on deaf ears. By 1962, the majority of the ships in the Pacific Fleet rated "barely satisfactory" in gunnery. That fall, plans went forward to consolidate the Fleet Gunnery School at San Diego with the Fleet Training Center even though the document proposing the merger acknowledged, "the elimination of FLEGUNSCOL SDIEGO . . . may have the effect of degrading emphasis on Fleet gunnery."[144] The former commanding officer of that school, John O. Stull, protested that the continual slighting references to gunnery had a debilitating effect on gunnery personnel. What ambitious individual would care to be associated with an obsolete weapons system—in the words of another analyst, "a professionally unfashionable backwater of naval capability, forced to the wall by more glamorous competing weapons"?[145] But Stull pointed out that most of the Navy's ships were still armed partly or wholly with guns. He then trenchantly noted, "our Navy-of-the-future is of no more use to us at this moment than one of Caesar's triremes; it is as unrealistic to live in the future as it would be to live in the past."[146]

A number of articles in the *Proceedings* backed Stull. Marines were especially concerned about faltering capabilities in shore bombardment. In one *Proceedings* piece entitled "The Gun Gap," Marine advocate Robert D. Heinl, Jr., ticked off a number of deficiencies: the comprehensive Naval Gunfire Officer Course formerly offered by Marine Corps schools had not been given for almost a decade; the annual Naval Gunfire Conferences, sponsored jointly by the Navy and Marines, had also fallen by the wayside; NATO had even stopped producing the specialized charts necessary to plot naval gunfire support for amphibious landings. To get more gunpower behind the Marines, Heinl called for the return of a battleship to active duty. This suggestion went nowhere for the time being. Nor did a plan to produce a new class of close-in fire support ships, called the LFS. Despite preliminary work in 1965, no final design materialized.[147]

Some surface line officers, as concerned as Heinl, noted that in time of war they would likely be called upon to attack a wide spectrum of targets ashore and afloat. Guns were essential not only to support landings but to combat small, fast craft in narrow waters. One 1963 weapons development group wrote that gunnery objectives ran the gamut from personnel to tanks to air strips to dams and tunnels. Certain hard targets were especially difficult to destroy by any means other than direct artillery fire. The team also observed that naval attack aircraft were increasingly resorting to higher speed or to standoff weapons to reduce their vulnerability to ground fire, with a consequent decrease in pinpoint accuracy.[148]

If aircraft were losing some of their effectiveness in the ground support role, the new missile ships seemed utterly ill-suited to fulfill this essential mission. One observer noted that the extensive and fragile electronics of missile frigates and destroyers made them vulnerable to return fire: "The susceptability [*sic*] of their topside antenna arrays to blast or fragment damage may resurrect for missile ships the old axiom that ships cannot fight forts."[149] Missiles were sometimes considered for shore bombardment, but they made a poor substitute for guns. The "birds" were inaccurate against most land targets because they lacked a sharply defined radar reflection for homing, and their range was consequently limited to line-of-sight. Also, of course, missiles were vastly more expensive than shells.[150]

The Ships Characteristics Board drew attention to the shore bombardment problem in 1962 by stating that the new missile ships of the *Leahy*, *Albany*, and *Long Beach* classes, which carried only the 3"/50 or the old 5"/38, "were critically deficient in gun power needed for amphibious assault operations."[151] Even as a last-ditch defense against aerial attack, these guns possessed only the most minimal capabilities.[152]

The 5"/54 Mk 42 was better in both areas. It was endowed with a high rate of fire and high-speed power drive systems. In summarizing its attributes, ordnance officers on command ship *Northampton* (CLC 1) called it "the best Anti-Aircraft Gun in the Navy today." Its competitors were not legion. *Northampton* officers noted too the ability of the Mk 42 to saturate with rapid fire targets ashore and afloat; at the same time, they asked for an armor-piercing projectile to enhance "the surface punch of this excellent weapon."[153]

Offsetting these virtues, training facilities ashore for the new weapon were utterly lacking on the West Coast. Moreover, the reliability of the Mk 42 mount was suspect, and it was also labor intensive, requiring a crew of twenty to operate. An improved weapon was on the way. In response to a 1961 directive from OPNAV, the Bureau of Naval Weapons started work on a new gun intended specifically for the support of amphibious operations:

the 5″/54 Mk 45. With the same 54-caliber gun as the Mk 42, the new mount differed from its predecessor in virtually every other respect. Its weight was barely one-third that of the Mk 42. The crewmen of the new weapon would enter the gunhouse only to conduct maintenance or to make repairs. Otherwise, a team of five men would feed the hoists; one gunner would fire the weapon from a remote control panel. Digital control promised much increased reliability.[154]

Coupled with the OPNAV requirement for a new gun was one for a matching fire control system which became the Mk 86. Intended to be compatible with all guns in the fleet from the 3-inch to the 16-inch, the digital Mk 86 possessed significant potentialities in areas other than directing fire support for amphibious operations. It could hook into NTDS, and it had a search capability against surface craft or low fliers. It was able to track four targets, engage two simultaneously, and switch rapidly from one threat to another. Typical of the solid state technology, the Mk 86 weighed half as much as the Mk 68 that it replaced. In contrast to the earlier system, the Mk 86 required a crew of three instead of the seven; its reliability was improved by 800 percent; and it demanded one-eighth of the maintenance.[155]

As development commenced on the new gun and fire control system, the Cuban Missile Crisis of 1962 drew attention to the *Komar* ships that Khrushchev had transferred to Fidel Castro. Their Styx missiles outranged all the guns in the U.S. Navy's active inventory. Some surface officers doubted the ability of carrier aviation to provide the counter. The only precision antiship weapon in carrier magazines was the Bullpup which required visual aiming and control. Night or foul weather seriously degraded its performance, especially against small craft. Many blackshoes felt the whole situation was dangerous and turned for a stopgap solution to the only weapons in their arsenals with the potential to hit *Komar*s at long range: the 3–Ts.[156]

True, OPTEVFOR had been experimenting since 1959, albeit in a rather desultory way, with Talos in an antiship mode. In one 1962 test in the Chesapeake Bay near Annapolis, a Bureau of Naval Weapons evaluation team fired four Talos variants successfully in the surface-to-surface mode. Too frequently, however, the missile suffered guidance problems as it closed its target; sea return often confused the missile's homing radar. As an added handicap to using Talos as an antisurface weapon, its range was limited to line-of-sight because its semiactive terminal seeker required that the parent ship illuminate the target with radar. In one test, BUWEPS evaluators expressed surprise that a Talos had successfully homed in on the masts and antennas of a hull-down ship. These limitations were serious, and of course only seven vessels could operate with the Talos. In 1964, BUWEPS dropped the requirement that this missile be effective as an antiship weapon; however, the cruisers, on rare occasions, shot Talos in the antiship mode into the 1970s. Cruiser *Albany* reportedly "obliterated" two surface targets with the big missile on the Atlantic Fleet Weapons Range in February 1971.[157]

The Navy worked harder and experienced more success with Terrier and Tartar. Two months after the Cuban Missile Crisis ended, BUWEPS began a series of tests from Roosevelt Roads, Puerto Rico, with the two missiles. Tartar performed quite well initially. Of the nine missiles fired against two targets configured to resemble *Komar*s, five Tartars flew successfully with three making direct hits. One, in fact, sank its target vessel. In contrast to Tartar, Terrier put on a dismal demonstration. In December 1962, OPTEV-FOR shot six Terriers at a target boat without making a single hit. Of a grand total of twenty beam-riding Terriers fired at shore and surface targets in the entire test series, the "birds" missed by an average of 110 feet. Only one came close enough to its objective to be considered a hit against a *Komar*. COMOPTEVFOR noted archly that, at this rate, a *Farragut*-class frigate could expect to obtain two hits by firing all the missiles in its magazines. Admiral Zumwalt later characterized the performance of Terrier in the antiship mode as "scandalous in its incapability." [158]

In hunting for causes, Navy evaluators found that land background frequently confused the missile guidance system, an especially serious matter in that the Styx-armed patrol boats would generally operate close inshore. In a calm sea, small boat targets were sometimes hit at ranges of up to 15 miles; in rougher weather, the missiles tended to lock on to wave return. Tests showed that in high seas, the chances of hitting a *Komar* boat were not good until the enemy vessel closed to within 6 miles—well inside the firing range of the Styx missile. Against much larger targets, like the hulked escort carrier *Makassar Strait* (ex-CVE 91), Terrier and Tartar did better. However, they were limited like Talos with their semiactive homers to the range within which the vessels firing them could illuminate the target.[159]

The missile warheads presented another set of problems. In the first place, they were small compared to those of the Soviets. Designed to bring down aircraft, the continuous-rod bundles and their proximity fuzes functioned in a less satisfactory fashion against surface targets. At very low altitudes, the fuze might well be triggered by wave return. Some officers wondered just how damaging a continuous-rod, which was designed to cut aircraft control surfaces, would be against a surface ship. Ultimately, tests showed that the best solution was to deactivate the proximity fuze so that the missile would crash directly into the ship rather than exploding close to it. COMOPTEVFOR proposed along this line to "inert" the sustainer motor of the Terrier so that its propellant would augment the power of the warhead. It is doubtful that this measure was ever implemented.[160]

Responding to the unsatisfactory test shots, the Naval Ordnance Laboratory at Corona undertook in 1963 a project to upgrade the antiship capabilities of Terrier. In light of the limited magazine space in most of the missile ships, the development of a specialized antiship missile was ruled out. COMOPTEVFOR argued: "Further dilution of these magazines with surface or shore bombardment special purpose missiles would be completely unacceptable."[161] Corona added a contact fuze to the rod warheads while retaining the proximity fuze. Ordnance technicians could then make the appropriate selection easily from the weapons console.[162]

*Long Beach* later tested the effectiveness of these alterations when, in February 1968, she fired her first surface-to-surface Terrier. The missile exploded inside the target ship *Abercrombie* (ex DE 343) with warhead fragments tearing through the main deck into the magazine. The boarding party who examined the ship agreed that had munitions been on board the ship, they would have detonated in the magazine, sinking the vessel.[163]

Missile guidance for antiship work also received attention. A long-term solution lay in the development of a homing version of Terrier. Analysts pointed out that such a modification, particularly if joined with the NTDS system, would give Terrier an antiship role well beyond the horizon of the radars of the firing ship. In fact, this capability would be worked into Terrier's descendant, Standard, although the latter would not be deployed until 1969.[164]

In the short term, surface warriors might be able turn to the nuclear versions of Terrier and Talos just becoming operational. Development had taken six years, which was not surprising given the difficulties involved in designing such nuclear devices. Specifications for the Terrier's warhead included the ability to withstand temperatures from $-100$ to $+500$ degrees Fahrenheit and an impact shock of 2,500 g's. The required reliability figure was 0.995. To fit into the cavity of a Terrier, the device had to be small and light. Because more powerful electronic equipment was entering the fleet, special care was essential to prevent the premature detonation of a warhead by electromagnetic radiation. One BUWEPS group cautioned on another matter, "As more nuclear warheads become available and more people become involved in weapon access and handling, every effort must be made to decrease the possibilities of a nuclear accident and preclude damaging action by the psychotic and saboteur."[165]

By 1962, the Navy produced for Terrier a warhead (the W–45) with a yield of about one kiloton. Approximately 750 of these were constructed. This nuclear capability alone kept Terrier in service well into the 1980s. Talos also came in a nuclear version. The Unified Talos (SAM–N–6c1) featured an interchangeable nuclear or high-explosive warhead and an improved low-altitude capability. About 300 of the Talos warheads (the W–30) were manufactured. An earlier design than the Terrier's, the Talos warhead gave a yield of about one-half kiloton.[166]

Flying the flag of Commander Seventh Fleet Vice Admiral Roy L. Johnson, the guided missile cruiser *Oklahoma City* (CLG 5) arrives at Saigon, 21 July 1964.

In the end, the observer must conclude that the 3–Ts provided the surface navy with only a modest antiship capability for conventional war. Suffering from numerous ailments, the missiles were little developed in this mode. OPTEVFOR shot Terrier at surface targets only thirty-four times between 1962 and 1968. One high-ranking surface sailor of the period, Vice Admiral David F. Emerson, said later that he never saw Talos, Terrier, or Tartar fired at a surface target during his entire career. A captain of cruiser *Topeka* remembered, "Our beam-rider Terrier had a supposed limited anti-surface capability, but we did not give it much credence and, as I recall, never trained in its use." [167] The experiences of these officers was merely symptomatic of the larger neglect of the surface branch in the McNamara era. Another top figure in the surface line, Vice Admiral Henry C. Mustin, reflected, "there was a design philosophy in the Navy which had been largely triggered by Mr. Robert McNamara, which said, essentially, that the main battery in every surface combatant was to be resident on the flight deck of an aircraft carrier. Therefore, the surface combatants would be built for predominantly defensive purposes."[168]

While this outlook prevailed at the highest levels in Washington, surface warships in distant waters began playing an important role once again in a limited war. Starting in December 1961, American units steamed in East Asian waters in support of the South Vietnamese government. In 1964, they began using their guns in earnest at sea. In August of that year, destroyers *Maddox* (DD 731) and *Turner Joy* (DD 951) fought North Vietnamese torpedo boats in the Tonkin Gulf, as did *Morton* (DD 948) and *Richard S. Edwards* (DD 950) later in the year. The enemy small craft sometimes ventured surprisingly far out to sea (on occasion over 100 miles from their bases). In rough weather or at night, the nimble torpedo boats made elusive opponents, and the gunnery performance of the American warships proved disappointing. CINCPAC reported that the August fighting "graphically portrayed a general deterioration in surface gunnery," a development that the commander of the Seventh Fleet attributed to "undue emphasis on nuclear warfare in the last few years. . . ."[169]

Remedial action was urgently needed. Following a series of range exercises firing at high-speed remote-control craft, the Cruiser-Destroyer Force of the Pacific Fleet concluded that the 5-inch projectile gave the best results when fuzed to burst about 100 feet above the PT boats. Still, spotting air bursts over one of these fast-maneuvering craft proved extremely difficult, and the boats presented a small radar target. Against a determined attacker, a destroyer would probably have to fire more than fifty rounds of 5-inch to achieve success. Evaluators judged that the performance of the 3-inch carried by many of the new missile ships would be "at best, only poor against these targets."[170] The commentators noted that some of the FRAM ships had dead spots astern where their guns would not bear.[171]

To drill, destroyermen lacked suitable targets, and in true Navy fashion, set about improvising some while the Bureau of Naval Weapons worked on a completely realistic model. Gunnery crews in forward areas began exercising their skills on a jury-rigged inflatable vinyl target 10 feet long. Costing $40 and repairable like a plastic swimming pool, the target was aluminized to give a radar reflection. It proved surprisingly hard to hit. One officer noted, "You may end up by going alongside with a bayonet if your aim is shaky or your procedures not thoroughly worked out."[172] During the summer of 1965, the Ryan Aeronautical Company, a maker of airborne drones, developed a remote-controlled fiberglass boat called the Firefish. In two exercises, cruiser *Boston* and and the destroyer *Conyngham* (DDG 17) found the 30-knot craft slippery; neither ship could put the Firefish out of action.[173]

In their summary, the analysts forecast: "There will doubtless be more 'Tonkin Gulfs' and the gunned ships will occupy a hub position in each such incident." [174] To meet the PT menace, Pacific Fleet headquarters reminded its surface warriors of Rear Admiral John Dahlgren's formula for gunnery success in the Civil War, "DRILL, ALIGN, SHOOT, ANALYZE, REPEAT." [175]

In the final reckoning, the years 1961–1965 featured for the surface navy both disappointments and positive steps. The surface line now had its Destroyer School at Newport. Effective antisubmarine weapons and sensors were entering the fleet. Work had begun on missile improvements that would ultimately bring the Navy a reliable, effective antiaircraft missile with secondary antiship capabilities—indeed a "Standard." The foundation had been laid, with the abortive Typhon, for a truly capable air defense system—Aegis. Sadly, almost two decades would pass before Aegis became operational. In the meantime, the surface navy would face the reality that the Soviets had stolen a march in cruise missile technology. It would also fight a hot war in Southeast Asia.

# 5

# Shocks to the System:
# Vietnam and the *Eilat,* 1965–1970

As President Lyndon Johnson committed large-scale American forces to Vietnam, surface warriors found themselves frustrated on several counts. The missiles they had spent two decades developing sat in the magazines largely unused. Instead, their guns, scorned as outdated and on the road to oblivion, got a real workout. While more and more of the surface navy's resources went to fulfill operational responsibilities in Southeast Asia, the number of ships in service declined dramatically. Then, in October 1967, three Styx missiles fatally damaged the Israeli destroyer *Eilat.* This event galvanized the surface warfare community in the U.S. Navy. Strapped for resources and seriously concerned that the North Vietnamese might shoot Styx missiles at U.S. destroyers and cruisers giving close support to American troops ashore, surface warriors pushed strongly for defenses against this suddenly defined threat—and for a way to strike back effectively.

Some of the surface navy's difficulties during the first part of the period can be traced to organizational upheavals within the U.S. Navy which directly affected the blackshoes' domain. This tumult in the Navy's structure was, in turn, partly attributable to the increased complexity of its warships. The lines differentiating such basic features of a new vessel as its hull, machinery, weaponry, and electronics were now so indistinct that even the bureau structure as revised in 1958 seemed unable to cope. The Dillon Board, a commission created to review the naval organization, decided in 1962 that the Navy's entire bureau system was obsolete. The board reached this conclusion in part because various pieces of equipment developed by the Bureau of Ships and the Bureau of Naval Weapons for new frigates were incompatible. In consequence, the vessels were running well behind schedule. After four more years of discussion, Secretary of Defense McNamara ordered a complete overhaul of the Navy's organizational structure in 1966. The bureaus were abolished and replaced by systems commands—a total reorganization that took four months to implement. Not unexpectedly, this McNamara-sponsored reform failed to give the surface branch equality with aviation's Deputy Chief of Naval Operations for Air. The proposal to add a DCNO for Surface Warfare to OPNAV was stillborn.[1]

On the larger stage, McNamara completely overhauled the planning and budgeting processes in the Department of Defense to tighten the links between military planners and those holding the purse strings in McNamara's office. The new scheme, called the Planning, Programming, and Budgeting System (PPBS), based its projections and allocations on a five-year time cycle, rather than planning year by year.[2]

Not that the McNamara reforms made for greater efficiency, at least in the opinion of many affected by them. One flag officer, David Emerson, called the resultant structure "a labyrinth." Committees proliferated; the review process stretched out; the acquisition process became arthritic. "The only way to keep track of any of this," said Emerson, "is to find the GS–7 secretary and find where all she had been, and then you'd know...."[3] Another officer, Claude P. Ekas, Jr., contrasted his experience as project manager for the A2F (later the A–6) attack plane in the late 1950s with the same job in the development of the Harpoon missile in the late 1960s. In the earlier post, he had had five staffers in his office and had given seven briefings to the Office of the Secretary of Defense and to OPNAV before his work was done. But for Harpoon, Ekas later said, "I probably conducted 150 briefings a year and to everyone in town."[4] One of the Navy's top scientists, Frederick C. Alpers, pointed in 1981 to the effects of the McNamara reforms on HARM (High-Speed Anti-Radar Missile) begun in the late 1960s: "That thing has been in and out of money and through...so many committee reviews and changes...that its story must almost read like a comedy. It's a darn shame, but I think it's gone on 12 years now. You cannot keep up with the Russians and do things in that manner!" McNamara intended his process to comb out wasteful practices; instead, claimed Alpers, it simply guaranteed the squandering of resources and energies.[5]

One astute observer, Vice Admiral Thomas R. Weschler, who pushed the innovative *Spruance*-class destroyer through the acquisition process in the latter part of the 1960s, contrasted that experience with the notably quick pace of the Polaris program. In just one decade, the nation had taken several retrograde steps in its weapons procurement process. "Mountains of paperwork" now loomed up.[6] Within the Navy, the process of acquiring surface weapons, Weschler said, became notably clumsy with an accounting system that made the development of new technology very difficult unless it was tied to a specific ship program already funded. Moreover, every program faced three distinct budget struggles: one within the Navy itself; the second within the Department of Defense; and the final one within Congress. As the purse strings tightened for defense during the late 1960s and the following decade, these battles became increasingly acrimonious and protracted. Alpers contrasted the twelve years it took to develop the HARM missile with the one year (1944–1945) for the antiship missile BAT.[7]

McNamara's 1966 restructuring brought in its wake a complete reordering of the Navy's laboratories. For instance, the ordnance facilities at China

NH 66153

A gathering of all living CNOs, spring 1968. From left, George Anderson, Louis Denfeld, Harold Stark, Robert Carney, Thomas Moorer, Arthur Radford, and Arleigh Burke. Radford never held the office of CNO, but had served as Chairman of the Joint Chiefs of Staff, 1953–1957.

Lake and Corona merged to form the Naval Weapons Center. During the attendant chaos, the aviators managed to make off with many of the best scientists and technicians from those two facilities. Admiral Isaac Kidd remembered that the top civilian scientists who had started in ordnance ended up with NAVAIR. His succinct analysis, using the terminology still favored by many old hands, was "BuAer got the best; BuOrd got the rest." [8]

This pecking order looked, of course, all too familiar by now to surface line officers. One advised his compatriots joining the staff of a carrier task group: "It may scuff your black-shoe ego to find that you are the Untouchable in this caste system, but most aviators are tactful enough not to remind you of this. Besides, in vast awe of themselves, they assume you realize it automatically." [9] At the higher levels, the surface officer continued to find his prospects of commanding a carrier task group remote. At the summit, all three CNOs approved by McNamara were aviators who paid too little attention to the needs of the surface navy, according to surface warfare officers. Rear Admiral Elmo Zumwalt, an effective spokesman for the surface line, believed that CNO Thomas Moorer picked him in 1968 to head the brown water navy in South Vietnam to get him out of Washington. [10]

Surface warriors jousted with a second union, the submariners. Both the nuclear attack and ballistic missile programs continued to fare well during the period, partly in response to the large Soviet submarine programs. In the eyes of many surface line officers, the submariners got more than their share of resources because of the influence Admiral Rickover exerted on Congress. In 1966, Rickover edged directly onto black-shoe turf by proposing a "fast escort" submarine to protect the carriers. The CNO killed the proposal for the time being, but this fight was one of the very few that Rickover lost during the period.[11]

Two short steps for the surface navy came late in the decade. In 1969, the destroyer school at Newport added a prospective commanding officer's course. The next spring, the Bureau of Naval Personnel established the designation of surface warfare officer with certain specific requirements and administrative procedures for qualification. Some surface officers objected to the 1970 changes on the grounds that the criteria were couched at such a low level as to be insulting.[12]

In the realm of national strategy, the surface navy's commitments remained heavy in both the Atlantic and Pacific. Following the first thorough review of NATO planning since 1956, the alliance formally announced in December 1967 the adoption of McNamara's strategy of Flexible Response: aggression short of nuclear war would meet initially with a conventional defense. One month later, a landmark strategic document, the Brosio Study, affirmed that NATO would have to wage a major campaign at sea to nourish its forces in Europe and to project power from the sea against the Soviets. Such a strategy would necessitate that the U.S. surface navy continue to pay close attention to antisubmarine warfare.[13]

Of course, this focus would vie with the demands of the Vietnam War which took a serious toll on the surface navy, although not in direct casualties to ships or men. In fact, the surface navy fought with efficiency and effectiveness. Units headed for the Far East in 1965 brushed up on their conventional warfare capabilities. For example, the commander of Cruiser-Destroyer Flotilla Seven, Rear Admiral Zumwalt, noted in his final report of Exercise Hot Stove in October 1965, "This war game was designed to prepare the participants for WESTPAC employment and was oriented toward operations off South East Asia."[14] Included in the exercise were missile site neutralization, live surface-to-air missile firing, underway replenishment, and anti-PT boat measures.

Surface warships deployed to North Vietnamese waters found that much of their work lay in backing up the aviators with their strike mission. Tasks included plane guard and general escort duties—and much steaming. Frigates and destroyers spent lengthy periods at sea—for example, the frigate *Reeves* in the two years starting with June 1966 was underway for 493 days, 312 of them in the Gulf of Tonkin. Continuous steaming was especially hard on the smaller escorts which frequently had to go to trial speeds to keep up with the carriers running at almost 30 knots in the light airs of the Gulf.[15]

Surface ships also patrolled close to the North Vietnamese coast to rescue downed American pilots. Often, the ships themselves went so near the beach that they exchanged gunfire with enemy artillery batteries. In the month of July 1966 alone, the frigate *King* saved five aviators, including one by the ship's helicopter from deep inside North Vietnam. During two months in 1967, the old destroyer *Wiltsie* (DD 716) picked up nine airmen, and in the same period refueled helicopters on search- and rescue missions 207 times. These rescues demonstrated the feasibility of operating the heavy SH–3 aircraft from frigates, even in poor weather.[16]

Beginning in April 1965, some G ships served as air control vessels in the Gulf of Tonkin. In June, destroyer *Joseph Strauss* (DDG 16) directed two F–4 Phantoms to a successful intercept of two North Vietnamese MiG–17s, thus helping to account for the first hostile aircraft downed by U.S. forces in aerial combat since the Korean War.[17]

As U.S. air operations over North Vietnam increased enormously in scope, the Navy continuously stationed a surface unit in the Gulf to track all aircraft over those waters and North Vietnam. This surveillance area was known by the unwieldy title of Positive Identification Radar Advisory Zone (PIRAZ). The tasks handed the warship serving as the PIRAZ unit were formidable: provide a stable and exact navigational reference point for friendly planes (a major problem in itself); check out every one of the hundreds of aircraft flying daily over the Gulf of Tonkin and parts of North Vietnam (and thereby to reduce the need for the carrier's CAP to identify radar contacts as friend or foe); warn American pilots of their proximity to the Communist Chinese border or of enemy fighters; vector search- and- rescue aircraft to downed aviators; and, with her own antiaircraft missiles, provide protection for friendly forces. To carry out these multitudinous chores, the PIRAZ ship had to be equipped with the NTDS and of course, with surface-to-air missiles. However, because of the exposed position of the PIRAZ ship and of the limited gun armament of the most modern ships with NTDS, an older vessel "rode shotgun" against enemy torpedo boat attack.[18]

The scale of this effort can be underlined by the performance of one of the PIRAZ warships, *Long Beach*. During four months on station in the Tonkin Gulf during 1967, the cruiser "was responsible for tracking, checking in, checking out, and rendering numerous services to approximately 30,000 United States aircraft sorties." Air controllers on board the PIRAZ ships also identified and tracked hundreds of MiG flights and guided U.S. fighters against the North Vietnamese aircraft. One controller on board cruiser *Chicago* won the Distinguished Service Medal for directing twelve successful interceptions in a single deployment.[19]

The ships scored less frequently in using their missiles directly against enemy aircraft, principally because of the restrictions originating in Washington. CINCPAC Admiral U. S. Grant Sharp tried on numerous occasions beginning in 1966 to get permission for a Talos cruiser to shoot at known MiGs. His requests were rebuffed by the Joint Chiefs of Staff for fear that an errant missile might destroy an American plane or fall into a North Vietnamese city. In May 1968, after tracking more than five hundred MiGs, *Long Beach* finally got clearance to fire. Although she missed on 11 May, twelve days thereafter the cruiser shot two Talos missiles two minutes apart at a pair of enemy aircraft 65 miles away. To quote from the CINCPAC summary of the episode, "Two minutes and 50 seconds [after the first missile left the rails], all of Talos directors recorded on their scopes the sudden blooming and the expanding clutter of debris associated with a direct hit. At the same instant, electronics signals from the MiG abruptly stopped. Two minutes later, the second Talos detonated on the falling wreckage." [20] This action was the first occasion in which a ship destroyed a hostile aircraft with guided missiles, and also the first time that a nuclear surface warship had scored against an enemy. In September, *Long Beach* repeated her May feat by hitting a second MiG at 61 miles. [21]

These successes were counterbalanced by several disappointments. In June, the frigate *Jouett* (DLG 29) fired two Terriers at a MiG which escaped by radical evasive action, and *Long Beach* missed on five additional Talos shots. [22] Worse, the JCS soon ordered that Talos be used only over the Gulf of Tonkin and not over land areas. Maintaining a Talos cruiser on station did keep North Vietnamese aircraft inland, but many sailors expressed frustration at the way the big missile was hobbled. Admiral Sharp later rendered his opinion of this decision: "Thus we denied ourselves an excellent weapon which could have made life very difficult for the MiGs over North Vietnam. *Long Beach* and her Talos missiles was perfectly capable of intercepting a MiG aircraft over the Hanoi-Haiphong area, and their accuracy was very good indeed...." [23] Vice Admiral Gerald E. Miller, an aviator who went on board *Long Beach* on occasion to check on her PIRAZ performance, later reminisced, "I've always said that if we could get it [the MiG] with Talos, why the hell are we going to put a guy over the beach up there and jeopardize him getting shot down...?" [24]

Talos also saw some action in another guise. Even though details are still sketchy, development started in 1965 on an antiradar version of the big missile, and by 1967 one hundred conversion kits had entered the Navy inventory. Seventh Fleet began planning for its use that fall. A potent weapon, the Talos ARM flew a high-altitude trajectory to a maximum range of 120 miles and, once in action, reportedly shut down North Vietnamese radar installations for an entire week. [25]

If the Vietnam War provided the first combat test for the surface navy's antiaircraft missiles, it did the same for the nuclear warships. *Bainbridge* escorted carrier *Enterprise* into the Tonkin Gulf in December 1965. *Long Beach* made her initial deployment in the fall of 1966. During her eight months on station, the cruiser was engaged principally in PIRAZ duties. In comparing her record to the conventional accompanying destroyer which refueled every three days, one officer estimated that the nuclear plant allowed *Long Beach* to spend an entire extra month on station by reducing transit time. He wrote to Admiral Rickover: "Had the recent flareup in the Middle East required Naval support to be sent from the Tonkin Gulf to the Red Sea, nuclear powered ships such as *Long Beach*, *Enterprise*, and *Bainbridge* would have been ideal for the purpose, since these ships could travel there in minimum time, operate there without immediate support and return in minimum time. These are the kinds of advantages that, in military crises, are of extreme value."[26]

While the Navy's most modern cruisers and frigates concentrated on the antiaircraft mission, other surface warships took on more mundane duties. Starting 11 March 1965, surface patrols put in countless hours to stop the southward flow of arms along the coast, an interdiction campaign dubbed Operation MARKET TIME. The work was constant, but mostly uneventful. For instance, *Kretchmer* (DE 329) in one year checked out 17,000 small craft, boarding 1,000 of them. An occasional large score punctuated the usual tedium, as when destroyers *Walker* (DD 517) and *Wilhoite* (DER 397) captured in 1967 a trawler with one million rounds of ammunition and 2 tons of TNT on board. *Wilhoite* hit the jackpot again when she drove an arms trawler ashore two years later, thereby effecting "the largest arms cache captured during the entire war."[27]

Surface warships also began providing gunfire support to friendly units ashore, with the first missions coming in the third week of May 1965 by cruiser *Canberra* and five destroyers. Shortly thereafter, *McMorris* became the first of her type involved in this duty. By the end of that year, seventy-two ships had shot almost 90,000 rounds at Viet Cong targets within range of the 850-mile coastline.[28]

The bombardment pace picked up in 1966, with the cruiser and destroyer types joined in April for close-in work by an inshore fire support ship (IFS). Within months, two of the rocket ships, *Carronade* and *St. Francis River* (LSMR 525), were providing area coverage at short ranges. The latter ship had fired 10,000 rockets by September. Although its effectiveness over the long haul was somewhat diminished by its age and lack of spare parts, *St. Francis River* was still serving in 1970. The larger ships also came to close quarters with the enemy. For instance, destroyer *Morton* steamed 22 miles up the Mekong River to back up the Army's First Division; *Bache* (DDE 470) closed to within 600 yards of shore to use her .50-

caliber machine guns. And, like the rocket ships, the bigger destroyers and cruisers fired a great many missions. Before her 1966 Vietnam tour, missile cruiser *Topeka* had practiced gunnery only infrequently. Once off South Vietnam, she shot so much that her commanding officer took his best men off missiles and put them on the guns—a switch criticized by BUPERS, but one that paid dividends. The cruiser's shooting drew such accolades from shore observers as "Your fall of shot is like a surgical tool instead of a sledge hammer . . . "; "They can't hide from these guns . . . "; "Accurate, even at long ranges . . . "; and "That sure shut them up!" [29] A precise accounting of the effectiveness of the gunfire was usually impossible, but the frequent calls for shore bombardment provided some index of its value. In supporting Operation PRAIRIE, *Canberra* expended over 2,900 rounds; *Towers* (DDG 9) in July alone shot off 3,266 5-inch shells. Ammunition scarcity forced ships headed for home to transfer high-capacity shells to "in-chopping" units. [30]

The enemy occasionally hit back at the gunships with punishing effect. On 25 March 1967, destroyer *Ozbourn* (DD 846) was assisting friendly troops just south of the Demilitarized Zone (DMZ). Steaming only 2 miles off the beach, the ship suddenly came under enemy mortar fire. Three rounds damaged the Mk 25 radar room and, more seriously, the ASROC magazine. Two rocket motors ignited, engulfing the magazine in flames. The crew extinguished the conflagration by prompt and heroic damage control measures and then disassembled the nuclear-tipped ASROC rounds. All were radiologically safe, but the incident moved Vice Admiral John Hyland, commander of the Seventh Fleet, to order the ships carrying nuclear weapons withdrawn from naval gunfire support duties. [31]

The years 1967 and 1968 saw even higher demands on an increasingly strained force. Typically, three cruisers and twenty destroyers worked along the coast in 1967; they spent 70 percent of their time underway, 20 percent on upkeep, and 10 percent on port visits. Then, the Tet offensive and the concurrent crisis when North Koreans seized the intelligence colection ship *Pueblo* (AGER 2) dictated an at-sea figure of 85 percent. Defending against the major enemy offensive in South Vietnam pushed ammunition expenditures to record levels: over 100,000 rounds per month, a pace maintained over the next quarter. At critical times, the big ships found more calls for help than they could answer, especially with the competing demands of the offensive against North Vietnam. [32]

That campaign, dubbed Operation SEA DRAGON, had initiated in October 1966 when two destroyers, *Mansfield* and *Hanson* (DD 832), entered North Vietnamese waters to interrupt the southward flow of munitions and to pressure the North at vital points along its coasts. Ranging northward from the DMZ 230 miles to the 20th parallel, U.S. warships shelled radar stations, coastal guns, and supply boats. Results were frequently gratifying. For instance, Surface Action Groups in May 1967 destroyed or damaged 160 of the 420 logistics craft detected. By the end of that year, one observer assessed the SEA DRAGON campaign as so effective that coastal traffic was reduced to "insignificance."[33]

Another index of the effectiveness of SEA DRAGON was a massive buildup along North Vietnamese shores of artillery pieces in both numbers and calibers (up to 130mm). Beginning in the summer of 1967, ships operating close to the coast were often forced to maneuver at flank speed to avoid the fire of the enemy artillery pieces. On 12 November of that year, destroyer *Goldsborough* (DDG 20) was ringed by some 150 shell splashes from five enemy guns off Song Giang. Surprisingly, the vessel escaped with only slight damage. Other ships were not so lucky. On 13 September, two 100mm shells did serious injury to the destroyer *Damato* (DD 871), putting her communications and ASROC launcher out of service. Shortly thereafter, destroyer *Mansfield* lost four crewmen to an 85mm projectile. In the course of these operations, North Vietnamese artillery hit twenty-nine ships on the gunline, killing five sailors, and wounding another twenty-six. As the CINCPAC review for August 1967 put the matter, "Like policemen covering a tough neighborhood, the ships patrolled in pairs or greater numbers, always on the alert for the sharp crack of sound, the puff of smoke and the shower of shrapnel—or the towering column of water—unmistakable signs that the North Vietnamese coastal batteries had commenced fire. The coastal batteries . . . were highly mobile and thus difficult to locate and destroy. . . . "[34]

Rumors abounded on the U.S. warships of more nefarious enemy weapons. Scuttlebutt had the North Vietnamese firing torpedoes from caves. Mines posed a more realistic threat; in fact, destroyer *Warrington* (DD 843) hit one and required yard work at Subic Bay. Some reports stressed the possibility that the SA–2 antiaircraft missile might be fired against the naval vessels. Of even greater concern was the possibility that the Soviets would supply the North Vietnamese with Styx antiship missiles.[35]

The very threat of the weapon kept SEA DRAGON vessels 20 miles off the North Vietnamese coast until they made their bombardment runs at high speed. Ships then followed a sinuous course in exiting the combat area. Truly effective defenses were meager indeed: neither chaff launchers nor ECM had attained a satisfactory stage of development. Certain types of ECM gear proved susceptible to shock damage from gunfire; spare parts remained in extremely short supply. One gunship active in 1968 waited six months for a key component necessary to fix her SLQ–12 radar jammer. Fortunately, Styx, despite many alarms, never reached North Vietnamese hands.[36]

Not all the danger came from the enemy: friendly fire proved a real menace on more than one occasion. The most serious such episode occurred in June 1968 when cruiser *Boston* and the Australian destroyer *Hobart* were attacked at night by unknown aircraft. The planes fired four guided missiles at the ships. *Boston* escaped with superficial damage, but *Hobart* suffered two direct hits which killed two of her men, wounded seven, and wrecked her weapons direction radars and missile system. Proof positive of the identification of the errant planes came when serial numbers from rocket fragments on board *Boston* matched those of Sparrow missiles fired that night by Air Force F–4s.[37]

Almost as challenging to the surface warriors as the stiffened North Vietnamese coastal defenses and the threat of advanced weaponry was simple wear-and-tear on the ships employed in SEA DRAGON. With the most sophisticated cruisers and frigates serving on PIRAZ or carrier escort duty, the workload closer to the Vietnamese coast fell to the older gunships, some of which were older than many of the crewmen serving on them. For instance, heavy cruiser *Saint Paul*, veteran of World War II and Korea, made five deployments to Southeast Asia. The *Fletcher*-class destroyer *Radford* (DD 446), having won twelve battle stars in World War II and five in Korea, garnered four more in Vietnam.[38]

Both north and south, the gunships did a great deal of shooting. From May 1965 to June 1968, U.S. surface warships fired 1.152 million rounds of ammunition at the enemy. One destroyer expended 48 tons of ammunition in a 26-hour mission. In 1968, the seven ships of Destroyer Squadron (DESRON) 22 fired 54,315 rounds—a daily average of 180 shells per ship on station. Among their successes were 123 secondary explosions, "many of them rather spectacular."[39]

But some of these vessels were fading under the press of continuous employment. After firing for four months during SEA DRAGON, the rifling of the 8-inch barrels on the veteran cruiser *Boston* was virtually worn smooth. The newer destroyer *Dupont* (DD 941) fired her guns well beyond their regulation lifespan until the "absolute end of gun barrel life was signaled by the ripping off of large pieces of the powder case mouths and a high incidence of flarebacks."[40] Ammunition and spare barrels for the fast-firing 5"/54 Mk 42 of the newer destroyers were in critical short supply. Regunning, usually done at Subic Bay, became a standard procedure for both destroyers and cruisers. Eight-inch–gun ships slated for retirement got a reprieve when Secretary McNamara announced they would remain on active duty. The wisdom of this decision was proved when heavy cruisers *Canberra* and *Newport News* gave sustained support to ground forces combating the enemy's Tet offensive. Destroyer escorts took over plane guard duty from destroyers to free up more 5-inch guns for coastal work; all gunships put in more time on the practice ranges before their deployments.[41]

Symbolic of the importance of the naval gun to the conflict was the recommissioning of *New Jersey* (BB 62) in 1968. Because no battleship had

NH 90639

Battleship *New Jersey* (BB 62) fires a 16″/50 round near Tuy Hoa, South Vietnam, during the last days of her deployment, March 1969.

been in the active fleet for a decade, the Navy had to tap the expertise of retired sailors and search the archives for information on operating the ship's systems. Relining the battleship's guns proved especially trying because all the special railroad flatcars capable of transporting the barrels had gone to the scrapyard. Fortunately, the 1940s drawings were in good shape—"a potent argument for proper documentation for record of all designs of ordnance items," noted one officer.[42]

Even as *New Jersey* was working up in April, President Johnson prohibited operations against North Vietnam above the 19th parallel, thereby reducing by one-third the SEA DRAGON area and placing some of the most tempting objectives beyond the battleship's aim. Reaching the theater in late September 1968, *New Jersey* still found plenty of targets. In backing up friendly troops ashore, her captain remembered, "Her record of performance...was exemplary. I had the fire control officer compute the average salvo error...[which] was 150 yards [in range] and about the same in deflection for the first salvos. That is GOOD shooting."[43] The ship was especially effective in counterbattery fire against North Vietnamese artillery

163

bedeviling American ground units on the south side of the DMZ. While *New Jersey* fired her shore bombardments against the North Vietnamese, her armor was a solace to her crewmen concerned about the Styx. One of her officers remarked that if the battleship were hit by a cruise missile, "I'd pipe sweepers."[44]

Abruptly on 1 November 1968, President Johnson halted all offensive operations against North Vietnam. Some surface officers looked forward to being able to accomplish long-deferred overhauls of their ships during the hiatus, but the press of naval gunfire support operations in the south kept them on line for a time. *New Jersey* continued to demonstrate the effectiveness of her big guns. In January, she hit a Viet Cong ammunition dump near Danang: "Red fireballs soared high above the target as the shells found their mark."[45] The next month, her shells on one occasion triggered seven huge secondary explosions among enemy rocket sites. The warship finished her seven-month deployment in March with a record expenditure of over 1,200 16-inch projectiles.[46] Although the battleship was slated for a second tour, the new Nixon administration, implementing a gradual withdrawal of American forces and the policy of Vietnamization, sent the ship to mothballs for the third time. When *Saint Paul* went home in September 1969, *Boston* was the only heavy gunship remaining on line in Southeast Asia.[47]

Those ships still in the theater shot sporadically. Demand could be heavy, as *Theodore E. Chandler* (DD 717) proved in December 1969 when she fired 4,300 rounds of 5-inch ammunition in twenty-two days. But as the war wound down and the focus shifted to Cambodian operations in the spring of 1970, the gunships shot fewer and fewer missions. By that point, only twelve destroyers—and not a single cruiser—were in the theater. *Saint Paul* returned in the summer for one last tour. The redoubtable cruiser fired her guns for the last time in the fall. Typically, her ammunition expenditure was heavy: 3,003 rounds of 8-inch added to her record as the cruiser "alleged to have fired more rounds than any gun ship in the U.S. Navy's history."[48] Seven of the destroyers in her task unit had also seen action during the Korean conflict.[49]

Twice in the late 1960s, another full-fledged war in Korea seemed very likely. On 23 January 1968, the North Koreans seized the intelligence collection ship *Pueblo*. Surface warships were among the naval forces diverted from Southeast Asia to the trouble spot. Two cruisers and eight destroyers escorted the two carriers dispatched to the scene; an antisubmarine group composed in part of six destroyers patrolled the Sea of Japan for the next forty-five days. *Chicago* took up PIRAZ station to conduct radar surveillance north of the 38th parallel and to control CAP. Although all ships returned to ordinary operations by the end of March, the diversion from SEA DRAGON operations had occurred at a critical moment in the Vietnam War.[50]

Then on 15 April 1969, North Korean fighters shot down a Navy EC–121 aircraft 90 miles off their east coast. The next day, the Seventh Fleet formed Task Force 71 made up of one antisubmarine and three attack carriers, three cruisers, and twenty-two destroyer types. Some of these units were rapidly pulled off the South Vietnamese gunline; for instance, *Waddell* (DDG 24) headed northeast at 22 knots. The first unit into the Sea of Japan, cruiser *Chicago*, was tailed by a Soviet *Kotlin*-class destroyer. Seventh Fleet planners seriously considered retaliating against the North Koreans by using the two Talos cruisers in the force, *Chicago* and *Oklahoma City*, to shoot down MiGs flying from Wonsan airfield. In the event, Washington rejected the military option.[51]

If the war in Vietnam proved anything to the surface navy, it was that a mix of capabilities remained essential in modern warfare. As one officer wrote in the *Proceedings*, guns were simply irreplaceable for "weight of fire, rapidity of response, [and] continuous availability during all weather conditions. . . ."[52] After a ten-year dry spell, the gun seemed worth developing again. However, in that decade, the Navy had lost a great deal of ground. Facilities most associated with gunnery such as Dahlgren had been, in the words of one ordnance specialist, "just meandering around aimlessly under the continuous threat of closure."[53] With all the emphasis

USN 1133001

Destroyer *Turner Joy* (DD 951) bombarding enemy positions, 20 June 1968, with her 5"/54 Mk 42. Note the shell casing ejected overboard.

on missilery, gun work had almost ground to a halt. By 1965, the few people at Dahlgren who understood aircraft gunnery were "worth their weight in gold."[54] European navies, not able to spend so heavily on missiles, had continued to invest in guns—as the success of the Italian 76mm OTO-Melara would later attest.

The U.S. neglect of gunnery also manifested itself in serious casualties. At the very beginning of regular naval gunfire support in South Vietnam, an in-bore explosion on destroyer *Somers* (DD 947) killed one man and inflicted moderate damage on the ship. *Turner Joy* later in the year lost three crewmen to a defective powder case. In December 1966 and again three months later, destroyer *Manley* suffered 5-inch Mk 42 explosions, one of which wrecked a mount beyond repair. Then in April 1967, *Bigelow* (DD 942) was "rocked" by a similar disaster. Corrective measures seemed to solve the problem until 1969, when in a five-month period, four more ships—*Boston*, *Lowry* (DD 770), *Hoel* (DDG 13), and HMAS *Brisbane*—suffered in-bore explosions in their 5-inchers. On destroyer *Hoel*, an "exploding projectile burst [a] barrel raining shrapnel and gun barrel fragments down on the forecastle. A large chunk of the barrel was hurled over the side by the force of the explosion carrying away life lines in the process."[55]

Experts conducted a detailed examination of ammunition from the suspect lots as well as sample projectiles from across a wide spectrum of the Navy's stockpiles. The results of the investigation were disturbing. Suppliers had produced a great deal of defective ammunition which had, in turn, been inspected and passed by naval personnel. Weak links existed all up and down the chain. Documentation was inadequate; improper waivers had been issued; operating procedures were sloppy; tooling was antiquated and improperly maintained. The frequent Navy reorganizations had compounded the problems by disrupting routines and transferring experienced personnel hither and yon. The official report on the matter hastened to add that negligence was not an issue. Rather, the problems grew out of a decade-long climate in which the money went to missiles and nuclear weapons with "vastly reduced emphasis and funding for conventional weapons."[56]

On the positive side of the ledger, improved guns for the Navy's cruisers and destroyers were entering the fleet. Work on the new 5-inch gun system, the Mk 45, under development with a low priority since 1961, was hastened. Specifically intended to support amphibious operations, the Mk 45 offered only a limited capability against aircraft. The weapon could elevate only to 65 degrees and fire only twenty rounds per minute. When it came into the fleet on frigate *California* (DLGN 36) in 1974, the Mk 45 (with its companion Mk 86 fire control system) was the first major shipboard gun system produced by the Navy in eighteen years.[57]

The Navy started an even more potent gun in early 1965: the lightweight 8-inch. With the gun cruisers retiring, the Navy anticipated facing

Soviet artillery pieces that could outrange the 5-inch. Initially a joint project with the Army and sized to fire the Army's 175mm projectile, the new gun was switched to accept the Navy's 8-inch ammunition when the Army terminated development on its weapon. By 1970, the design, similar in appearance to the streamlined 5-inch Mk 45, was well along. Planners hoped to fit one mount forward in each of the new *Spruance*-class destroyers. The reduced ammunition supply of three hundred rounds (vice six hundred for the 5-inch the larger gun would replace) seemed worth the sacrifice to gain the 8-inch shell.[58]

At the same time that work began on this new weapon, the Navy initiated a longer-term program to make radical advances in gunnery. Nothing if not ambitious, its authors stated its overall goal as "reestablishing the gun as the primary weapons system of the Navy through the application of technology developed for missiles over the last fifteen years."[59] Called Project Gunfighter, the program's work was centered at the Naval Ordnance Station (until 1966, the Naval Propellant Plant), Indian Head, Maryland. Specific aims included extending the range of guns, improving their efficiency, and reducing barrel erosion.[60]

In meeting the first goal, Indian Head hoped for major gains by boosting the range of the artillery pieces in the Navy and Marine Corps from 65 percent to more than 150 percent. Testing at White Sands, ordnance technicians fired 5-inch subcaliber rounds from a smooth-bore gun to distances of over 50 miles. They achieved surprising accuracy by stabilizing the projectiles with fins. With requests for longer ranges coming from the forces operating in Southeast Asia, Project Gunfighter began development of a long-range round for those 8-inch cruiser guns still in the active fleet. In February 1968, an 8-incher at the Wallops Island test facility shot a round almost 40 miles. Program advocates enthusiastically wrote: "This was one of the most outstanding feats performed by a gun since 1918 when the Germans astonished the world by shelling Paris. It marked the beginning of a new era for US Navy Gunnery."[61] These new rounds reached the fleet; in 1970, *Saint Paul* fired these long-range shells for the first time against Viet Cong targets 35 miles inland. Air Force pilots who questioned why a naval spotter was so far from the coast were convinced he was "deranged" when informed that he was spotting for *Saint Paul*—a ship 60,000 yards away. Air Force skepticism changed to belief when some of the cruiser shells landed within a few feet of the target. In February of the same year, destroyers on the gunline fired 5-inch rocket-assisted projectiles (RAP) to 23,000 yards. The Gunfighter team also started work on a 280mm saboted round to double the range of battleship *New Jersey*.[62]

To improve accuracy, researchers at the University of Virginia developed a velocimeter to measure the speed of projectiles as they left the muzzle—a calculation essential in refining fire control solutions. Indian Head also experimented with the more exotic solution of guided shells. Dahlgren called this area of inquiry critical, concluding "that naval guns were not worth pursuing unless we could improve the intelligence in the bullet."[63]

To cut barrel erosion, potentially a serious problem given the high velocities necessary for the extended ranges, the naval ordnance teams pulled from the shelf and put into production the Navy Cool propellant developed in the late 1950s. Tests showed that NACO quadrupled barrel life for the 5″/54 and provided double that benefit for the 3″/50. NACO began reaching the fleet in 1968 and demonstrated the additional benefit of lessened muzzle blast pressures—an important consideration given the fragile electronics on the newer surface warships. Project Gunfighter technicians advanced an additional remedy to bore erosion with a wear-reducing compound, titanium dioxide. Called Swedish additive, this material "teflon-coated" the inside of a gun barrel and further diminished the problem.[64]

All of these advances taken together were promising enough that the Navy established a Gunnery Conclave. Composed of staffers from the Navy labs and ranges, the panel also incorporated experts from the Applied Physics Laboratory, Texas Instruments, and the Space Research Company. The conclave would lead to the Naval Gunnery Improvement Program of the 1970s. Project Gunfighter technicians also looked ahead to unconventional employment for the gun. Among the exotic areas they considered were applications for antiballistic missile defenses, antisubmarine warfare, orbital missions, and near space probes. In 1969, a Gunfighter report concluded, "the potential of the US Navy gun has just begun to be exploited."[65]

If the naval gun seemed to have almost endless long-term possibilities, of immediate menace was the antiship missile. On 25 October 1967, the Israeli *Eilat*, formerly a Royal Navy destroyer completed in 1944, was cruising about 15 miles off Port Said, Egypt. A veteran crew, *Eilat* sailors had participated in a successful action against Egyptian torpedo boats during the Six Day War of the preceding summer. In the uneasy truce of the fall, the Egyptians suddenly retaliated with their Soviet-supplied missiles. Fired from the sanctuary of the harbor, two Styx closed to within 6 miles of the Israeli ship before *Eilat* radars detected them in the land clutter. *Eilat*'s crew barely had time to initiate a turn and to open fire with antiaircraft guns when the first missile struck high in the ship, destroying the radio antennas. The second demolished the engine room. Dead in the water and unable to communicate, the destroyer was helpless when, ninety minutes later, a third missile inflicted fatal damage. As the ship capsized, a fourth Styx crashed into the blazing debris. Ninety-nine of the Israeli sailors were killed or wounded.[66]

Her loss—the first vessel ever sunk by an antiship missile—created a sensation in naval circles, especially in the U.S. Navy. As one black-shoe officer later related, "From a surface officer's view . . . it was reveille."[67] Another said, "Everybody went to General Quarters."[68] A third remembered, "The *Eilat* ... was the one that really began to wake people up."[69] One analyst forecast that the event would revolutionize naval warfare like the *Monitor-Virginia* duel of 1862.[70]

Not only were the Soviets deploying large numbers of missile boats themselves, they were supplying significant numbers of them to client nations. By one count, eleven of these countries had *Komar* boats in 1968. As destroyer officers noted, "While the short-range, surface-to-surface threat can be countered by ordering all units to remain clear of its sphere of influence, this only keeps us out of another slice of the world's oceans."[71]

Despite initial agonizing within the Navy, its public comment at first was oddly muted. The Secretary of the Navy's annual reports for FYs 69 and 70 simply did not mention the cruise missile. The first significant article to appear on *Eilat* in the *Proceedings* was published two years after the event and focused almost totally on the sort of aid the United States should provide its allies to enable them to cope with the new threat.[72]

This *Proceedings* piece drew a pointed rejoinder from one officer who wrote that the *Eilat* incident required not just a reexamination of American aid packages but a profound reassessment of "our basic naval posture and development program."[73] The writer pointed out that expensive surface ships were vulnerable to a much cheaper weapon. Moreover, given the range of cruise missiles, enemy ships equipped with them could attack with impunity any vessel not backed up by an aircraft carrier. As for the carriers, they were overcommitted in Vietnam and declining rapidly in numbers with the older *Essex* class headed for retirement. In fact, the Styx threat had already begun constraining the movement of American surface forces; cruisers and destroyers "couldn't go anywhere without an aircraft escort," in the words of one officer.[74]

Whatever the Navy's public stance, the *Eilat* affair caused immediate repercussions on board U.S. ships operating in Southeast Asian waters. Surface warfare officers there were most concerned that the Russians, who were lavish in equipping the North Vietnamese with antiaircraft missiles, would pass Styx on to their allies. The North Vietnamese might conceivably fit it into their PT boats; more probably, they would simply fire it from shore. Following the sinking of *Eilat*, rumor went around the American ships that the North Vietnamese had taken delivery of the Styx and were simply awaiting the right opportunity to use it. Admiral Zumwalt considered the Styx threat from North Vietnam "his worst nightmare."[75] Captain Mark W. Woods, the commanding officer of *Canberra*, would end his shore bombardment missions with a high-speed retreat along a sinuous course in an attempt to make it as difficult as possible for enemy missileers. But officers caught in this situation basically felt that they were "sitting ducks."[76]

Styx was just the beginning of the nightmare. The Soviets in the late 1960s were deploying ever more capable antiship missiles on board improved platforms. The SS–N–9 for patrol craft was an improved version of the Styx with a quadrupled range of 60 miles. The SS–N–7 Siren could be launched from a completely submerged submarine located as far as 35 miles from its American targets. Introduced in 1968, both could carry a 200-kiloton nuclear warhead. Two advanced air-launched antiship missiles, the AS–4 Kitchen and the AS–5 Kelt, added another dimension to the Soviet threat. The Kitchen flew high and fast. As it neared its target, it went into a nearly vertical dive, "coming down the stovepipe," in sailors' slang. All four of these missiles were large, with conventional or nuclear warheads from one-half to one ton in weight. In types and numbers of antiship missiles, the Soviets were "just coming along like gang busters," said one officer.[77]

Those American ordnance specialists who were able to examine the Soviet missiles over the years were impressed. One expert evinced toward them "a healthy respect," adding that they were simple and durable as if "made of cast iron."[78] After looking over a Styx, an aviator thought, "There wasn't any question that this was the weapon system that was going to give fits to a lot of people."[79] Naval officers in open testimony before Congress in 1970 concluded that the antiship missile possessed "great current capability and future potential."[80] All ships were vulnerable to it, with unarmored vessels most at risk. Carriers with their elaborate protective features had somewhat less to fear. Officers debated just how many missile hits a carrier could absorb and keep operating. Some experts maintained that two to four of the large Soviet weapons could put a carrier out of action. One of the top carrier advocates, Rear Admiral James L. Holloway III, disputed this contention, saying that "a large number" of hits would be necessary. His assessment seemed to be borne out by an Operations Evaluation Group (OEG) calculation that the damage *Enterprise* suffered when nine large-caliber bombs accidentally exploded on the flight deck in 1969 was the equivalent of six antiship missiles hitting the ship. It was a well-known fact that *Enterprise* resumed flight operations within hours. Nonetheless, the same OEG study concluded that a Soviet cruiser could put a carrier out of action for several hours with only half its missile battery, assuming perfect system reliability.[81]

Increasing Soviet successes in developing their cruise missiles led Admiral Gorshkov to brag that his navy could defeat the American carrier forces. In public pronouncements, he gave his surface ships status equal to Soviet navy's air and submarine units. Then, in February 1968, he termed the cruisers and destroyers armed with antiship missiles, "the pride of the fleet."[82] And this fleet was building up fast. In the last half of the decade,

USN 1146092

A Shaddock launcher elevated to firing position on a *Kresta*-class cruiser, c. 1970.

the Soviets constructed more than two hundred warships; the United States, sixty-eight.[83]

The Soviets matched the variety of new missiles that they were sending to sea with a wide array of new strike craft. The first Soviet aviation ships, two helicopter carriers of the *Moskva* class, commissioned in 1967 and 1968. The first *Yankee*-class ballistic missile submarine similar to the Polaris boats completed in 1967. In a test, *Charlie*-class submarines launched their eight SS–N–7 Siren cruise missiles while submerged. One Soviet author compared their salvo firing to "a flock of geese leaving the water."[84] Improved coastal boats of the *Osa II* type gave the Soviets increased capabilities in the narrow seas. Four "rocket cruisers" of the *Kresta* type reinforced the four *Kynda*s in the anticarrier role. Larger ships of 7,500 tons, the *Kresta I*s carried four Shaddock missiles supported by a targeting helicopter. The eight cruisers of these two classes, characterized by one American admiral as "especially innovative and potent,"[85] were often deployed to waters frequented by American carriers. Moreover, the first of the follow-on *Kresta II* cruisers entered service in 1970. Ten of these were ultimately

171

constructed; they were armed with eight big launchers thought by Western analysts to carry a new type of antiship missile.[86]

Soviet vessels now operated as far afield as the Indian Ocean and the Gulf of Guinea. By the end of the decade, some were on station constantly in the Mediterranean; others appeared off Guam. Submarines cruised off Hainan Island. The Soviet ships were behaving much more aggressively, which reflected their increasing professionalism and strength as well as a U.S. fleet spread ever more thinly. Just three months after the *Eilat* sinking, in January 1968, the Soviets sortied sixteen ships during the *Pueblo* crisis and interposed them between North Korea and a U.S. carrier task group. In 1970, the Soviets capped a decade of naval growth with the Okean exercise involving 206 ships—the largest deployment in their history and the first exercise on a global scale ever mounted by any nation.[87]

New Soviet submarines looked particularly threatening. As the commissioning officer of *Sample* (DE 1048) assessed the situation: "Seemingly fantastic improvements in deep-diving, high speed attack submarines and in stand-off weapons from air, surface or sub-surface platforms sorely challenged not only the particular ships but also the whole mission of escort forces."[88] Exercises frequently showed that the ASW craft were hard-pressed. Against diesel submarines firing torpedoes, the escorts did well until a submarine penetrated the screen. Main body units then became "sitting ducks"—a situation leading to the desperate counsel that ships tow anchors until more of the short-range Mk 46 torpedoes entered service. And against nuclear submarines firing standoff missiles, one commander concluded, "it is evident that the force would have had essentially no capability against such an attack."[89] ASW sailors needed improved sensors, longer-range weapons, and more ships.[90]

Variable depth sonar (VDS) and towed passive arrays held out the hope of much greater detection ranges. Under development from 1959, the SQS–35 VDS went to sea in 1967; it was especially valuable in detecting submarines hiding below temperature layers. Unfortunately, the towed "fish" endangered submarines during exercises, and escort commanders, to their great frustration, were often forbidden use of the device while training.[91]

Promising for both detection and prosecution of submarines was the helicopter. With a dipping sonar, it could "sanitize" a corridor 10 kilometers wide and 100 kilometers long, sufficient to protect a task force moving at 30 knots. The helicopter could carry sonobuoys and acoustic homing torpedoes as well as ECM gear useful against cruise missiles whether fired from surface craft or submarines. As DASH experienced increasingly serious problems, the Navy turned toward providing escorts with the manned helicopter—the LAMPS program (for details, see below).

As for ASW ships themselves, coming into the fleet were large numbers of escorts ordered early in McNamara's tenure: the *Garcia*, *Brooke*, and

*Knox* classes. The seventeen ships of the first two types were commissioned between 1964 and 1968; they performed a wide variety of duties, including serving as trials ships for towed arrays, automated ASW systems, and the Sea Sparrow short-range missile. Some saw duty off Vietnam where they were tasked with such chores as plane guard, search and rescue, shore bombardment, and even PIRAZ. Their limited gunnery capabilities and lack of engineering redundancy made Seventh Fleet loath to use them for SEA DRAGON. On the other hand, their performance in the ASW arena earned plaudits. Especially outstanding was *Voge* (DE 1047), which in 1969 trailed a *Yankee*-class ballistic missile submarine so ably that she received a Meritorious Unit Commendation. Three years later, *Voge*, on special assignment at the Straits of Gibraltar to track Soviet submarines entering and leaving the Mediterranean, dogged one boat 300 miles out into the Atlantic before breaking contact.[92]

Forty-six of the follow-on *Knox* class were eventually commissioned between 1969 and 1974. By earlier standards, they were certainly large for escorts at 4,066 tons. Like their immediate predecessors, their single shaft and 5-inch gun made them the object of suspicion, a view hardly mollified when the second ship of the class, *Roark* (DE 1053), experienced in January 1971 a serious fire in her engineering plant which left her dead in the water. Wet ships forward, they ultimately needed raised bulwarks to cure that defect. Despite their modest speed, they often were pressed into service as escorts for fast carriers.[93]

On the plus side, they received the rapid-fire 5″/54 Mk 42 mount; their machinery returned to the 1,200-pound plant rather than the pressure-fired boilers. Their sonar gear was the state-of-the-art SQS–26. Most ships eventually were fitted with the SQS–35 towed array. With ample hangar space, the ships could easily accommodate manned helicopters when DASH left the fleet. The Spanish thought enough of them to build five similar vessels of the *Baleares* class.[94]

Regarding the threat from the rapidly increasing Soviet surface fleet, most top American officers, such as Admirals Horacio Rivero and Harry D. Felt, still expressed public confidence about their ability to defeat it with their trump of carrier aviation, if given adequate warning of hostilities. Some high-ranking surface officers, such as Stansfield Turner, agreed with this assessment. Particularly worrisome, however, was the prospect of the Soviets initiating hostilities by a concerted, surprise blow. Soviet cruisers sometimes trailed the carriers rather closely, on occasion with missiles trained on the American ships. At other times, smaller Soviet ships, the "tattletails" or "trailers," would tag along with the American task groups while the *Kynda*s and *Kresta*s stayed in the distance. In either case, American strategists thought that the Soviets might try to eradicate the principal American naval tool, the carrier, with a coordinated launching of their antiship missiles by all available delivery platforms. American doctrine called for surface units to interpose themselves between the Soviet missile ships and the carrier. In a crisis atmosphere, American commanders might have significant advance warning as to Soviet intentions, signaled in part by the rigid command and control sequence common to Soviet operating procedures.[95]

Defenses against antiship missiles quickly became a top U.S. Navy priority. Up to the *Eilat* sinking, the Soviet antiship missile, while hardly new, had been largely overlooked. No longer. The Navy commissioned several groups to examine various facets of the problem. The more the naval analysts studied the menace, the more threatening they found it. Because the antiship missile could be launched from shore, patrol boats, surface ships, submarines, and aircraft, it made every enemy platform a potential ship killer. The Navy had long recognized that very low-level air attacks were especially dangerous, but until the advent of the cruise missile, these challenges had entered the equation only when naval forces were close to enemy airbases. One study by the Center for Naval Analyses concluded, "The threat is so great to all combatant ships of the Navy that a revolution in naval tactics may be required."[96]

In July 1968, the Navy's Office of Program Appraisal made a formal presentation entitled the "Anti-Ship Missile Defense Study" to Secretary of the Navy Paul R. Ignatius. The study concluded that the monetary cost of absorbing one cruise missile hit was on the order of $50 million. The study then assessed the antiship missile threat as most dangerous coming from, in order of importance: aircraft; submarines; patrol boats; and cruisers and destroyers. So serious was the matter that in April 1969, Ignatius's successor, John H. Chafee, testified before the Senate Armed Forces Committee that the Navy had assigned to cruise missile defense a priority equal to that accorded antisubmarine warfare. Of course with the Soviet *Charlie*-class submarines, the two problems were even more intertwined than before.[97]

An "effective defense" needed to be an airtight one. Naval Ordnance Systems Command (NAVORDSYSCOM) pointed out in August 1969, "A single penetrator per ship is sufficient to effect unacceptable losses."[98] Even near misses could cause severe damage to a ship's sensors or to its hull and propulsion system. However, building a really good defense would prove complicated; to make matters worse, defense budgets began to decline precipitously as the Vietnam War ground on.[99]

A series of exercises in the second half of the decade showed how much progress the fleet had made in antiaircraft effectiveness—and how far it had to go. In the summer 1965 test called Hot Stove, surface warships, including cruiser *Chicago*, which had just been equipped with NTDS, were subjected to attacks by aircraft, some of which simulated air-launched missiles. Thirty-seven actual raids generated 150 bogey reports; only eight of the attackers were downed—and so were numerous friendly and nonexercise aircraft. The flotilla commander blamed this dismal showing on poor intership and intraship communications which allowed enemy raiders to slip through unopposed. Several months later, First Fleet surface warships in Exercise Rag Weed shot down more of the enemy (38 percent), but once again "fired" a distressingly large number of missiles at friendly aircraft: 57 out of the 104 "shot." This unsatisfactory level of performance was essentially repeated in Exercises Base Line and Range Bush when ships downed fewer friendlies but killed only about one raider in four.[100] In Exercise Eager Angler, November 1966, surface warships employed PIRAZ procedures to good effect for the first time. Raid destruction improved daily from 50 percent to 72 percent; far fewer "Blue" aircraft fell victim to friendly missiles.[101]

Antiship missiles presented an even tougher target than planes. Five months before Styx hit *Eilat*, the commander of the First Fleet, Vice Admiral Bernard F. Roeder, directed a test of carrier task force defenses against cruise missiles. A number of commands and agencies, such as Port Hueneme, China Lake, Corona, APL, and the Center for Naval Analyses, cooperated with the project. Results were disquieting. The final report listed among its conclusions:

> Shaddock, Samlet and Styx missile systems would pose a serious threat to U.S. ships if used in a sustained aggressive attack. Samlet and Styx missiles are particularly serious threats to forces such as Sea Dragon/SAR [search and rescue] due to the extremely short time of flight (thirty seconds to about four minutes) during which the ship must detect, evaluate and destroy the missile.[102]

A similar exercise by the Second Fleet a year later reinforced these findings. Of the twenty-three missiles shot at drones simulating cruise missiles, only ten were successful. The officer in charge, Rear Admiral Frank H. Price, Jr., reported, "Currently, fleet units cannot successfully respond to short range anti-ship cruise missile attack from a condition of electronic silence."[103]

The phrase "to shoot down a bullet with a bullet" expressed the difficulty of the task. One of the toughest parts of the problem was the detection and positive identification of the threat, especially in the case of low fliers. The Navy began work on a specialized radar, the SPS–58, for this purpose. Eventually deployed, the rotating antenna of the SPS–58 suffered from the drawback that two or more rotations were necessary before sufficient evidence existed that a target was present. Once a target was detected, it had to be interrogated via identification friend or foe (IFF) to ascertain if it was actually an enemy. Time, of course, was at a premium: a Styx would cover 10 miles in about one minute, and the newer Soviet missiles were much faster. Deciding whether to open fire became a major problem.[104]

As it had for some time, the Navy emphasized a multilayered defense, preferring to break up attacks at maximum range before they could threaten individual ships. As an integral part of this strategy, the Navy in the late 1960s began development of the F–14 Tomcat fighter with its Phoenix missile system to strike at the most dangerous Soviet launching platforms—the long-range aircraft. Aviators and surface warriors put in extra hours at China Lake and other missile ranges coordinating the airplanes and air defense missiles which would oppose the attackers that escaped the combat air patrol. The Soviet cruise missile submarine mandated intense efforts by the Navy to refine its underwater countermeasures. The Navy also accelerated its efforts on close-in, or point, defenses, against "leakers" fired by any Soviet platform.[105]

In 1968, against those attackers that evaded the fighters, the Navy could use the 3–Ts. By this point they were working well against manned aircraft. For instance, of the six missiles fired at drones in Exercise Rag Weed, five destroyed their targets. However, a more typical score was recorded by Pacific Fleet G ships over the period November 1967 to April 1968: twenty-two Terriers splashed ten drones; of the eleven Tartars fired, seven hit their mark. *Long Beach* during Exercise Eager Angler killed a drone with Talos at 85 miles. In their latest versions, Tartar, Terrier, and Talos had nominal ranges of 17, 40, and 100 miles; in clear conditions they would do better than the advertised figures. Experiments with mid-course guidance, started in 1969 for Tartar and Terrier, promised significantly longer ranges and higher rates of fire. Reliability improved. By 1970, Talos was turning in a particularly enviable record: over 180 consecutive flights without a single propulsive failure. Unfortunately its production ended that year. Talos would remain in the fleet until 1980, but it was too big to be fitted to new ships. Additionally, the cruisers that carried it were reaching the end of their useful lives.[106]

If the 3–Ts remained a viable defense against the Soviet airplane, they were inadequate against the newer Soviet cruise missiles. Closing rates against the most modern, supersonic versions might exceed Mach 6. Smaller Soviet missiles would not present a large enough radar reflection to allow the 3–Ts to engage at maximum range. Those versions of the American missiles with infrared homing might find their performance seriously degraded by heavy fog or rain. Weather or land clutter could cause problems for 3–T radar, as might Soviet jamming. The systems were vulnerable to swamping by a large-scale simultaneous attack. Especially troublesome was the sea-skimmer. Even before *Eilat*, surface officers recognized that, in the words of one expert, "the 3–T's couldn't hack it against a cruise missile after launch."[107] Consequently, the production lines shut down. The last buy of Terrier and Tartar came with FY 66; the last Talos left the Bendix Corporation plant in Mishawaka, Indiana, in 1970.[108]

Replacing all three missiles was the aptly named Standard. An evolutionary development of the Terrier and Tartar, the new weapon came in two versions: the model with medium range that used the Tartar rocket motor; the extended-range (or ER) type that used the Terrier booster and sustainer. Otherwise all elements of the two versions were interchangeable. Aside from the lower cost and simplified support facilities that this change engendered, the Standard missile contained a number of advanced features. With solid state electronics and an improved inertial guidance system, the missile offered much-improved performance against low-altitude and surface targets. It also required no warm-up either in the magazine or on the launcher. In March 1967, the Navy issued a five-year contract for the new weapon.[109]

To bring down any "leakers," the Navy concentrated in the late 1960s on two disparate point defense systems: a short-range missile and a gun system. The Navy had early in the decade considered versions of Army missiles like Redeye or Chaparral for the task. Only after the *Eilat* sinking did the matter take on urgency. Requirements for the Basic Point Defense Surface Missile System (BPDSMS) demanded a weapon that was small, simple, and cheap. The resultant Sea Sparrow system, approved for operational use in November 1967, was largely cobbled together out of existing pieces including the 3"/50 gun mount, fire control elements from the Mk 63 gun and the F–4 aircraft weapon systems, and a modified version of the Sparrow air-to-air missile produced for the Air Force. Proposed as an alternative to Tartar as early as 1955, the Sea Sparrow system featured new elements, including a simple computer, a continuous-wave illumination radar, and an eight-cell launcher.[110]

Able to detect and track targets at 20 miles, initial versions of the Sea Sparrow could intercept them within a range band of 5 miles to one-half mile and at altitudes from 3 miles down to 50 feet. The last limitation would prove a serious one. The system suffered from other drawbacks: it possessed only a slight ability to engage surface craft; sailors found that reloading the eight-cell launcher was a laborious and lengthy task. Notwithstanding these deficiencies, tests showed Sea Sparrow to be promising, and the first went to sea in 1969. In service, the weapon performed well enough that a number of friendly countries, including Italy, Denmark, Norway, and the Netherlands, also bought a modified version of it, giving rise to the name NATO Sea Sparrow.[111]

But both the minimum altitude and range limitations of the missile were tough problems. To cover the space closest to the warship, the Navy turned to guns. The 3-inch and 5-inch seemed virtually worthless for the purpose, an assessment validated by numerous exercises. Fatal drawbacks against low fliers included the three-second minimum flight time of the "bullet" before arming and the slow rate of fire of the guns. One officer

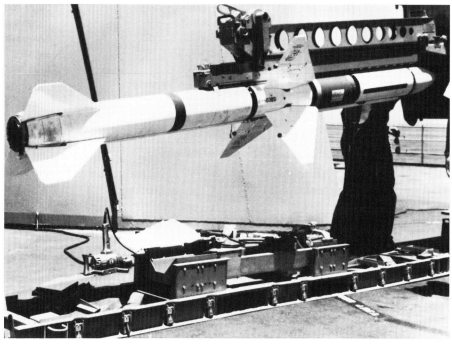

A RIM–7 NATO Sea Sparrow. The missile's fins fold to fit the compact Mk 29 launcher.

pointed out that the only possibility for using the weapons was to fire a barrage into the ocean and hope the cruise missile would fly into it. A Navy study early in 1970 admitted that the two calibers had such a low kill probability against cruise missiles that "their effects have not been modeled very carefully. . . ." [112]

Existing foreign weapons might provide the solution. The Swedish Bofors Company, whose fine 40mm piece had been a U.S. Navy mainstay in World War II, produced a 120mm gun that some officers wanted to evaluate. Another promising weapon was the Italian OTO-Melara 3"/62. This lightweight weapon fired in excess of a round per second and required a crew of only three men in comparison with the fourteen who served the old U.S. 3"/50. By 1967, the Italian, German, and Israeli navies had acquired the OTO-Melara, and the Italian concern offered to loan the U.S. Navy a sample for evaluation without charge. Initially, the Navy had turned this offer politely aside until *Eilat* caused second thoughts. The OTO-Melara gun would eventually make its way into the *Oliver Hazard Perry*-class frigates of the 1970s.[113]

178

The Navy was also considering a lightweight gun system to destroy incoming targets at the closest ranges. Under development was a high-velocity, rapid-fire machine gun which would ultimately become the Close-In Weapon System (CIWS) or the Phalanx gun. A mixed breed, the weapon traced its ancestry to an Army initiative of the 1950s. The Army's prototype achieved a remarkable rate of fire of six thousand rounds per minute by using the principle of multiple rotating barrels pioneered by Richard J. Gatling during the Civil War. Naval officers first examined the piece at Fort Bliss in 1958. With a range-only radar, the system did not seem to fit Navy needs at the time. However, the Air Force, pursuing it during the mid-1960s as a fighter gun and an air-to-ground weapon for AC–130 gunships, developed for the latter use a special flechette to penetrate enemy bunkers and armor plate. Made of depleted uranium, a metal over twice as heavy as steel, the projectile compounded its striking power by its high velocity of 4,200 feet per second which was attained through encircling the subcaliber round with a discarding sabot. Such a projectile could completely shatter an attacking missile's airframe and warhead so that the incoming weapon would be unable to continue on, damaged, into the ship's structure.[114]

In a 1964 experiment pregnant with long-term consequences, APL at White Sands Missile Range began tracking outgoing bullets with a Doppler radar. In 1967, the Bureau of Naval Weapons showed the weapon at Dahlgren to Thomas Weschler, the coordinator for the new destroyer program. By coincidence, he had seen the Army's prototype at Fort Bliss nine years earlier. *Eilat* added urgency to the project, as did the specter of submerged *Charlie*-class submarines firing their missiles at close range. By 1968, the gun had been developed to track both the outgoing bullets and the incoming missile, and then to make the requisite corrections so that the following rounds struck the missile. Its trials were quite successful, and in 1969, the Navy awarded a contract to General Dynamics, Pomona, for the refinement of CIWS.[115]

Until Sea Sparrow and CIWS came on line, the only terminal defense the Navy possessed against the antiship missiles that evaded the combat air patrol and the 3–Ts were the electronic countermeasures of jamming and deception. In the former, jammers transmitted either deceptive or high-powered signals on the incoming missile's radar frequency band. In the latter, chaff launchers or special gun projectiles created a false target by firing reflective materials to fool the missile's radar and decoy the weapon away from the ship. The Navy found that the 5-inch shell carried too small a chaff load and settled eventually on the special Zuni chaff rocket which could establish a large target quickly. An obvious challenge facing ECM personnel was that they had to become familiar with the characteristics of the enemy electronics. Also, certain missiles could be programmed to home in on infrared emissions or the jamming signals themselves. Counters for these existed too, at least in theory: ships could tow radar transponders or infrared decoys.[116]

Certain aspects of Soviet missile technology frustrated officers charged with ECM defenses against them. The early models were difficult to fool despite (or perhaps because of) their simple guidance systems. And well into the Vietnam era, key details regarding their radar settings remained clouded.[117] Despite such uncertainties, some officers thought that advanced ECM measures could provide adequate defense against antiship missiles. Following the *Eilat* sinking, a great debate lasting almost a decade flared within the Navy over the issue, dubbed by one of the participants as the "Soft-Kill vs. Hard-Kill Controversy."[118]

In the interim, ships operating off Vietnam were fitted with chaff launchers and jammers, and these were the only realistic defenses the vessels had against enemy antiship missiles. One destroyer, *Rich* (DD 820), reported in 1969 the measures it was taking to defeat a Styx attack in the Gulf of Tonkin. The ECM officer played a central part because he would most likely be the one to detect the incoming missile. With time of the essence, watch officers would activate the defense measures without seeking permission from their superiors. The destroyer operated continuously in a high state of readiness with one 5"/38 twin gun mount and a director manned. One of the projectile hoists was loaded with antiaircraft projectiles; the other, with chaff shells. During drills, *Rich* took about 13 seconds from the supposed detection of the Styx to firing the chaff. Five rounds, requiring about 15 seconds to fire and 15 seconds more for the chaff strips to "bloom," were needed to establish a destroyer-sized target. Thus, almost 45 seconds went by from initial warning to the establishment of the chaff decoy—and this in a ship in the highest state of training. Because the Styx would fly about 8 miles during that time, a ship operating closer than that distance from the North Vietnamese coast would be unable to set up an effective decoy. One analyst has noted, "*Rich's* arrangements, however well-meaning, had almost no chance of success."[119]

The whole electronics field continued to occupy a vast portion of the surface navy's attentions and resources. Exercises pointed to the inadequacy of the older AN/SPS–6 air search radar still equipping many ships. The drills also demonstrated that the current IFF was far too slow for the demands of modern warfare: a good operator might take a minute to determine whether a "blip" was friendly or otherwise. NTDS was still a relative rarity in the fleet; radar data from the Tonkin Gulf showed that the Navy's older equipment and manual tracking methods simply were not adequate for the crowded air environment of modern warfare. Tardy correlation and dissemination of data allowed even surface raiders to surprise carriers in task groups. One study concluded, "Although Navy radars have become more sophisticated, the actual process of using the radar to detect and track targets is, on most ships, similar to that employed in the 1940s."[120]

Providing a partial solution was the digital revolution which went on apace, with the accustomed benefits. For instance, when *Albany* was rebuilt over a twenty-one-month period during 1967 and 1968, her Talos fire control system was converted from analog to digital. The ship reported that her mean time between failures then multiplied more than tenfold. During the same refit when NTDS came on board, the tracking capabilities of *Albany* increased terrifically. When the cruiser left the yards in 1968, her new NTDS system allowed her to keep up with 272 targets and to share them with other NTDS-equipped ships in her vicinity. Previously, *Albany* had been able to track only 24 targets. One 1966 report ranked the NTDS ship present as "sine qua non" to the antiaircraft exercise. As more and more ships received the NTDS, its functions were expanded from the aerial sphere to the surface and submarine elements by processing data from sonars and even satellites.[121]

New and much more capable radars and fire control equipment were entering the fleet. Of special importance was the AN/SPS–48, a three-dimensional radar which first went to sea on board frigate *Worden* (DLG 18) in 1965. "A super piece of gear," recalled the commanding officer of *Albany* of

K–119189

Secretary of the Navy W. Graham Claytor watches as cruiser *Albany* (CG 10) fires a Talos, September 1977.

the new radar.[122] In tandem with the AN/SPG–55 fire control system, this equipment offered much enhanced capability against "very fast, very low, very high, or very small targets." [123] By the end of the decade, APL was developing an automatic detection and tracking system for the AN/SPS–48. Designed to go on board those Terrier and Tartar ships that could not be fitted with a radically new radar, the AN/SYS–1 was tested at sea by *Somers* in 1973. The AN/SYS–1 met with much skepticism, but ultimately proved successful beyond all expectation.[124]

Of course the revolutionary system was Aegis. It also made significant strides during this period, in large part because the antiship missile threat demanded a quantum jump in capability. Called initially the Advanced Surface Missile System, the Navy tapped the expertise of industry and APL to develop it. In 1967, APL initiated work on a promising multifunction fixed-array radar. Capable of tracking both air and sea targets, the new radar was specifically designed to counter low fliers. To form the fully automatic Aegis system, the radar with its steerable beams would be combined with digital computers, the new Standard missile, and a fast-response launcher. Plans called for a reaction time from detection of the antiship missile to the launching of the Standard of no more than 15 seconds. In 1969, the Navy let a multiyear contract with RCA for the new system, now named Aegis after the shield of Zeus. The Navy hoped to have Aegis at sea by the middle of the next decade.[125]

The electronics systems being added in the late 1960s made increasing demands on ship layout. Destroyers by this point were carrying 250 tons of electronics, much of it high in the ship. Power demands were prodigious: 2,000 kilowatts for electronics alone in destroyers. Cruiser *Albany* recommissioned with four 750-kilowatt generators, yet her commanding officer stated, "If the ship had an Achilles heel it was the electrical generating capacity." With the missile systems and radars, the ship steamed routinely with three of the generators on line. General Quarters required all four. So, "if one went down, we were operating on the ragged edge. Fortunately this did not happen often." [126]

Better defenses against cruise missiles were essential, but naval officers preferred, of course, to hit the enemy launching platforms before they could shoot. Increasing American involvement in the Vietnam conflict deepened Navy concern over its lack of a dependable antiship missile. As more of the Navy's dollars went to operations, the size of the fleet shrank, a trend that was distressingly obvious by the late 1960s. With virtually all of the Navy's firepower tied up in the carriers and with the number of carriers on active duty decreasing, each carrier became increasingly valuable. Shore-based antiship missiles forced the carriers farther out to sea, thereby reducing their effectiveness in the power projection role. Analysts feared that Soviet vessels and aircraft, with their large antiship missiles, might well be able to inflict unacceptable losses on American carriers by concentrating on those few high-value units. In fleet exercises, some American submarine commanders, simulating the Soviets, went by the simple expedient "If it doesn't ping, shoot it." [127] Carriers did not "ping" and were therefore the valuable targets. In the initial stages of an exercise, the cruisers and destroyers of a carrier task force could be safely ignored as long-range offensive threats. To alter this equation, the Navy in 1968 began an accelerated program to endow all the Navy's surface combatants with offensive capabilities by developing antiship missiles capable of negating the three principal Soviet threats: the fast missile boats, the larger cruisers, and the missile-firing submarines. [128]

The CNO in 1967, Admiral Moorer, was an aviator. In the 1950s, he had worked with the winged torpedo Petrel and thus had experienced the hurdles associated with antiship missiles. Less than a week after the *Eilat* sinking, Moorer directed that increased efforts be made to devise an effective antiship weapon. The CNO felt that a future major naval war would be global with widely dispersed encounters. As the Soviets improved their antiaircraft capabilities, American carrier pilots could expect to take heavier casualties. Moorer wanted a weapon that could be fired from the maximum number of platforms. But the United States had paid little heed to this area for a decade, and even though a new missile, Harpoon, was on the drawing board, it would take years to bring it to fruition. In the meantime, with the need so pressing, Moorer asked for an interim solution, one that included consideration of buying from "more or less" friendly navies. [129] Specifically charged with the job of finding a stop-gap solution was the Division of Systems Analysis headed by Rear Admiral Zumwalt after an abbreviated tour commanding a cruiser-destroyer flotilla off Vietnam. His evaluators looked closely at the Ryan Firebee, a reconnaissance drone frequently used in Vietnam. At the instigation of NAVORD, an antiship version called the Fireflash was tested in the summer of 1968. The missile showed certain positive attributes: it was reliable, having made over seven thousand flights by 1968; it could fly at altitudes from 50 to 50,000 feet, at speeds up to Mach .95, and to a maximum range of 180 miles. To heighten its destructive effects, it could carry two bombs under its wings. Offsetting these advantages, Fireflash was so large that most destroyers could carry only two (generally in the DASH hangar). Worse, readying the missile was a clumsy process requiring up to 45 minutes. Nonetheless, it was an index of the Navy's desperation to get an antiship missile to sea that Fireflash was the subject of experiments and controversy for three years until the Navy canceled it in 1971. [130]

Far superior would be a smaller missile designed specifically for the antiship mission. In the interests of a speedy remedy, the Navy took a close look at several foreign designs: the Israeli Gabriel, the Italian Otomat, and the French Exocet. The Gabriel had enjoyed extensive development. The Israelis had started work on it in the late 1950s, but from the American standpoint, the missile suffered a number of crippling defects. Despite its small size, the Gabriel required a large crew of from ten to fifteen to operate. Worse, it possessed a range of barely 12 miles and relied partially on optical guidance. It was thus undependable in bad weather.[131]

The other two foreign missiles were better. Both possessed certain important assets, especially longer range. Two top Navy experts, Captain Claude Ekas and Rear Admiral Frank Price, thought highly of the Otomat, but it would not fit in U.S. Navy launchers. The Exocet was another top choice. In its container it required no maintenance for a year at the end of which time it could be off-loaded and checked out by a shore establishment. One missile technician could operate the whole Exocet system—the missile, container, and control console—and fire all four missiles virtually simultaneously. In the air, the Exocet missile was "especially sinister" in its ability to fly at an extremely low altitude of no more than 19 feet above the water. One Navy assessor who examined all the missiles available at the time concluded of Exocet, "In surface engagements, this weapon is the best available."[132] Unfortunately, it would not fit the standard American missile launcher either. At almost $200,000 per missile, it was expensive. Moreover, it was French. Bias in Congress weighed especially heavily during the early 1970s against going abroad for military hardware.[133]

Zumwalt's team turned instead to Standard for an interim solution and found this antiaircraft missile amenable to the new mission. By the early 1970s, an antiship version was in production (for details, see Chapter 6). Nonetheless, Standard was a makeshift solution. It lacked the range and killing power that the surface navy wanted.[134]

Under development was a missile with twice the reach and more than double the warhead size—Harpoon. The origins of this weapon antedate the *Eilat* sinking and are befogged by controversy, perhaps because, as one observer noted, "Success has a thousand fathers."[135] One view contends that Harpoon, a weapon which gave back to the surface community its offensive punch, was, in a neat irony, originated by Naval Air Systems Command (NAVAIR).

Admiral Moorer remembers pushing for an antiship missile when he was CINCPAC in 1965, mainly to enable his patrol planes to strike at Soviet surface ships. Other analysts point out that the Soviets, in their anticarrier strategy, were obviously banking heavily on shooting the big SS–N–3 Shaddock from their *Whiskey Long-Bin*s, *Juliett*s, and *Echo*s. However, in order to fire their missiles, all three classes of submarines had to surface and then remain there for up to 25 minutes to guide the Shaddocks on the initial stages of their flight. As a counter, American aviators wanted a weapon that could catch the submarines on the surface, preferably before they had fired their missiles, but certainly before the submarines fed in the mid-course corrections from the coordinating Bear D aircraft. "Harpoon" was a particularly appropriate name then for a missile that would spear the surfaced whale. NAVAIR began development of the Harpoon as early as 1965. So did a potential contractor, McDonnell Douglas, which privately financed studies on the desirability of such a weapon.[136]

Simultaneously, surface sailors were pursuing independently an antiship weapon to be fired from their vessels. A key figure was Rear Admiral Zumwalt. Long concerned about the "emasculation" of surface warships, Zumwalt struck an alliance with Captain Worth Bagley, the executive assistant to Secretary of the Navy Nitze. Nitze, at Bagley's urgings, wrote a directive to OPNAV ordering a concept formulation study for an antiship missile. Shortly thereafter, Moorer became CNO and handed the task to Zumwalt with an informal warning that the missile's range be kept to 50 miles, or it would not get funding. Zumwalt attributed this requirement to the "bias against giving the surface Navy an independent capability for fear that that would impact on the future of the aircraft carrier."[137] Publicly then, Harpoon was credited with a range of 50 miles although the missile in its original design could fly 20 miles farther. No matter; Zumwalt remarked that at last the Regulus cancellation had been rescinded.[138]

The *Eilat* sinking put the Harpoon program into high gear. NAVORD and APL rushed forward a study for a ship-launched missile; NAVAIR and China Lake sketched an air-launched weapon. Given the downward trend in defense spending, the DCNO (Development) suggested in the spring of 1968 that the basic missile be developed for both air and ship launch. The initial requirement for the Harpoon then specified an air-dropped version for a variety of aircraft including the P–3, S–3, A–6, and A–7, as well as a boosted version for several ship classes. NAVAIR became the lead agency, with NAVORD the deputy. The Harpoon program office was set up in 1969, with Claude Ekas as the director. Ekas set a tone of cooperation between the government and chief contractor, McDonnell Douglas, by demanding a minimum of detailed oversight of the company.[139]

The surface navy sorely needed a versatile missile to even the odds against the Soviet navy which by 1970 was a modern force with only one percent of its vessels dating back more than two decades. In sharp contrast, the U.S. Navy was getting long in the tooth with 58 percent of its ships older than twenty years. During Admiral Moorer's tenure as CNO (1967–1970), the total size of the Navy dropped from over 900 warships to 760. With the Nixon cutbacks in Navy allocations for 1969, nineteen CRUDESLANT ships alone joined the mothball fleet. Frigate *Wilkinson*, having just completed a nine-month overhaul in June 1969, was ordered the next month into retirement. A mark of the times was the demotion of

USN 1178473

Nuclear cruiser *California* (DLGN 36) returns from an Indian Ocean deployment with carrier *Nimitz* (CVN 68), 26 May 1980.

the Navy's first missile ships, *Boston* and *Canberra*, from CAG to CA when they did not receive scheduled refits.[140]

A few new ships were entering the fleet, the most notable being the nine frigates of the *Belknap* class and their nuclear cousin *Truxtun*. With their ASROC and SQS–26, they were potentially fine antisubmarine ships. Because NTDS, standard equipment in all but the first two, was coupled with Terrier and SPG–55 and SPS–48 radars, they possessed first-class antiaircraft capabilities, as *Wainwright* (DLG 28) demonstrated on her trials in 1966. The ships also made up partially for the deficiencies of the "double-enders" by mounting a 5"/54 Mk 42. Able to maintain 28 knots in rough waters, their seaworthiness was "magnificent," although their length, narrow beam, and single rudder made them slow to pivot in certain wind conditions. Their habitability was significantly improved over their predecessors.[141]

The new frigates could expect few reinforcements in the near future. A large-scale plan to upgrade many of the Navy's ships from the 1950s fell to the budget ax. McNamara told CNO Moorer to buy to replace attrition; thus funds were available for new helicopters but not ships. For 1969, the money allotted to ship construction dropped below $1 billion for the first time in over a decade; inflation, just beginning, would significantly erode the purchasing power of that sum.[142]

At the urging of Admiral Rickover, Congress aggravated the situation by putting its few eggs into fewer baskets. In June 1968 the legislature, despite administration objections, insisted on ordering two nuclear frigates, *California* and *South Carolina* (DLGN 37). Unquestionably capable ships, these 10,000-ton vessels were armed with two Tartar/Standard missile launchers and two of the new 5-inch Mk 45 gun mounts. The missile launchers located at either end far from the superstructure enjoyed excellent arcs of fire. The digital electronics suite was the most modern available with the SPS–48A three-dimensional radar and a missile guidance system capable of controlling four missiles simultaneously. For ASW work, the ships carried the SQS–26 and a quick-reload ASROC launcher. They could steam twenty-five times around the world without refueling; the reliability of their power plant was beyond reproach.[143]

*California*, completed in 1974, represented the United States at the Jubilee Spithead review two years later in Britain where she made a great impression with her size and graceful lines. Some observers commented on the seeming skimpiness of her armament, but before Aegis, she was the most capable antiair ship in the fleet. One of the commanding officers of the "Golden Grizzly" recalled,

> Our normal mode of operation would be to put the carrier in EMCON, have aircraft from the carrier fly low on a vector toward us where they would pop up as though we had launched them. With the electronic wizards making our emissions look like those of the carrier, we would act as a missile trap against the threat, using the aircraft under our control to shoot the archer before he could let fly his air to surface arrows.[144]

Unhappily, the *California*s cost so much—$200 million each—that a third unit authorized in 1968 was canceled. Zumwalt bitterly noted in 1976, "Those pets of Rickover's, the enormously expensive nuclear-propelled guided-missile frigates (DLGNs) remained almost purely defensive ships without cruise missiles." [145] At the time they were ordered, Zumwalt, as head of Systems Analysis, put together a paper entitled the "Major Fleet Escort Study" calling for building large numbers of ships, particularly with antisubmarine (DE/DX) and antiaircraft (DXG) capabilities but also with the qualities necessary to gain sea control against enemy surface warships. Included in the study were plans for continued nuclear frigate (DXGN) construction as well.[146]

Zumwalt's project would ultimately result in four ships of the *Kidd* class (the DXG) and thirty-one ships of the *Spruance* class (the DX), the latter being the largest single class of destroyers constructed in the West after World War II. The escort ship (the DE) would metamorphose into the patrol escort (PF) and ultimately the *Oliver Hazard Perry*-class guided missile frigate (FFG). The first ship ordered was destroyer *Spruance* (DD 963) in FY 70. It was long overdue. Except for the two *California*s, Congress had not authorized a single new frigate or destroyer since FY 62.[147]

The DX mission statement dictated that the ship be able to operate in the face of air, surface, and subsurface threats as an escort to carrier task groups, amphibious forces, or convoys; the destroyer's design would stress antisubmarine features. The DXG was tasked with similar missions; in addition, it would be able to operate independently in an area of air threat. Consequently, the DXG design emphasized antiaircraft weaponry. The Navy regarded the DX/DXG as so important that the program coordinator was ordered to report directly to the CNO and the Secretary of the Navy, as had the manager of the Polaris program a decade earlier.[148]

Tapped for this hot seat early in 1967 was Rear Admiral Raymond Peet, the former commander of *Bainbridge* and a man who, with his large reputation in the destroyer force, would give credibility to the project. However, Peet quarreled with Secretary Nitze, in part over the nuclear power issue. When Thomas Weschler took over from Peet he found himself the beneficiary of some powerful patronage: both the CNO, David McDonald, and Secretary Nitze were personally interested in the project. Weschler also found significant foes in Secretary of Defense McNamara and Admiral Rickover. McNamara wanted a cheap ship with one screw, a single gun, and only an ASW capability. In Weschler's words, "They were seeing a DE 1052 class [the *Knox* class]—smaller than that . . . cheaper than that." [149] Weschler intended to build a much more potent ship for the surface navy. In the intense bureaucratic wrangling attendant on these negotiations, Weschler found himself every two weeks in the CNO's conference room briefing a host of staffers and frequently top policymakers such as the CNO and the Secretary of the Navy. Rickover, guarding his bailiwick, reluctantly gave his support for a new destroyer without nuclear propulsion in exchange for the promise that his reactors would power any major combatant over 8,000 tons (the so-called Korth agreement).[150]

The DX/DXG design pushed that 8,000-ton limit, in part to buy high speed in bad weather. When the lead ship commissioned in 1975, she displaced 8,040 tons at full load, the largest vessel ever listed as a destroyer by any navy. The *Spruance* class boasted a host of innovations. First priority went to antisubmarine characteristics, and in this area the ships shone from the outset with a new sonar (SQS–53) and extensive quieting. In pursuit of the latter, the ships featured special mounts under the engines and reduction gears, plus low-speed propellers. Weschler reserved space and weight in the plans for a passive sonar suit with a towed array which was then only in the experimental stages. Similarly, the layout allowed, as early as 1968, for more computer installations to marry inputs from the ac-

Rear Admiral Thomas R. Weschler as Commander U.S. Naval Support Activity, Danang, South Vietnam, 25 February 1966.

NH 74469

tive and passive sonars and from helicopter sensors. Antisubmarine armament included ASROC with reloads and short-range torpedo tubes.[151]

Impressive as ASW ships, the early *Spruance*-class destroyers were outfitted with little in the way antiaircraft defenses. Impressed with the Close-In Weapons System, Weschler did make provisions for it in the ship's designs. He also saved space for Mk 26 antiaircraft launchers, fore and aft. Although CIWS was still ten years away and the Mk 26 launchers were never fitted, the reserved space in the plans was more than adequate for the vertical launch missile containers fitted in the mid-1980s.[152]

The DXG with its "conversion suit" provided the antiaircraft firepower that the basic DX design lacked. Essentially, the DXG married the *Spruance* hull with the most modern antiaircraft system. Although never ordered as such by the U.S. Navy because of cost, four were built for the Shah of Iran. Almost complete at the time of his fall, they entered American service as the *Kidd* class. Conversion to U.S. standards went smoothly: the helicopter hangar was enlarged and the living spaces revamped, although the ships operated for their first year with Iranian computer programs. Frequently called the *Ayatollah* class, the *Kidd*s proved to be a marked success in U.S. hands.[153]

Additionally, the architects of the *Spruance* made provision for upgrading the gun armament. As built, the ships carried two of the new 5-inch Mk 45 gun mounts. Good as that weapon promised to be, Weschler was in-

*Spruance* (DD 963) preparing for builder's trials at Ingalls Ship-building Division, Pascagoula, Missis-sippi, c. January 1975. the large dome at the foot of her bow en-closes the new SQS–53 sonar; the gun is the 5″/54 Mk 45.

NH 93230

trigued in 1967 with the 8-inch lightweight gun that Dahlgren was developing. In consequence, the ship was laid out so that there were no solid girders or strength members in the way of the larger weapon if it were adopted. Also, Weschler's team provided from the beginning the extra electrical power that the bigger gun would require.[154]

Weschler further believed the ships might need longer-range striking power. He heeded a footnote in Zumwalt's Major Fleet Escort Study that warned of Soviet advances in missilery so rapid that the U.S. Navy should make preparations to convert its ASW ships to missile shooters by the 1980s, if the need arose. From the beginning of the project then, Weschler intended that the *Spruances* would carry the Harpoon when it became available, either in an ASROC launcher or in separate canisters.[155]

The *Spruance* design team also made provision for a sizable helicopter. With DASH a failure, the DX-DXG office lobbied for a multipurpose aircraft—one that could prosecute submarine contacts as well as carry out search and rescue missions. Weschler envisioned an aircraft with an additional capability for over-the-horizon attack against surface ships, especially *Komar*s and *Osa*s. The Weschler team called the concept the Light Airborne Multi-Purpose System (LAMPS), a name reflecting its versatility. Weschler had been impressed with a number of NATO helicopters, especially the British Wasp and Wessex in their *County*-class cruisers. Weschler remarked later, "We could have gotten [the capability] if we had been willing to accept any of their birds, but the not-invented-here syndrome and not-built-in-the-United States syndrome were strong, and we never were able to take any of the overseas equipment." [156]

Consequently, the LAMPS I system that emerged in the early 1970s was based on the light Seasprite utility helicopter, the SH–2. Introduced to the fleet by *Belknap* (DLG 26) in 1971, the LAMPS I demonstrated good performance in spotting for shore bombardment missions in Vietnam, although the little SH–2 suffered from the limitations inherent in its size. Fortunately, the *Spruance*-class was planned from the outset to take a larger helicopter, and in the end, the ships operated the more capable SH–3 and the SH–60 (LAMPS III). [157]

The *Spruance* destroyers offered other distinctions. They would be the first major U.S. Navy ships powered by gas turbines, essentially marinized versions of jet aircraft engines. The Navy had considered the new engineering plant as early as 1938, but had not adopted it, partly because of the opposition of Admiral Rickover and, conversely, the proponents of steam plants. For the *Spruance*s, Weschler examined over fifty experimental versions of the three basic propulsion systems: diesel, steam, and gas. The gas turbine offered significant advantages including reduced maintenance and personnel requirements, quiet operation, instant response, and great power. It was only one-tenth the weight of its two principal competitors, but it was thirsty and demanded a high-quality fuel, called Navy Distillate Fuel, free from particulate and water contaminants. To get the gas turbine, Weschler had to argue its case before the House Armed Services Subcommittee. [158]

Adding to the responsiveness of the ships were their variable-pitch propellers. Hardly new (screw frigate *Merrimack* had carried the first in 1856), the propeller in the *Spruance*s increased fuel economy, improved maneuverability, and—essential for the gas turbine plant—enabled the ship to back down without changing the direction of shaft rotation. Prototypes were tested in *Patterson* (DE 1061) and *Barbey* (DE 1088). [159]

Special consideration went into providing the ships with a lower infrared signature and features, such as water wash-down, for operations in a radioactive environment. New was the pollution control equipment. Habitability also received significant attention, largely as a result of the influence of Admiral Charles K. Duncan, Chief of the Bureau of Personnel. Naturally, some officers felt the sailors were being coddled.[160]

As the *Spruances'* characteristics became known in the Navy, the design was attacked on a variety of other fronts. Some destroyer traditionalists objected on aesthetic grounds to the gas turbines and the propeller shafts that "rotated the wrong direction."[161] More substantive was the criticism that the *Spruances* violated the destroyer tradition of "jack-of-all-trades." The new class seemed far too narrowly focused on the antisubmarine mission. One analyst wondered if such an expensive ship with such a "tender" bow sonar would ever be used for fire support close inshore.[162]

The most fiercely adverse comments from both officers and enlisted men centered on the ship's armament. For an 8,000-ton ship, the *Spruances* looked to be woefully underarmed, especially in comparison with their Soviet counterparts which fairly bristled with weapons. One officer later remarked, "When they [the *Spruances*] first hit the water, you had to walk a mile in those ships before you ever stumbled over a weapon."[163] Some analysts attributed the paucity of offensive power to a design philosophy that left attack firepower to carrier aviation.[164]

Weschler admitted that this criticism seemed warranted on its face. At the same time, he saw a certain irony in the whole situation. When the design process had started, the Secretary of Defense wanted a one-gun escort of the *Knox* type. Instead, the surface navy was going to take delivery of a two-gun destroyer with real room for growth when the weapons and funds were available. As Weschler later remarked, "Those who said, 'She's naked,' didn't know how naked she was supposed to be. And to us, she looked like she was really set for the ball."[165] Without doubt, the *Spruances* sported handsome lines with a blocky, purposeful superstructure and a sharp clipper bow.

Virtually everything about the ship was new, including her design and contracting processes. For the first time, the Navy went to an outside firm for the entire program, both development and production. This concept derived from the McNamara revolution with his Total Package Procurement plan. The Defense Department would accept only binding bids for the whole class. Winning it was Litton/Ingalls, a newcomer to the field of warship construction. The contract, awarded in June 1970, specified that Litton took total responsibility for the design and production of the entire run of thirty ships (an additional unit was ordered later), to include the combat systems, with their electronics and computer programs. The shipbuilder would even provide logistic support for and share in the training of the officers and enlisted men assigned to the destroyers. The crew would join the ship only shortly before its commissioning and take virtually no part in builders or acceptance trials.[166]

Many "old hands" in the procurement process doubted the feasibility of McNamara's Total Package Procurement approach, modeled on the acquisition of military aircraft. Once the ship design was hammered out, it would supposedly be frozen. Construction would proceed with no change orders to disturb the orderly building of the entire class. Navy doubters pointed out that ships were much more complex than aircraft and that during the protracted construction period change orders were inevitable. Some top officers in the new Naval Ships Systems Command reportedly felt so sure that McNamara's system was doomed to failure that they resigned in protest. Nonetheless, the Total Package Procurement approach was first tried with amphibious craft and then extended to the *Spruance* class.[167]

Before building any ships, Litton had to build a shipyard, which it did at Pascagoula, Mississippi. A computerized facility, the yard constructed the ships as modules with the hulls built in three sections instead of one. The electronics equipment went on board on pallets, a time-saving construction method adopted extensively for later classes. Clauses in the Litton contract allowed for bonuses if the ships exceeded Navy specifications in certain areas. For example, because Litton went significantly beyond the minimum in quieting the destroyers, the firm received a bonus of $1 million per ship. A land-based test facility ironed out about 65 percent of the potential problems before the ships actually entered service. Although the Navy hoped to take delivery of the lead ship in July 1974, *Spruance* did not hoist her commissioning pennant until September 1975.[168]

Trials revealed troubles, some perhaps inevitable given the radical nature of the design and construction process. But many officers blamed the worst of the problems on McNamara's ill-conceived Total Package Procurement scheme. Certain unproved items, such as auxiliary boilers and generators, broke down so frequently that they were replaced. The LM 2500 gas turbines balked at full-power trials. Metal fatigue afflicted the bolts holding the propeller blades onto the hub. The contractor, beset by inflationary woes, was notably uncooperative. The Navy accepted ships with major waivers, and "Post Shakedown Availabilities became almost a second construction period to correct many of the discrepancies."[169] But these problems were eventually overcome. In 1975, *Spruance* during her trials set records on the AUTEC range for her ASW weaponry.[170]

By that year, her class was one of the keys to rejuvenating the surface navy. The later 1960s had seen a sharp decline in the size of this force in the face of a rapid Soviet buildup, and budget cutters had failed to replace most of the vessels worn out by arduous duty in Southeast Asia. Yet the period had also contained the seeds for a turnaround. In critical areas of ordnance, blackshoes had made important advances in such key weapons systems as CIWS, Sea Sparrow, Standard, Harpoon, and Aegis. Unfortunately, the deployment of most of these systems was years away. In the interim, the Navy would confront grave threats from an antimilitary mood at home and an aggressive and competent enemy on the high seas. In the summer of 1970, a surface warrior took the helm to shepherd the Navy through the trough.

# 6

# The Zumwalt Years and Their Immediate Aftermath: Troubles and Triumphs, 1970–1975

On 1 July 1970, Elmo R. Zumwalt, Jr., was sworn in as Chief of Naval Operations. The first surface line officer to head the Navy since Arleigh Burke had retired nine years earlier, Zumwalt faced challenges of the most difficult sort. Arguably, Zumwalt's tenure brought to the Navy changes as significant as those imparted by his illustrious predecessor. In addition, Zumwalt made a greater and more beneficial impact on the surface navy community.

Like Burke, Zumwalt was something of a surprise selection. Plucked from far down the list of flag officers, he was at forty-nine the youngest man ever to hold the Navy's top job. His three predecessors in the post had been aviators, and Admiral Moorer who was heading upstairs in 1970 to chair the Joint Chiefs of Staff recommended to Secretary of Defense Melvin Laird that the next CNO come from the same branch. Despite this counsel, Laird and Secretary of the Navy John H. Chafee selected Zumwalt for his innovative thinking and his background in surface warfare.[1]

A 1942 graduate of the Naval Academy, Zumwalt had been decorated with the Bronze Star for heroic service on *Robinson* (DD 562) during that destroyer's attack on Japanese warships at Surigao Strait in October 1944. He also saw combat in Korea as navigator of battleship *Wisconsin*. Destroyer commands followed; in 1959, Zumwalt commissioned the first ship built for the purpose as a guided missile ship, frigate *Dewey*. In 1964, he became the youngest officer ever promoted to the rank of rear admiral. Two years later he organized the Systems Analysis Division, and in 1968 went back to his third war, this time as Commander U.S. Naval Forces, Vietnam.[2]

If Laird and Chafee wanted a CNO who would shake up the organization, they had selected the right man. Zumwalt felt that the Navy was facing a crisis. The Nixon administration publicly enunciated a policy of being able to fight a major and a minor war simultaneously (the "1½ wars" concept). But the Vietnam War was damaging the military in the eyes of the country as a whole; the conflict's voracious demands on the naval budget had hamstrung the building programs. The great majority of the Navy's warships were coming to the end of their useful lives while the Soviets

CNO Admiral Elmo R. Zumwalt, Jr., at the commissioning ceremony for *Brewton* (DE 1086), 8 July 1972.

K–94847

were accelerating their construction. Shockingly, Zumwalt was convinced that his service had reached the point where it could no longer guarantee victory in a major war.

Major initiatives were mandatory, but Zumwalt felt that the Navy's planning processes were so cumbersome that he had to sidestep the bureaucratic maze. He set up a special team that was to submit its recommendations in two months, hence "Project Sixty." His initial choice for a principal assistant was Rear Admiral Bagley, picked in Zumwalt's words "for his brains, but it was no accident that I picked a brainy destroyerman rather than a brainy aviator or a brainy submariner." [3] But Bagley was stuck in his current job until late August, and Zumwalt turned to another surface officer with a reputation for his broad outlook and innovative thinking: Captain Stansfield Turner. Zumwalt asked Turner to look afresh at the Navy's raison d'être and to develop a conceptual framework for a modernized force structure. Zumwalt intended to sell Project Sixty to Chafee and Laird on 10 September. Turner later described his labors on Project Sixty as the "most frantic" period of his entire career. [4]

Turner's presentation to these top policymakers specified four principal roles performed by the Navy essential to national security: strategic deterrence, sea control, peacetime presence, and projection of power ashore. Although none of these missions was new, Turner's formulation was unusually

196

The controversial Z-grams.

clear and persuasive in helping Zumwalt convince Chafee and Laird to buy most of his revisions in force structure and procurement. Zumwalt also had to stimulate the Navy bureaucracy to act. To this end, he frequently went outside the chain of command with his famous directives called "Z-grams." Controversial in the extreme, especially those dealing with personnel issues, the Z-grams nonetheless imparted a sense of urgency to the whole Navy.[5]

In allocating scarce resources to fulfill the missions articulated by Turner, Zumwalt stressed sea control, without which power projection would be impossible to achieve. But this emphasis forced Zumwalt to make difficult choices in dealing with the three "unions." He quickly found himself locked in a bitter contest with an old rival, Hyman Rickover. Earlier in his career, Zumwalt had weathered one of Rickover's infamous interviews and had then rejected command of a nuclear warship, largely because he loathed Rickover's style. Zumwalt discovered in 1970 that he had to bargain with his ostensible subordinate as an equal. The new CNO offered Rickover five attack submarines annually for the next three years in return for a reduction to three beginning in 1974. Zumwalt would then spend the difference on innovative surface warships whose designs he hoped to ready in the interim. According to Zumwalt, Rickover accepted this deal only to renege on it later. Rickover disputed the charge through one of his deputies who claimed that no deal had ever been struck. The bitterness

197

USN 1143716

Frigate *Coontz* (DLG 9) trails a Soviet *Kresta*-class guided missile cruiser in the Sea of Japan, April 1970, during the worldwide Soviet naval exercise Okean. Note the frigate's blocky ASROC launcher.

that Zumwalt harbored toward Rickover surfaced in the remarkably candid memoirs *On Watch* published soon after the CNO's retirement while Rickover still held sway over his nuclear empire. Zumwalt wrote: "A final malady that afflicted—and continues to afflict—the whole Navy, though the surface Navy was and is the greatest sufferer, can be described in one word . . . : Rickover."[6]

Zumwalt also struggled with the aviation community over its share of the budgetary pie and over the nature of its weaponry. The CNO saw the health of naval aviation as critical to America's command of the sea, and he managed to wring from Congress authorization for supercarrier *Carl Vinson* (CVAN 69). Zumwalt also pushed hard for the F–14 fighter with its Phoenix missiles—a combination intended to strike at Soviet long-range bombers carrying antiship missiles. Nonetheless, many brownshoes saw Zumwalt as hostile to their union. One top aviator remembered:

> When Zumwalt came in, it was obvious he'd been sitting there suffering . . . and he's a fighter, a damn effective one. He'd been watching the surface community take the short end of the stick, and aviation getting everything for a long period of time. It was very obvious he was going to fix the surface warfare community, and he was going to make naval aviation pay for it.[7]

Zumwalt did slice the number of carriers drastically by laying up all the specialized antisubmarine carriers. These ships were aged veterans of the *Essex* class nearing the end of the line. Zumwalt sent them into mothballs and ordered the "big bird farms," the supercarriers, to take on the antisubmarine mission by flying squadrons of ASW aircraft.[8]

This decision, unpopular with aviators, was reinforced by Zumwalt's proposal to build a small carrier that he labeled the Sea Control Ship (SCS). Zumwalt worried that the Soviets would cripple the big carriers by a surprise attack with their antiship missiles. During times of tension, he intended to deploy the much smaller Sea Control Ship in forward areas while holding the large carriers back in the broad oceans. Once a shooting war began and the danger of a Soviet first strike had passed, the positions of the two types of ships would be reversed. Although some officers wondered about the practicality of this strategy, Zumwalt's unusual choice of nomenclature—the Sea Control Ship—reflected his conviction that the Navy had paid far too much attention since World War II to power projection ashore and far too little to maintenance of its sea control capabilities. This imbalance he intended to redress with many of the other innovations proposed in Project Sixty.[9]

Zumwalt would be rowing against a fast-rising Soviet tide. The Soviets, according to an estimate made later in the decade, outspent the United States by 50 percent in naval missiles. U.S. Navy analysts anticipated that the Soviets intended in their massive surprise attack to overwhelm the American protective shield. As this disintegrated, the missiles arriving later would find the defenses shattered and inflict lethal damage.[10]

Characteristically, the Soviets continued sending to sea purposeful new warships with advanced missiles. The *Nanuchka*, which ONI dubbed a "missile gunboat" or PGG, represented a step up in capability from the *Osa*s and *Komar*s in that the 770-ton type could operate in the Barents or Mediterranean Seas. American analysts credited a new frigate, the *Krivak*, with an improved type of antiship missile in a massive quadruple launcher. The new cruisers of the *Kresta II* and the *Kara* types seemed designed for antiship operations. A modified version of the *Kashin*-class destroyer with aft-firing missiles began trailing American carriers, often at very close range. By 1975, Admiral Gorshkov, the commander of the Soviet navy, was spending more of his navy's resources on major surface vessels than on ballistic missile submarines. In their Okean exercises in 1970 and 1975, the Soviets aimed at global coordination of strikes in several oceans within a 90-second response time. These advanced antiship weapons led some American strategists in 1972 to fear that the Soviets might directly challenge any American attempt to blockade Haiphong.[11]

In fact, the Soviet antiship capability was overestimated by U.S. naval intelligence which misidentified the missile carried by eighteen major new

Russian warships. Analysts evaluated the new type, which they dubbed the SS–N–10, as an antiship missile. In actuality, the weapon carried by cruisers of the *Kresta II* and *Kara* classes and by frigates of the *Krivak* type was an antisubmarine device. One U.S. officer has noted: "We in the intelligence community at the time knew that the Soviets classified *Kynda* and *Kresta* as 'rocket cruisers' and *Kresta II* as 'Large ASW Ships,' but we simply did not believe them." [12] By 1975, most Western analysts concluded that the lack of supporting guidance radars strongly suggested that the SS–N–10 was not an antiship weapon. In early 1976 American naval authorities publicly announced their new findings and redesignated the missile as the SS–N–14. The upshot of the matter was that the threat from Soviet surface warships, serious as it was in reality, was overstated during the Zumwalt years. [13]

Top U.S. officers also worried that antiship missiles launched from shore or by coastal craft might deny the United States the use of a major trump card—its superior amphibious forces. As these missiles proliferated among Third World countries, American surface warships without the backing of carrier aviation found themselves pushed out of coastal waters by Soviet client states. For example, when Cuba seized a Panamanian freighter in 1972, President Nixon responded by ordering American destroyers from Guantanamo to protect Panamanian vessels. Admiral Weschler, COM-CRUDESLANT at that time, felt that the United States "was setting itself up to have a terrible black eye" because none of his ships could fight an *Osa or Komar* successfully. [14] Prudence dictated that Weschler ask for fighters at Guantanamo to be kept on strip alert ready for immediate takeoff to back up his destroyers. Weschler later recalled, "It drove home to me how defenseless we were against the *Osas* and *Komars* unless we had air cover." [15]

Meanwhile, antiship missiles with other navies were showing just how effective this weapon could be when used properly. In the Indo-Pakistani War of 1971, three Indian *Osas* sank one Pakistani destroyer and disabled a second by a salvo of nine Styx. Then, in the first actions ever fought solely with antiship missiles, the Israeli navy in 1973 obtained revenge for the *Eilat*. In four engagements against Egyptian and Syrian *Osas* and *Komars*, Israeli missile boats shooting Gabriel missiles sank nine vessels without loss to themselves. The Israeli achievement was all the more impressive in light of the range advantage of the Styx over the Gabriel. The Israelis decoyed most of the Styx with ECM (supposedly as many as fifty-five in one battle). Other accounts ascribed the Arab impotence to the failure of the Styx crews to run up their missiles' gyros in advance, or to the "fast maneuvering" of the Israeli boats. [16]

There was no denying the capability of the antiship missile when used by competent crews. Were the Soviets competent? American sailors found ample opportunities to form their own conclusions as the Soviet flag went farther to sea and stayed for longer periods. When the Royal Navy withdrew from east of Suez in 1971, the Soviets made Berbera, Somalia, a regular port of call. In early 1972, a Soviet cruiser armed with antiship missiles began trailing an American task group south of Sri Lanka until the American forces were ordered out of the Indian Ocean. During the period, Soviet units operated regularly off the west coast of Africa.[17]

In the Mediterranean, carriers of the Sixth Fleet were accompanied at very short ranges and around the clock by "tattletails" armed with cruise missiles. Zumwalt felt that two could play the same game and dispatched for the mission two *Asheville*-class gunboats "small enough to be expendable, fast enough to keep up." [18] He laid out his rationale in pithy terms:

> The Russians trail us closely in order to be able to destroy most of a carrier's planes or disable the carrier herself before aircraft can take off. We adopted the retaliatory technique of trailing the trailer so as to prevent them from preventing us from launching our planes by knocking out most of their cruise missiles before many of them took off. In the words of the poet, "Great fleas have little fleas upon their back to bite 'em/And little fleas have lesser fleas, and so ad infinitum." [19]

American sailors thus got to know their opponents quite well. One *Kynda* stayed close to *Belknap* for almost six months; occasionally the American ship would flash across a "Good Morning." [20] The interchange was sometimes less friendly as when the Russian would illuminate *Belknap* with fire control radars. In times of tension, Sixth Fleet commanders tried to keep a Talos ship between the carrier and the Soviet cruiser. At extended range, the Soviet cruiser would have to launch the Shaddocks at a high angle, and the Talos would have the best chance of interception. Still, some officers regarded the Soviet antiship missiles as virtually unstoppable and thought the only solution lay in preventing their launch. Navymen agonized over ways to ensure that the Soviets could not get their missiles into the air; Admiral Gerald Miller later recalled, "I sure had my fingers crossed a lot as to whether or not we...had a realistic capability." [21]

In October 1973, some officers thought they were about to find out. When the Yom Kippur War flared up between Israel, Syria, and Egypt, American naval forces in the crisis area found themselves for the first time at a numerical disadvantage in a confrontation with Soviet ships. Sixty U.S. Navy warships, including three carriers, faced ninety-six Soviet vessels carrying an estimated eighty-eight antiship missiles (a figure not including those on long-range Soviet aircraft). Although some of these Soviet ships were obsolescent or of marginal military utility, others were potent adversaries. In particular, the smaller *Nanuchkas* presented serious targeting problems. One American surface officer recalled, "We had a real stand-off with them." [22] Zumwalt's verdict: "I doubt that major units of the U.S. Navy were ever in a tenser situation since World War II ended...." [23]

One Talos ordnance technician on *Little Rock* was shocked to see "white birds on the rails"—combat missiles ready to shoot.[24]

Having held the CNO's post for three years by this point, Zumwalt was more pessimistic than ever about the chances of the Navy to win a war at sea against the Soviets. In 1970, he had estimated that his service had a 55 percent chance of seizing a conventional victory. The next year, he told Chafee the edge had gone to the Soviets by a 65–35 margin. In March 1971, one senator asked Zumwalt during a formal congressional session, "What would happen if we had a bilateral conventional naval war with the USSR in 1972?" Zumwalt replied that in his judgment "we would lose"—a reply the senator called "devastating." In 1972, when another crisis brewed over the mining of Haiphong, Zumwalt told one of his principal subordinates, "We are going down hill so fast that I feel it's better to have a confrontation [with the Soviets] now than two years from now." His feeling was borne out by a more methodical study conducted the following year by the Systems Analysis Division. The division's findings concluded that of the fifteen critical warfare areas (such as strike warfare, surveillance, and amphibious lift), the U.S. Navy was ahead in five while the Soviets led in ten. By some estimates, NATO had only half the forces it would need to guarantee the resupply of Europe. Again in 1974, Zumwalt told a Senate subcommittee that "the judgement of our Fleet commanders and my own personal judgement, indicate that the odds are that we would be unable today to succeed in these goals"[25] of protecting the sealanes and flanks of NATO.[26]

In the event of a war with the Soviets, some top U.S. naval officers were banking on the American advantages of quality of personnel and training to offset the growing disparity in numbers and equipment. Stansfield Turner recalled that, in his experience, it seemed that the Soviets "sat at anchor all the time." He concluded that their philosophy was to avoid exercising their equipment to keep from wearing it out. After visiting a Soviet ship, he noted caustically that the officers wore pins signifying their various deployments—hardly a reason to award medals in the U.S. Navy.[27] Gerald Miller shared the impression of most American officers that the new Soviet ships were handsome and impressive with their purposeful armaments above decks on full display. But Miller remarked on how little the Soviets exercised their systems: "I doubt if they ever fired . . . anything in the Mediterranean. Maybe a .45-caliber pistol. . . ." He decided after watching Soviet ships and armaments for lengthy periods, "In our hands . . . they would be pretty good systems." He remembered thinking, "Hell, these guys are a bunch of amateurs. They haven't gotten around to the first phase of professionalism in warfare."[28]

American practice usually ran directly counter to the Soviet: U.S. sailors drilled equipment and technique constantly. Turner's philosophy was common throughout the Navy: "If I've got a gun on this ship and it hasn't fired a round through the bore this week, I don't want to count on that gun." [29] Miller expressed the same philosophy in somewhat more colorful terms:

> I used to send ships down to this contested area off Libya where we have to protect freedom of the seas. Shoot a Talos. I don't give a goddamn what you shoot it at, but shoot it. Go down there and shoot one. I used to do the same thing in the Pacific, as far as that goes. But if you don't practice and exercise—besides, that's what the fun is. It's dull as hell if you just sit. [30]

Rather than sitting still, the surface navy was wearing out from lack of resources and overuse. Maintenance was deferred so often and spares were in such short supply that cruisers and destroyers found their readiness and safety records debilitated. For instance, the failure of hydraulic piping in destroyer gun systems became so prevalent as to be accepted as a standard operating condition. Navy investigators were shocked at how widespread the breakdowns had become. One officer noted the "profoundly adverse effects" such trends had on the work habits of the personnel. [31] In 1972, the Pacific Fleet ran short of 5-inch ammunition—hardly an esoteric item; the Atlantic Fleet was stripped of certain types of antiaircraft weapons to fill the needs of the ships operating off Vietnam. [32]

With the Arab oil embargo beginning in October 1973, fuel shortages led to cutbacks in the operating tempos of both ships and aircraft. In 1974, CINCLANT warned Congress of impending severe shortages of fuel for the fleet. Ships limped through exercises or missed them altogether. As training funds dried up, U.S. Navy ships were beginning to look suspiciously like their Soviet counterparts. After a deployment to the Sixth Fleet, the commander of one cruiser-destroyer group complained that of the fifteen ships under his command during the six-month period, only cruiser *Columbus* had fired either missiles or ASW weapons. Spare parts shortages were so widespread that the time required to repair combat systems was averaging almost a month. [33]

Stretching assets even thinner were increased commitments, especially far from U.S. bases. With the British withdrawal from east of Suez, American ships picked up the slack. In August 1970, frigate *Bainbridge* made a surveillance sweep into the Indian Ocean, beginning occasional American forays into these waters. In November 1973, a carrier task group spent the month in the Indian Ocean. Surface warships spelled the carriers, with *Bainbridge* cruising there for the first two months of 1974, and *Chicago* for part of the summer. Seventh Fleet especially appreciated nuclear power following *Bainbridge*'s first venture: "With the Soviet Navy on the move in all oceans of the world and with the reduction in the size of the U.S. Navy, it is even more essential that our ships be capable of operating for extended periods in far-flung areas on an independent basis, free from logistics ties." [34]

K–109535

Cruiser *Chicago*, frigate *Sterett*, and dock landing ship *Fort Fisher* (LSD 40) during exercises, 26 June 1975. Both *Chicago* and *Sterett* had engaged North Vietnamese aircraft with their missile batteries three years earlier.

For the first half of Admiral Zumwalt's watch, the war in Southeast Asia continued to eat up an inordinate share of the surface navy's resources, despite Nixon's policy of Vietnamization. In 1972, surface warships played a significant role in thwarting the Communist Easter offensive and in isolating North Vietnam from outside Communist help. *Waddell* fired so many missions during April that she had to be regunned at Subic. So did *Towers* following Linebacker strikes north of the DMZ in late July and early August. The Navy's last active all-gun cruiser, *Newport News*, by now nicknamed "Thunder" for her rapid fire turrets, led a night surface bombardment of targets around Haiphong on 10 May.[35]

Casualties in the U.S. surface forces during 1972 were few, although not insignificant. During the first strike on Haiphong, 15 April, *Worden* was hit by two ARM missiles fired by U.S. aircraft. The most famous incident occurred on 1 October when an explosion wracked *Newport News*. While the ship was firing on North Vietnamese troops near Quang Tri, a defective projectile in turret two ignited more than 700 pounds of powder in the hoists. The fire killed twenty sailors and permanently damaged the turret.[36]

As before, surface warships supported the airmen with PIRAZ tours and by search and rescue. *Towers* even picked up six aviators from a downed B–52 near Guam in July. Nuclear frigate *Truxtun* during one week in October directed CAP to six successful MiG interceptions. On several occasions, surface warships were attacked by the enemy planes. During the aerial mining of Haiphong in May, *Chicago* was tasked with principal responsibility for protecting the aircraft involved. When these were challenged by MiGs, *Chicago* hit one of the North Vietnamese planes with a Talos at a range of 48 miles. Two months later, five MiGs made the mistake of jumping *Biddle* (DLG 34) on PIRAZ duty in the Gulf of Tonkin. The frigate downed two; the others turned tail.[37]

These exchanges were not totally one-sided. On 19 April, MiGs off Dong Hoi, North Vietnam, dropped a 250-pound bomb on the old destroyer *Higbee* (DD 806), demolishing the ship's aft gun mount and magazine. With *Higbee* were cruiser *Oklahoma City*, destroyer *Lloyd Thomas* (DD 764), and the *Belknap*-class frigate *Sterett* (DLG 31). In the confused action, *Sterett* claimed with her missiles a certain kill on the MiG that did the damage and a probable kill on a second, fleeing aircraft. As the frigate covered the retirement of the other warships, she fired two Terriers at what her captain believed to be a Styx. Later in the day, she picked up two PT boats on radar and claimed to have sunk both with her 5-inch.[38]

Many officers believed *Sterett* overoptimistic in her assessments, particularly the one about the Styx (the claim about the first MiG is generally conceded as accurate). Whatever the truth of the matter, the frigate's action report drew some cogent lessons from the affair. For instance, the commanding officer, H. E. Reichert, recommended in a "short fuze" environment placing missiles on the rails early and giving subordinates weapons release authority. Reichert maintained, "The Captain that tries to run a one man show will lose his ship." Reichert asked for specific items of hardware. Among them were rocket pods for the LAMPS helicopter to use against hostile surface craft; Sea Sparrow instead of the 3"/50; new chaff launchers; and cassette recorders to pick up conversations in key areas of the ship for later evaluation. Reichert added, "An urgent requirement exists for a heavy impact (approximately 500 pounds high explosive) surface-to-surface missile." He also suggested as "a crucial need" the development of tactical doctrine for surface forces confronting a coordinated air and surface attack. Despite all the shortcomings listed in his report, Reichert's concluding remarks echoed with pride in his ship: "Combatant ships with the size, speed and weapons capabilities of a Guided Missile Frigate are an entity unto themselves, having the capability to defend against multiple air/surface/subsurface threats from any direction."[39]

There just were not enough of these ships, and Zumwalt had to face deep retrenchment in defense spending by the Nixon administration. The administration cut the number of projected *Spruances* in half; to compensate, some FRAM *Gearings* were kept on well past their allotted span. Given this climate, Project Sixty emphasized a mix of ships, the so-called "high-low" solution. Zumwalt sought funding for a few very capable and expensive ships such as nuclear frigates and a nuclear carrier. He also asked for a larger number of much cheaper vessels useful in a lower threat environment, of which the Sea Control Ship was only one. Similarly, Zumwalt emphasized weapons useful in asserting sea control at the expense of weapons devoted to power projection ashore.[40]

As Arleigh Burke had done over a decade earlier, Zumwalt intended to pay for his initiatives partly by decommissioning worn-out units and culling the mothball fleet. Overall, the active navy declined during his four years from 769 warships to 512. The majority of these cuts hit the surface fleet. The number of destroyer types in reserve fell from 267 to 70. During Zumwalt's tenure, the Navy struck from its rosters ten heavy and eight light cruisers. Retired were some of the Navy's most famous ships, such as *Saint Paul*, the heavy cruiser that had fired the last shots by a major warship against Japan on 9 August 1945 and the last shots of the Korean War on 27 July 1953. Nicknamed fondly the "King Maker," nineteen of her twenty-five captains had made flag rank. Some of the first missile ships—*Boston*, *Galveston*, and *Topeka*—also were broken up. By the time Zumwalt left office in mid-1974, just one gun cruiser, *Newport News*, remained in commission; she decommissioned early the following year.[41]

K–121961

The end of the line. Three cruisers await the breakers at Philadelphia in October 1978. From left, *Newport News*, *Springfield*, and *Northampton*.

Spared the cutter's torch, oddly enough, were the four *Iowa*-class battleships. In 1974, when the first steps were taken to scrap them, Zumwalt intervened and explained later, "They were just too valuable potentially. The day would come when we would have to regain power quickly, and the only way [we] could do it was with something that was already built." [42] Having been posted to *Wisconsin* during the Korean War, Zumwalt was intimately familiar with the capabilities of the battleships. [43]

For new surface ship construction, nuclear frigates (designated DLGN) would make up the "high-end" of the spectrum. Congress added two 11,300-ton ships, *Texas* (DLGN 39) and *Mississippi* (DLGN 40), to the *Virginia* class, the lead ship of which had been authorized in FY 70. Originally intended to be the first ships with Aegis, their advocates hoped to see as many as twenty-three of them built. However, they were far too expensive for the times especially when Aegis was slow in coming along. By this point, only one shipyard, Newport News Shipbuilding and Dry Dock Company, could build nuclear vessels, and that yard was falling well behind its construction schedules. In FY 75, Congress funded but one more nuclear warship, *Arkansas*, redesignated from a frigate to a cruiser (CGN 41). To economize on the construction costs of the *Virginia*s, their designers deleted the strengthened forward structure the ships needed for Aegis. Capable vessels notwithstanding, they were armed with two of the new Mk 26 launchers for Tartar/Standard. They were also the first surface warships since World War II to be fitted with a hangar at the stern, in their case for helicopters. Unfortunately, the hangar roof leaked, and the space was ultimately given over to Tomahawk long-range cruise missiles. [44]

One last nuclear surface ship received serious consideration—a 17,000-ton strike cruiser (CSGN) equipped with Aegis, Standard, Tomahawk, Harpoon, the 8-inch gun, LAMPS, and a towed array. Pushed hard by Zumwalt's successor, Admiral James Holloway III, who hoped for eight of the warships, the CSGN was configured to carry out independent operations, thereby taking some of the strain off the hard-pressed carrier task forces. However, the Carter administration killed the project (as well as a proposal to refit *Long Beach* to strike cruiser standards), and the *Virginia*s thus proved to be the last of the Navy's surface warships built with reactors. [45]

Zumwalt very much wanted Aegis, but he preferred that it be mounted in a much cheaper hull than the nuclear cruisers. He advanced a gas turbine destroyer which was designated DG/Aegis. An austere ship (some of its design variants displaced barely 5,000 tons), the DG/Aegis ran afoul of Rickover and was ultimately killed after Zumwalt left office. [46]

Coming along almost on schedule was Weschler's *Spruance*-class destroyer, in Zumwalt's acerb words, "that modest escort vessel that Paul Nitze had seen miraculously metamorphose into DD 963." [47] By this point, Congress had ordered thirty of the 8,000-ton ships, but the surface navy needed a larger program of escort vessels for convoy work. Project Sixty called for a new design. The result was the FFG 7, or *Oliver Hazard Perry*-class, a descendant of the DE/PF envisioned in Zumwalt's Major Fleet Escort Study of 1968 that had spawned the *Spruance* class. Not surprisingly, the *Perry* class emphasized the qualities needed to combat the latest high-speed, missile-firing Soviet submarines. To locate these at a distance, the escort eventually mounted as its main sensor the SQR–19 towed array; the hull-mounted active sonar, the SQS–56, was of much shorter range. To tackle submarines at the greater distances made possible by the towed array, the *Perry*s were outfitted with a hangar commodious enough for two LAMPS helicopters. ASROC was dropped; the only short-range weapons were the Mk 32 torpedoes. The hangar contributed substantially to the relatively large size of the *Perry* class: 3,486 tons full load.[48]

Having "great open-ocean ASW capability," the *Perry*s were also armed with a Standard missile launcher, giving a modest antiaircraft capability directed against cruise missiles launched by submarines. For this mission, the ships suffered from the lack of a height finder radar. The Standard launcher could also fire Harpoon. The ships came under criticism for their single screw; some officers found their design too skewed toward the anti-submarine mission. Nominally slower at 28 knots than the FRAM destroyers they were replacing, the *Oliver Hazard Perry*s did later serve with the fast carriers. Moreover, they were affordable; fifty-one were ultimately constructed with the lead ship running her trials in 1977.[49]

Project Sixty also visualized an important role for a much smaller vessel: the high-speed hydrofoil. Armed with the Harpoon missile, the hydrofoil could keep up with Soviet tattletails and, Zumwalt argued, provide striking power in narrow seas like the Aegean and Adriatic. This capability, he envisioned, would give "a chance to pull your carriers back, ready to come in fighting, instead of having them forward exposed to the first blow, not ready to fight. So I realize that the whole low end of the mix, including the sea control ship, would give you the small increments of power that would let you keep your big muscle outside the Mediterranean until you needed it."[50]

The end product was the *Pegasus*-class fast attack craft, developed in cooperation with Germany and Italy. Up on its foils, it could run at 50 knots and carry eight Harpoons, once the missile had been perfected. Zumwalt wanted thirty of the 230-ton craft, but inflation and cost overruns drove their price sky-high. After their sponsor left office, the hydrofoil was truly an endangered species. The Navy proposed that only the lead vessel be completed although Congress saw to it that six ultimately entered service.[51]

Even more radical than *Pegasus* was Zumwalt's dream of a 100-knot Navy. If surface ships could operate at such a speed, their vulnerability would be much reduced and their offensive power multiplied. Thus, the surface warship would become more competitive with the submarine in its virtues of stealth and surprise. A number of surface warriors shared Zumwalt's enthusiasm for attaining a quantum jump in speed. The flag officer directing the Navy's Tactical Air, Surface, and Electronic Warfare Development Division maintained that ultra-high speed would "restore the primacy of the surface ship over the submarine."[52] Articles in the *Proceedings* relished the prospect of a 100-knot navy which Zumwalt himself thought would rival in significance the transition from sail to steam. To achieve such extraordinary increases in speed, the CNO saw a number of possible approaches: hydrofoils, hovercraft, and Small Waterplane Area Twin Hull (SWATH) vessels. He thought that the first of these new craft might be on active duty as early as the 1980s. In retrospect, these plans must be judged as visionary given the fiscal realities of the time.[53]

During the first half of the 1970s, developments in weaponry paralleled those in ship design as older systems were retired to be replaced by smaller numbers of more capable types. A count of the guns in the fleet revealed in stark figures how the surface navy's gunfire capabilities were dwindling.[54]

|  | 1970 | 1975 | 1980 (estimated) |
|---|---|---|---|
| 8-inch in active fleet | 18 | 1 | 1 |
| 6-inch | 12 | 6 | 0 |
| 5-inch | 657 | 267 | 212 |
| 5-inch in reserve | 104 | 132 | 33 |

Sheer numbers of barrels alone did not tell the whole story. A conclave called in response to "dismaying" troubles with the 5-inch Mk 42 mount initiated the Gunnery Improvement Program in 1972. Zumwalt approved the next spring its ambitious objectives to provide the Navy with gun systems that would allow surface vessels to counter small high-speed combatants, major surface ships, and antiship missiles. Part of the effort went to upgrading the 5-inch Mk 42 with its own improvement program which eventually brought about significant advances in that weapon's reliability and accuracy.[55]

Coming on line at long last was the 5-inch Mk 45. During tests in *Norton Sound*, misfires ran at one-third of the contract rate. The rugged mount could function in winds gusting to 113 knots, wild extremes of temperatures, and green water over the gun. Teaming up with the gun was the new digital Mk 86 fire control system which allowed for simultaneous tracking of air, surface, and land targets. The first of the sleek-looking mounts reached Newport News, Virginia, in the fall of 1972 for installation in *California*. By 1980 this gun went to sea on six cruisers and thirty destroyers; it was also fitted on board *Arleigh Burke*-class destroyers which began entering serivce in 1991.[56]

Counterbalancing the success of the new 5-inch mount was the "failure" of the eagerly awaited 8-inch lightweight gun (officially the Mk 71 Major Caliber Lightweight Gun, or MCLWG). Having many of the same features as the 5-inch Mk 45, the weapon fired a shell weighing almost five times that of the 5-inch, and its range of 15 miles could be extended with rocket-assisted projectiles. Ashore, its tests were a great success; the *Forrest Sherman*-class destroyer *Hull* carried out her sea trials in 1975. These shoots attracted much attention with some skeptics questioning whether a lightly framed destroyer could withstand the dynamic loads from the firing. Soothsayer Jeanne Dixon had predicted that the Navy would lose a ship armed with a big gun. Surely *Hull* was that vessel, said some sailors. In the event, the tests went without a hitch. In further exercises, the weapon showed great accuracy, scoring five hits out of five shots on a ship target, and an excellent rate of fire for such a big piece: eleven rounds per minute.[57]

After this promising start, the 8-inch lightweight gun went nowhere. It was never tied adequately to a program that could help finance it; in other words, it had no effective sponsor. Additionally, it received evaluation reports from the Operational Development Force that some surface officers thought biased. Admiral Weschler remembered, "I thought that the 8-inch lightweight gun was every bit as good as anything we had before. They [the evaluators] simply were saying, in essence, 'No gunnery is any good,' rather than just, 'The 8-inch lightweight gun isn't any good.'"[58]

Peculiarly, just as the Navy was rejecting a very good homemade product, it was arranging to buy its first foreign gun since World War II: the OTO-Melara 76mm. In January 1971, Zumwalt directed that the Navy conduct an extensive review of foreign ordnance, especially to discern what weapon best suited the *Oliver Hazard Perry* escort and the *Pegasus* hydrofoil on the drawing boards. An acceptable lighter gun and fire control system was not in the American inventory for either. The selection team settled on the Italian OTO-Melara with a fire control system (designated the Mk 92 by the U.S. Navy) made by Signaal of the Netherlands. The Italian weapon, already in service with a number of NATO countries, pared off weight by extensive use of aluminum alloys in the magazine and by a fiberglass gun shield. Fully automatic with a rate of fire of 85 rounds per minute, the weapon during its evaluation on *Talbot* (FFG 4) knocked down three drones on the first pass. Both *Oliver Hazard Perry* (FFG 7) and *Pegasus* (PHM 1) introduced it to the fleet in 1977.[59]

Some ordnance experts continued to advocate the guided projectile as having great potential for gunnery. Dahlgren worked early in the decade on an 8-inch shell with a tracking head and simple control surfaces. The lab also experimented with upgrading the 5-inch shell by adding a passive infrared homing guidance system to shoot down cruise missiles.[60]

Through Zumwalt's tenure and beyond, the antiship missile remained a major threat and a principal determinant of the Navy's research and spending. Project Sixty mandated a close look at defenses against it. Despite almost three years of work since the *Eilat* sinking, the Navy did not possess an effective defense against the burgeoning Soviet capabilities in antiship missiles. In Zumwalt's words, "We were desperately looking for something."[61] Certainly some of the projects under consideration hinted at desperation: water monitors to deceive or destroy antiship missiles; 20mm saboted thermite pellets; a light gas gun to fire a .22-caliber projectile at 27,000 feet per second. Another Rube Goldberg concoction contemplated directing electromagnetic pulses in a narrow beam to disable the solid state circuitry of the incoming weapon. Perhaps more realistic was the laser. If it could be harnessed, it offered great potential advantages: instantaneous delivery of destructive power, no lead angle computations, and no acceleration limitations. However, the laser required enormous amounts of electrical power and was degraded by bad weather.[62]

Aegis was much closer at hand. It promised nothing short of a new era in surface warfare. Designed to defend against both air and surface threats in all environments, Aegis would perform a number of major functions hitherto controlled by many disparate systems. For example, it would detect, track, and engage all targets by automatic threat evaluation and response, especially important against low-fliers. Aegis was designed to track more than one hundred targets simultaneously and to control more than ten missiles in the air at one time. To achieve this capability, Aegis would employ a multifunction radar system with fixed faces, a digital weapon direction system, and advanced missilery.[63]

NAVORD, charged with overseeing its development, established the Aegis Weapons System project office. Picked for the tough job was Captain Wayne E. Meyer, the director of missile systems engineering at Port Hueneme. A veteran of enlisted service in World War II, Meyer had gone on to earn a commission from the Navy and an advanced degree from MIT. His missile work began at Fort Bliss in 1951 and continued on board *Galveston* which he joined as fire control and weapons officer when that cruiser brought Talos into the fleet. Meyer's work at Hueneme attracted the attention of Rear Admiral Arthur R. Gralla, the head of NAVORD. Meyer hoisted his flag in 1970 as Aegis project manager, a position that he held until 1983. Concurrently, he served as the last head of the Surface Missile Systems office (the 3–T Get Well office) from 1972 to 1974 and then was named first Director of Surface Warfare, Naval Sea Systems Command.[64]

Meyer provided the right mix of technical expertise and political acumen in shepherding Aegis from concept to reality. His name became something of a legend in the surface warfare community. Admiral Stansfield Turner assessed his performance as director of the Aegis project as "superb."[65] Vice Admiral Henry Mustin called Meyer the "Rickover of the surface navy's weapons."[66] Following his retirement, he garnered numerous awards, perhaps the most deserved being the naming of the Aegis schools at Dahlgren as the RADM Wayne E. Meyer Aegis Education Center.[67]

In moving Aegis ahead, Meyer endorsed the construction of a special test facility ashore at Moorestown, New Jersey. In 1973, this site began tracking its first targets with the SPY–1 radar. Disassembled, the equipment was then flown to California and installed in the trials ship *Norton Sound*. The following May, this vessel successfully defended against two Talos drones simulating a cruise missile attack on a carrier. Over the next six years, Aegis on board *Norton Sound* engaged fifty targets "with an extraordinary success rate."[68]

Despite this promising start, getting Aegis to sea in operational warships proved surprisingly difficult. Funding for all Navy projects was very tight, and some analysts saw Aegis as threatening the Navy's premier fighter, the F–14, which was under scrutiny. As Mustin recalled, "an either-or argument [had] been created in the SECDEF's office and [was] *furiously* debated in the Navy."[69] CNO Zumwalt saw that Aegis (and the F–14) remained in the budget. The engineers working on Aegis had taken great pains to shave its size and power requirements so that it would fit into a variety of warships, including carriers, most of the newer frigates, *Spruance*-class destroyers, and Zumwalt's DG/Aegis of under 6,000 tons. By 1973, the weight of the system was down from 220 tons to 158 tons; its personnel requirements, from thirty-four to twenty-one; and its expense, from $61 million to $43 million.[70]

Originally slated for the *Virginia*-class frigates, Aegis was not far enough along when the lead ship of that class neared its commissioning date. Worse, in 1975, Aegis became mired in the Rickover swamp. It might fit into a variant of the *Spruance* class, but then the ship would exceed 8,000 tons and fall under that category of "major combatant vessels" requiring nuclear power. The expense of both Aegis and reactor would be too great; in the face of severe funding cuts, Secretary of the Navy J. William Middendorf II and new CNO Holloway moved to strike money allotted for the system. But surface warfare officers, after a series of studies, argued strongly that the new carrier, *Carl Vinson*, just authorized in FY 74, needed additional air defenses in a very high threat environment. Admiral Holloway, a former commanding officer of *Enterprise*, had been favorably impressed with the potentialities of the fixed-array radar that the first nuclear carrier had mounted. Holloway reversed course and personally began lobbying Congress for Aegis. President Gerald R. Ford gave Holloway support, and Aegis was narrowly saved.[71]

SDAN DY–ST–84–01890

Prominent in this 1983 view of cruiser *Ticonderoga* is the eight-sided fixed array of the SPY–1A radar, part of the Aegis system.

In commenting on the system shortly after this narrow escape, Meyer argued, "Cruise missiles are worldwide. Modern defenses against them are a generation ahead in the U.S. Navy alone. We have an advantage to exploit [with Aegis]."[72] The top officer in the surface branch from 1974 to 1981, Vice Admiral James H. Doyle, Jr., made it his "number one priority" to get Aegis on board as many ships as possible.[73] His first success was with a derivative of the *Spruance* destroyer just entering service. Originally designated as the DDG 47 class, the first of these *Ticonderoga*-class missile ships was authorized by Congress in 1977. To reflect the strengths provided by Aegis (and the costs which inflation had shoved to almost $1 billion per vessel), the ships were redesignated missile cruisers, the CG 47 class.[74]

In many ways, the most capable surface combatant ever constructed, one Aegis cruiser alone more than doubled the effectiveness of the antiaircraft screen of any carrier task group. Admiral Isaac Kidd wrote, "Aegis made such an improvement in our ability to handle hostile air targets that it should be considered revolutionary."[75] Aviators welcomed the vessels because they filled the gap in the middle zone of the task group's layered defenses. The principal drawback to Aegis was that its lead ship *Ticonderoga* (CG 47) did not commission until 1983—eight years late according to original projections for the system.[76]

Although no one in the early 1970s envisioned such a protracted gestation, it was clear that Aegis would not enter the fleet on schedule. Top officers, therefore, viewed an interim defense against cruise missiles as absolutely essential. Of necessity, this defense would be cobbled together from existing programs and equipment. One fundamental task was to increase the warning time against sea-skimmers. The surface navy made major gains in this area by using its LAMPS helicopter in an early warning mode. Stationed along the axis of probable threat, the helicopter could hope to spot the launching platform and perhaps even employ chaff to deceive incoming missiles.[77]

The 3–Ts, close to phase-out from the fleet, would have to shoulder their share of the burden despite their limitations in reaction time and inability to handle multiple simultaneous attacks. Four of the six Talos cruisers remaining (*Albany*, *Chicago*, *Long Beach*, and *Oklahoma City*) were upgraded in availability, reliability, and reduced maintenance by the addition of digital fire control equipment. A digital electronics package in the missile itself allowed for more propellant and thus an extension in range. By switching to a denser fuel, the last versions of Talos exceeded the 200-mile mark. At White Sands, some flew right out of the range. The men who worked with final versions of Talos held a high opinion of their missile. One later recalled, "Talos was not out of date; its platforms were."[78] On 6 November 1979, *Oklahoma City* fired her 6-inch guns and Talos missiles—the last time for both Navy weapons. Altogether, the Navy had purchased 2,404 Talos missiles; the seven Talos ships had fired 887 of them; and White Sands had shot 462 more. The missile alone scored a success rate of over 80 percent, but the figure for the entire system ran about 40 percent. Orphaned Talos missiles soldiered on throughout the next decade as high-speed targets. Called Vandal, the 320 missiles flown in this guise amassed a success record of 98 percent.[79]

Most of the Terrier and Tartar ships outlasted the Talos cruisers. Prodded particularly by the threat of the Soviet supersonic long-range Tu–22 Backfire bomber with its AS–4 antiship missile, the Naval Sea Systems Command began a program in the mid-1970s called the New Threat Upgrade to modernize the surveillance radars and weapons control systems of the thirty-one Terrier and the ten newest Tartar ships.[80]

By 1973, the Terriers and Tartar missiles were phasing out in favor of a newer "bird," the Standard SM–1. Adaptable to either magazine or launcher with a simple change of propulsion, Standard offered other advantages: better performance in the face of ECM, faster reaction times, and an increased kill probability. The SM–1 still used the continuous-rod warhead but with a new fuze whose sensing cones and digital logic triggered it to cause maximum damage depending upon whether the target was a surface ship, jet bomber, or cruise missile. Under development was the Standard SM–2 with a range of 100 miles and a programmable autopilot. Although SM–2 was intended principally for the Aegis ships, the Terrier and Tartar vessels could benefit from its assets as well when the new missile was coupled with better target detection and tracking equipment. The older ships required only minor electrical modifications; SM–2 was deployed first on board *Wainwright* (CG 28, exDLG 28) in 1976.[81]

Adding to the effectiveness of the Standard was the Mk 26 launcher which first appeared on *Virginia* (CGN 38). Even in the worst sea conditions with heavy pitch and roll, the launcher could fire in rapid succession several kinds of missiles, including all variants of Standard, Harpoon, and ASROC. To accomplish this flexibility without using adapters (and thus slowing down the rate of fire), the launcher featured a unique retracting rail to give the requisite length of guided travel which varied according to the type of missile fired (the lighter antiaircraft "birds" needed less time on the guides than did the cumbersome ASROC). A jettison device could shove dud missiles overboard.[82]

Two especially significant and novel features of the Mk 26 launcher were its fault isolating equipment and its modular design. The former permitted a technician to track down failures quickly through displays showing the status of every switch and solenoid. The modular design of the system allowed the entire launcher with its magazine to be "plugged in" to the ship. The base of the module rested on prepared foundations within the vessel. Once the module was lowered into the ship, the system needed only electrical power and utility connections for operation.[83]

The Mk 26 went first into the *Virginia*s and then into the *Kidd* destroyers. The modular concept proved especially fortunate because it allowed the Navy in the mid-1980s to begin superseding the Mk 26 with the vertical launch system (VLS) in new construction and conversions. In the words of Admiral Doyle, the VLS was "a big breakthrough."[84] Each missile canister with its zero-length rail segment served as a separate launcher, independent of the others. VLS allowed for the entire missile battery to be fired in rapid succession. The VLS obviated the dangerous problem of disposing of defective missiles on the launching rails. Because the missiles were shot straight from their VLS boxes, the ordnance technicians would, in the event of a dud, simply select another missile. VLS offered a number of daunting technical challenges, especially the management of the missile exhaust stream with its highly abrasive particles and its temperature in excess of 2,000 degrees Kelvin. First planned for the Aegis DDG 47/CG 47 class, the VLS would eventually be fitted in several types of surface ships in the 1980s.[85]

For short-range antiship missile defense in the early 1970s, Zumwalt placed great emphasis on upgrading the Sea Sparrow point defense missile, in the same way that Terrier/Tartar had been improved into Standard. As could be expected, the Sea Sparrow advances shared many of the same features as those of the larger missiles: a computer, an automatically controlled director, and a modified missile. Its better launcher accepted the canister in which the missile was shipped. Developed by the Naval Ordnance Station, Louisville, the canister allowed the missile to be packaged at an ordnance facility or a tender. The canister was then shipped sealed to the warship where it was slipped into the launcher, and the electrical leads were plugged in. This simple, effective system greatly enhanced readiness through reduced maintenance and easier testing. By the end of the decade, the Sea Sparrow was vastly improved in its ability to take on low-altitude targets.[86]

Paralleling Sea Sparrow was the Close-In Weapon System, looking "like something out of Buck Rogers" or like R2D2 of the film *Star Wars*. Of modular design as well, CIWS only required from the ship electricity, sea water for cooling, and the vessel's course inputs. Weighing 5 tons, the mount could be bolted onto almost any spot that gave it a suitable vantage point. With its high rate of fire, dense bullet, and ability to make quick corrections to match bullet and target, CIWS was so promising that Zumwalt afforded it high priority. Some officers wanted a larger projectile, like the 30mm fired by the Dutch Goalkeeper, but in tests against mockup Soviet missiles, the 20mm round generally smashed the enemy warhead to fragments. By 1972, development had reached the halfway point, and introduction into the fleet was scheduled for 1974.[87]

Important as improvements were in antiaircraft defense, they took second place to the development of effective antiship missiles. Of all Admiral Zumwalt's initiatives listed in Project Sixty, he ranked this "the most urgent task by far."[88] The first production versions of the weapon were to go on board his surface warships, with aircraft and submarines receiving them as soon thereafter as possible. Only the Mk 48 advanced torpedo stood on the same level of priority.[89]

Planners considered two routes to Zumwalt's goal: a surface-to-surface version of the Standard as a quickly achievable stop-gap measure; for the long term, Harpoon. Standard proved quite amenable to modification for this mission. Three variants differed only in guidance with active, semiactive, and antiradiation homers being developed. The active version allowed the missile to travel an "up-and-over" trajectory so that it arrived at the target in a steep descent. The antiradiation variant was based on the battle-tested Shrike missile with the addition of a memory so that if the enemy shut down its emitter, the Standard ARM would still possess a reasonable chance of hitting the target. Moreover, the missile was already in production, and costs were reasonable at about $50,000 per copy.[90]

To place the Standard on active units, the surface navy modified the ASROC launcher on escort ships and developed a coffin-like box launcher for patrol craft. By giving the small patrol gunboats the Standard, the Navy endowed them with the ability to strike at the Soviet tattletails. The large addition to the firepower of both the escorts and the patrol craft demanded surprisingly few alterations to the ships themselves. New fire control computers came on board; the superstructure of the escort ships required reworking to take the hotter blast of the Standard as compared to the ASROC.[91]

Endowing these smaller combatants with some brawn was popular with the surface warfare community. The few criticisms focused on the relatively short range of the missile and on its 219-pound warhead, quite small compared to those carried by Soviet missiles. Still, Standard packed a punch. In its first tests, three of the missiles scored direct hits on destroyer hulks at the Pacific Range. Even without warheads, two of the Standards penetrated into the engine rooms and magazine spaces. To magnify the missile's destructive effects, Dahlgren produced a warhead specifically intended for use against surface targets. When triggered, the device scattered high-velocity fragments and burning materials in a pattern calculated to destroy the combat capability of larger Soviet warships and to wreck smaller missile boats. Standard worked well, both in practice and later in action in 1988 in the Persian Gulf.[92]

Harpoon was even more eagerly awaited by the black-shoe community. Zumwalt pushed up its priority in September 1970. Two months later, the program office, headed by Rear Admiral Ekas, presented a ten-volume report to a review committee proposing the production of two versions of Harpoon: one, air-launched; the other, ship-launched. The two differed only in the booster required on the ship version to get the missile up to flying speed. In January 1972, the Navy added submarines to the list of Harpoon platforms. The missile development effort involved the work of the prime contractor, McDonnell Douglas, and various other subsidiaries such as Teledyne, Lear, Honeywell, and Texas Instruments. Ten Navy labs and field stations participated in the project, as did APL. Ekas had flexibility unusual for the time in reprogramming his resources.[93]

A "fire-and-forget" missile, the Harpoon was dependent for guidance on initial course inputs from its launching platform. It would then fly to a predetermined spot and turn on its active radar seeker only at the last moment in order to lessen the opportunity for the enemy to deploy countermeasures. The homing radar was "frequency agile," making jamming difficult. Its turbojet engine gave it a range of almost 70 miles. At the end of its low-level flight, Harpoon was programmed to climb and then dive steeply onto the target, thus penetrating the lightly protected upper works of a warship.[94]

The initial requirements also specified that the missile be capable of disabling targets ranging in size from a *Komar* boat to a cruiser. The Harpoon's 570-pound blast warhead could punch through the pressure hull of a surfaced *Juliett* or *Echo*, although Program Manager Ekas noted that "these targets did not...dominate any of the design features of the

*Knox* (DE 1052) fires a Harpoon from her ASROC launcher, c. 1975.

missile."[95] If the warhead could not guarantee the sinking of a larger surface warship, it would nonetheless do significant damage to the vessel's topside sensors; in other words, the missile would be able to achieve a mission kill against a Soviet cruiser. As a sign of the times, there was no provision for a nuclear-tipped version of Harpoon.[96]

From the beginning, the missile was designed for maximum reliability—to be a "wooden round." In part, this emphasis on reliability came from the CNO's office; in part, it was due to operational considerations. Initially, there was no thought given to forward replenishment of the weapon to destroyers and other surface craft. Consequently, Harpoon had to be absolutely dependable considering the small numbers that any single vessel would carry. As one officer associated with the project said, "You couldn't carry five around in the hope of getting three off."[97] The price paid for this reliability was that Harpoon was manufactured with the best components available. In mid-1972, the price tag for the missile was estimated at $255,000 per copy, excluding any money for modifications to the ships that would carry it.[98]

Ekas spurred McDonnell Douglas on with a contract that carried incentives for fulfilling two simple goals: keeping costs under control and producing missiles that would hit their targets during tests. The first prototype flew in December 1972, only eighteen months after the contract award. The missile made a direct hit, setting a standard upheld by over 90 percent of the following test missiles. So successful were these trials that a 1973 General Accounting Office study anticipated emergency use of prototypes in the event of a war. The escort *Downes* (DE 1070) shot the first Harpoon at sea in 1974.[99]

With strong backing from Secretary Laird and Admiral Zumwalt who "fenced" funding for production, an order went out in June 1974 for 150 production missiles. In the meantime, work was well underway on modifying those surface vessels that would carry the missile. In most cases, the alterations required were minimal. The missile was tailored for the Standard missile launchers. It also could be shot from the ASROC boxes, although here the fit was snug. The loader crane on the *Garcia*-class escorts, for instance, was rated at 1,200; the missile weighed 1,260 pounds, requiring acceptance of a 5 percent overload. The magazine for ASROC could not take Harpoon with booster fins and control surfaces attached, so these were clipped on at the time of launching.[100]

For the hydrofoils and other small patrol craft, the Navy developed a sealed canister which both housed the missile and served as its launcher. The canister turned out to be a real success. For instance, the *Pegasus* hydrofoil was slated originally for four Harpoons, but the launcher, as produced, was much lighter than anticipated. In consequence, the patrol craft could carry eight missiles giving it extraordinary striking power for a vessel of its size. In the early 1980s, armored and reusable canister launchers—and by mid-decade, the vertical launch system—would ease Harpoon on board a wide variety of warships from the refurbished *Iowa*-class battleships to the *Spruance*s.[101]

The missile also proved tractable for use from other platforms. By the 1980s, Harpoon entered the inventory of certain long-range patrol squadrons of P–3 Orions. Two types of carrier planes, the S–3 Viking submarine hunter and the A–6 Intruder attack bomber, also employed the weapon. Submarines could shoot Harpoons from their torpedo tubes; attack boats theoretically were able to carry up to twenty missiles but at substantial sacrifice in torpedo capacity. Zumwalt even asked the Air Force to give the Navy long-range help by installing Harpoons on B–52s—a proposal that ultimately led to a positive response by the 1980s.[102]

By 1977, only a few Harpoons had reached operating units, but the pace quickened substantially later in the decade. In 1979, the thousandth missile left the factory. Within the next three years, U.S. orders topped the 1,800 mark and were supplemented by 1,300 for a host of allies (Australia, Denmark, Great Britain, Greece, Israel, Japan, Netherlands, Saudi Arabia, South Korea, Spain, Turkey, and West Germany). Officers of all navies liked the missile's reliability and its handiness. If the Harpoon had a defect, it was the quarter-ton warhead which seemed small to some ordnance specialists.[103]

Nonetheless, the surface navy especially appreciated the offensive force Harpoon gave their warships from patrol boats to cruisers. By extension, blackshoes knew full well how Harpoon complicated the picture for Soviet tacticians who could no longer concentrate solely on the carriers as the source of all American offensive power. Harpoon also boosted the morale of the American surface warrior. As the commanding officer of one of the much maligned *Knox*-class frigates remarked, "Now everyone can be a shooter."[104]

One naval authority has summarized what Harpoon meant in the broader picture of strategic affairs:

> The Harpoon program symbolized the shift from an American navy so powerful it could ignore Soviet surface-ship interference and concentrate on carrier-strike warfare against land targets, to a force that might have to face the Russian fleet in sea battles and might not always be able to supply carrier aircraft to protect its surface ships against those of the enemy.[105]

A similarly important shift was presaged during Zumwalt's tenure by the beginning of serious work on a cruise missile aimed at land or sea targets at very long range. Originally known as the Sea Launched Cruise Missile (SLCM), the weapon would eventually become the Tomahawk. It would give the surface navy a real strategic attack capability against targets far inland for the first time.

The origins of this weapon date to early 1971 when the Navy began considering submarine-launched cruise missiles. Very low-altitude flight conferred on such weapons a virtual immunity to detection that made them extremely attractive to strategists. During the later stages of the Vietnam War, drones flying at altitudes under 200 feet foiled Soviet radar systems with ease. One reportedly accomplished sixty-eight reconnaissance missions before it was shot down. One authority noted, "Considering the dense antiaircraft defenses in North Vietnam, and that the drones flew in the most dangerous areas, this record is outstanding."[106]

The SLCM program received formal approval in June 1972; the prototype flew for the first time in December 1976, two years after Zumwalt's retirement. The missile offered many new advantages to the surface line. It could carry a nuclear warhead or a conventional one almost twice as heavy as that of Harpoon. With its small turbofan engine and dense fuel, the Tomahawk had a range of 800 to 1,500 miles, depending on the warhead. The entire missile at 2,700 pounds weighed less than the nuclear warhead of the Regulus I. Although hitting ship targets at great distances in a crowded ocean environment proved to be the toughest problem in the development of Tomahawk, its guidance system based on a terrain map-matching technique yielded precise results against land targets. For this reason, Zumwalt later called Tomahawk a revolutionary weapon: "It meant that any surface ship could then do the job that only an aircraft carrier could do, namely reach way over the horizon in warfare at sea and play a role in the land battle." [107]

For this reason, some aviators opposed the missile. The brownshoes feared the loss of defense dollars if the cruise missile seemed capable of usurping the job of the carrier aircraft. Their concerns were heightened during Jimmy Carter's presidency when Secretary of Defense Harold Brown suggested buying more cruise missiles and cutting the number of carriers. Aviators had feared such a trade-off as early as Regulus I. When the issue of funding SLCM was first raised in 1971 at a NATO meeting of military commanders in Norfolk, the commander of the Second Fleet, Gerald E. Miller, distributed brochures on the A–7. In a colorful spiel, Miller pointed to the attack aircraft as "one of the best cruise missiles that's ever been designed." Like Thomas Moorer in the late 1950s, Miller argued that the airplane was reusable, fast, and cost effective; he added that the only reason the Soviets had developed cruise missiles was that they could not produce carriers.[108]

An early Tomahawk over White Sands Missile Range, 1976.

Miller later claimed that aviators were not hostile to the cruise missile, just confident in the ability of their aircraft. He specifically dismissed complaints by surface sailors that without the offensive power of the cruise missile their surface ships were vulnerable. The attack planes could provide the coverage the vessels needed, he said. Miller's was not a lone voice; in 1972, aviators argued to Zumwalt, "The carrier with its present mix of aircraft and weapons is fully capable of effectively countering other surface units with acceptable attrition." [109]

At least one conspicuous figure in the surface navy agreed: Stansfield Turner. In 1970 during the Project Sixty debates, he maintained that carrier aviation could cope with the Soviet missile ships and that Harpoon was therefore unnecessary. Turner argued that the surface navy should concentrate on antisubmarine warfare. He reminisced in 1988: "I always viewed the destroyer force as a servant of the carriers, and I didn't worry about fighting *Kyndas*. I was counting on the carrier to fight the *Kyndas* for me.... [After a war had started] with the Soviet Union, my concept was always that there would be a carrier there, that he would [keep] anybody from getting within firing range of me, and that my job was to protect the carrier." [110] But Turner's opinion was certainly a minority one which a shrinking number of carriers made more dubious. The *Pueblo* affair of 1968 highlighted the uncertainty of the aviation argument. Would a carrier always be within range to provide cover?[111]

Ordnance and capabilities were not the only issues under debate among the Navy's branches during Zumwalt's tour. The CNO felt that OPNAV had for decades given inadequate representation to surface warfare. The type commanders (such as for cruisers or destroyers) might advance projects, but in OPNAV, the surface navy had no overall office to present a coordinated view from its various segments. One top surface warfare officer recalled, "In the late 60s, there wasn't any surface community; it was an amorphous mass." [112] The aviators, on the other hand, had benefited since 1921 from the representation that the Bureau of Aeronautics and its descendant (OP–05) gave them within OPNAV. The submariners carved out their own niche with the OP–32 office under DCNO (Fleet Operations and Readiness). In 1966, a Navy task force had proposed, unsuccessfully, a revamping of OPNAV with a "Four Force" structure composed of deputy chiefs for undersea, air, surface, and amphibious/logistics warfare. Similar suggestions for such a configuration dated back to before 1950.[113]

In March 1971, Zumwalt ordered the implementation of the Four Force concept. The surface navy at last gained a permanent voice equal to aviation's with the creation of the Deputy Chief of Naval Operations for Surface, or OP–03; the office would later be called DCNO (Surface Warfare). OP–05 continued to represent aviation; OP–02, the submariners; and OP–04, logistics. Serving as the first DCNO for one year was Vice Admiral

Jerome H. King, Jr., succeeded in 1972 by Robert E. Adamson, Jr. Adamson served a two-year tour before his relief by James Doyle in July 1974. As one of its first tasks, the OP–03 office produced a study called the Surface Warfare Plan to lend some coherence to various surface warfare projects and to aid in winning funding for them.[114]

This major organizational shift was only the first of many key changes in surface warfare initiated while Zumwalt was CNO and which culminated the year after he left office. Complaints from the surface community about a plethora of issues were finally coming to a head. The way command opportunities were parceled out had long rankled surface officers. For example, Turner noted that black-shoe officers, even when commanding carrier task groups, were still forced to fly their flags from cruisers, not carriers— "the height of parochialism."[115]

At lower levels, surface line officers also felt the sting of discrimination. Aviators continued to command most of the larger amphibious and service ships to obtain the deep draft seasoning they needed before taking over a carrier; the commander of the Pacific Fleet's Service Force protested to Zumwalt that all his new ships were going to aviators.[116] These officers needed to "check the boxes" on shiphandling maneuvers and thus personally directed major evolutions like anchoring, mooring, or conning the ship during underway replenishment, thereby depriving the junior surface officers of these opportunities. Young surface officers charged that throughout the Navy their jobs infrequently vested them with real responsibility, with the stringent fiscal times bearing some of the blame. For instance, the commander of a destroyer or cruiser was often reluctant to put green officers in charge of hazardous maneuvers for fear of damage to his ship and his career.[117]

In fact, junior officer grievances were legion and were reflected in the 14 percent retention rate for surface line officers in 1970. Zumwalt called eleven full and junior-grade lieutenants to Washington to form the Surface Warfare Officer Retention Study Group. Their final report to the CNO pulled no punches. Assuring the CNO that a "dedicated SWO core exists," the young officers made almost one hundred separate recommendations.[118] Because their ships were shorthanded, the officers endured lengthy separations from their families, a situation exacerbated by encroachments upon their annual leave. Among the personnel changes the panelists wanted were expanded early promotion opportunities and more attention from their detailers. They identified shortsighted planning as leading to crisis management (the "flap of the day" syndrome) and complained of the ballooning of directives from multilayered staffs. Many of the training exercises seemed contrived or, worse, were rigged to allow substandard units to "meet" qualifications.

The junior officers argued that their specialty lacked an identifiable image in the eyes of the general public. More degrading, surface warfare was seen within the Navy as the refuge for the second-rater. To combat this problem, they suggested more rigorous standards, better schooling, and a surface warfare pin equivalent to the dolphins worn by submariners or the wings by the aviators. The panelists also urged that dropouts from those two communities be allowed to leave the Navy rather than be forced into surface warfare. The surface sailors argued, "No one wants to be part of a second rate outfit."

According to the panelists, "widespread feeling" existed that the surface navy was incapable of meeting modern Soviet threats due to low personnel levels and poor equipment. In the latter area, they cited the lack first of a surface-to-surface missile and second of an inadequate antiaircraft capability. Of course, these ordnance deficiencies were hardly news to the CNO and, in any case, were being tackled on a number of fronts.[119]

Zumwalt had also taken action already to remedy some of the personnel issues that this committee raised. He felt the surface warfare officer designation did need strengthening. Established in April 1970 by the Bureau of Naval Personnel, the SWO designation meant little initially because of its minimal standards. Just one year later, Zumwalt tightened the requirements by adding to the SWO qualifications such significant demands as a one-year tour in an operational surface ship and successful service as both CIC watch officer and officer of the deck.[120] In 1974, to "dispel any thought of the surface navy as a second career, unless an officer is willing to undertake a rigorous qualification program," entry and exit guidelines were stiffened. A billet review routed junior officers into responsible jobs earlier in their careers.[121]

Younger officers soon found their training tougher and more meaningful. Zumwalt, through his vaunted Z-grams, called for increased junior officer shiphandling. The CNO went so far as to ensure commanding officers that they would not be held responsible for the inevitable minor scrapes and dents. In 1975, the Destroyer School at Newport was upgraded and redesignated the Surface Warfare Officer School. It would now offer courses which qualified officers to head departments in surface ships.[122]

At a higher level, the more senior officers detailed to the Naval War College faced a revitalized curriculum starting in 1972. That year, Zumwalt dispatched Stansfield Turner to Newport to reenergize the institution. Tactics had almost vanished from its offerings; in fact, the very word "tactics" had not appeared in a Naval War College course description since 1958. This state of affairs changed in 1973 when the senior students took a tactics course in the College of Naval Warfare. Major themes among the new studies were discussed in the context of Turner's strategic matrix of nuclear deterrence, naval presence, power projection overseas, and sea control. Antiship missile defenses and ECM figured prominently in the sea control problems.[123]

Captain Stansfield Turner during
Project Sixty, 19 August 1970.

USN 485667

Zumwalt also made sure that top surface officers regularly received the
jobs hitherto almost monopolized by aviators. For instance, Admiral Doyle
early in the 1970s flew his flag from *Forrestal* when he commanded a carrier task group. Doyle then took over the Third Fleet in the Pacific before
moving to the post of DCNO (Surface Warfare) in Washington. Similarly,
Turner commanded a carrier task group in the Sixth Fleet and later the
entire Second Fleet. Raymond Peet flew his vice admiral's flag over the
First Fleet in 1970.[124]

A most controversial proposal in the surface line was the move to amal-
gamate the cruiser-destroyer forces with the amphibious, service, and mine
warfare elements of the Navy. The initial impetus for this change came in
1972 as an attempt to cut administrative overhead; the proposal met with
significant resistance at each type commander conference. All four of the
specialties believed that their requirements were so technical that the
cross-training of officers would be a waste of time. Moreover, the cruiser-
destroyer forces regarded themselves as the elite of the surface type commands and feared that their quality, already suspect in the minds of the
air and subsurface communities, would be further diluted by association
with the "slow-movers." [125]

Other opponents of the shift argued persuasively that the Navy was
abolishing a structure that had stood the test of three wars; that the Navy

80–G–462831

80–G–706197

NH 89463

Naval aviation, submarine, and surface warfare insignia.

needed to concentrate on getting its house in order after the Vietnam trauma; and that the sheer size of the new organizations would make them unwieldy. Standing powerfully against these points was the contention that amalgamation would further the prestige of the entire black-shoe community. It would also strengthen the surface navy in its Pentagon battles for funds. Debate ended in 1973 when the Secretary of Defense demanded further reductions in staff. Zumwalt directed the establishment on 1 January 1975 of two naval surface commands that would encompass the four diverse naval elements.[126]

Called Naval Surface Force, U.S. Atlantic Fleet and Naval Surface Force, U.S. Pacific Fleet, the new organizations were large commands. NAVSURF-LANT, for instance, contained 220 ships and 80,000 men and women. Among the disparate elements under the command of its first head, Vice Admiral Adamson, were amphibious and mine forces; cruisers and destroyers; replenishment ships; salvage vessels; tenders; Naval Inshore Warfare Command; Beachmaster Unit Two; Seal Team Two; Underwater Demolition Team 21; Coastal River Squadron Two; Navy Parachute Team; Explosive Ordnance Disposal Group Two; Harbor Clearance Unit Two; Cargo Handling and Port Group; and a variety of other organizations. Adamson clearly faced a major challenge as did his counterpart in California, Vice Admiral Robert S. Salzer. NAVSURFPAC was somewhat smaller, listing on its rosters 184 ships staffed and supported by 58,000 personnel.[127]

Ashore, the laboratories that principally supported surface warfare underwent the same amalgamation. In 1974 for example, the Naval Ordnance Laboratory (NOL), White Oak, Maryland, and the Naval Weapons Laboratory (NWL), Dahlgren, merged to form the Naval Surface Weapons Center (NSWC), Dahlgren Laboratory and White Oak Laboratory.[128]

Surface warfare officers hoped to garner from the new setup some important advantages, including more efficient analysis of surface needs at all levels of the chain of command. Zumwalt's successor, Admiral Holloway, believed the new organizations would further training and readiness as well as enhance the status of all elements of the Surface Force. The reconfiguration did open a variety of different career paths for officers in all its branches by mandating that every officer should serve split tours, spending half the time in the cruisers/destroyers and the other half in service/amphibian/minecraft.[129]

In the first tests for the integrated surface navy, warships from the Pacific Fleet removed American and friendly personnel from Cambodia and Vietnam as that conflict ended with victory for the Communist forces. In May 1975, U.S. surface warships took part in the recovery and rescue of the American containership SS *Mayaguez* and her crew, seized by the Cambodians. The new publication *Surface Warfare* editorialized, "The interaction of the cruiser-destroyer, amphibious, and service-type ships dur-

227

ing these operations was an example of the one-force/one-team concept that consolidation was designed to accomplish." [130]

On the negative side, the new commands established by the reorganization were so large as to be unwieldy. Nor did the restructuring eradicate the pecking order among the different types of ships. Some cruiser-destroyer officers wriggled out of spending time with their "low and slow" cousins, who in turn resented being so stigmatized when their jobs were as essential to the national security as those of their more visible counterparts. A third drawback lay in the loosening of traditional ties between the Fleet Marine Forces and the former Amphibious Forces. [131]

Also the subject of considerable controversy was the establishment of the surface warfare pins. For a long time, surface sailors had noted that their branch of the line Navy was the only one without a distinctive insignia. True, skippers could wear the Command at Sea badge, but so could the heads of aviation units. Irritatingly, once a surface officer advanced to flag rank, he could no longer wear the Command at Sea badge while his peers continued to wear dolphins and wings. [132]

Some within the surface community, like Turner, opposed a surface warfare device on the grounds that it was "Mickey Mouse" or that it furthered parochialism in the Navy. In fact, Zumwalt considered for a time banning pins on all flag officers' uniforms on just that last ground. However, a number of the most prominent surface officers, such as Adamson, Doyle, Walters, and Weschler, wanted the pin. Their victory came in 1975 when the surface line finally won a distinctive insignia. Designed by Adamson, the crest featured crossed cutlasses framing a surface warship with a bone in her teeth. Although some felt it looked too much like the submariners' dolphins, most surface officers wore it with pride. [133]

If surface warriors won one old fight, they lost another: sea pay equivalent to flight pay or dive pay. They pushed for it on the grounds that some of the most talented officers were lured to the other branches partly for the monetary compensation. However strong the logic of this argument, it had not compelled Congress to grant a special allowance. This lack remains a sore point with the surface line. [134]

Reflecting the vast changes that had taken place during Zumwalt's tenure were the wholesale redesignation of the principal surface warships and the evolution of publications dedicated to the advancement of the surface sailor. At the end of 1974, *Cruiser-Destroyerman* ceased publication after more than a decade. It was replaced by *Surface* and then by *Surface Warfare* which first came out in September 1975. *Surface Warfare* offered a larger forum than *Cruiser-Destroyerman,* which had been essentially a newsletter for the Atlantic Fleet's surface forces. [135]

Finally, in 1978, the Naval Education and Training Support Command published a volume entitled *Surface Ship Operations* which focused principally on shiphandling, navigation, weather, and the like. Other chapters discussed antiaircraft and antisubmarine warfare; oddly, antiship operations received little attention.[136]

The 1975 redesignation of most of the surface warships was a natural outgrowth of the movement to give increased prominence to the surface warfare community. Contrary to practice abroad, the U.S. Navy since 1955 had termed "frigates" (DL/DLG/DLGN) its largest new surface warships (with the exception of *Long Beach*). The result was twenty-four years of confusion with such anomalies as *Truxtun*, a "frigate," being considerably larger than a *Kynda*-class "cruiser." In fact, one tongue-in-cheek definition of "frigate" was "a warship which, if the Soviets built it, we would call a cruiser." [137]

As of 1 July 1975, a new system went into effect. Frigates (DLG or DLGN) were henceforth to be called cruisers (CG or CGN). Destroyer escorts (DE or DEG) were now frigates (FF or FFG). All ships kept their original hull numbers except for the ten DLGs of the *Farragut*-class which had up to this time been the smallest of the Navy's "frigates." Because of their size and because their skippers were not captains but rather commanders, the *Farragut*s were reclassified as guided missile destroyers (DDG). They had to be renumbered to avoid confusion with ships of the *Charles F. Adams*-class.[138]

In looking back over the Zumwalt years, the analyst can only be impressed at how much was done during a time when it was difficult—for financial, political, and organizational reasons—to make any headway at all. Unquestionably, some of the solutions Zumwalt advanced to recover the U.S. Navy's supremacy gave great strength to aviation (another nuclear carrier and the F–14) and a new capability to submariners (Harpoon).[139]

But many of Zumwalt's remedies focused on bolstering the Navy's surface forces in meaningful ways. In hardware, a number of pivotal programs were either begun or accelerated: the Point Defense Missile System; CIWS; the *Perry*-class frigate; LAMPS; Standard; Harpoon; and Aegis. The organizational steps (the creation of the Deputy Chief of Naval Operations for Surface Warfare and the establishment of the Surface Commands) ultimately gave the surface line greater internal coherence and more clout within and without the Navy. Better schooling, stricter qualifications, and a distinctive insignia boosted the professional abilities and self-respect of surface warriors, most especially of the junior officers. As one blackshoe noted with pride at the end of 1974: "Recruiters will soon be faced with a problem of recruiting for three separate branches. No longer will it be submarines, aviation, or 'other.'" [140] Credit for these changes must go, in large part, to Admiral Elmo R. Zumwalt, Jr.[141]

# Postscript:
# The Surface Navy Resurgent, 1975–1991

From the mid-1970s, the surface arm of the Navy underwent a renaissance. At the start of President Ronald Reagan's defense buildup, the Congressional Budget Office felt compelled to pose the question, "Are present-day surface combatants merely the vestigial remnant of a long tradition, or are they still a vital component of naval forces whose place remains secure in logic as well as in tradition?"[1] That the committee affirmed the latter was due in large part to the efforts made by black-shoe officers in the first part of the 1970s. These advances had laid the groundwork for a renewal of surface warfare professionalism.[2]

In large part, this rebirth was tied to the long-delayed fruition of advanced weapons systems. In 1978, one naval analyst pointed out that a full decade after the *Eilat* sinking, "The U.S. Navy does not have a viable shipboard Anti-Ship Missile Defense (ASMD) system, and an effective jamming/decoy capability is only now entering the Fleet."[3] Admiral Thomas Weschler looked back with similar frustration: "I was on the source selection board to pick the Aegis contractor in the spring of 1967. Then we saw it [Aegis] go to sea in *Ticonderoga* in 1985, about 18 years later."[4]

Late Aegis might have been, but when the reliable and effective defensive system came onto line, exercises showed Aegis to be remarkably capable. An early trial pitted twenty-two Norwegian F–16s in a coordinated attack on the lead Aegis cruiser, *Ticonderoga*, operating in a fjord. All of the Norwegian aircraft "knew the real estate" and appeared over the walls of the fjord within ninety seconds of one another. In this extraordinarily demanding test, judges ruled that *Ticonderoga* "hammered" every one of the F–16s before they had reached release points for their weaponry. One surface officer highlighted Aegis as the most important single element in the revivification of surface warfare.[5]

Nonetheless, it is essential to note that Aegis was only part of the solution to the air problem; it was supplemented by capable point defenses like NATO Sea Sparrow and CIWS and by much improved electronics and decoy measures. When rounded out with the longer-range systems of the F–14 and airborne radar aircraft, Aegis helped give task groups a multi-layered and coordinated set of shields. One analyst maintained that these defenses returned "the fleet to much the position at the Battle of the

Philippine Sea, in which it could reasonably accept the possibility of air attack in expectation of destroying the attacking force in the air." [6]

Coupled with the shield was a new sword—the cruise missile. The restoration of an offensive capability gave the surface navy a sense of uplift that is hard to overstate. Like the improvements in defense, the provision of strike weaponry in surface warships produced a synergistic relationship with the carrier navy. The cruise missile made all ships an offensive threat and thus complicated the enemy's targeting problems. The cruise missile could hit enemy radar installations and command posts, thereby clearing the way for the carrier air strikes. If the tactical situation dictated, Harpoon and Tomahawk could carry a heavier portion of the offensive load, allowing the carrier to reduce its number of strike planes in exchange for more fighters. On the other side of the equation, the carrier helped the surface warships employ their cruise missiles. The greatest problem in shooting cruise missiles at naval targets remained in distinguishing the "red" (enemy) from the "white" (neutral) from the "blue" (friendly). Here, electronics aircraft with their radars could provide essential assistance. One top surface line officer, Vice Admiral Henry C. Mustin, summarized, "The combination of aircraft and missiles is better than either by several orders of magnitude." [7] In antisubmarine warfare too, the surface navy added to its capabilities since 1975. During the 1960s, some pessimists were saying that "surface ships can't do ASW." [8] That situation, if it ever truly existed, began changing in the 1970s. New passive towed arrays were augmented by improved active sonars. LAMPS helicopters on board cruisers, destroyers, and frigates could prosecute long-range contacts. Some surface officers also pointed out that LAMPS had the potential for attacking enemy missile boats in narrow seas. [9]

The completion of a large number of capable new warships went a long way to upgrading the surface navy. *Spruance* was followed by thirty more ships of her class and by the four antiaircraft derivatives of the *Kidd* class. Carrying Aegis to sea were two new classes: the *Ticonderoga* cruisers (twenty-seven ships) and the *Arleigh Burke* destroyers (with twenty-five hulls on order in 1994). Both the *Ticonderoga* and *Burke* designs were based directly on *Spruance*, reaffirming that ship as one of the most significant in naval history.

The performance of the surface navy was also enhanced by improvements in its schooling and in its qualification procedures. Vice Admiral J. F. Parker delineated the vast strides made in these areas. Parker entered the surface navy in the 1950s when the ensign "learned by doing." That system disappeared, especially with the Zumwalt reforms. Additional time set aside for exercises produced major benefits. In 1988, Parker concluded that "only the very best ships [of the early 1970s] achieved anything approaching the quality of the ships we have today." [10] Even the most dedicated leadership of the earlier period lacked the time to reach the levels of training that surface officers routinely realized by the 1980s. Ironically, the much more thorough schooling resulted in a situation where the least qualified officers on board surface warships are, in many cases, the senior officers who began their careers before the institution of these reforms. A commentator noted, "The faults of the SWO [Surface Warfare Officer] concept, and these are surprisingly few, stem from the fact that no conscious effort has been made to 'requalify' those officers who were ahead of this movement." [11]

As the surface navy improved, its standing within the Navy as a whole went up correspondingly. Aviators and submariners became more supportive of the blackshoes. The second DCNO for Surface Warfare, Vice Admiral Robert Adamson, remarked of the implementation of his Surface Warfare Plan, "I had a hell of lot of cooperation from the air and submarine communities.... There was an increasing realization in the air and submarine communities that you can't have a stool with two legs." [12] Another top surface warfare officer, Vice Admiral Robert L. Walters, concluded that the Navy of the 1980s was "a much more unified service than in the Sixties and Seventies." [13]

Frictions did remain. Some aviators resented the money spent on Tomahawk. Aviators on their way up the ladder still obtained their deep draft experience by taking the conn of fast combat support ships, replenishment oilers, combat stores ships, and amphibious ships. On occasion, some surface sailors sounded defensive about their specialty: "Our people are not second rate citizens, never have been, and never will be. Our insignia is not a black hole lying between shining aviation and submarine devices!" [14]

Intramural rivalries persisted within the surface branch, albeit to a reduced degree. Officers of amphibious ships still harbored the feeling that their brethren in cruisers and destroyers looked down their noses at the "Gator Navy." Perhaps the best judgment regarding this touchy matter was the one rendered by Admiral Parker who in his career commanded a tank landing ship, a support ship, and a guided missile frigate. Parker said that these different types of vessels made varying but approximately equal demands on their officers, with amphibious operations being possibly the most complex evolution that a junior officer would face in the surface navy. Clearly, split tours and a closer cooperation among the four elements of the surface warfare community muted, if not eliminated, intramural tensions. [15]

The establishment in 1988 of the Surface Navy Association reflected the tighter integration of the branches of the surface line. The organization held annual meetings and established chapters in a number of cities like Norfolk and San Diego. It published a newsletter, and helped to fund with a cash award advances in damage control. It also provided scholarships and recognized with its Old Salt Award the serving officer whose commission listed the earliest date.

If measured against the Soviets, the U.S. surface navy during the 1980s gained appreciable ground despite the fact that the Soviets introduced several new types of antiship missiles and impressive ships of the *Kirov* and *Slava* classes. With the disintegration of the Soviet Union, these vessels and their missiles became more of academic interest rather than the deadly menace that they would have been earlier. Instead, the immediate threat pressed from the navies of erratic Third World countries like Libya, Iraq, Iran, and North Korea. And these forces were frequently armed with a wide variety of weaponry, especially ex-Soviet equipment. Styx, for instance, was employed by twenty-one different nations in the early 1980s. As one commentator noted, the threat of very sophisticated arms technology was "apparent to anyone who looks at advertisements in the front and back of *Jane's* [*Fighting Ships*]." [16]

During the 1980s and early 1990s, the U.S. surface navy confronted several Third World challenges. In September 1982, the lead Aegis cruiser *Ticonderoga*, only nine months from her commissioning, deployed in a combat environment off Lebanon for over a month with marked success for her combat system. During the Gulf of Sidra incident in 1986, *Ticonderoga* and her sister *Yorktown* (CG 48) used Aegis to maintain a complete air picture and to direct surface and air strikes against Libyan patrol boats, aircraft, and missile sites. The Iraqi attack on frigate *Stark* in 1987 revealed once again the potency of the antiship missile, as well as the high state of damage control that U.S. surface warriors had achieved. The latter was demonstrated again when frigate *Samuel B. Roberts* (FFG 58) struck an Iranian mine in 1988. In both cases, the warships were operating in a quasi-war environment close to hostile bases from which the enemy could launch air and small craft attacks.[17]

The surface navy eventually obtained retribution for both these episodes. In retaliation for the *Samuel B. Roberts* mining, American naval forces struck back in Operation PRAYING MANTIS at Iranian targets. During this April 1988 action, both American offensive and defensive measures worked effectively. The performance of the Standard and Harpoon missiles proved especially satisfying. Cruiser *Wainwright* downed an Iranian F–4 with a Standard. U.S. surface ships fired five Standards at an Iranian vessel, *Joshan*; all five missiles struck the patrol boat, mortally damaging it. One Harpoon aimed at *Joshan* passed over the wreck. The derelict was finished off with 5-inch gunfire. The three Harpoons fired at patrol craft *Sahand* all hit. Iranian missile shots, on the other hand, were decoyed by American chaff.[18]

Only months later, cruiser *Vincennes* (CG 49) created a furor by shooting down an Iranian airliner in the Persian Gulf. This episode prompted a sharp debate within the surface navy, not over the value of Aegis, but over its handling in this particular incident. Less problematic was the performance of the surface navy in the 1991 war against Iraq. Battleships, cruisers, and destroyers fired some of the first shots of the war with their Tomahawks. The missiles helped clear the way for attack aircraft, just as their proponents had long anticipated. The last two battleships in service, *Missouri* and *Wisconsin*, showed once again the devastating power of the big-bore naval gun. Three Aegis cruisers—*Bunker Hill* (CG 52), *Mobile Bay* (CG 53), and *Princeton* (CG 59)—kept track of over 65,000 aircraft sorties without a single "blue-on-blue" loss.[19] These actions certainly bore out the conclusions of the 1981 Congressional Budget Office review that reasserted the value of surface warships: "Cruise missiles, autonomous aviation capability, and substantial technical improvements in radar, sonar, and command and control systems are among the factors combining synergistically to improve the combat potential of modern surface warships."[20] If history can serve as a guide, conflicts with Third World nations from 1987 to 1991 are certain to be repeated—and the Navy will continue to project American power abroad. Of the more than two-hundred international incidents affecting the United States during the period covered by this study, 1945 to 1975, the Navy played a role in 80 percent of the crises.[21]

For the foreseeable future then, surface warships will remain a key component of the U.S. Navy because of their capacious magazines, hard-hitting armament, sensors, endurance, and command and control facilities. Only the surface warship can carry out all four missions advanced by Admiral Stansfield Turner for the Navy: strategic deterrence, sea control, naval presence, and projection of power.[22]

Nonetheless, there are recurrent predictions that the surface warship is in its dying days—that the future lies with the submarine. Were this true, we would see the end of sea power as it has traditionally been exercised. If the surface warship cannot stay afloat in a hostile environment, then neither can the carrier that it protects. The merchant ship, in such circumstances, would be hopelessly vulnerable, and this country could no longer make its sustained presence felt in areas outside the Western Hemisphere.[23]

The black-shoe community has heard its doom forecast in earlier times by both submarine and air power enthusiasts. Surface warships have, in the end, survived all of the threats arrayed against them. There is every reason to believe that the surface navy will do so in the future. It simply must. There is no alternative if the United States is to remain a major force in world affairs.

# Abbreviations

| | |
|---|---|
| AAW | Antiair Warfare |
| APL | Applied Physics Laboratory (Johns Hopkins University) |
| ARM | Anti-Radiation Missile |
| ASROC | Antisubmarine Rocket |
| ASMS | Advanced Surface Missile System |
| ASW | Antisubmarine Warfare |
| AUTEC | Atlantic Underwater Test and Evaluation Center, Bahamas Islands |
| AVM | Guided Missile [Trials] Ship |
| BB | Battleship |
| BPDSMS | Basic Point Defense Surface Missile System |
| BUAER | Bureau of Aeronautics |
| BUORD | Bureau of Ordnance |
| BUPERS | Bureau of Naval Personnel |
| BUSHIPS | Bureau of Ships |
| BUWEPS | Bureau of Naval Weapons |
| CA | Heavy Cruiser |
| CAG | Guided Missile Heavy Cruiser |
| CAP | Combat Air Patrol |

*Abbreviations*

| | |
|---|---|
| CB | Large Cruiser |
| CG | Guided Missile Cruiser |
| CGN | Nuclear-powered Guided Missile Cruiser |
| CIC | Combat Information Center |
| CINCLANT | Commander-in-Chief, Atlantic |
| CINCPAC | Commander-in-Chief, Pacific |
| CIWS | Close-In Weapon System |
| CL | Light Cruiser |
| CLC | Command Ship |
| CLGN | Nuclear-powered Guided Missile Light Cruiser |
| CLK | Antisubmarine Warfare Cruiser |
| CNA | Center for Naval Analyses |
| CNO | Chief of Naval Operations |
| COMCRUDESLANT | Commander Cruiser-Destroyer Force, Atlantic |
| COMCRUDIV | Commander Cruiser Division |
| COMOPTEVFOR | Commander Operational Test and Evaluation Force |
| CRUDESFLOT | Cruiser-Destroyer Flotilla |
| CSGN | Strike Cruiser |
| CV | Aircraft Carrier |
| CVA | Attack Aircraft Carrier |
| CVAN | Nuclear-powered Attack Aircraft Carrier |
| CVE | Escort Aircraft Carrier |

| | |
|---|---|
| CVN | Nuclear-powered Aircraft Carrier |
| *DANFS* | *Dictionary of American Naval Fighting Ships* |
| DASH | Drone Antisubmarine Helicopter |
| DCNO | Deputy Chief of Naval Operations |
| DD | Destroyer |
| DDG | Guided Missile Destroyer |
| DE | Escort Ship (or Destroyer Escort) |
| DEG | Guided Missile Escort Ship |
| DESDIV | Destroyer Division |
| DESRON | Destroyer Squadron |
| DL | Destroyer Leader (from 1955–1975, Frigate) |
| DLG | Guided Missile Frigate |
| DLGN | Nuclear-powered Guided Missile Frigate |
| DTRC | David Taylor Research Center |
| EAG | Experimental Auxiliary |
| ECCM | Electronic Counter-Countermeasures |
| ECM | Electronic Countermeasures |
| FFG | Guided Missile Frigate |
| FRAM | Fleet Rehabilitation and Modernization |
| FY | Fiscal Year |
| G Ships | Any of the guided missile cruisers, frigates, destroyers, or escorts |

| | |
|---|---|
| HARM | High-speed Anti-Radiation Missile |
| IFF | Identification Friend or Foe |
| JCS | Joint Chiefs of Staff |
| LAMPS | Light Airborne Multi-Purpose System |
| LST | Landing Ship, Tank |
| MCLWG | Major Caliber Lightweight Gun |
| NACO | Navy Cool (propellant) |
| NARA | National Archives and Records Administration |
| NATO | North Atlantic Treaty Organization |
| NAVAIR | Naval Air Systems Command |
| NAVORD | Bureau of Naval Ordnance |
| NAVORDSYSCOM | Naval Ordnance Systems Command |
| NAVSURFLANT | Naval Surface Force, U.S. Atlantic Fleet |
| NAVSURFPAC | Naval Surface Force, U.S. Pacific Fleet |
| NHC | Naval IIistorical Center |
| NOL | Naval Ordnance Laboratory |
| NROTC | Naval Reserve Officer Training Corps |
| NSWC | Naval Surface Weapons Center |
| NTDS | Naval Tactical Data System |
| NWC | Naval War College, Newport, RI |
| NWL | Naval Weapons Laboratory, Dahlgren, VA |
| NWP | Naval Warfare Publication |

| | |
|---|---|
| OA | Operational Archives (of the Naval Historical Center) |
| OCS | Officer Candidate School |
| OEG | Operations Evaluation Group |
| ONI | Office of Naval Intelligence |
| OPDEVFOR | Operational Development Force |
| OPNAV | Office of the Chief of Naval Operations |
| OPTEVFOR | Operational Test and Evaluation Force |
| PGG | Missile Gunboat |
| PHM | Patrol Combatant Missile Hydrofoil |
| PIRAZ | Positive Identification Radar Advisory Zone |
| PT | Patrol Torpedo Boat |
| SCS | Sea Control Ship |
| SH | Ships Histories Branch (of the Naval Historical Center) |
| SLCM | Sea Launched Cruise Missile |
| SOSUS | Sound Surveillance System |
| SS | Submarine |
| SSBN | Nuclear-powered Ballistic Missile Submarine |
| SSN | Nuclear-powered Submarine |
| SWATH | Small Waterplane Area Twin Hull |
| SWO | Surface Warfare Officer |
| VLS | Vertical Launch System |

# Glossary

**Aegis:** Integrated fleet weapon control system, using automatic detect-and-track phased-array AN/SPY–1 radar and computerized decision and command element; able to operate simultaneously against multiple high-performance air, submarine, and surface threats, and to coordinate the weapon systems of a task force.

***Albany* (CG 10) class**: U.S. guided-missile cruisers, three ships completed as *Baltimore/Oregon City*-class gun cruisers 1945–46. Extensively modernized, rearmed with Talos and Tartar missiles, and recommissioned 1962–64.

***Arleigh Burke* (DDG 51) class:** U.S. guided-missile destroyers. *Arleigh Burke* commissioned 1991; 41 or more projected. 466 feet; 8,300 tons; Standard, ASROC, Tomahawk, Harpoon, (1) 5″/54, ASW torpedoes. Later production blocks will incorporate current improvements. Designed as antiair/antisurface warfare destroyers with Aegis weapon system to supplement *Ticonderoga*-class of CGs well into the next century.

**AS–2 Kipper:** Soviet air-launched standoff antiship missile, introduced 1961.

**AS–4 Kitchen:** Advanced Soviet air-to-surface missile, produced with alternative nuclear and antiship warheads.

**AS–5 Kelt:** Soviet air-to-surface naval aviation missile, designed primarily for antiship use.

***Asheville* (PG 84) class:** U.S. gunboats, 17 completed 1966–70. 165 feet; 245 tons; gas turbine and diesels; 37.5 knots; (1) 3″/50. One tested Standard missile in SSM mode; four more backfitted with them. Some served in Vietnam.

**ASROC:** Surface-ship antisubmarine weapon, introduced 1961; ballistic rocket armed with nuclear depth charge (no longer in service) or acoustic homing torpedo.

***Bainbridge* (DLGN 25):** U.S. nuclear-powered missile frigate (DLGN), completed October 1962 as fast, high-endurance antiaircraft ship to operate with aircraft carriers. Reclassified missile cruiser (CGN) 1975. 550 feet; 8,580 tons; Terrier, ASROC, (2) twin 3″/50.

***Baltimore* (CA 68) class:** U.S. heavy cruisers, 14 completed 1943–45. 674 feet; 16,800 tons; (9) 8″/55, (12) 5″/38, 40mm and 20mm AA. Some mothballed after WWII; others served in Korea and after. *Saint Paul*, last active ship of the class, served in Vietnam. *Boston* and *Canberra* received a partial missile conversion. *Chicago* and *Columbus* became *Albany*-class missile cruisers. Three *Oregon City*-class ships, modified *Baltimore*s with single stacks and superstructure, grouped for better AA fire, completed 1946. *Albany* became a missile ship; the unfinished *Northampton* was completed as a command ship.

**Bat:** U.S. air-launched, radar-guided glide bomb, used against Japanese shipping in 1945.

**Battleships (BB):** During WWII older, slower ships, completed 1912–23 and later modernized, provided heavy firepower for the amphibious forces. The *North Carolina*, *South Dakota*, and *Iowa* classes, completed 1941–44, were fast enough to operate with the carrier striking force. The *Iowa*s were the only active postwar BBs. Other fast BBs and "newer" old BBs remained in reserve but were disposed of by 1962.

***Belknap* (DLG/CG 26) class:** U.S. guided-missile frigates (DLG), reclassified missile cruisers (CG) 1975, nine ships completed 1964–67. 547 feet; 7,940 tons; Terrier, ASROC, (1) 5″/54, ASW torpedoes. Now out of commission.

***Boston* (CAG 1) class:** U.S. guided-missile heavy cruisers, two ships built as *Baltimore*-class gun cruisers during WWII. When two Terrier missile launchers replaced one gun turret, they recommissioned 1955–56 as missile ships. Their missile suits were obsolescent by the time of the Vietnam war, but they provided extensive gunfire support to ground forces.

***Bronstein* (DE/FF 1037) class:** U.S. escort ships, two completed 1963. 372 feet; 2,560 tons; (3) 3″/50, ASROC, ASW torpedoes. The *Garcia* class was an enlarged version of this design. Reclassified frigates 1975; both decommissioned 1990.

***Brooke* (DEG/FFG 1) class:** U.S. missile escort ships, six completed 1966–68. 414 feet; 3,426 tons; (1) 5″/38, Tartar, ASROC, ASW torpedoes. Missile version of the *Garcia* design. Reclassified missile frigates 1975.

**Bullpup:** Supersonic air-to-surface standoff missile, radio-guided by the launching plane. Operational in 1959, it remained in use through the Vietnam War, carried by P–3 patrol planes as well as fighters and attack planes. Original Bullpup carried a 250-lb bomb; later version took a 1,000-lb bomb. Air Force version could also carry a nuclear warhead.

**Bumblebee:** Surface-to-air missile project, begun by Bureau of Ordnance December 1944 to meet threat of standoff aircraft weapons such as

German Hs.293 and PC 1400 FX. It eventually led to the Talos, Terrier, and Tartar missiles of the 1950s.

*California* **(DLGN/CGN 36) class:** Nuclear-powered missile frigates, two completed 1974–75 for high-endurance operation with carrier task forces; reclassified cruisers 1975. 596 feet; 11,100 tons; Tartar, ASROC, (2) 5″/54, ASW torpedoes.

*Chapaev* **class:** Soviet light cruisers, planned before WWII as a 12-ship class; only six were laid down and five completed 1948–51. 659 feet; 15,000 tons; (12) 5.9″/50, (8) 3.9″/60, 37mm AA. Fitted for minelaying.

*Charles F. Adams* **(DDG 2) class:** U.S. missile destroyers, 23 completed 1960–64. 437 feet; 4,500–4,900 tons; Tartar, (2) 5″/54, ASROC, ASW torpedoes. Missile version of the *Forrest Sherman* design, they were the first U.S. keel-up missile destroyers. Considered versatile warships and good sea boats. Now out of service.

*Charlie* **class:** Soviet nuclear-powered cruise missile submarine, first identified 1969. 300 feet; 4,500 tons surfaced; (8) SS–N–7 missiles, torpedoes.

**CIWS (Close-in Weapon System):** Phalanx all-weather, automatically controlled close-in gun system for point defense of ships against missiles and aircraft, using an electrically powered Vulcan 20mm Gatling-type gun with a cyclic rate of 3,000 rounds/minute. Its radar guidance system tracks target and gun projectiles to correct aim. Operational 1980, CIWS is used throughout the fleet.

*Claud Jones* **(DE 1033) class:** U.S. escort ships, four completed 1959–60. 312 feet; 1,777 tons; (2) 3″/50, (2) Hedgehog. Designed as mass-producible diesel ASW ships, but proved unable to carry modern antisubmarine systems. Two ships tested Norwegian Terne III ASW missile in the 1960s; one received VDS. Sold to Indonesia 1973–74.

*Cleveland* **(CL 55) class:** U.S. light cruisers, 27 completed 1942–46. 610 feet; 13,000 tons; (12) 6″/47, (12) 5″/38, 40mm and 20mm AA. War production rapid-fire 6″-gun cruisers, result of design process begun with the *Brooklyn* (CL 40) class of the late 1930s. All but one were in reserve by Korea. Six were converted to missile ships (CLG) during 1956–60. Two modified *Cleveland*s completed 1945–46 as the single-stack *Fargo* class.

**Condor:** Long-range air-to-surface missile, TV-guided using a two-way data link to attack point targets with a conventional warhead. Development and evaluation were successful, with 1976 production planned, but Condor was canceled by Congress for its high cost.

**Continuous-rod warhead:** Warhead casing made up of parallel rods connected accordion-fashion at their ends. On detonation, instead of fragmenting, the rods open up into an expanding ring of metal designed to cut into a target.

***Coontz* class:** *See Farragut* (DLG 6) class.

**Corvus:** Long-range standoff nuclear air-to-surface missile, begun 1957 and canceled 1960.

**CSGN:** *See* Strike cruiser.

**DASH (Drone Antisubmarine Helicopter):** Small drone helicopter developed for antisubmarine use by destroyer types. The QH–50A (redesignated DSN–1, 1962) could carry one homing torpedo; the production versions QH–50C (DSN–3) and QH–50D (DSN–4) carried two.

***Dealey* (DE 1006) class:** U.S. escort ships, five ships completed 1954–57. 315 feet; l,950 tons; (4) 3″/50, Weapon Able, ASW torpedoes. First post-WWII U.S. frigate types, with geared turbines for higher speed. *Dealey* completed with two British Squid ASW mortars in lieu of Weapon Able.

***Decatur* (DDG 31) class:** U.S. missile destroyers, four converted 1964–68 from *Forrest Sherman*-class DDs. A Tartar launcher and ASROC replaced two 5″/54. All were inactivated in the late 1980s.

***Des Moines* (CA 134) class:** U.S. gun cruisers, three completed 1948–49. 717 feet; 21,500 tons; (9) 8″/55 rapid-fire, (12) 5″/38. With the *Worcester* class, these were the last U.S. all-gun cruisers. Guns were a new rapid-firing model using metal cases in lieu of the powder bags used in all previous 8″ guns. Served in Atlantic Fleet through thc 1950s. *Des Moines* inactivated 1961, *Salem* 1959. *Newport News* later served in Vietnam, inactivated 1975. Being disposed of.

**Destroyer (DD):** Surface warship, ranking in size between a DE and a DL. WWII DDs mounted 5″ guns, torpedo tubes, depth charges; were primarily used to screen carrier and surface task forces. Postwar DDs grew in size, added new electronics and ASW weapons. Some received missile armament (DDG).

**Destroyer Escort (DE):** Surface warship, smaller than a destroyer, produced during WWII primarily for antisubmarine patrol and escort. Redesignated escort vessel (DE) 1948. *See also* Escort ship; Frigate.

**DG/Aegis:** Design concept advanced by CNO Admiral Elmo Zumwalt for an austere, economical fleet air defense destroyer. Scheduled for construction FY 77, it was canceled as impracticable within desired cost and size limits.

**DX–DXG Project:** Concept project that ultimately resulted in the *Spru-ance* (DD 963) and *Kidd* (DDG 993) classes.

**ECCM (Electronic Counter-Countermeasures):** Actions taken to frustrate an opponent's electronic warfare measures.

***Echo II* class:** Soviet nuclear-powered missile submarines. Prototype *Echo I* class built in early 1960s; experience incorporated into improved *Echo II* design, armed with four twin launching tubes for SS–N–3 Shaddock surface-to-surface missiles.

**ECM (Electronic Countermeasures):** Active and passive systems and techniques used to prevent an opponent from effectively using radio or radar. ECM may include detection, deception, and jamming.

***Eilat:*** Israeli destroyer sunk during the 1967 Six-Day War by Egyptian Styx missiles, the first warship so lost.

***Enterprise* (CVAN 65):** First U.S. nuclear-powered aircraft carrier, completed 1961. 1,102 feet; 89,600 tons; 84-plus aircraft. Like *Long Beach*, built with fixed-array radars that dictated a unique boxlike superstructure. Began Vietnam service 1965 as first nuclear-powered ship to see combat. Modernized 1979–82, phased-array radars replaced by conventional electronics. Had neither guns nor missiles as built; CIWS and Sea Sparrow later added.

**Escort ship (DE):** Surface warship type, between destroyer and corvette, designed primarily for antisubmarine warfare. First built during WWII as destroyer escorts (DE); many wartime ships served postwar. New DEs began joining fleet mid-1950s; first missile ships (DEG) commissioned 1966–68. Escort ships were redesignated frigates (FF, FFG) 1975. Modern FFGs have some antiair and antisurface capabilities.

**Escort vessel (DE):** WWII destroyer escorts redesignated escort vessels (DE) 1948, escort ships (DE) 1960, and frigates (FF) in 1975.

***Essex* (CV–9) class:** U.S. aircraft carriers, 24 completed 1942–50; eight more canceled unbuilt. 876–888 feet; 33,000 tons; 80-plus aircraft. Production fleet carriers of WWII formed part of the backbone of the Fast Carrier Force 1943–45, and were the strength of TF 77 in Korea 1950–53. Active *Essex*es were extensively modernized in the 1950s and early 1960s; used as attack carriers (CVA) and antisubmarine carriers (CVS); some served through Vietnam.

***Fargo* (CL 106) class:** *See Cleveland* class.

***Farragut* (DLG 6) class:** U.S. missile frigates, ten completed 1959–61. 513 feet; 5,350 tons; Terrier, (1) 5"/54, ASROC. Built as AAW ships to screen carriers, they were modernized in the 1970s and redesignated the DDG 37 class in 1975. Often referred to as the *Coontz* class.

**Fireflash:** Proposed antiship missile version of the Ryan BQM–34A Firebee target and reconnaissance drone aircraft.

***Forrest Sherman* (DD 931) class:** U.S. destroyers, 18 completed 1955–59. 418 feet; 3,950–4,050 tons; (3) 5″/54, (4) 3″/50, (2) Hedgehog, ASW torpedoes. First U.S. destroyers built after WWII, incorporating war experience. Eight ships received an ASW modernization in the late 1960s. Four were converted to Tartar DDGs, 1964–68; conversion of the rest of the class was canceled. All decommissioned in the 1980s.

***Forrestal* (CVA 59) class:** U.S. aircraft carriers, four completed 1955–59. 1,066–1,071 feet; 75,900–79,300 tons; (8) 5″/54; 70-plus aircraft. First post-war-designed "supercarriers," and first carriers designed to handle jet planes. Guns were removed by late 1960s; later armed with Sea Sparrow. Three of the class have been inactivated.

**FRAM destroyers:** 131 WWII-built U.S. destroyers extensively modernized in the early 1960s under the Fleet Rehabilitation and Modernization (FRAM) program to improve weapon and sensor capabilities and extend service lives. 95 *Gearing*s (DD 710), 33 *Allen M. Sumner*s (DD 692), and 3 *Fletcher*s (DD 445) were FRAMmed.

**FRAS–1:** Soviet ballistic antisubmarine rocket with a nuclear warhead, introduced 1967 and designated FRAS–1 (Free Rocket Antisubmarine) by NATO.

**Frigate:** Term used in two different senses during this period. Post-WWII U.S. frigates (DL) and missile frigates (DLG, DLGN) ranked between destroyers and cruisers. Later frigates grew in size, blurring frigate/cruiser distinction; also, U.S. nomenclature differed from NATO's and all other navies. In 1975 smaller DLG became DDG; DLGN and larger DLG became CGN, CG; by then "gun frigates" (DL) had passed out of service. The term was applied, in its contemporary sense, to former escort ships (DE, DEG), now called frigates (FF, FFG). *See also* Escort ship.

**FX 1400:** *See* PC 1400 FX.

***Galveston* (CLG 3) class:** Term sometimes refers to the six *Cleveland*-class cruisers converted to missile ships in 1956–60. These actually break down into four groups according to flagship or non-flagship configuration and whether armed with Talos or Terrier. All six were "single-enders," with missile launchers aft. Four flagships (two Talos, two Terrier) kept one 6″/47 triple turret to make room for enlarged bridge structures. Two non-flagships (one Talos, one Terrier) kept two turrets. The CLGs, redesignated CG in 1975, saw gunfire support service in Vietnam.

*Garcia* **(DE 1040) class:** Escort ships, ten completed 1964–68. 415 feet; 3,403 tons; (2) 5″/38, ASROC, ASW torpedoes. Enlarged *Bronsteins*, originally using DASH but later modified to handle LAMPS II. Reclassified FF 1975; decommissioned in the late 1980s.

**Grebe:** Post-WWII folding-wing ASW missile carrying an acoustic torpedo. The first U.S. attempt to develop a standoff antisubmarine weapon; Grebe was canceled in the early 1950s. The concept led to RAT and later to ASROC.

**Guidance, missile:** The means by which a missile is directed to its target. These included preset, command, beam-riding, homing, inertial, and composite guidance. Preset guidance is set into a control system before launch. In command guidance, the missile is controlled by radio or radar from the launcher. In beam-riding guidance, the firing ship aims a control radar at the target and the missile guides itself along the radar beam. Homing guidance can be active, semiactive, or passive. In active guidance, the missile has its own radar and steers itself. A semiactive system holds the target in a radar beam from an external source, such as a ship, and the missile homes on the reflection. A passive system homes on heat or radar energy generated by the target. In inertial guidance, the firing ship's navigational system programs directions to the target into the missile's digital computer. After launch, gyroscopes and accelerometers sense and measure the missile's movements to keep it on its programmed trajectory. In terrain-matching guidance the missile senses the terrain below, matching it to a computer "map" to fix its position and adjust its course. Composite guidance combines features of two or more of the systems cited above.

**Guns:** A modern gun is, essentially, a rifled steel tube closed at its breech end and mounted on a carriage that trains and elevates the gun and accommodates its recoil. Guns may fire fixed (projectile and metal powder case combined in one unit), semifixed (projectile and metal powder case loaded separately), or bag (projectile and cloth powder bag loaded separately) ammunition. During 1945–75 penetrating projectiles were armor-piercing (AP) for armored ships or fortified land targets and common (COM) for lightly protected ships or targets. Fragmenting projectiles included high capacity (HC) for unprotected sea or land targets, antiaircraft (AA) for aircraft in flight, and AA common (AAC) for aircraft and lightly protected surface targets. Special-purpose projectiles included illuminating (ILLUM), also called star shell; white phosphorus (WP), or smoke; and chaff (W), dispensing foil strips formerly called "window" to confuse an enemy's radar. Five-inch rocket-assisted projectiles (RAP), sacrificing some explosive load for rocket propellant, were used in Vietnam. Projectiles dispensing numbers of "bomblets" were developed in the 1980s for 16″ battleship guns. Shells were detonated by impact, mechanical time, or proximity fuzes.

During this period, the U.S. Navy had the following larger guns in its inventory:

| | |
|---|---|
| 16″/50 | *Iowa*-class BB |
| 16″/45 | *North Carolina*, *South Dakota*, *Colorado*-class BB |
| 14″/50 | *Tennessee*-class BB |
| 12″/50 | *Alaska*-class CB |
| 8″/55 | *Des Moines*-class CA |
| 8″/55 | *Baltimore*-class CA, and CAG conversions |
| 8″/55 | Major-Caliber Lightweight Gun (MCLWG). Tested 1970s to improve gunfire support capability, considered for *Spruance* class; canceled. |
| 6″/47 | *Cleveland*-class CL, and CLG conversions |
| 5″/54 | Postwar CV, DLG/DLGN, DD, DDG |
| 5″/54 | Lightweight automatic gun. CG/CGN, *Spruance*-class DD, *Arleigh Burke*-class DDG, LHA |
| 5″/38 | BB, WWII CV, CA/CL, CAG/CLG, WWII DD, DE/DEG, auxiliaries |
| 3″/50 | Automatic AA gun. Combatants, auxiliaries |
| 76mm/62 | Oto Melara automatic gun. FFG, PHM |

**Gyatt (DDG 1):** *Gearing*-class destroyer (DD 712), completed 1945 and converted 1955–56 to a prototype missile destroyer, with fin stabilizers and a twin Terrier launcher. Missiles were removed in 1962.

**HARM (High-Speed Anti-Radiation Missile):** U.S. air-to-surface missile for use against enemy radars, developed from the earlier Shrike and Standard ARM missiles with improved seeking capability.

**Harpoon:** U.S. antiship cruise missile, launched by submarines, surface ships, and patrol planes. Introduced 1979, it saw combat in the Persian Gulf. The missile flies a programmed low-altitude course to its target, with active target acquisition and active or passive homing. Improved versions have been produced or are being developed.

**Heavy cruiser (CA):** Ship classification originated by the London naval limitation treaty of 1930, based on gun caliber; in the U.S. Navy, a cruiser armed with 8″ guns.

**Hs.293:** Henschel Hs.293, German WWII antishipping glide bomb, launched from a medium bomber and steered to its target by radio. *See* PC 1400 FX.

**Iowa (BB 61) class:** U.S. battleships, four ships completed 1943–44. 887 feet; 57,216–57,540 tons; (9) 16″/50, (20) 5″/38, 40mm, 20mm. Last, and fastest (33 knots) U.S. battleships. All served in WWII and Korea. *New Jersey* (BB 62) reactivated 1968–69 for one Vietnam tour. All four reactivated and modernized in 1980s with Harpoon and Tomahawk missiles; now out of commission in reserve.

***Joshan*:** One of 11 *Combattante II* type missile attack craft completed in France for Iran 1977–81. Sunk by U.S. naval forces 18 April 1988 during the Persian Gulf "tanker war."

***Juliett* class:** Soviet cruise missile submarines, about 15 built early 1960s. 280 feet; 2,500 tons surfaced; SS–N–3, torpedoes. Diesel-electric submarines, thought to have been experimental prototypes for the larger nuclear-powered *Echo* class.

***Kara* class:** Soviet missile cruisers, seven completed 1973–80. 571 feet; 10,000 tons; SS–N–14, SA–N–3, SA–N–4, (4) 76.2mm, (4) 30mm Gatling, ASW rockets, torpedoes. Gas turbine ships, similar in concept to the *Kresta II* class.

***Kashin* class:** Soviet missile destroyers, 20 completed 1962–73. 472 feet; 4,750 tons; SA–N–1, (4) 76.2mm, ASW rockets, torpedoes. Capable of minelaying. The first gas turbine warships. Six ships had SS–N–2C missiles added in the 1970s.

***Kidd* (DDG 993) class:** U.S. missile destroyers, four completed 1981–82. 563 feet; 8,300 tons; Standard ER, ASROC, Harpoon, (2) 5″/54, (2) CIWS, ASW torpedoes. Missile version of the *Spruance* class; originally built for Iran and acquired by the U.S. in 1979 after the fall of the Shah.

***Kildin* class:** Soviet missile destroyers, four completed late 1950s from unfinished *Kotlin*-class hulls. 425 feet; 3,800 tons; SS–N–l, (16) 57mm AA, ASW rockets, torpedoes. Apparently used to test the missile installation later used in the *Krupnyy* class.

***Kirov* class:** Soviet heavy cruisers, six completed 1938–1944. 627 feet; 11,500 tons; (9) 7.1″/57, (6) 3.9″/60, 37mm AA, torpedoes. Capable of minelaying. Italian-designed, the last Soviet heavy cruisers.

***Knox* (FF 1052) class:** U.S. frigates, 46 completed 1969–74. 438 feet; 3,877 tons; (1) 5″/54, ASROC, ASW torpedoes. Later modifications added Sea Sparrow, CIWS, towed sonar, Harpoon, and Standard missile capability to all or some ships. Some became Reserve training ships. All are now out of commission, with some transferred to other navies.

***Komar* class:** Soviet fast missile attack craft, 42 completed 1959–61. 85 feet; 75 tons; SS–N–2, (2) 25mm AA. Cruise missile version of the P–6 torpedo boat design of the 1950s, smaller than the *Osa* class with two missile launchers to the *Osa*'s four. Some transferred to other navies.

**Kotlin** **class:** Soviet destroyers, 19 ships completed 1954–58. 418 feet; 3,885 tons; (4) 5.1″/50, (16) 47mm AA, torpedoes, depth charges. Capable of minelaying. Later ships had fewer torpedoes, ASW rockets in lieu of depth charges. Considered a successful, seaworthy design. Some were converted to handle SA–N–2 missiles in the 1960s, designated the *Kotlin*-SAM class. Four *Kotlin*s were completed with SS–N–1 missiles as the *Kildin* class.

**Kresta I class:** Soviet missile cruisers, four completed 1967–69. 508 feet; 7,500 tons; SS–N–3, SA–N–1, (4) 57mm AA, torpedoes, ASW rockets. A Hormone B helicopter provides over-the-horizon missile targeting. Thought to be designed for long-range operation against NATO carriers. One ship extensively refitted 1973–75 with new electronics and four 30mm Gatlings.

**Kresta II class:** Soviet missile cruisers, 10 completed 1970–78. 518 feet; 7,600 tons; SS–N–14, SA–N–3, (4) 57mm AA, (4) 30mm Gatlings, torpedoes, ASW rockets. *Kresta I* variant with enhanced ASW and AA capabilities.

**Krivak** **class:** Soviet frigates, 21 completed 1970–82. 410 feet; 3,575 tons; SS–N–14 & SA–N–4 missiles, (4) 76.2mm, torpedoes, ASW rockets. Capable of minelaying. Gas turbine antisubmarine ships with limited AA capability, used extensively in the Baltic. Eleven *Krivak II* ships completed 1975–82 with two 100mm in lieu of 76.2mm guns.

**Krupnyy class:** Soviet missile destroyers, 8 ships completed 1961–63. 456 feet; 4,560 tons; SS–N–1, (16) 57mm AA, torpedoes. Developed from the *Kildin* class. Later converted to ASW ships, SS–N–1 missiles replaced by SA–N–1 AA missiles and ASW rockets; this version was dubbed the *Kanin* class by NATO.

**Kynda class:** Soviet missile cruisers, four completed 1962–65. 466 feet; 5,600 tons; SS–N–3, SA–N–1, (4) 76.2mm, torpedoes, ASW rockets. First new-design Soviet missile ships, designed to counter NATO carriers.

**LAMPS:** Light Airborne Multi-Purpose System. Integrated combination of surface warship and antisubmarine helicopter, designed to increase ship effectiveness by using the aircraft to extend the range of the ship's sensors and weapons. The original LAMPS Mark I system used the SH–2F Seasprite helicopter; the current computer-integrated LAMPS Mark III uses the SH–60B Seahawk.

**Large cruiser (CB):** *Alaska* class, six ordered; CBs 1–3 laid down during WWII, two completed. 808 feet 6 inches; 34,250 tons; (9) 12″ guns. Designed as an intermediate type between the 8″-gun heavy cruiser and the 16″-gun battleship, they compared to the German *Scharnhorst* and French

*Dunkerque* classes. *Alaska* and *Guam* saw brief service and were inactivated after V-J Day. *Hawaii*, nearly complete by 1945, was later considered for missile or fleet flagship conversion.

***Leahy* (DLGCG 16) class:** U.S. missile frigates, nine completed 1962–64. 533 feet; 8,200 tons; Terrier, ASROC, ASW torpedoes. First U.S. keel-up double-ender missile ships, emphasizing carrier task force AA defense. Modernized 1967–72. All modified to use Standard missiles; six ships also got Harpoon. Reclassified as cruisers 1975. Out of commission.

**Light cruiser (CL):** Ship classification based on gun caliber (*See also* Heavy cruiser). U.S. light cruisers usually mounted 6″ guns. Some small WWII CLs designed prewar as destroyer flotilla leaders had 5″ main batteries, were used as AA ships during the war, and were classified as antiaircraft light cruisers (CLAA) in 1949.

***Lion* class:** *See Tiger* class.

***Long Beach* (CGN 9):** U.S. missile cruiser, completed 1961. 721 feet; 17,525 tons; Terrier, (2) 5″/38, ASROC, ASW torpedoes. Aegis installation planned for FY 77, but canceled. Midlife modernization 1980–83 replaced Terrier with Standard and added Harpoon with new electronics. Out of commission.

**Loon:** Post-WWII U.S. Navy experimental version of the German V–1 pulse-jet "buzz bomb."

***Mitscher* (DL 2) class:** U.S. frigates, four completed 1953–54. 493 feet; 4,730 tons; (2) 5″/54, (4) 3″/70, ASW torpedoes. Oversized conventional destroyers, begun as DDs 927–930 and redesignated DLs 2–5 in 1951. Two ships converted to DDG 1966–69; Tartar and ASROC added. Now disposed of.

***Moskva* class:** Soviet ASW helicopter carriers, two ships completed 1967–68. 625 feet; 19,200 tons; 15–18 Hormone helicopters; FRAS–1, SA–N–3, (4) 57mm AA, torpedoes, ASW rockets. "Helicopter cruisers" to counter Polaris strategic missile submarines as part of ASW task groups.

***Nanuchka* class:** Soviet small missile ships, 37 completed 1969–91. 194 feet; 675–685 tons; SS–N–9, SA–N–4, (2) 57mm AA (*Nanuchka I*) or (1) 76.2mm, (1) 30mm Gatling (*Nanuchka* III). Ten export ships, the *Nanuchka II* class, were built for other navies.

***Nimitz* (CVN 68) class:** U.S. nuclear-powered aircraft carriers, six completed 1975–92; three building. 1,092 feet; 93,300–96,836 tons; Sea Sparrow, three or four CIWS; 90-plus aircraft. Designed for maximum resistance to battle damage. Later ships incorporate detail improvements.

***Norfolk* (DL 1):** U.S. frigate, completed 1953. 540 feet; 7,300 tons; (8) 3″/70, (4) Weapon Able/Alfa, ASW torpedoes. Two "ASW cruisers," designed for all-weather offensive work against high-performance submarines, were authorized in FY 48 as hunter-killer ships, CLKs 1–2. CLK 2 was canceled. CLK 1, *Norfolk*, was completed as a frigate (DL 1) and served as flagship for various Atlantic commands; decommissioned 1970.

***Northampton* (CLC 1):** U.S. command ship, converted from the unfinished hull of an *Oregon City*-class heavy cruiser and completed 1953. Used as flagship for various Atlantic commands; decommissioned 1970.

***Oliver Hazard Perry* (FFG 7) class:** U.S. missile frigates, 51 ships completed 1977–89. 445 feet; 3,658–4,100 tons; Standard, Harpoon, (1) 76mm/62, ASW torpedoes; 1 LAMPS I or 1–2 LAMPS III. Designed as low-cost escort ships with numerous improvements added to fit them for fleet duty to replace older destroyers and frigates. Some are assigned to Reserve training.

***Oregon City* (CA 122) class:** *See Baltimore* class.

***Osa* class:** Soviet missile attack craft, approximately 110 completed 1959–70. 132 feet; 200 tons; SS–N–2, (4) 30mm AA. Built in two configurations, identified as the *Osa I* and *Osa II* classes; larger than the *Komar* class, with four missile launchers to the *Komar*s' two. Many *Osa*s were transferred to foreign navies.

**PC 1400 FX:** German WWII air-launched radio-controlled armor-piercing glide bomb. It sank the Italian battleship *Roma* 1943. *See also* Hs.293.

***Pegasus* (PHM 1) class:** U.S. hydrofoil missile craft, six completed 1977–83 for U.S. Navy. 145 feet; 240 tons; Harpoon, (1) 76mm/62. Developed in cooperation with West Germany and Italy. Gas turbine craft, capable of 50 knots foilborne. Thirty ships originally projected; also NATO construction planned but dropped as not cost-effective. Operated out of Key West, Florida; used for drug interdiction. Out of commission, slated for disposal.

**Petrel:** U.S. air-launched antiship missile carrying a homing torpedo, in service 1955 but soon discarded in favor of antisubmarine weapons.

***Providence* (CL 82):** Cleveland-class cruiser, completed 1945. Decommissioned 1949 after Atlantic and Mediterranean service, converted to a missile cruiser (CLG 6) 1957–59. (*See also Galveston* class.) Saw gunfire support service in Vietnam 1966–72. Decommissioned 1973; sold for scrapping 1980.

**Proximity fuze:** Fuze containing a miniature radio transmitter activated when a gun projectile is fired. When radio signals are reflected by a nearby target, the fuze detonates. Called variable time (VT) fuzes for security when introduced by the U.S. Navy in 1942, they proved valuable anti-aircraft weapons in the Pacific.

**Regulus I:** Air-breathing turbojet cruise missile capable of carrying a nuclear warhead. Some carriers, cruisers, and submarines were fitted to launch Regulus I.

**Regulus II:** Supersonic cruise missile for submarines and surface ships with range over 1,000 miles. Nuclear-capable, it was guided by command from ship or plane, or by self-correcting inertial navigation system.

***Riga* class:** Soviet frigates, 80 completed late 1950s. 299 feet; 1,600 tons; (3) 3.9"/50, 37mm AA, torpedoes; fitted for minelaying. Most later modernized, with new electronics and ASW weapons.

**SA–N–1 Goa:** Soviet command guided, Mach 2, medium-range antiaircraft missile, introduced 1962 as naval version of the land SA–3. Used in surface warships.

**SA–N–3 Goblet:** Soviet command guided, supersonic antiaircraft missile, introduced 1967. Used in large warships; standard area defense missile until SA–N–6 introduced in 1980.

**SA–N–4 Gecko:** Soviet short-range low-altitude command guided anti-aircraft missile, introduced 1969. Principal AA missile in smaller warships, secondary AA missile in larger types.

**SA–N–6:** Soviet vertical-launch, long-range, terminal homing Mach 5 antiaircraft area defense missile, introduced 1980.

**Sea Control Ship (SCS):** A small (610 feet), relatively inexpensive (under $100 million) aircraft carrier to operate V/STOL airplanes and helicopters. The concept was studied by the U.S. Navy in the early 1970s, and eight ships were projected for completion by 1977–80 before the project was dropped. The large-deck amphibious assault ship *Guam* was tested as an "interim SCS," and ships of that general type have operated AV–8 Harriers as well as helicopters.

**Sea Sparrow:** U.S. short-range antiaircraft missile for surface ships, derived from the Sparrow III air-to-air missile. Designed to give individual ships short-range defense capability against high-performance aircraft and missiles. It has been followed by the jointly developed NATO Sea Sparrow, with an improved missile and control system.

***Skoryy* class:** Soviet destroyers, 72 completed 1949–54. 400 feet; 3,180 tons; (4) 5.1"/50, (2) 85mm/50 AA, 37mm and 20mm AA, torpedoes, depth charges. The first post-WWII Soviet destroyers. Eight ships later received new electronics and 57mm AA guns.

**SOSUS (Sound Surveillance System):** Array of fixed undersea listening devices intended to detect the passage of Soviet submarines.

*Spruance* **(DD 963) class:** U.S. destroyers, 31 ships completed 1975–83. 563 feet; 8,040–8,250 tons; Harpoon, NATO Sea Sparrow, (2) 5″/54, ASROC, ASW torpedoes; LAMPS I or LAMPS III. Large, highly automated gas turbine destroyers, their basic hull and engineering plant also led to the designs of the *Kidd* and *Ticonderoga* classes. Seven *Spruances* received armored box launchers for Tomahawk missiles; the rest of the class have received, or will receive, a vertical launching system (VLS) for Tomahawk. One of the class launched missiles at Iraqi targets during Desert Storm.

**SS–N–1 Strela:** Small, short-range Soviet antiship cruise missile used by *Krupnyy*- and *Kildin*-class DDGs.

**SS–N–2 Styx:** Soviet surface-launched subsonic antiship missile, in service with fast attack craft since late 1950s. First used in combat by Egypt 1967 (*see Eilat*) and by India 1971. Used by many foreign navies; also manufactured in China as HY–2.

**SS–N–3 Shaddock:** Soviet nuclear/conventional cruise missile, improved naval version of a coast defense missile used by land forces. Used in submarines and missile cruisers.

**SS–N–7:** Soviet submarine-launched cruise missile, capable of submerged launch with conventional or nuclear warhead.

**SS–N–9 Siren:** Soviet ship-launched conventional or nuclear cruise missile, used in small combatants and submarines.

**SS–N–10:** NATO designation for what was at first thought to be a Soviet ship-launched antiship missile. Later discovered to be an ASW weapon, it was then redesignated SS–N–14.

**SS–N–14 Silex:** Soviet surface-ship antisubmarine missile, armed with a homing torpedo or nuclear warhead. NATO originally evaluated this as an antiship weapon and designated it SS–N–10.

*Stalingrad* **class:** Soviet large cruisers, generally comparable to the U.S. *Alaska* class, four or more projected. One ship, *Stalingrad*, laid down at Nikolaev 1949. Canceled when about 60 percent complete, 1953 after Stalin's death. Used as a missile test target.

**Standard:** Surface-to-air missile, produced in medium-range (MR) and extended-range (ER) versions. The single-stage MR replaced Tartar; the two-stage ER superseded Terrier. Both can be used against surface targets.

**Strike cruiser (CSGN):** Concept designation for a large nuclear-powered Aegis cruiser, capable of independent operation and armed with Standard, Tomahawk, Harpoon, (1) 8″/55, and ASW torpedoes. Inclusion of V/STOL capability was suggested. Eight CSGN were planned, beginning in FY 78, but slipped and were finally canceled.

***Sverdlov* class:** Soviet light cruisers, 13 laid down after WWII and completed 1952–58. 689 feet; 19,000 tons; (12) 5.9″/50, (12) 3.9″/60, 37mm AA. Fitted for minelaying. 24 ships planned, 20 laid down, 13 completed. One was converted to a missile ship armed with SA–N–1 Guideline SAMs 1961; two were converted to command ships 1972.

**SWATH:** Small Waterplane Area Twin Hull. Catamaranlike design in which the platformlike upper hull is supported by two submerged pontoons, which provide buoyancy and house the electrically driven propulsion system. This configuration is designed for superior seakeeping and stability. Ocean surveillance ships, beginning with the *Victorious* (T-AGOS 19) class, are built to a SWATH design.

***Tallinn*:** NATO designation for the experimental Soviet destroyer *Nastoichivyi*, first observed 1955. This was the first ship to test rocket depth charge projectors.

**Talos:** Long-range ramjet beam-riding surface-to-air missile with semiactive terminal homing, introduced 1957 and taken out of service 1979. Large and heavy, it could only be used by cruiser-size ships. Later versions had improved warheads and guidance systems; some had nuclear capability.

**Tartar:** Supersonic surface-to-air missile, developed 1950s for frigates (DLG) and destroyers. Entered service with the *Charles F. Adams* (DDG 2) class. Later Tartars extended range from original 7.5 miles to 17.5 miles, had improved warheads and surface-to-surface capability. Replaced by Standard I (MR).

***Tennessee* (BB 43):** U.S. battleship, one of two ships of the class, completed 1920. Slightly damaged at Pearl Harbor, but thoroughly modernized 1942–43. With extensive added hull protection, modern fire control systems, and new secondary and AA armament, the ship served in the Pacific from Kiska to Okinawa. Decommissioned 1947; sold for scrapping 1959.

**Terrier:** Medium-size rocket surface-to-air missile. Development began late 1940s, evaluation completed 1955 after many changes to resolve problems. First operational 1956, arming cruisers and missile frigates. Later missiles had semiactive homing. Production ended 1966; replaced by Standard I (ER).

***Ticonderoga*** **(CG 47) class:** U.S. missile cruisers, 27 ships completed 1983–94. 568 feet; 9,407–9,589 tons; Standard, ASROC, Harpoon, Tomahawk (CG 52–73), (2) 5″/54, CIWS, ASW torpedoes; 1 or 2 LAMPS I (CG 47–48), 1 or 2 LAMPS III (CGs 49–73). Based on *Spruance*-class hull and machinery, they were originally classed as destroyers (DDG 47 class), redesignated cruisers (CG) 1980. Considered highly capable general-purpose cruisers, successive production blocks have incorporated improvements. CGs 47–51 have topside missile launchers, later ships have VLS. Some launched Tomahawk strikes during Desert Storm.

***Tiger*** **class:** British cruisers, three completed 1959–61. 556 feet; 11,700 tons; (4) 6″/50 rapid-fire, (6) 3″. Begun as wartime *Swiftsure*-class gun cruisers, suspended 1945, resumed to revised design 1955. Automatic 6″ dual-purpose guns, improved engineering and habitability. Two ships modified to helicopter carriers in the late 1960s.

**Tomahawk:** U.S. all-weather ship- or submarine-launched cruise missile carrying a 1,000-lb explosive warhead. Its land-attack version uses inertial and terrain-matching guidance; the antiship version flies a programmed low-altitude course and uses active terminal guidance to acquire and hit its target. Tomahawk saw combat in Desert Storm. A 1991 presidential order directed retirement of a strategic nuclear version.

***Triton*** **(SSR(N) 586):** U.S. nuclear-powered submarine, completed 1959. 447 feet; 5,800 tons surfaced; torpedoes. Built as a radar-picket submarine, *Triton* circumnavigated the globe submerged in 1960. Radar-picket capability was removed 1962–64. Decommissioned 1969.

***Truxtun*** **(DLGN 35):** U.S. nuclear-powered missile frigate, completed 1967. 564 feet; 9,127 tons; Terrier, ASROC, (1) 5″/54, ASW torpedoes. Standard, Harpoon, CIWS added later. Redesignated a missile cruiser (CGN 35) 1975. Decommissioned 1994.

**Typhon:** U.S. long-range ramjet missile for use against high-performance aircraft and missiles as well as surface ships. Its control system, designed to operate against multiple targets, was large and costly; Typhon was canceled 1963, as was a large DLG designed to carry it. The basic concept was pursued and eventually developed into the Aegis system.

***United States*** **(CVA 58):** U.S. aircraft carrier, laid down and canceled 1949. 1,050 feet. Designed to operate aircraft capable of carrying the large atomic weapons of that time, *United States* would have been the first of the post-WWII "supercarriers." The intense interservice debate over strategic missions led the Secretary of Defense to terminate construction only days after the keel was laid.

***Vanguard***: Britain's last battleship, completed 1946. 814 feet; 51,420 tons; (8) 15/42″, (16) 5.25/50″, 40mm AA. To expedite construction, armed with turrets removed from WWI "light battle cruisers" *Courageous* and *Glorious*. Reputed to be a good Atlantic seakeeper and steady gun platform. Inactivated 1954, sold 1960.

***Virginia*** **(CG 38) class:** U.S. nuclear-powered missile cruisers, four completed 1976–80. 585 feet; 10,420 tons; Standard/Tartar, Harpoon, ASROC, (2) 5″/54, ASW torpedoes. Improved version of the *California* class. Two inactivated.

**VLS (Mark 41 Vertical Launching System):** Integrated system for stowage and launching of missiles, combining in one unit the functions of magazine and launcher. Missiles are carried in vertical below-deck tubes, called cells. Any needed mix of missiles can be fired in quick succession without the delays involved in reloading earlier weather-deck launchers. The *Ticonderoga* and *Arleigh Burke* classes are armed with VLS; most of the *Spruance* class has, or will have, it.

***Whiskey*** **class:** Soviet submarines, 236 completed 1951–59. 248 feet; 1,050 tons surfaced; torpedoes. Capable of minelaying. First post-WWII Soviet submarines, produced in six variants. Four or five were later converted to radar picket submarines called *Whiskey Canvas Bag* by NATO. Six became *Whiskey Single-Cylinder* or *Whiskey Twin-Cylinder* missile submarines, armed with one or two deck-mounted SS–N–3 surface-to-surface launchers; six later *Whiskey Long Bin* conversions received a streamlined superstructure containing four SS–N–3 launchers. The last *Whiskey*s were disposed of 1989–91.

***Worcester*** **(CL 144) class:** U.S. light cruisers, two completed 1948–49, inactivated 1958. 680 feet; 18,500 tons; (12) 6″/47, (12) 5″/38. Ordered in 1943, their new automatic 6″ guns had dual-purpose capability. *Worcester* served in Korea.

# Notes

## 1. Sinking Fast

1. Lecture, Captain S. Teller, "Guided Missiles for Naval Operational Employment," 27 Jul 1946, 2, RG 15, Naval War College (NWC), Newport, RI.

2. Agenda, 13 Sep 1945, Secretary of the Navy—Cabinet Folder, PSF, Truman Papers, Harry S. Truman Library, Independence, MO (hereafter Truman Library).

3. Vincent Davis, *The Admirals Lobby* (Chapel Hill, 1967), 186. For a detailed look at the scale of the U.S. Navy's triumph, see Malcolm Muir, Jr, "The United States Navy in World War II: An Assessment," in *Reevaluating Major Naval Combatants of World War II*, ed. James J. Sadkovich (New York, 1990), 15–16.

4. James V. Forrestal to the President, 11 Sep 1945, Secretary of the Navy—Cabinet Folder, PSF, Truman Papers, Truman Library.

5. Davis, *Admirals Lobby*, 187.

6. Ibid., 188–89

7. Lloyd J. Graybar, "The Buck Rogers of the Navy: Admiral William H. Blandy," in William R. Roberts and Jack Sweetman, eds. *New Interpretations in Naval History: Selected Papers from the Ninth Naval History Symposium Held at the United States Naval Academy, 18–20 October 1989* (Annapolis, 1991): 340–41.

8. *Brassey's Annual, 1947*, (New York, 1947), 146–47.

9. Ibid., 152–53, 156–57.

10. "Estimate of Russian Intentions," 10 Jan 1950, 36, 38, 57, CNO Command Files, Operational Archives (OA), Naval Historical Center (NHC), Washington, DC; Michael A. Palmer, *Origins of the Maritime Strategy: American Naval Strategy in the First Postwar Decade* (Washington, 1988), 4.

11. Davis, *Admirals Lobby*, 187.

12. True, this Soviet navy was so weak that it drew sarcastic comments from the Air Force. One general said in 1947, "To maintain a five-ocean navy to fight a no-ocean opponent . . . is a foolish waste of time, men and resources." Steven L. Rearden, *History of the Office of the Secretary of Defense*, vol. 1, *The Formative Years 1947–1950* (Washington, 1984), 390.

13. Arthur W. Radford, *From Pearl Harbor to Vietnam: The Memoirs of Admiral Arthur W. Radford*, ed. Stephen Jurika, Jr. (Stanford University, 1980), 78.

14. Carl Boyd, "Radford, Arthur William," in *Dictionary of American Military Biography*, ed. Roger J. Spiller, vol. 3, *Q–Z* (Westport, CT, 1984), 899–901.

15. Edwin B. Hooper, Dean C. Allard, and Oscar Fitzgerald, *The United States Navy and the Vietnam Conflict*, vol. 1, *The Setting of the Stage to 1959* (Washington, 1976), 73.

16. Davis, *The Admirals Lobby*, 197.

17. Joseph Zikmund, "James V. Forrestal," in *American Secretaries of the Navy*, ed. Paolo E. Coletta, vol. 2, *1913–1972* (Annapolis, 1980), 736; Thomas C. Hone, *Power and Change: The Administrative History of the Office of the Chief of Naval Operations, 1946–1986* (Washington, 1989), 12; BUPERS memo, 1 Oct 1949, Secretary of the Navy—Cabinet Folder, PSF, Truman

Papers, Truman Library; Clark G. Reynolds, *The Fast Carriers: The Forging of an Air Navy* (New York, 1968), 69; and Henry H. Adams, *Witness to Power: The Life of Fleet Admiral William D. Leahy* (Annapolis, 1985), 328.

18. Reynolds, *Fast Carriers*, 391.

19. For details, see Reynolds, *Fast Carriers*, 385, 391–94; and Clark G. Reynolds, *Admiral John H. Towers: The Struggle for Naval Air Supremacy* (Annapolis, 1991), 513–15, 531–33.

20. Graybar, "Admiral Blandy," 339, 341; and Richard Hallion, *The Naval Air War in Korea* (Baltimore, 1986), 13.

21. Robert G. Albion and Robert H. Connery, *Forrestal and the Navy* (New York, 1962), 46–47.

22. Zikmund, "James V. Forrestal," in Coletta, *Secretaries of the Navy* 2:735; and Hone, *Power and Change*, 18.

23. John S. McCain, Jr., "Where Do We Go from Here?" U.S. Naval Institute *Proceedings* (hereafter *Proceedings*) 75 (Jan 1949): 49.

24. Albion and Connery, *Forrestal and the Navy*, 46.

25. Frederick H. Schneider, Jr. to author, 5 Apr 1993.

26. James L. Holloway III, interview with author, 28 Aug 1992, Admiral James L. Holloway III File, OA (hereafter Holloway interview).

27. Robert L. Brandenburg, "Destroyer Command: Critical ASW Subsystem," *Proceedings* 90 (Jul 1964): 39.

28. Richard G. Alexander to author, 7 Jul 1992.

29. John H. Hitchcock, "Discrimination in Selections: Fact or Fancy?" *Proceedings* 86 (Sep 1960): 73–74.

30. Coletta, "Francis Matthews," in Coletta, *Secretaries of the Navy* 2:811.

31. Frank M. Hertel, "The Naval Academy and Naval Aviation," Proceedings 74 (Jan 1948): 37; James L. Holloway, Jr., "The Holloway Plan—A Summary View and Commentary," *Proceedings* 73 (Nov 1947): 1300; and McCain, "Where Do We Go from Here?" 51.

32. Paul B. Ryan, *First Line of Defense: The U.S. Navy Since 1945* (Stanford, CA, 1981), 11–12, 28.

33. Stansfield Turner, interview with author, 4 May 1988 (hereafter Turner interview).

34. McCain, "Where Do We Go from Here?" 47.

35. Thomas B. Buell, *The Quiet Warrior: A Biography of Admiral Raymond A. Spruance* (Annapolis, 1987), 418.

36. Granville A. Moore, "The Naval War College Takes a New Look at Its Courses," *Proceedings* 81 (Jan 1955): 70–71; Edward L. Katzenbach, Jr., "The Demotion of Professionalism: The War Colleges," *Proceedings* 91 (Mar 1965): 34; and Buell, *Quiet Warrior*, 418–19, 421–23.

37. Lecture, A. G. Pelling, "Employment of Ships' Weapons," 2 July 1946, RG 14, NWC.

38. Coletta, "John Lawrence Sullivan," in Coletta, *Secretaries of the Navy* 2:749, 763; Davis, *Admirals Lobby*, 188; Rearden, *Formative Years*, 393; and Paolo E. Coletta, *The United States Navy and Defense Unification, 1947–1953* (Newark, 1981), 57.

39. Frederic S. Withington, 1972, 150, U.S. Naval Institute (USNI) Oral History Collection, OA (hereafter Withington oral history).

40. Davis, *Admirals Lobby*, 206.

41. Graybar, "Admiral Blandy," 336.

42. Lecture, C. V. Ricketts, "Battleships and Cruisers," 26 Jul 1947, 8, RG 14, NWC; J. W. Stryker, "The Battleship as an Auxiliary Supply Ship," *Proceedings* 73 (Oct 1947): 1181–84; and Palmer, *Origins of the Maritime Strategy*, 6–7.

43. John B. Colwell to author, 16 Jul 1992; and Charles K. Duncan to author, 22 Aug 1992.

44. Lecture, R. J. Woodaman, "Employment of Ships' Weapons," 21 July 1947, 12, RG 14, NWC; Folder 2577H, "Board Maneuver Rules; Supplement to Maneuver Rules," Aug 1946, 19, RG 4, NWC; James V. Forrestal to the President, 10 Jan 1946, OF 18, Truman Papers, Truman Library; Stephen G. Xydis, "The Genesis of the Sixth Fleet, *Proceedings* 84 (Aug 1958): 41–43; and William H. Hessler, "The Battleship Paid Dividends," *Proceedings* 72 (Sep 1946): 1154.

45. Lecture, R. R. Hartung, "Cruisers," 12 Jul 1946, 21, RG 14, NWC; Frederick H. Schneider, Jr. to author, 31 Jul 1992; William R. St. George to author, 6 Jul 1992; *Dictionary of American Naval Fighting Ships* (Washington, 1968), 3:289–90 (hereafter *DANFS*); and *DANFS* 6:236, 252.

46. Frederick H. Schneider, Jr. to author, 17 Feb 1993; and Thomas C. Buell, interview with author, 7 Oct 1992 (hereafter Buell interview).

47. W. M. Montgomery to author, 28 Sep 1992.

48. Report, 21 Jun 1948, "Navy Dept Tentative Basic Naval Establishment Plan for Jan 1950," Navy Department, Richards Files, RG 200; Robert L. Dennison to the President, 12 Mar 1948, Secretary of the Navy—Cabinet Folder, PSF, Truman Papers; and A. C. Wedemeyer, Director of Plans and Operations to Chief of Staff, 5 Oct 1948, Richards Files, RG 200, all in Truman Library.

49. Report, 21 Jun 1948, "Navy Dept Tentative Basic Naval Establishment Plan for Jan 1950," Navy Department, Richards Files, RG 200; and Robert L. Dennison to the President, 12 Mar 1948, Secretary of the Navy—Cabinet Folder, PSF, Truman Papers, Truman Library.

50. CO, USS *Davis* (DD 937) to Chief of Naval Operations (CNO), 23 Dec 1962, "Unsatisfactory Personnel Situation," 7, Personal Files of Allan Slaff, Naples, FL.

51. Buell interview, 7 Oct 1992; Douglas C. Plate to author, 13 Aug 1992; Robert Foreman, interview with author, 22 Aug 1992 (hereafter Foreman interview); Robert C. Peniston to author, 25 Jun 1992; Harold L. Young, "Techniques and Practices in Recent Naval Steam Turbine Construction," *Journal of the American Society of Naval Engineers* 71 (Nov 1959): 712; and *DANFS* 1 (rev.):91.

52. Roger W. Paine, Jr. to author, 29 Oct 1992.

53. Robert L. Dennison to the President, 12 Mar 1948, Secretary of the Navy—Cabinet Folder, PSF, Truman Papers, Truman Library.

54. *DANFS* 1 (rev):131, 396; 7:219; 8:397; and *Brassey's Annual, 1967*, 76.

55. William J. Manning, interview with author, 2 Apr 1993 (hereafter Manning interview).

56. Commander Western Pacific Striking Force to Commander Naval Forces Western Pacific, 18 Jun 1948, "Task Force Exercises, 7–11 June 1948," 1, Western Pacific Striking Force File, Post 1 Jan 1946 Report Files, OA.

57. Commander Task Force (CTF) Seventy-One to Commander Naval Forces, Western Pacific, 3 Oct 1948, "Report of Task Force Seventy-One Exercise," 1; CO, USS *Ozbourn* (DD 846) to Commander Cruiser Division Three, "Report of Task Force Exercises conducted 22–26 April, 1947," Destroyer Flotilla Three File; "Report of CONVEX ONE—Surface Raider Action," 1–2, Cruiser Division Four File; and CO, USS *Hamner* (DD 718) to CTF 71, "Report of Task Force Exercises," 2, Destroyer Flotilla Three File, all in Post 1 Jan 1946 Report Files.

58. CTF 71 to Commander Naval Forces, Western Pacific, 7 Nov 1948, "Report of Task Force Seventy-One Exercise," 1–7.

59. "Study of Nature of Warfare within Next Ten Years and Navy Contributions in Support of National Security. G.B. No. 425, Part 3: Seizure of an Advanced Base (Iceland)," 30 Apr 1948, 21, XWAG, RG 8, NWC.

60. "Search and Screening and Task Force Dispositions Exercises," 12 Jul 1948, Folder 2686, RG 4, NWC; Hone, *Power and Change*, 27; Norman Friedman, *U.S. Destroyers: An Illustrated Design History* (Annapolis, 1982), 241; J. L. Moulton, "NATO and the Atlantic," in *Brassey's Annual, 1973* (New York, 1974), 149; Jürgen Rohwer, "The Confrontation of the Superpowers at Sea," in *R.U.S.I.* and *Brassey's Defence Yearbook, 1974* (New York, 1975), 167; Jan Breemer, *Soviet Submarines: Design, Development and Tactics* (Coulsdon, Surrey, 1989), 78–80; and Norman Polmar and Jurrien Noot, *Submarines of the Russian and Soviet Navies, 1718–1990* (Annapolis, 1990), 141.

61. Commander Western Pacific Striking Force to Commander Naval Forces Western Pacific, 18 Jun 1948, "Task Force Exercises, 7–11 June 1948," 4.

62. CTG 71.4 to CTF 71, 29 May 1947, "Comments and Recommendations, Task Force Exercises, period 22–26 April," 3, Destroyer Flotilla Three File.

63. Sokolsky, "Seapower in the Nuclear Age," 47–48; and Naval Ordnance Laboratory, Corona, *From Sky to Sea: Twenty Years of Guided Missile Development at NBS and NOLC* (Corona, CA, 1959), 26.

64. A. L. Danis, "Offensive ASW: Fundamental to Defense," *Proceedings* 83 (Jun 1957): 586–87; *DANFS* 8:440; and Willem Hackmann, *Seek & Strike: Sonar, Anti-Submarine Warfare and the Royal Navy, 1914–54* (London, 1984), 350.

65. Friedman, *U.S. Destroyers*, 258–63; *Conway's All the World's Fighting Ships 1947–1982, Part I: The Western Powers* (Annapolis, 1983), 222–23; *DANFS* 3:267; *Brassey's Annual, 1967*, 69; and Coletta, *United States Navy and Defense Unification*, 58.

66. *Conway's* 1:222–23.

67. *ONI Review*, Dec 1949, 8, in OA.

68. "Estimate of Russian Intentions," 10 Jan 1950, 22, CNO Command Files, OA.

69. "Study of Nature of Warfare within Next Ten Years and Navy Contributions in Support of National Security. G.B. No. 425, Part 3: Seizure of an Advanced Base (Iceland)," 30 Apr 1948, 21, XWAG, RG 8, NWC.

70. "Operations Problem 3J," Nov 1946, Folder 2606 A–D, RG 4, NWC; "Operations Problem 3-48, BLUE-RED Staff Solution," Sep 1947, 49–50, Folder 2644B, RG 4, NWC. BLUE has one missile battleship, RED none. "No intelligence has shown PURPLE to have any of these ships. However, it is known that PURPLE has given emphasis to guided missiles and it is believed that guided missile-rocket weapons are ready for use on a large scale. BLUE-RED plans, therefore, must accept the possibility that one or more PURPLE battleships may be a missile-launching type." Lecture, G.B.H. Hall, "Guided Missiles," 10 Jan 1951, 3, RG 15, NWC.

71. "The Soviet Navy," *ONI Review*, Mar 1950, 99.

72. Jürgen Rohwer, Direktor of Bibliothek für Zeitgeschichte, to author, 3 Mar 1990; and "The Development of the Soviet Navy Since World War II," *ONI Review*, Oct 1960, 425.

73. Lecture, H. D. Felt, "Russian Naval Power," 30 Dec 1950, RG 14, NWC.

74. "The Soviet Navy," 94–95.

75. "Study of Nature of Warfare within Next Ten Years and Navy Contributions in Support of National Security. G.B. No. 425, Part 2: Answers to Red Check Items in the Agenda," 26 Apr 1948, 64–66, 82, XWAG, RG 8, NWC.

76. Omar N. Bradley to Armed Service Committee, House, c. 1949, Clifford Papers, Truman Library.

77. Norman Friedman, *The Postwar Naval Revolution* (Annapolis, 1986), 82, 83, 120.

78. "Study of Nature of Warfare within Next Ten Years and Navy Contributions in Support of National Security. G.B. No. 425, Part 3: Seizure of an Advanced Base (Iceland)," 30 Apr 1948, 10, XWAG, RG 8, NWC; Wedemeyer to Chief of Staff, 5 Oct 1948, Richards Files, RG 200, Truman Library; Report, Navy Department to JCS Special Budgetary Assistants, 24 Aug 1948, Richards Files, RG 200; Allard, "An Era of Transition, 1945–1953," 293; and Clark G. Reynolds, *Command of the Sea: The History and Strategy of Maritime Empires* (New York, 1974), 556–57.

79. Initially, the Atlantic Fleet's Cruiser Force was known as the Battleship-Cruiser Force, U.S. Atlantic Fleet, but with the mothballing of the battleships the unit was redesignated in November 1948. Ironically, the first vice admiral commanding Cruiser Force, William M. Fechteler, flew his flag in *Missouri*, the only battleship in commission. In the Pacific, COMCRUDESPAC would remain in existence, with alternations in title, until March 1975; nineteen flag officers would take the helm. See *Cruiser-Destroyerman*, Jan 1970, 5, NDL; *Surface*, Oct 1975, 11, NDL; and Commander Naval Surface Force, Pacific Fleet to Director of Naval History, 18 Jun 1975, "Commander Cruiser-Destroyer Force, U.S. Pacific Fleet Command History 1974 and to 'Secure the Watch,' March 31, 1975," 6, Naval Surface Force, Pacific Fleet File, Post 1 Jan 1946 Report Files.

80. Coletta, *United States Navy and Defense Unification*, 255; Commander Cruiser Division Three to Commander Hawaiian Sea Frontier, 11 Apr 1948, "Report of Joint Training Exercises 7–9 April 1948," 2, Cruiser Division Three File; Report, Navy Department to JCS Special Budgetary Assistants, 24 Aug 1948, Richards Files, RG 200, Truman Library; and "Anti-Aircraft Fire Effect and Rules Governing Damage Inflicted by Aircraft," Aug 1946, Folder 2577J, RG 4, NWC. Not until the 1960s would the Soviets deploy effective air-launched antiship missiles.

81. Walter Millis, ed., *The Forrestal Diaries* (New York, 1951), 467.

82. Hone, *Power and Change*, 27; and Norman Friedman, *U.S. Cruisers: An Illustrated Design History* (Annapolis, 1984), 374.

83. Friedman, "The '3–T' Programme," in *Warship*, ed. John Roberts (Annapolis, 1982), 6:160; and Lloyd M. Mustin interview, 24 Jun 1992.

84. BUORD, *Bulletin of Ordnance Information*, 30 Jun 1946, 14, OA; Thomas R. Weschler, interview with author, 24 Mar 1988 (hereafter Weschler interview); Norman Friedman, "USS *Worcester*," in *Warship*, ed. Roberts, 4:142; and *DANFS* 6:119; 8:464.

85. OPNAV, NWIP 21-2 (A), "Naval Weapons Selection—Ships," c. 1960, 4–9, OA; *DANFS* 4:647; 6:260; and *Bulletin of Ordnance Information*, 30 Jun 1946, 14.

86. *Combat Readiness*, "The 8″/55 as an AA Weapon," Apr–Jun 1954, 23–24, OA.

87. *Bulletin of Ordnance Information*, 31 Dec 1945, 18; *DANFS* 6:259; "Report of CONVEX ONE – Surface Raider Action," 1–2, Cruiser Division Four File; and Weschler interview, 24 Mar 1988.

88. Robert L. Baughan, Jr. to author, 18 Jul 1992.

89. Weschler interview, 24 Mar 1988; Jewett O. Phillips, Jr. to author, 24 Jun 1992; OPNAV, NWIP 1–4: "Experimental Tactics for U.S. Navy Ships and Aircraft," Jul 1954, 81–4, OA; *Bulletin of Ordnance Information*, 30 Sep 1955, 16; and Friedman, *U.S. Cruisers*, 355–60.

90. "Operations Problem 3–48," May 1948, Folder 2644–B, RG 4, NWC; "Operations Problem 3–48, BLUE-RED Staff Solution," Sep 1947, 49–50, Folder 2644B; Friedman, *U.S. Battleships: An Illustrated Design History* (Annapolis, 1985), 390; and Friedman, "The US Command Cruiser," in *Warship*, ed. Roberts, 5:209.

91. *Combat Readiness*, "Destroyer Leaders," Jan–Mar 1955, 9–10; Scheina, "Search for a Mission," 262; and Friedman, *U.S. Destroyers*, 243.

92. "Study of Nature of Warfare within Next Ten Years and Navy Contributions in Support of National Security. G.B. No. 425, Part 2: Answers to Red Check Items in the Agenda," 26 Apr 1948, 65–66; and *Bulletin of Ordnance Information*, 30 Jun 1946, 67.

93. *Bulletin of Ordnance Information*, 31 Dec 1945, 15.

94. Ibid., 30 Jun 1947, 7; Ibid., 31 Dec 1947, 17; and Scheina, "Search for a Mission," 268.

95. OPNAV, NWIP 21–2 (A), "Naval Weapons Selection--Ships," c. 1960, 4–9, OA; *Bulletin of Ordnance Information*, 30 Jun 1946, 21; Buford Rowland and William B. Boyd, *U.S. Navy Bureau of Ordnance in World War II* (Washington, 1953), 516; *DANFS* 6:97; and LT Joseph H. Herlihy, "Use of the 30/50 in Gunfire Support," *Combat Readiness*, Apr–Jun 1967, 1–2. During the July 1988 RIMPAC exercise, the author noted that the 3″/50s on the *Cleveland* (LPD 7), temporary flagship of the Third Fleet, had the most elementary ring sights.

96. Laurence W. Ferris, Richard A. Frey, and James L. Mills, Jr., "The Ship Launched Projectile," *Naval Engineers Journal* 75 (Feb 1963): 97.

97. Friedman, *U.S. Destroyers*, 388; Scheina, "Search for a Mission," 262; *Bulletin of Ordnance Information*, 31 Mar 1948, 8–9; OPNAV, NWIP 21–2 (A), "Naval Weapons Selection—Ships," c. 1960, 4–9; and Gary L. Pickens, "5-Inch, 54 Gun Reliability Improvement Program," *Naval Ordnance Bulletin*, Jun 1973, 44.

98. William D. O'Neil III, "Gun Systems? For Air Defense?," *Proceedings* 97 (Mar 1971): 45–46; *Bulletin of Ordnance Information*, 30 Jun 1946, 22; and Ibid., 30 Sep 1954, 26, 31.

99. Lecture, D. V. Gallery, "Guided Missiles," 13 Feb 1950, 6, RG 15, NWC; Review of the Naval Guided Missiles Program, 1 Aug 1947, 23–24, OPNAV, CNO Command Files, OA; Semi-Annual Progress Report of the Guided Missiles Program, 31 Oct 1949, 21, OPNAV, CNO Command Files; and "Control of Gun Launched Guided Missiles," Lark Seminar, 13 Mar 1947, Fahrney Source Materials, Records of the Bureau of Aeronautics (RG 72), National Archives and Records Administration (NARA), Washington, DC.

100. Kenneth G. McCollum, ed., *Dahlgren* (Dahlgren, VA, 1977), 58.

101. Ibid., 140.

102. *Bulletin of Ordnance Information*, 31 Mar 1957, 16.

103. *Bulletin of Ordnance Information*, 30 Jun 1946, 67; Ibid., 31 Mar 1957, 16; Ibid., 31 Mar 1951, 60–61; and Review of the Naval Guided Missiles Program, 1 Aug 1947, 9–10.

104. Jacob Neufeld, *The Development of Ballistic Missiles in the United States Air Force, 1945–1960* (Washington, 1990), 21–22, 26; *Bulletin of Ordnance Information*, 31 Dec 1947, 4; Review of the Naval Guided Missiles Program, 1 Aug 1947, 13, 18; Weschler interview, 24 Mar 1988; and Alexander Kossiakoff, "APL—Expanding the Limits," *Johns Hopkins APL Technical Digest* 13 (Jan–Mar 1992): 9.

105. Lecture, Dr. G. I. Welch, "Naval Implications of Guided Missiles, 13 Sep 1948, 3, 17–18, 22, RG 15, NWC.

106. Review of the Naval Guided Missiles Program, 1 Aug 1947, 10–11; and Gallery lecture, "Guided Missiles," 13 Feb 1950, 11.

107. Semi-Annual Progress Report of the Guided Missiles Program, 31 Oct 1949; Review of the Naval Guided Missiles Program, 1 Aug 1947, 17, 18; and Frederick C. Alpers (with Robert C. Fletcher), interview by Leroy Doig III, 27 Jan 1981, 13, copy in David Taylor Research Center (DTRC), Carderock, MD (hereafter Alpers oral history).

108. D. V. Gallery to Duncan, 14 Mar 1947, Pilotless Aircraft Division, Guided Missile Development Progress Report, Fahrney Source Materials, RG 72, NARA.

109. Review of the Naval Guided Missiles Program, 1 Aug 1947, 12–13.

110. Gallery to Duncan, 14 Mar 1947.

111. J. D. Gerrard-Gough and Albert B. Christman, *History of the Naval Weapons Center, China Lake, California*, vol., 2, *The Grand Experiment at Inyokern* (Washington, 1978), 277, 279.

112. Kossiakoff, "APL—Expanding the Limits," 10; Review of the Naval Guided Missiles Program, 1 Aug 1947, 22; Louis A. Gebhard, *Evolution of Naval Radio-Electronics and Contributions of the Naval Research Laboratory* (Washington, 1979), 237; Friedman, *US Naval Weapons*, 150–53; and James Reckner to author, 29 Oct 1991.

113. *Bulletin of Ordnance Information*, 31 Mar 1957, 16.

114. Ibid., 30 Jun 1948, 49; Semi-Annual Progress Report of the Guided Missiles Program, 31 Oct 1949, 16.

115. Semi-Annual Progress Report of the Guided Missiles Program, 31 Oct 1949, 16; George F. Emch, "Air Defense for the Fleet," *Johns Hopkins APL Technical Digest* 13 (Jan–Mar 1992): 41; and *Bulletin of Ordnance Information*, 30 Sep 1949, 61–62.

116. *Bulletin of Ordnance Information*, 31 Dec 1949, 46.

117. Ibid., 30 Sep 1948, 54; and Gallery lecture, "Guided Missiles," 13 Feb 1950, 5. The Terrier's diameter of 13.5 inches determined the size of the Navy's launchers for over thirty years—and of its successor, the Standard. See Marion E. Oliver and William N. Sweet, "Standard Missile: The Common Denominator," *Johns Hopkins APL Technical Digest* 2 (Oct Dcc 1981): 285.

118. "Estimate of Russian Intentions," 10 Jan 1950, 26–27, CNO Command Files; O'Neil, "Gun Systems? For Air Defense?," 45; "Board Maneuver Rules; Supplement to Maneuver Rules," Aug 1946, 19, Folder 2577H, RG 4, NWC; and "Anti-Aircraft Fire Effect and Rules Governing Damage Inflicted by Aircraft," Aug 1946, Folder 2577J.

119. Semi-Annual Progress Report of the Guided Missiles Program, 31 Oct 1949, 17; and Gallery lecture, "Guided Missiles," 13 Feb 1950, 3.

120. *Bulletin of Ordnance Information*, 30 Sep 1948, 52–54; and Gallery lecture, "Guided Missiles," 13 Feb 1950, 6.

121. "A Guided Missile Electronic Countermeasures Plan for a Naval Task Force of 1955," 1950, 1–3, Antiaircraft and Guided Missile Branch, Fort Bliss, TX, Artillery School, File #23996, Center for Naval Analyses (CNA), Fairfax, VA; Review of the Naval Guided Missiles Program, 1 Aug 1947, 18; Albert A. Gallotta, Jr., "Navy EW and C3CM," in *Naval Tactical Command and Control*, ed. Gordon R. Nagler (Washington, c. 1985): 213; and Norman Friedman, *Naval Radar* (Greenwich, 1981), 129.

122. Edward J. Fahy, "Pushbuttons Need Men," *Proceedings* 75 (Feb 1949): 149.

123. "Airborne Early Warning System," May 1948, Folder 2637–C & D, RG 4, NWC.

124. W. H. Blandy, "The Future Value of Sea Power," *Transactions of The Society of Naval Architects and Marine Engineers* 55 (1947): 498.

125. Gallery lecture, "Guided Missiles," 13 Feb 1950, 8; and Semi-Annual Progress Report of the Guided Missiles Program, 31 Oct 1949, 114.

126. Chester W. Nimitz, "The Future Employment of Naval Forces," in *Ironclad to Trident: 100 Years of Defence Commentary: Brassey's, 1886–1986*, ed. Bryan Ranft (London, 1986), 204–5; Semi-Annual Progress Report of the Guided Missiles Program, 1 Aug 1947, 87; Ibid., 31 Oct 1949, 82; "Answers to Red Check Items in the Agenda," 26 Apr 1948, 68; and Ross R. Hatch, Joseph L. Luber, and James H. Walker, "Fifty Years of Strike Warfare Research at the Applied Physics Laboratory," *Johns Hopkins APL Technical Digest* 13 (Jan–Mar 1992): 114.

127. Alpers oral history, 14–17.

128. Review of the Naval Guided Missiles Program, 1 Aug 1947, 15–16.

129. "Operations Problem 3–48, BLUE-RED Staff Solution," Sep 1947, 49–50, Folder 2644B; "Answers to Red Check Items in the Agenda," 26 Apr 1948, 68; and Review of the Naval Guided Missiles Program, 1 Aug 1947, 99–100.

130. Monthly Progress Report, 1 Mar 1947, Pilotless Aircraft Division, Guided Missile Development Progress Report, Fahrney Source Materials, RG 72, NARA; Review of the Naval Guided Missiles Program, 1 Aug 1947, 22–23; and Gebhard, *Evolution of Naval Radio-Electronics*, 240.

131. Review of the Naval Guided Missiles Program, 1 Aug 1947, 11.

132. Ibid., 11; Friedman, *U.S. Battleships*, 389; and OP–601 to OP–06, 19 Jun 1946, Pilotless Aircraft Division, Guided Missile Development Progress Report, Fahrney Source Materials, RG 72, NARA.

133. Report, 21 Jun 1948, "Navy Department Tentative Basic Naval Establishment Plan for Jan 1950," Richards Files, Navy Department, RG 200, Truman Library; *DANFS* 2:387; Stefan Terzibaschitsch, "Mothball Fleet: The United States 'Naval Inactive Ships Maintenance Facilities,'" in *Warship*, ed. Andrew Lambert (Annapolis, 1987), 11:98; John L. Sullivan to Kenneth McKellar, 2 Feb 1949, Secretary of the Navy—Cabinet Folder, PSF, Truman Papers, Truman Library; and Dean C. Allard, "An Era of Transition, 1945–1953," in *In Peace and War: Interpretations of American Naval History, 1775–1984*, ed. Kenneth J. Hagan, 2d ed. (Westport, Conn, 1984), 293.

134. Robert W. Love, Jr., *History of the U.S. Navy*, vol. 2, *1942–1991* (Harrisburg, 1992), 321–24; Coletta, *United States Navy and Defense Unification*, 224; and Coletta, "Francis Matthews," in Coletta, *Secretaries of the Navy* 2:815–16.

135. Davis, *Admirals Lobby*, 224; and Russell S. Crenshaw, Jr. to author, 19 Jun 1992. Crenshaw maintains that Sherman as CNO "quickly started the ball rolling to place fellow Aviators in as many key positions in the Navy as possible. They openly initiated a program to convert as many Flag and Captain billets to Aviation billets as possible."

136. David A. Rosenberg, "Burke, Arleigh Albert," in *Dictionary of American Military Biography*, ed. Roger J. Spiller, vol. 1, *A–G* (Westport, CT, 1984), 131; Hallion, *Naval Air War in Korea*, 21–21; and Love, *History of the U.S. Navy* 2:320.

137. Clark G. Reynolds, "Forrest Percival Sherman," in *The Chiefs of Naval Operations*, ed. Robert W. Love, Jr. (Annapolis, 1980), 215. President Truman had vowed earlier to keep *Missouri* out of mothballs; Sherman thus had a powerful ally in the wings if he needed assistance.

## 2. The Surface Navy Enters the Missile Age

1. William W. Kaufmann, *Planning Conventional Forces, 1950–80* (Washington, 1982), 2; and William W. Kaufmann, *The McNamara Strategy* (New York, 1964), 18.

2. Allard, "An Era of Transition, 1945–1953," 299; Ernest M. Eller, *The Soviet Sea Challenge* (New York, 1971), 105; and Hallion, *Naval Air War in Korea*, 30.

3. *DANFS* 3:290; 6:137–38; 8:397.

4. COMCRUDIV 5 to CNO, 5 Nov 1950, "Action Report of Amphibious Landing Inchon, Korea," 26, Cruiser Division Five File, Post 1 Jan 1946 Report Files, OA; and *DANFS* 7:220.

5. Doris M. Condit, *History of the Office of the Secretary of Defense*, vol. 2, *The Test of War, 1950–1953* (Washington, 1988), 225, 227; Coletta, *United States Navy and Defense Unification*, 241, 256; and Henry C. Mustin, interview with author, 27 May 1992 (hereafter Henry C. Mustin Interview).

6. *DANFS* 1(rev.):485–86; 4:187; Stefan Terzibaschitsch, *Cruisers of the US Navy, 1922–1962*, trans. Harold Erenberg (Annapolis, 1984), 308; and Friedman, *U.S. Destroyers*, 443–72.

7. Commander Cruiser-Destroyer Force to CNO, 25 Jan 1951, "Reactivation of destroyers," KK2–KK4, CINCPAC Interim Evaluation Report No. 1, Period 25 June to 15 November 1950, Korean War—Pacific Fleet Operations File, Post 1 Jan 1946 Report Files.

8. Richard G. Alexander to author, 7 Jul 1992.

9. Daniel J. Carrison, "Reserves—What Kind?" *Proceedings* 81 (May 1955): 529; and COM-CRUDIV 1 to CNO, 4 Apr 1952, "Action Report for period 21 February to 2 April 1952," 6, Cruiser Division One File, Post 1 Jan 1946 Report Files.

10. Malcolm W. Cagle and Frank A. Manson, *The Sea War in Korea* (Annapolis, 1957), 299; Malcolm Muir, Jr., *The Iowa Class Battleships: Iowa, New Jersey, Missouri & Wisconsin* (Poole, Dorset, 1987), 94–99; "Characteristics of Naval Gunfire Support in Korea," 1, Operations Evaluation Group Study 506, CNO Command Files, OA; and COMCRUDIV 1 to CNO, 4 Apr 1952, "Action Report for period 21 February to 2 April 1952," 4–5.

11. "Characteristics of Naval Gunfire Support in Korea," 1, Operations Evaluation Group Study 506; *Bulletin of Ordnance Information*, 30 Jun 1953, 32; Ibid., 31 Dec 1953, 10; COM-CRUDIV 5 to CNO, 5 Nov 1950, "Action Report of Amphibious Landing Inchon, Korea," 18; *DANFS* 3:290; 6:137–138; and "The Elements of Naval Gunfire for use in connection with the Surface Action Study," Naval Warfare (I), Class of June 1955, Nov 1954, 13, Folder 2912, RG 4, NWC.

12. Love, *History of the U.S. Navy* 2:355; *DANFS* 3:290; 6:137–38; 8:465.

13. "USS *Saint Paul* (CA–73)," *Proceedings* 86 (May 1960): 159–60; Raymond E. Peet, 1984, 73, USNI Oral History Collection in OA (hereafter Peet oral history); and *DANFS* 6:138; 8:465.

14. *DANFS* 6:567; 1(rev.):177; Muir, *The Iowa Class*, 86; COMCRUDIV 5 to CNO, 5 Nov 1950, "Action Report of Amphibious Landing Inchon, Korea," 17; Tamara Moser Melia, *"Damn the Torpedoes": A Short History of U.S. Naval Mine Countermeasures, 1777–1991*, Contributions to Naval History Series No. 4 (Washington, 1991), 155; *DANFS* 8:59, 465; and "USS *Saint Paul* (CA–73)," 159–60.

15. Alastair Buchan, "The United States and the 'New Look,'" in *Brassey's Annual: The Armed Forces Yearbook, 1954*, ed. H. G. Thursfield (New York, 1954), 172; Davis, *Admirals Lobby*, 225; and *Brassey's Annual, 1967*, 72.

16. Kaufmann, *McNamara Strategy*, 21; and Buchan, "The United States and the 'New Look,'" 172–73.

17. Kaufmann, *McNamara Strategy*, 22–23.

18. Montgomery quoted in Moulton, "NATO and the Atlantic," 151.

19. Kaufmann, *McNamara Strategy*, 22–23.

20. Buchan, "The United States and the 'New Look,'" 174, 177.

21. Karl Lautenschläger, *Technology and the Evolution of Naval Warfare, 1851–2001* (Washington, 1984), 43; and Rohwer, "The Confrontation of the Superpowers at Sea," 168. Huntington quoted in Carl H. Amme, "Naval Strategy and the New Frontier," *Proceedings* 88 (Mar 1962): 29.

22. Alexander to author, 7 Jul 1992.

23. Brian B. Schofield, "The Role of the NATO Navies in War," *Proceedings* 87 (Apr 1961): 66, 68; and Daniel J. Carrison, "Defense Against Nuclear Attack at Sea," *Proceedings* 90 (May 1964): 36–39.

24. Carrison, "Defense Against Nuclear Attack at Sea," 39.

25. Robert B. Carney, "Always the Sea," *Proceedings* 81 (May 1955): 503.

26. Love, *History of the U.S. Navy* 2:373–74.

27. Carney, "Always the Sea," 500, 502.

28. Breemer, *Soviet Submarines*, 83, 86; and Polmar and Noot, *Submarines of the Russian and Soviet Navies*, 154.

29. COMCRUDIV 1 to Commander Cruiser-Destroyer Force, U.S. Pacific Fleet, 29 Aug 1951, "Report of Air Defense and Anti-Submarine Exercises 3–9 August 1951," 6, encl. 2, 3, Cruiser Division Three File, Post 1 Jan 1946 Report Files.

30. COMCRUDIV 1 to Commander Cruiser-Destroyer Force, Pacific Fleet, 20 Oct 1951, "Report of Air Defense and Anti-Submarine Exercises 6–11 October 1951," 3–2, Cruiser Division One File.

31. Commander Cruiser-Destroyer Force, Pacific Fleet to CINCPAC, 14 Apr 1954, "Report of Operation PACTRAEX 54R," 3–5, Cruiser-Destroyer File, Pacific Fleet, Post 1 Jan 1946 Report Files.

32. COMCRUDIV 1 to Commander Cruiser-Destroyer Force, U.S. Pacific Fleet, 29 Aug 1951, "Report of Air Defense and Anti-Submarine Exercises 3–9 August 1951," encl. 4, 1.

33. Ibid., 6, encl. 2, 3; Friedman, *US Naval Weapons*, 106; and Ronald T. Kelly to author, 16 Feb 1993.

34. Wayne L. Jensen, "Helicopters in Antisubmarine Warfare," *Proceedings* 89 (Jul 1963): 36, 38; Commander Cruiser-Destroyer Force, Pacific Fleet to CINCPAC, 14 Apr 1954, "Report of Operation PACTRAEX 54R," 1.

35. Allan N. Glennon, "An Approach to ASW," *Proceedings* 90 (Sep 1964): 50.

36. Friedman, *US Naval Weapons*, 126–27; and Glennon, "An Approach to ASW," 54. Project Hartwell quoted in Sokolsky, "Seapower in the Nuclear Age," 135.

37. Scheina, "Search for a Mission," 263; Norman Polmar, *The Ships and Aircraft of the U.S. Fleet*, 11th ed. (Annapolis, 1978), 101; and *DANFS* 5:104–5.

38. Alexander to author, 7 Jul 1992.

39. Allan P. Slaff to author, 25 Jun 1992.

40. *Brassey's Annual, 1967*, 70; Sokolsky, "Seapower in the Nuclear Age," 62; and Alexander to author, 7 Jul 1992.

41. C. N. Crandall, Jr. to author, 21 Jul 1992.

42. Robert H. Rossell to author, 15 Jul 1992; Alexander to author, 7 Jul 1992; Joseph J. Doak, Jr. to author, 3 Jul 1992; and William R. St. George to author, 6 Jul 1992.

43. *DANFS* 2:248; 3:545, 554, 561; 4:94.

44. Everett A. Parke, "The Unique and Vital DER," *Proceedings* 86 (Feb 1960): 91; and *DANFS* 7:456.

45. Robert C. Peniston to author, 25 Jun 1992.

46. Ibid; and Parke, "The Unique and Vital DER," 91.

47. Peniston to author, 25 Jun 1992.

48. Friedman, *U.S. Destroyers*, 229–33; and *DANFS* 4:361.

49. *ONI Review*, Dec 1949, 5–6, 8, 95, 220, OA.

50. Norman Polmar, *Guide to the Soviet Navy*, 4th ed. (Annapolis, 1986), 192.

51. *ONI Review*, May 1955, 217; Ibid., Autumn, 1954, n.p.; and James W. Kehoe and Kenneth S. Brower, "Warship Design in the Future," in *The U.S. Navy: The View from the Mid-1980s*, ed. James L. George, (Boulder, CO, 1985), 141.

52. OPNAV; NWP 20, "Striking Force Operations," May 1953, 5–23, OA; "Operations Problem 8-51, Operation Peppermint," May 1951, 100, Folder 2761a; and "Operations Problem 7–52," Jun 1952, 5, Folder 2811, both in RG 4, NWC.

53. "Strength and Disposition of Foreign Navies," Oct 1951, 31, 38, ONI, CNO Command Files; and "Operations Problem 2–53," Sep 1952, Folder 2843, RG 4, NWC.

54. "Developments and Trends in the Soviet Fleet During 1952," *ONI Review*, Summer 1953, 16.

55. Memo, Arleigh Burke, Director, Strategic Plans Division; "Attack Carrier Force Levels," 13 Oct 1953, 35–36, OP-30S/OP-60S; Strategic Plans Division Records, OA (hereafter Strategic Plans).

56. "Developments and Trends in the Soviet Fleet During 1952," 13.

57. Ibid., 10.

58. Ibid.; "The Development of the Soviet Navy Since World War II," *ONI Review*, Oct 1960, 423, 425; and Jürgen Rohwer to author, 3 Mar 1990.

59. *ONI Review*, May 1955, 219.

60. Ibid, 12; and "Soviet Technical Capabilities, Part 2," *ONI Review*, Autumn 1953, 28.

61. *ONI Review*, Spring 1954, 24, 29; and Ibid., Summer 1954, 7.

62. Weschler interview, 24 Mar 1988. Weschler was Arleigh Burke's aide for a time when Burke was CNO. Joseph Metcalf III, interview with author, 1 Oct 1987 (hereafter Metcalf interview); David F. Emerson, interview with author, 26 Apr 1988 (hereafter Emerson Interview). Emerson maintained that the *Iowa*-class battleships would have given foul weather coverage in the Arctic. Henry C. Mustin interview, 2 May 1988. Mustin especially pointed out that the *Sverdlov*-class had no surface-to-air missiles and thus the Navy did not see high aircraft attrition involved in attacking those ships with aircraft. "We didn't think it was going to be easy, but . . . we had a lot of people who had done that in World War II, and who knew how to do antiship warfare." "An Estimate of the Threat Posed by the Sino-Soviet Bloc to U.S. and Allied Control of the Seas," 3 Feb 1956, 32, ONI, OA; "Operations Problem 1–53," Jun 1952, Folder 2842, RG 4, NWC; "Operations Problem 7–52," Jun 1952, 31; "Directive for Surface Action Study," 3–5 Nov 1954, Folder 2912, RG 4, NWC; and OPNAV, NWIP 1–4; and "Experimental Tactics for U.S. Navy Ships and Aircraft," Jul 1954, 81–5, OA.

63. "Operations Problem 5–53 Annex," n.d., p. 15, Folder 2846, RG 4, NWC.

64. "Operations Problem 1–53," Jun 1952; "Operations Problem 7–52," Jun 1952; "Operations Problem 8–51, Operation Peppermint," May 1951; and "Operations Problem 2–53," Sep 1952. *Tennessee* had been rebuilt after Pearl Harbor with modern fire control equipment.

65. "The Elements of Naval Gunfire for use in connection with the Surface Action Study," Naval Warfare (I), Class of June 1955, Nov 1954, 10; "Directive for Surface Action Study," 3–5 Nov 1954; Senior Member, Committee on Evaluation of Curriculum Items to Curriculum Board, 7 Dec 1954, "Evaluation of Surface Action Study," Folder 2912, RG 4, NWC; Director, Surface Action Study to Head, Strategy and Tactics Department, 2 Dec 1954, Folder 2912, RG 4, NWC; Lecture, M. J. Lousey, "Surface Action Principles, Tactics and Doctrine," 3 Nov 1954, 2, RG 14, NWC; Committee on Evaluation of Curriculum Items to Naval Warfare I students, 2 Nov 1954, "Evaluation Report 'Surface Action Study,'" Folder 2912, RG 4, NWC; and Francis J. McHugh, "Gaming at the Naval War College," *Proceedings* 90 (Mar 1964): 52–53.

66. OPNAV, NWIP 1–4; "Experimental Tactics for U.S. Navy Ships and Aircraft," Jul 1954, 81–6, 81–7.

67. Commander Cruiser-Destroyer Force, Pacific Fleet to CINCPAC, 26 Oct 1953, "Report of Operation DESTRAEX 54L," 2–5, Cruiser-Destroyer Force, Pacific Fleet File; COMCRUDIV 1 to Commander Seventh Fleet, 10 Mar 1954, "Report of Seventh Fleet Exercise 1–54," 1, Cruiser Division One File; COMCRUDIV 1 to Commander Cruiser-Destroyer Force, U.S. Pacific Fleet, 29 Aug 1951, "Report of Air Defense and Anti-Submarine Exercises 3–9 August 1951," encl. 2, 11; COMCRUDIV 2 to Commander Second Fleet, 1 Mar 1955, "Report of Phases II and III INTEX 1–55," 7–8, Cruiser Division Two File; COMCRUDIV 6 to Commander Second Fleet, 14 Jun 1951, "Report of Surface Raider Exercises during CONVEX II," 4, Cruiser Division Six File; COMCRUDIV 3 to Commander Seventh Fleet, 1 Jan 1955, "Task Force Seventy-Five Operations during Seventh Fleet Exercise 2–54, 6–14 December 1954," 4, Cruiser Division Three File, all in Post 1 Jan 1946 Report Files.

Into the mid-1960s, major fleet exercises occasionally featured surface ships employed as raiders. In such cases, they often were markedly successful in attacks on convoys or even on the carriers themselves. For *Saint Paul* against *Bon Homme Richard* (CVA 31) in 1965, see Commander Cruiser-Destroyer Flotilla Eleven to Commander First Fleet, 3 May 1965, "Exercise TEE SHOT Final Report," 2, Cruiser-Destroyer Flotilla Eleven File, Post 1 Jan 1946 Report Files.

Six months later, the same cruiser attacked *Kitty Hawk* (CVA 63) and *Yorktown* (CVS 10). See Commander Cruiser-Destroyer Flotilla Eleven to Commander First Fleet, 22 Oct 1965, "Exercise RAG WEED Final Report," 5, Cruiser-Destroyer Flotilla Eleven File.

During Exercise Belaying Pin, destroyer *Shields* (DD 596) acting as a raider was able to approach within 4,200 yards of *Coral Sea* (CVA 43) before being challenged. See Commander Cruiser-Destroyer Flotilla Three to Distribution List, 19 Aug 1966, "'Highlights' of Final Report of Fleet Exercise 'BELAYING PIN,'" 2–3, Cruiser-Destroyer Flotilla Three File, Post 1 Jan 1946 Report Files.

In a "real life" situation, when a carrier task force entered the Sea of Japan following the North Korean destruction of an American EC-121 reconnaissance plane in April 1969, a Soviet destroyer approached to within 21 miles of *Enterprise* before being detected. See U.S. Seventh Fleet, "Monthly Historical Summary," Apr 1969, 66, OA.

68. "Operations Problem 7-52," Jun 1952; "The Elements of Naval Gunfire for use in connection with the Surface Action Study," Naval Warfare (I), Class of June 1955, Nov 1954; "A Solution to Surface Action Problem," Nov 1954, Folder 2912, RG 4, NWC; CTF 75 (COMCRUDIV 1) to Commander Seventh Fleet, 3 Sep 1954, "Report of Task Force Seventy-Five Operations 4–12 August 1954," 1–2, Cruiser Division One File; and COMCRUDIV 6 to Commander Second Fleet, 14 Jun 1951, "Report of Surface Raider Exercises during CONVEX II," 1–5.

69. Ibid.; OPNAV, NWIP 21-2 (A), "Naval Weapons Selection—Ships," c.1961, B–4, OA.

70. "Directive for the Study of Extra-Ordinary Weapons and Techniques," Sep 1952, 5, Folder 2860, RG 4, NWC.

71. Elmer D. Robinson, "The Talos Ship System," *Johns Hopkins APL Technical Digest* 3 (Apr–Jun 1982): 162.

72. *Bulletin of Ordnance Information*, 31 Dec 1954, 38;

73. NOL, Corona, *From Sky to Sea*, 36.

74. "Navy Guided Missile Program," 11 Mar 52, CNO, Post 1 Jan 1946 Command File, OA; Public Relations Release, Sep 1954, Regulus File, Naval Aviation History Branch (AVH), NHC; Ibid., Nov 1952; Annual Progress Report, Guided Missile Program, Regulus XSSM–N–8, 1 July 1953, Guided Missile Division, OPNAV Files, OA; and Commander

Cruiser-Destroyer Force, Pacific Fleet Representative, Guided Missile Evaluation Unit #1 to Officer-in-Charge, Guided Missile Evaluation Unit #1, Naval Air Station, San Diego, 8 Nov 1954, "REGULUS Flight Test Conducted from U.S.S. *Los Angeles* (CA–135), 18 October 1954," 1–2, Cruiser-Destroyer Force, Pacific Fleet File.

75. "Navy Guided Missile Program," 11 Mar 1952; Memo for Director of Guided Missile Division, 17 Mar 1959; Chuck Hansen, *US Nuclear Weapons: The Secret History* (New York, 1988), 190–91; Friedman, *US Naval Weapons*, 218; and Alpers oral history, 20–22.

76. "Navy Guided Missile Program," 11 Mar 1952; Annual Progress Report of the Guided Missile Program, 1 Oct 1953, Guided Missile Division, OPNAV Files; and Armament for Regulus, 1 July 1953, Guided Missile Division, OPNAV Files.

77. Robert Walters, interview with author, 17 Dec 1987 (hereafter Walters interview); As quoted in Berend Derk Bruins, "U.S. Naval Bombardment Missiles, 1940–1958: A Study of the Weapons Innovation Process." (Ph.D. dissertation, Columbia University, 1981), 256. The Air Force was having similar problems. In Dec 1956 a Snark (with inertial guidance) "jumped the fence" and flew off to Brazil where a farmer found its carcass in 1982. See Kenneth P. Werrell, *The Evolution of the Cruise Missile* (Maxwell Air Force Base, AL, 1985), 92.

78. Bruins, "U.S. Naval Bombardment Missiles," 257; J. H. Sides to OPNAV Staff, 19 May 52, Regulus File, AVH, NHC; Regulus XSSM–N–8a Supplement 10, 1 Jul 1953; Annual Progress Report of the Guided Missile Programs, Regulus XSSM–N–8, 31 Oct 1949, Guided Missile Division, OPNAV Files; and Friedman, *Naval Radar*, 182.

79. Bruins, "U.S. Naval Bombardment Missiles," 260, 290–91; and Friedman, *Naval Radar*, 182.

80. *Combat Readiness*, Apr–Jun 1954, 11–12, OA; and Bruins, "U.S. Naval Bombardment Missiles," 243, 254–55.

81. OPNAV, NWIP 1–4, "Experimental Tactics for U.S. Navy Ships and Aircraft," Jul 1954, 82–3; and David K. Stumpf, "Blasts from the Past," *Proceedings* 119 (Apr 1993): 62–63.

82. NWIP 1–4, 82-3, 82–4, 81–5; Author's observations during FLTX–1–88 while on board USS *Stump* (DD 978), Jan 1988.

83. OPNAV, NWP 20, "Striking Force Operations," May 1953, 1–10.

84. Ibid., 1–10, 1–12.

85. Ibid., 7–1 to 7–33.

86. COMCRUDIV 6 to Commander Second Fleet, 14 Jun 1951, "Report of Surface Raider Exercises during CONVEX II," 1; COMCRUDIV 4 to COMCARDIV 4, 21 Nov 1951, "Report of Phase II, LANTFLEX 52," 1, Cruiser Division Four File, Post 1946 Report Files, OA; COMCRUDIV 3 to CINCPAC, 9 Dec 1953, "Report of Operation REX 54Q, Phase BAKER," 9–11, Cruiser Division Three File; Philip D. Gallery, "A Few Ideas of a Cruiser Skipper," *Proceedings* 81 (Jul 1955): 787; and David Rosenberg to author, 29 Oct 1987.

87. OPNAV, NWP 20, "Striking Force Operations," May 1953, 1–8, 1–12, 7–3.

88. Ibid., 1–12, 1–13; and COMCRUDIV 1 to COMCARDIV 3, 10 Sep 1955, "Report of Task Force Seventy-Seven Operations, 30 August–6 September 1955," 1–2, Cruiser Division One File.

89. COMCRUDIV 4 to Commander Amphibious Force, Atlantic Fleet, "Report of Phases III and IV, LANTFLEX 52," 6–7; COMCRUDIV 4 to Commander Sixth Fleet, 30 Jul 1951, "Report of MEDLANDEX XVI," 1, both in Cruiser Division Four File; John O. Stull, "Guns Have Not Gone Yet!" *Proceedings* 90 (Apr 1964): 82; Robert D. Heinl, Jr., "The Gun Gap and How to Close It," *Proceedings* 91 (Sep 1965): 32–34; *Brassey's Annual, 1967*, 72; and Norman Friedman, "Amphibious Fire Support: Post War Development," in *Warship*, ed. Roberts, 4:238.

90. McCollum, *Dahlgren*, 58; Peet oral history, 80–81; and *Bulletin of Ordnance Information*, 31 Dec 1953, 43–44.

91. OPNAV, FXP 5, "Conduct of Fleet Exercises," 3–6, OA; Hallion, *Naval Air War in Korea*, 76; "Operations Problem 8–51, Operation Peppermint," May 1951, 103; OPNAV, FXP 5, "Conduct of Fleet Exercises," Appendix 1–19, 1–20; and "An Estimate of the Threat Posed by the Sino-Soviet Bloc to U.S. and Allied Control of the Seas," 3 Feb 1956, 22–23.

92. COMCRUDIV 1 to Commander Cruiser-Destroyer Force, U.S. Pacific Fleet, 29 Aug 1951, "Report of Air Defense and Anti-Submarine Exercises 3–9 August 1951," 4.

*93. COMCRUDIV 2 to Commander Second Fleet, 1 Mar 1955, "Report of Phases II and III INTEX 1–55," 2; COMCRUDIV 4 to Commander Amphibious Force, Atlantic Fleet, "Report of Phases III and IV, LANTFLEX 52," 2–3; COMCRUDIV 1 to Commander Cruiser-Destroyer Force, Pacific Fleet, "Report on Air Defense Standardization Exercise, 26 May 1954, Cruiser Division One File; COMCRUDIV 1 to Commander Cruiser-Destroyer Force, Pacific Fleet, 20 Oct 1951, "Report of Air Defense and Anti-Submarine Exercises 6–11 October 1951," 1–3; and CTG 14.6 to CINCPAC, 26 Sep 1952, "Report of Operation, 15–21 September 1952," 2–3, Cruiser Division Five File.

94. Edmund B. Mahinske, Joseph S. Stoutenburgh, and Erick N. Swenson, "NTDS: A Chapter in Naval History" (ASNE Day Papers, 1988), 1, 4. The Air Force suffered from similar problems. For instance, in 1951, a pair of MiGs escaped detection and boldly overflew Seoul before leisurely turning north again. See Hallion, *Naval Air War in Korea*, 76.

95. Thomas J. Misa, "Military Needs, Commercial Realities, and the Development of the Transistor, 1948–1958" in *Military Enterprise and Technological Change: Perspectives on the American Experience*, edited by Merritt Roe Smith (Cambridge, MA, 1985): 265; Mahinske, Stoutenburgh, and Swenson, "NTDS: A Chapter in Naval History," 4; and David K. Allison, "U.S. Navy Research and Development Since World War II," in *Military Enterprise and Technological Change*, 321–22.

96. Commander Cruiser-Destroyer Force, Pacific Fleet to CINCPAC, 23 Jul 1951, "Report of Air Defense and Submarine Exercises 11–14 June 1951," 6, 12, Cruiser Division Three File.

97. Hallion, *Naval Air War in Korea*, 160; Friedman, *U.S. Destroyers*, 228–29; *DANFS* 8:356; Gerald W. Rahill, "Destroyer Duty," *Proceedings* 78 (Oct 1952): 1082; COMCRUDIV 4 to Commander Amphibious Force, Atlantic Fleet, "Report of Phases III and IV, LANTFLEX 52," 2–3; COMCRUDIV 4 to COMCARDIV 4, 21 Nov 1951, "Report of Phase II, LANTFLEX 52," 1, 3; Commander Cruiser-Destroyer Force, Pacific Fleet to CINCPAC, 14 Apr 1954, "Report of Operation PACTRAEX 54R," 3–5.

98. Hallion, *Naval Air War in Korea*, 76.

99. "The 8″/55 as an AA Weapon," *Combat Readiness*, Apr–Jun 1954, 23.

100. "The Elements of Naval Gunfire for use in connection with the Surface Action Study," Naval Warfare (I), Class of June 1955, Nov 1954; and "The 8″/55 as an AA Weapon," 23–24.

101. Emerson interview, 26 Apr 1988.

102. R. S. Wentworth, Jr. to author, 28 Jun 1992; Author's observations during FLTX-1-88 while on board *Thomas C. Hart* (FF 1092), Jan 1988; Frederick H. Schneider, Jr. to author, 31 Jul 1992; Alexander to author, 7 Jul 1992; Friedman, *U.S. Destroyers*, 245; Polmar, *Ships and Aircraft of the U.S. Fleet*, 11 ed., 453; and Edward J. Marolda, "By Sea, Air, and Land" (MS), 15, 45.

103. Action Report, USS *Los Angeles* (CA 135), "East Coast Korea, 21 November–17 December 1952," OA; *Bulletin of Ordnance Information*, 30 Sep 1950, 6, 12, 14; and Ibid., 30 Jun 1950, 6.

104. Rowland and Boyd, *Bureau of Ordnance*, 517.

105. James H. Doyle, interview with author, 28 Mar 1988 (hereafter Doyle interview).

106. *Bulletin of Ordnance Information*, 31 Dec 1955, 7; Ibid., 30 Jun 1956, 62; and Ibid., 30 Sep 1954, 22, 26. No 3″/70 armed warships operated off Vietnam.

107. *DANFS* 3:550; and Polmar, *Ships and Aircraft of the U.S. Fleet*, 136.

108. Garnett Laidlaw Eskew, *Cradle of Ships* (New York, 1958), 242; Schneider, Jr. to author, 31 Jul 1992; and Peniston to author, 25 Jun 1992.

109. Harold G. Bowen, *Ships Machinery and Mossbacks: The Autobiography of a Naval Engineer* (Princeton, 1954), 125; Reuven Leopold, "Surface Warships for the Early Twenty-First Century," in *Problems of Sea Power as We Approach the Twenty-First Century: A Conference Sponsored by the American Enterprise Institute for Public Policy Research*, ed. James L. George (Washington, 1978): 278; J. D. Oliver and A. W. Slifer, "Evaluating the DDG," *Proceedings* 91 (Jul 1965): 81–82; Wentworth to author, 28 Jun 1992; Alexander to author, 7 Jul 1992; and H. H. Ries to author, 23 Jun 1992.

110. Young, "Recent Naval Steam Turbine Construction," 713; Wentworth, Jr. to author, 28 Jun 1992; Stansfield Turner to author, 23 Jul 1992; Foreman interview, 28 Aug 1992; and U.S. Seventh Fleet, "Monthly Historical Summary," May 1969, 38, OA.

111. William R. St. George to author, 9 Jul 1992. Making the same point was Ronald T. Kelly to author, 16 Feb 1993.

112. Alexander to author, 7 Jul 1992.

113. Ibid.

114. Eskew, *Cradle of Ships*, 241–42; and Schneider to author, 29 Dec 1992.

115. Alexander to author, 7 Jul 1992; and Schneider to author, 29 Dec 1992.

116. Alexander to author, 7 Jul 1992.

117. Ries to author, 23 Jun 1992.

118. Alexander to author, 7 Jul 1992.

119. Douglas C. Plate to author, 13 Aug 1992.

120. *DANFS* 8:318, 320, 380–81.

121. Alexander to author, 7 Jul 1992.

122. David F. Emerson to author, 20 Aug 1992.

123. Peniston to author, 25 Jun 1992.

124. *BuShips Journal*, Nov 1952, 12; CO, USS *Timmerman* (EAG 152) to Chief of Information, "Material for the Navy Almanac," 26 Sep 1955, both in Timmerman File, Ships Histories Branch (SH), NHC; Young, "Recent Naval Steam Turbine Construction," 711; and Eskew, *Cradle of Ships*, 240–41.

125. Robert J. Knox, "The Twentieth Century Clermont," *Journal of the American Society of Naval Engineers* 66 (Feb 1954): 44–45.

126. Eskew, *Cradle of Ships*, 241; Robert J. Knox, "Twentieth Century 'Clermont's' First Cruise," *Journal of the American Society of Naval Engineers* 68 (May 1956): 245–48, 251, 253; and Friedman, *U.S. Destroyers*, 123.

127. Terzibaschitsch, *Cruisers of the US Navy*, 290–91; J. Laurence Craig, "USS *Northampton* (CLC–1)," *Proceedings* 86 (Jul 1960): 155, 156, 158; Friedman, "The US Command Cruiser," 211; Ephraim P. Holmes to author, 5 Aug 1992; *DANFS* 5:112; and George F. Emch and Glenn I. Kirkland, "Search Radar Automation: AN/SYS–1 and Beyond," *Johns Hopkins APL Technical Digest* 13 (Jan–Mar 1992): 93.

128. Polmar, *Ships and Aircraft of the U.S. Fleet*, 99; and Friedman, *U.S. Destroyers*, 246, 249.

129. W. M. Montgomery to author, 28 Sep 1992.

130. Ibid.

131. *DANFS* 4:220.

132. Ries to author, 23 Jun 1992.

133. St. George to author, 6 Jul 1992; Ries to author, 23 Jun 1992; Young, "Recent Naval Steam Turbine Construction," 717; and R. T. McGoldrick, "Rudder-Excited Hull Vibration on USS *Forrest Sherman* (DD 931)....(A Problem in Hydroelasticity)," *Transactions of the Society of Naval Architects and Marine Engineers* 67 (1959): 341.

134. Alexander to author, 7 Jul 1992.

135. Russell S. Crenshaw, Jr. to author, 19 Jun 1992.

136. Alexander to author, 7 Jul 1992.

137. "The Elements of Naval Gunfire for use in connection with the Surface Action Study," Naval Warfare (I), Class of June 1955, Nov 1954, 12–13C; and *Bulletin of Ordnance Information*, 30 Sep 1954, 26, 29, 32. The gun calibers involved for the variable depth rifling were 5″/70 and 6″/70; for the squeeze-bore, 4″/3″, with a designed muzzle velocity of 6,000 feet per second; for the saboted projectile, 3.75″ shot at 3,800 feet per second from a 5″/54. BUORD experimented with a variety of liquid propellants such as hydrazine, ammonia, hydrogen, and aniline.

138. McCollum, *Dahlgren*, 143, 146; OPNAV, NWIP 21–2 (A), "Naval Weapons Selection—Ships," c.1960, 1–3, 4–13; and "Directive for the Study of Extra-Ordinary Weapons and Techniques," Sep 1952, 5.

139. Charles R. Brown and Charles F. Meyer, "The Talos Continuous-Rod Warhead," *Johns Hopkins APL Technical Digest*, 3 (Apr–Jun 1982): 157; and "OPNAV Conference Report: CAG Conference," 22 Apr 1955, 2, Admin. Services Div., File #38493, CNA.

140. Lecture, G.B.H. Hall, "Guided Missiles," 10 Jan 1951, 5, 6, 12, RG 15, NWC; and *Bulletin of Ordnance Information*, 31 Mar 1951, 62.

141. Edward A. Ruckner, interview by John T. Mason, Jr., 1977, 245, USNI Oral History Collection, OA (hereafter Ruckner oral history); *Bulletin of Ordnance Information*, 30 Jun 1954, 66–67; "Guided Missiles: Production of Cast Double-Base Propellants for Guided Missiles," *Bulletin of Ordnance Information*, 30 Jun 1953, 60; Rodney Carlisle, *Powder and Propellants: Energetic Materials at Indian Head, Maryland, 1890–1990* (Washington, 1990), 146; and Kossiakoff, "APL—Expanding the Limits," 11.

142. Ruckner oral history, 273; Hall lecture, "Guided Missiles," 10 Jan 1951, 12; "Guided Missiles: Production of Cast Double-Base Propellants for Guided Missiles," *Bulletin of Ordnance Information*, 30 Jun 1953, 60; Ibid., 30 Jun 1951, 56; and Friedman, "The '3-T' Programme," 161.

143. BUORD, Annual Progress Report: Guided Missile Program, 1 Oct 1953, 16.

144. *Bulletin of Ordnance Information*, 30 Jun 1954, 64–65; and Ibid., 31 Mar 1955, 49–50.

145. *Bulletin of Ordnance Information*, 31 Mar 1955, 49.

146. Ibid., 30 Jun 1958, 16.

147. Ibid., 31 Mar 1955, 49–50; and Ibid., 30 Jun 1954, 18, 19, 60, 62.

148. Kossiakoff, "APL—Expanding the Limits," 11.

149. Emch, "Air Defense for the Fleet," 42.

150. Lecture, L. L. Frank, "Guided Missiles," 18 Jan 1952, 11, RG 14, NWC.

151. Hall lecture, "Guided Missiles," 10 Jan 1951, 6; BUORD, Annual Progress Report: Guided Missile Program, 1 Oct 1953, 141; *Bulletin of Ordnance Information*, 30 Sep 1951, 37–38; David R. Frieden, *Principles of Naval Weapons Systems* (Annapolis, 1985), 437; and Wilbur H. Goss, "Talos in Retrospect," *Johns Hopkins APL Technical Digest* 3 (Apr–Jun 1982): 116.

152. BUORD, Annual Progress Report: Guided Missile Program, 1 Oct 1953, 145; Ruckner oral history, 273; Robinson, "Talos Ship System," 162; Brown and Meyer, "Talos Continuous-Rod Warhead," 157; Goss, "Talos in Retrospect," 116; and William Garten, Jr. and Frank A. Dean, "Evolution of the Talos Missile," *Johns Hopkins APL Technical Digest* 3 (Apr–Jun 1982): 116.

153. R. J. Tamulevicz, "Standard Missile: A Brief History," *Naval Ordnance Bulletin*, Jun 1969, 32; BUORD, Annual Progress Report: Guided Missile Program, 1 Oct 1953, 141–45, 147; Emch, "Air Defense for the Fleet," 43; and Preston N. Shamer to author, 27 Sep 1992. *Hawaii* was briefly considered for conversion to a Talos ship. See T. Blades, "USS *Galveston*: The First Talos Guided Missile Cruiser," in *Warship*, ed. Roberts, 4:228.

154. *Bulletin of Ordnance Information*, 31 Dec 1955, 50.

155. Ferris, Frey, and Mills, "The Ship Launched Projectile," 97; *Bulletin of Ordnance Information*, 31 Dec 1952, 24; Ibid., 31 Dec 1955, 50; and Kleber S. Masterson, interview by John T. Mason, Jr., 1973, 253, USNI Oral History Collection, OA (hereafter Masterson oral history).

156. *Bulletin of Ordnance Information*, 31 Dec 1955, 50.

157. Ibid., 30 Jun 1951, 56; and Ibid., 31 Dec 1955, 50.

158. Eli T. Reich, interview by John T. Mason, Jr., 1982, 462, USNI Oral History Collection, OA (hereafter Reich oral history).

159. *Bulletin of Ordnance Information*, 31 Dec 1955, 50; and Ibid., 30 Jun 1951, 56.

160. Ibid., 30 Jun 1953, 53–55; Ibid., 30 Jun 1954, 64–65; Ferris, Frey, and Mills, "The Ship Launched Projectile," 100–101; and CO, USS *Boston* (CAG 1) to Chief BUORD, 20 Oct 1959, "Terrier Weapons System Performance Report, 1st quarter, fiscal year 1960," 1–1, *Boston* File, Post 1 Jan 1946 Report Files.

161. *Destroyerman*, Apr 1962, 7, NDL; and *Bulletin of Ordnance Information*, 31 Dec 1955, 50.

162. "OPNAV Conference Report: CAG Conference," 22 Apr 1955, 1, Admin Services Div, File #38493, CNA; and "The Elements of Naval Gunfire for Use in Connection with the Surface Action Study," Naval Warfare (I), Class of June 1955, Nov 1954, 13.

163. P. M. Shepherd, "The Black Shoe: Back in Fashion," *Proceedings* 100 (Dec 1974): 39.

164. Turner interview, 4 May 1988.

165. Shepherd, "The Black Shoe," 39.

166. Ralph Gerber, "The Choice of a Career within the Navy," *Proceedings* 79 (Jun 1953): 622.

167. P. W. Rairden, "What Is a Line Officer?" *Proceedings* 80 (Jan 1954): 53.

168. Gallery, "A Few Ideas of a Cruiser Skipper," 784, 787.

169. Reynolds, *Fast Carriers*, 393–94; and Gerber, "The Choice of a Career within the Navy," 622.

170. Manning interview, 2 Apr 1993.

171. Palmer, *Origins of the Maritime Strategy*, 73; and Gerald Kennedy, "William Morrow Fechteler," in *Chiefs of Naval Operations*, ed. Love, 238–39.

172. Robert B. Carney, interview by Michael J. Palmer, 2 Jul 1987, NHC Oral History, OA.

173. Paul R. Schratz, "Robert Bostwick Carney," in *Chiefs of Naval Operations*, ed. Love, 247–48; David Rosenberg to author, 29 Oct 1987; and Hone, *Power and Change*, 33.

## 3. The Burke Years

1. "An Estimate of the Threat Posed by the Sino-Soviet Bloc to U.S. and Allied Control of the Seas," 3 Feb 1956, 36, ONI, OA; *ONI Review*, Oct 1956, 402, OA; and "Reinforcement of the Soviet Pacific Fleet," *ONI Review*, Fall 1955, 3–5, 10.

2. "An Estimate of the Threat Posed by the Sino-Soviet Bloc to U.S. and Allied Control of the Seas," 3 Feb 1956, 2.

3. Ibid., 37.

4. Ibid., 1–2, 16, 19; Polmar, *Guide to the Soviet Navy*, 25; and *ONI Review*, Feb 1956, 75.

5. "Aboard a Soviet Cruiser," *ONI Review*, Autumn 1956, 35.

6. *ONI Review*, Aug 1956, 354.

7. Norman Polmar, ed., *Soviet Naval Developments* (Annapolis, 1979), 4.

8. "Developments and Trends in the Soviet Fleet During 1955," *ONI Review*, Spring 1956, 5; and "Developments and Trends in the Soviet Fleet, 1957," *ONI Review*, May 1958, 192–93, 197.

9. "The Soviet Surface Guided Missile Navy in 1960," *ONI Review*, Jul 1960, 301; Rohwer, "The Confrontation of the Superpowers at Sea," 170; and Polmar, *Guide to the Soviet Navy*, 190–92.

10. Rohwer, "The Confrontation of the Superpowers at Sea," 170; and John E. Moore and Richard Compton-Hall, *Submarine Warfare: Today and Tomorrow* (Bethesda, MD, 1987), 67.

11. "An Estimate of the Threat Posed by the Sino-Soviet Bloc to U.S. and Allied Control of the Seas," 3 Feb 1956, 26–27; and "The Transition Period in Soviet Naval Construction," *ONI Review*, Sep 1958, 375–78.

12. "Naval Strategy from the Soviet Viewpoint," *ONI Review*, Nov 1958, 485; Ibid., Oct 1956, 432; and "Developments and Trends in the Soviet Fleet During 1956," 9–10; and "As the Soviets See Us: Admiral Vladimirskiy on Rocket Weapons," 77–79, *ONI Review*, Spring–Summer 1957.

13. "Significant Developments in Soviet Surface Ordnance and Fire Control," *ONI Review*, Dec 1959, 513–15.

14. "Developments and Trends in the Soviet Fleet, 1958," *ONI Review*, May 1959, 183–84; and "Sighting of a Soviet DD with Guided Missile Launcher," *ONI Review*, Jan 1959, 27.

15. "Significant Developments in Soviet Surface Ordnance and Fire Control," *ONI Review*, Dec 1959, 513–15; "Developments and Trends in the Soviet Fleet, 1959," *ONI Review*, Apr 1960, 149; "Intelligence Briefs," *ONI Review*, Jun 1960, 294–95; "The Soviet Surface Guided Missile Navy in 1960," 299, 301; Michael K. MccGwire, "The Background to Russian Naval Policy," in *Brassey's Annual: The Armed Forces Yearbook 1968*, 150; and Polmar, *Guide to the Soviet Navy*, 426.

16. Weschler interview, 24 Mar 1988.

17. "Developments and Trends in the Soviet Fleet, 1959," 153, 158; "Intelligence Briefs," *ONI Review*, Sep 1960, 418; and "Missile Armament in the Soviet Navy," *ONI Review*, Dec 1960, 511.

18. "The Development of the Soviet Navy Since World War II," *ONI Review*, Oct 1960, 427–29.

19. Polmar and Noot, *Submarines of the Russian and Soviet Navies*, 154, 155; Breemer, *Soviet Submarines*, 85; and Moore and Compton-Hall, *Submarine Warfare*, 66, 72.

20. "Naval Strategy from the Soviet Viewpoint," 487–88; "Developments and Trends in the Soviet Fleet, 1957," 198; "Missile Armament in the Soviet Navy," 510; John Jordan, *Soviet Warships: The Soviet Surface Fleet, 1960 to the Present* (Annapolis, 1983), 12–13; *Jane's All the World's Aircraft 1975–76* (New York, 1975), 639; Polmar, *Guide to the Soviet Navy*, 3d ed., 356; and General Dynamics, *The World's Missile Systems*, 7th ed. (Pomona, CA, 1982), 113.

21. Rosenberg, "Burke, Arleigh Albert," 131–33.

22. Burke quoted in Malcolm W. Cagle, "Sea Power and Limited War," *Proceedings* 84 (Jul 1958): 24; and Rosenberg, "Burke, Arleigh Albert," 132.

23. Edward J. Marolda and Oscar P. Fitzgerald, *The United States Navy and the Vietnam Conflict*, vol. 2, *From Military Assistance to Combat, 1959–1965* (Washington, 1986), 3. Burke was the most prominent naval officer to voice these concerns. For assenting Navy views, see Laurence B. Green and John H. Burt, "Massive Retaliation: Salvation or—?" *Proceedings* 84 (Oct 1958): 23; and Amme, "Naval Strategy and the New Frontier," 30.

24. Francis Duncan, *Rickover and the Nuclear Navy: The Discipline of Technology* (Annapolis, 1990), 101. The Berlin Crisis of 1959 reinforced Burke in his view that the Navy should be a useable instrument to retaliate for Soviet harassment on the ground. See Sokolsky, "Seapower in the Nuclear Age," 138.

25. D. D. Lewis, "The Problems of Obsolescence," *Proceedings* 85 (Oct 1959): 27–28; *Cruiser-Destroyerman*, Jan 1970, 3, NDL; and Marolda and Fitzgerald, *From Military Assistance to Combat*, 9.

26. R. B. Laning, "The *Seawolf*: Going to Sea," *Naval History* 6 (Summer 1992): 57.

27. Hackmann, *Seek & Strike*, 354.

28. Laning, "The *Seawolf*: Going to Sea," 55–56; and Edward A. Morgan, "The DASH Weapons System," *Proceedings* 89 (Jan 1963): 151–52.

29. *DANFS* 3:553; Friedman, *U.S. Destroyers*, 193; and Friedman, *US Naval Weapons*, 264.

30. Danis, "Offensive ASW," 583–84, 588. Some analysts doubted that persistent tactics would be necessary. See W. P. Hughes, "The Split-Level Bridge," *Proceedings* 88 (May 1962): 77.

31. Thomas D. McGrath, "Antisubmarine Defense Group ALFA," *Proceedings* 85 (Aug 1959): 49–55.

32. Commander Cruiser Force Atlantic Fleet to CINCLANT, 29 Oct 1960, "Conclusions and recommendations based upon consecutive operating periods in the Second, First, Seventh and Sixth Fleets," 3–4, Cruiser Force Atlantic Fleet File, Post 1 Jan 1946 Report Files, OA.

33. Martin M. Zenni to author, 31 Jul 1992.

34. *Brassey's Annual, 1967*, 79.

35. Lewis, "The Problems of Obsolescence," 31; James C. Hay, "The Attack Submarine," in *U.S. Navy: The View from the Mid-1980s*, ed. George, 218.

36. Friedman, *U.S. Destroyers*, 285.

37. For details of the convoluted FRAM story, see Friedman, *U.S. Destroyers*, 285–90; *Conway's* 1:195–96, 223–24; and *DANFS* 3:551; 1 (rev.):178, 396; 6:567–68.

38. *Conway's* 1:223–24; E. J. Hannon, Jr., "Destroyers in Their Sixtieth Year," *Proceedings* 88 (Nov 1962): 138–39; and Baker, "Historic Fleets," 61.

39. J. Stan III, to C. F. Meyer, APL, "Missions, Design Tasks, and Contingent Tasks of United States Combatant Naval Vessels," 24 May 1956, 1–3, File #43770, CNA.

40. Elmo R. Zumwalt, Jr., interview with author, 20 Apr 1988 (hereafter Zumwalt interview); Hansen, *US Nuclear Weapons*, 173; Friedman, *U.S. Battleships*, 390, 392; "Report of Battle Readiness Exercises, Battleship-Cruiser Force, U.S. Atlantic Fleet, FY 1956," 8 Sep 1956, File #42397, CNA; and *Cruiser-Destroyerman*, Jan 1970, 6. *Missouri*, on continuous active duty since her commissioning in 1944, had retired in early 1955.

41. *Cruiser-Destroyerman*, Jan 1970, 6; and Polmar, *Ships and Aircraft of the U.S. Fleet*, 11th ed., 79.

42. Frederick H. Schneider, Jr. to author, 17 Feb 1993.

43. Ibid.; and "USS *Saint Paul* (CA–73)," 161.

44. Rosenberg, David A., "Arleigh Albert Burke," in *Chiefs of Naval Operations*, ed. Love, 276; *Bulletin of Ordnance Information*, 31 Dec 1956, 9, OA; and Friedman, *U.S. Cruisers*, 396.

45. *DANFS* 6:591; 1 (rev.):131.

46. *DANFS* 3:12–13; Friedman, "The '3–T' Programme," 181; and Blades, "USS *Galveston*," 231–33.

47. Friedman, *U.S. Cruisers*, 382–85; *Bulletin of Ordnance Information*, 31 Mar 1958, 6; Ibid., 30 Sep 1951, 37–38; Ibid., 31 Mar 1957, 19–21; "Bureau of Ships Research and Development Program Highlights," 24 Oct 1958, Naval Sea Systems Command (NSSC) Command File, OA; and Robinson, "Talos Ship System," 162–63.

48. Commander Cruiser-Destroyer Flotilla Eleven to Commander First Fleet, 3 May 1965, "Exercise TEE SHOT Final Report," encl. 10, 2, Cruiser-Destroyer Flotilla Eleven File, Post 1 Jan 1946 Report Files.

49. W. M. Montgomery to author, 28 Sep 1992; and H. H. Ries to author, 22 Oct 1992.

50. John B. Colwell to author, 16 Jul 1992; Ries to author, 22 Oct 1992; and Frank L. Pinney, Jr. to author, 10 Sep 1992.

51. Roger W. Paine, Jr. to author, 29 Oct 1992.

52. Frederick E. Janney to author, 28 Sep 1992.

53. Robert C. Peniston to author, 25 Jun 1992.

54. Jack E. Mansfield to author, 29 Sep 1992; Ries to author, 22 Oct 1992; Montgomery to author, 28 Sep 1992; Jewett O. Phillips, Jr. to author, 24 Jun 1992; Russell S. Crenshaw, Jr. to author, 19 Jun 1992; and Blades, "USS *Galveston*," 230.

55. *DANFS* 6:591; Friedman, "The US Command Cruiser," 211; and Ries to author, 22 Oct 1992.

56. Crenshaw to author, 19 Jun 1992.

57. Blades, "USS *Galveston*," 233; and *Conway's* 1209. *Little Rock* remains a museum ship at Buffalo.

58. Harry D. Felt, interview by John T. Mason, Jr., 1973, 1:305, USNI Oral History (hereafter Felt oral history).

59. *Bulletin of Ordnance Information*, 30 Sep 1959, 19, 21, 22, 23; Friedman, *U.S. Cruisers*, 393–94; and Terzibaschitsch, *Cruisers of the US Navy*, 267–68. Some officers anticipated the replacement of carrier aircraft with missiles. See, for example Allan P. Slaff, "Time for Decision," *Proceedings* 82 (Aug 1956): 809–13. Slaff argued that "the guided missile must replace the piloted aircraft as the primary vehicle for the application of fleet offensive and defensive power, just as the aircraft replaced the battleship as the main strength of the fleet fifteen years ago.... The battleship of the fleet of the future may well resemble the beauties currently covered with grease and preservatives... because it appears that the battleship embraces many of the required attributes of the future ship of the line. The toughness, stability, capacity, and endurance of the battleship modified, of course, by the removal of obsolete armament and other equipment and the addition of guided missiles and guided missile installations, appears to make it a fine candidate for the primary offensive guided missile ship of future fleets." These remarks, given the events of the Gulf War, strike one as prescient.

60. *Bulletin of Ordnance Information*, 31 Mar 1955, 49–50; Ibid., 30 Sep 1956, 15, 17–18; Friedman, *U.S. Destroyers*, 297; Christopher C. Wright, "The Tall Ladies: *Columbus, Albany* & *Chicago*," *Warship International* 14, no. 2 (1977): 108; and *Cruiser-Destroyerman*, Dec 1965, 18.

61. *DANFS* 3:195; C. R. Calhoun, "The Destroyer—Key Ship of the Fleet," *Proceedings* 85 (Feb 1959): 50–51; and Oliver and Slifer, "Evaluating the DDG," 80.

62. Friedman, *U.S. Destroyers*, 249, 308; and Polmar, *Ships and Aircraft of the U.S. Fleet*, 14th ed., 148.

63. Polmar, 14th ed., 129–30, 145; and *Bulletin of Ordnance Information*, 31 Dec 1959, 36–37.

64. *Bulletin of Ordnance Information*, 30 Sep 1959, 13.

65. "The Elements of Naval Gunfire for use in connection with the Surface Action Study," Naval Warfare (I), Class of June 1955, Nov 1954, 13–14, Folder 2912, RG 4, NWC.

66. *Bulletin of Ordnance Information*, 30 Sep 1959, 17–19; Friedman, "The '3–T' Programme," 163, 185; and Schofield, "The Role of the NATO Navies in War," 69.

67. Ibid., 19, 21–23; Terzibaschitsch, *Cruisers of the US Navy*, 278–79; Friedman, *U.S. Cruisers*, 404.

68. Robinson, "Talos Ship System," 163–64; Mahinske, Stoutenburgh, and Swenson, "NTDS," 9, 12; and Holloway interview, 28 Sep 1992.

69. Friedman, *U.S. Cruisers*, 405–6, 411; and Rosenberg, "Arleigh Albert Burke," in *Chiefs of Naval Operations*, ed. Love, 301–2.

70. Polmar, *Ships and Aircraft of the U.S. Fleet*, 14th ed., 131–32; Friedman, *U.S. Cruisers*, 410; Duncan, *Rickover and the Nuclear Navy*, 102–5; and Norman Polmar & Thomas B. Allen, *Rickover* (New York, 1982), 261.

71. Polmar & Allen, 259; and Friedman, *U.S. Destroyers*, 311, 327, 330.

72. Duncan, *Rickover and the Nuclear Navy*, 101, 106–7, 113.

73. OPNAV, NWIP 21-2 (A), "Naval Weapons Selection—Ships," c.1960, 4–19, OA; and Terzibaschitsch, *Cruisers of the US Navy*, 21.

74. Robert H. Wertheim, interview by John T. Mason, Jr., 1981, 85, 87, 88, USNI Oral History Collection, OA (hereafter Wertheim oral history).

75. Commander Cruiser-Destroyer Force, Pacific Fleet to CINCPAC, 5 Apr 1956, "Report of Regulus Strike Operations on 11 and 14 January," 1–5, Cruiser-Destroyer Force, Pacific Fleet, Post 1 Jan 1946 Report Files.

76. Wertheim oral history, 88–89.

77. CDR First Fleet to CINCPACFLT, "Fleet Guided Missile Operations," 21 Feb 1956, CNO Command File, OA; Commander Cruiser-Destroyer Force, Pacific Fleet to CINCPAC, 5 Apr 1956, "Report of Regulus Strike Operations on 11 and 14 January," 7.

78. Wertheim oral history, 90.

79. CDR First Fleet to CINCPACFLT, "Fleet Guided Missile Operations, 21 Feb 1956; Withington oral history, p. 149; Stumpf, "Blasts from the Past," 64; and OPNAV, NWIP 21–2 (A), "Naval Weapons Selection—Ships," c.1960, 4–19.

80. W. D. Brinckloe, "Missile Navy," *Proceedings* 84 (Feb 1958): 27.

81. Commander Cruiser-Destroyer Force, Pacific Fleet to CINCPAC, 5 Apr 1956, "Report of Regulus Strike Operations on 11 and 14 January," 1–2; *DANFS* 4:187; and Stumpf, "Blasts from the Past," 62–63.

82. CDR First Fleet to CINCPACFLT, "Fleet Guided Missile Operations, 21 Feb 1956; Office of Naval Research, Systems Analysis Division, "Cruiser Missile Guidance," vol. 2, Mar 1958, File #62305, CNA; George H. Miller, interview by John T. Mason, Jr., 1975, 267, USNI Oral History Collection, OA (hereafter George H. Miller oral history); Robert Walters, interview

with author, 17 Dec 1987 (hereafter Walters interview); Weschler interview, 24 Mar 1988; and Bruins, "U.S. Naval Bombardment Missiles," 302–3.

83. Rosenberg, "Arleigh Albert Burke," in *Chiefs of Naval Operations*, ed. Love, 277–78. Among those officers were the director of the Guided Missile Division, the DCNO (Air), and the DCNO (Fleet Operations and Readiness).

84. CNO to Chief BUAER, 9 Sep 1958; CNO to BUAER, 2 Feb 1955; and CNO to Naval Research, 1 Feb 1957, all in Regulus File, Naval Aviation History Branch (AVH), NHC.

85. CNO to C/S AF, 11 Jul 1956; NAVMISTESTCEN, Pt Mugu to BUAER, 11 Dec 1958, both in Regulus File; Joseph Metcalf III to author, 11 Aug 1992; and Werrell, *Evolution of the Cruise Missile*, 117.

86. Air War Division to DCNO (Air), 1 Jul 1957, Regulus File. Polaris also soaked up funds intended for *Leahy*-class frigates. See Friedman, *U.S. Destroyers*, 303.

87. Gates to LBJ, Chair, Preparedness Investigating Subcommittee of Armed Forces Committee, 20 Jan 1959, Regulus File; Arleigh Burke, interview by John T. Mason, Jr., 1973, 92–93, USNI Oral History Collection, OA (hereafter Burke oral history).

88. Gates to LBJ, Chair, Preparedness Investigating Subcommittee of the Armed Forces Committee, 20 Jan 1959; Director, Guided Missile Division to Director, Undersea Warfare, 3 Feb 1959, Regulus File; and Friedman, *US Naval Weapons*, 220.

89. Mark W. Woods, interview with author, 19 April 1988 (hereafter Woods interview).

90. Zumwalt interview, 20 April 1988.

91. Calhoun, "The Destroyer—Key Ship of the Fleet," 50–51; Hatch, Luber, and Walker, "Fifty Years of Strike Warfare Research at the Applied Physics Laboratory," 114–15; Lecture, W. T. Luce, "Navy Guided Missiles Program," 30 May 1957, 10, RG 14, NWC; *Bulletin of Ordnance Information*, 31 Mar 1958, 15; and Philip A. Beshany, interview by John T. Mason, Jr. 1983: 2: 856–57, USNI Oral History Collection, OA (hereafter Beshany oral history); Beshany to author, 15 Nov 1991. For the opinion of VADM Benedict J. Semmes, see Ronald Huisken, *The Origin of the Strategic Cruise Missile* (New York, 1981), 21. For similar views, see Masterson oral history, 304; Peet oral history, 143; Wertheim oral history, 94; George H. Miller oral history, 266–67; and Withington oral history, 2:149–50. Another extremely advanced cruise missile called LOBLO never got beyond the initial conception stages. See U.S. Naval Air Development Center, Johnsville, PA, "A Review of LOBLO," Sep 1961, File #75924, CNA.

92. Elmo R. Zumwalt, Jr., *On Watch: A Memoir* (New York, 1976), 81.

93. Weschler interview, 24 Mar 1988.

94. Zumwalt interview, 20 Apr 1988; Woods interview, 19 Apr 1988; Gerald E. Miller, interview with author, 1 Jun 1988 (hereafter Gerald E. Miller Interview); "Missile Armament in the Soviet Navy," 510; and *ONI Review*, Jul 1956, 271–72.

95. Petrel File, AVH, NHC; *Bulletin of Ordnance Information*, 31 Mar 1956, 64–65; Ibid., 30 Sep 1956, 13–14; "Guided Missile Systems of the Department of the Navy," Mar 1958, 64–65, BUSHIPS File, OA; Thomas H. Moorer, interview with author, 26 May 1992 (hereafter Moorer interview); and Alpers oral history, 17–18.

96. Claude P. Ekas, c.1975, 9–10, USNI Oral History Collection, OA (hereafter Ekas oral history).

97. "Guided Missile Systems of the Department of the Navy," Mar 1958, 68–69, 72–73, BUSHIPS File; and Lautenschläger, *Technology and the Evolution of Naval Warfare*, 43, 48.

98. "The *Barry* Incident," *ONI Review*, Oct 1960, 430–32; and Zumwalt interview, 20 Apr 1988.

99. Minutes of the Twentieth Meeting of the Composite Design Research Panel, APL-JHU, 8–9 Feb 1956, 16, File #46041, CNA.

100. Ibid.; Friedman, *U.S. Destroyers*, 308; Surface Missile Systems, Quarterly Progress Report, 31 October 1962, NSSC Command File, OA; and Masterson oral history, 252.

101. OPNAV, NWIP 21–2 (A), "Naval Weapons Selection—Ships," c.1960, 4-16; *Bulletin of Ordnance Information*, 31 Mar 1957, 9, 10, 12, 13; and Bruins, "U.S. Naval Bombardment Missiles," 338.

102. Lecture, M. A. Iiams, "Introduction to Surface Force Operations," 17 Oct 1958, 1, RG 14, NWC.

103. Mahinske, Stoutenburgh, and Swenson, "NTDS," 5, 18.

104. Ivar E. Highberg, interview by Leroy L. Doig III, 1 Apr 1981, 13, NHC Oral History (hereafter Highberg oral history); and Mahinske, Stoutenburgh, and Swenson, "NTDS," 7, 8, 11.

105. Edward C. Svendsen and Donald L. Ream, "Design of a Real-Time Data Processing System," paper presented to International Federation for Information Processing, 29 May 1965, 291; Mahinske, Stoutenburgh, and Swenson, "NTDS," 7–9; and Naval Education and Training Program Development Center, Surface Ship Operations (Washington, 1978), 213.

106. Allison, "U.S. Navy Research and Development since World War II," 322–24; Edward C. Svendsen and Donald L. Ream, "What's Different about the Hardware in Tactical Military Systems," paper presented to the National Computer Conference, 1973, 797; Mahinske, Stoutenburgh, and Swenson, "NTDS," 13–14; and Friedman, *U.S. Destroyers*, 318, 329.

107. Weschler interview, 24 Mar 1988; Felt oral history, 1:305; Peet oral history, 98; and *Bulletin of Ordnance Information*, 30 Jun 1956, 9–10.

108. Crenshaw to author, 19 Jun 1992.

109. Commander Cruiser-Destroyer Force, U.S. Pacific Fleet to Commander First Fleet, 23 Apr 1960, "Report of Anti-Air Warfare Exercise 11–14 Apr 1960," 4, Cruiser-Destroyer Force, Pacific Fleet File.

110. Masterson oral history, 252; G. G. Beall, "Standard Missile," *Naval Ordnance Bulletin*, Jun 1973, 29; COMCRUDIV 3 to CINCPAC, 26 Mar 1958, "Full Scale Air Defense Exercise (ADEX 10) 12 March 1958," 1–3, Cruiser Division Three File, Post 1 Jan 1946 Report Files; Walters interview, 17 Dec 1987; Friedman, *U.S. Destroyers*, 221; *Brassey's Defence Yearbook, 1987* (New York, 1988), 472; Frieden, *Principles of Naval Weapons Systems*, 479–80; Naval Education and Training Command, *The Weapons Officer* (Washington, 1982), 203; Alvin R. Eaton, "Bumblebee Missile Aerodynamic Design: A Constant in a Changing World," *Johns Hopkins APL Technical Digest* 13 (Jan–Mar 1992): 69, 73, 77; M. E. Bustard, "USS *King* (DLG–10)," *Proceedings* 87 (Mar 1961): 164; and Foreman interview, 28 Aug 1992.

111. Walters interview, 17 Dec 1987.

112. Robert E. Adamson, Jr., interview with author, 10 Mar 1988 (hereafter Adamson interview).

113. Charles J. Smith, interview with author, 10 Dec 1987 (hereafter Charles J. Smith interview).

114. William Seltzer, interview with author, 12 Jun 1991 (hereafter Seltzer interview).

115. BUORD, Annual Progress Report: Guided Missile Program, 1 Oct 1953, 141; and *Cruiser-Destroyerman*, Jan 1966, 9.

116. Commander Cruiser Force, Atlantic Fleet to Commander Second Fleet, 8 Jan 1960, "Report of Weapons Systems Evaluation Group WEXVAL 8 Operations," Cruiser Force Atlantic Fleet File.

117. *DANFS* 3:13.

118. Brinckloe, "Missile Navy," 28.

119. *Bulletin of Ordnance Information*, 31 Mar 1957, 9, 10, 12, 13; Ibid., 31 Dec 1956, 17–20; "Guided Missile Systems of the Department of the Navy," Mar 1958, 20; Ferris, Frey, and Mills, "The Ship Launched Projectile," 100; Thomas J. Christman, "Naval Ordnance Today

and Tomorrow," *Naval Ordnance Bulletin*, Sep 1972, 17; COMCRUDIV 1 to Commander Seventh Fleet, 27 Jun 1960, "Report of Anti-Air Warfare Exercises 15-21 June 1960," 1–3, Cruiser Division One File, Post 1 Jan 1946 Report Files; Foreman interview, 28 Aug 1992; Robinson, "Talos Ship System," 166; Todd Blades, "The Bumblebee Can Fly," *Naval History* 2 (Fall 1988), 50–51; and Garten and Dean, "Evolution of the Talos Missile," 121.

120. COMCRUDIV 1 to Commander Seventh Fleet, 17 Jul 1960, "Report of Anti-Air Warfare Exercises 28 June–1 July 1960," 3, Cruiser Division One File.

121. Commander Cruiser-Destroyer Force, U.S. Pacific Fleet to Commander First Fleet, 23 Apr 1960, "Report of Anti-Air Warfare Exercise 11–14 Apr 1960," 1–4.

122. CO USS *Gyatt* (DDG 1) to Commander Destroyer Flotilla Six, 18 Dec 1958, "Final Exercise Report for DESAIRDEX 2–58," 6, Destroyer Flotilla Six File, Post 1 Jan 1946 Report Files; CO USS *Boston* (CAG 1) to Chief BUORD, 20 Oct 1959, "Terrier Weapons System Performance Report, 1st quarter, fiscal year 1960," 1–2, *Boston* File, Post 1 Jan 1946 Report Files; Oliver and Slifer, "Evaluating the DDG," 84; and Janney to author, 28 Sep 1992.

123. COMCRUDIV 1 to Commander Seventh Fleet, 17 Jul 1960, "Report of Anti-Air Warfare Exercises 28 June–1 July 1960," 4.

124. Ibid.; CO USS *Gyatt* (DDG–1) to Commander Destroyer Flotilla Six, 18 Dec 1958, "Final Exercise Report for DESAIRDEX 2–58," 1; and Commander Cruiser Force Atlantic Fleet to CINCLANT, 29 Oct 1960, "Conclusions and recommendations based upon consecutive operating periods in the Second, First, Seventh and Sixth Fleets," 1–4.

125. COMCRUDIV 1 to Commander Seventh Fleet, 27 Jun 1960, "Report of Anti-Air Warfare Exercises 15–21 June 1960," 4–5.

126. *Bulletin of Ordnance Information*, 31 Dec 1956, 10–11; Ibid., 31 Mar 1956, 60–64; Beall, "Standard Missile," 31; Kossiakoff, "APL—Expanding the Limits," 12; Friedman, "The '3–T' Programme," 164; and Eaton, "Bumblebee Missile Aerodynamic Design," 74.

127. Ibid., 31 Dec 1956, 16.

128. Ibid., 10–11, 15–18; OPNAV, NWIP 21–2 (A), "Naval Weapons Selection—Ships," c.1960, 4–18; R. J. Tamulevicz, "Standard Missile: A Brief History," *Naval Ordnance Bulletin*, Jun 1969, 33; and Billy D. Dobbins and George W. Luke, "From Kamikaze to Aegis: An Introduction," *Johns Hopkins APL Technical Digest* 2 (Oct–Dec 1981): 234.

129. Crenshaw to author, 19 Jun 1992.

130. Blades, "The Bumblebee Can Fly," 50–51; Gerald E. Miller interview, 1 Jun 1988; Walters interview, 17 Dec 1987; Weschler interview, 24 Mar 1988; Marion E. Oliver, "Terrier/Tartar: Pacing the Threat," *Johns Hopkins APL Technical Digest* 2 (Oct–Dec 1981): 256–57; Robinson, "Talos Ship System," 166; and Beall, "Standard Missile," 29.

131. "Naval Strategy from the Soviet Viewpoint," 487; Tamulevicz, "Standard Missile: A Brief History," 33; and *Bulletin of Ordnance Information*, 30 Sep 1959, 14–15.

132. R. J. Tamulevicz, "Standard Missile: A Brief History," 33; W. Coleman Hyatt, "Fleet Air Defense: Countermeasures," *Johns Hopkins APL Technical Digest* 13 (Jan–Mar 1992): 106; James D. Flanagan and William N. Sweet, "Aegis: Advanced Surface Missile System," *Johns Hopkins APL Technical Digest* 2 (Oct–Dec 1981): 243; APL/JHU, "Future Fleet Defense: An Advanced Weapon System Study," 7 Jan 1958, File #54763, CNA; Dobbins and Luke, "From Kamikaze to Aegis," 234; James D. Flanagan and George W. Luke, "Aegis: Newest Line of Navy Defense," *Johns Hopkins APL Technical Digest* 2 (Oct–Dec 1981): 237–39; James L. Keirsey, "Airbreathing Propulsion for Defense of the Surface Fleet," *Johns Hopkins APL Technical Digest* 13 (Jan–Mar 1992): 60–61; James H. Doyle and Wayne E. Meyer, "Cruisers," unpublished paper, 9 Mar 1992, 7; and Milton Gussow and Edward C. Prettyman, "Typhon—A

Weapon System Ahead of Its Time," *Johns Hopkins APL Technical Digest* 13 (Jan–Mar 1992): 82–84.

133. *Bulletin of Ordnance Information*, 31 Mar 1958, 63.

134. Ibid., 31 Dec 1958, 50; Ibid., 30 Sep 1958, 42–43; and "Naval Ordnance Station, Indian Head, Maryland," *Naval Ordnance Bulletin*, 11 Dec 1967, 9–10.

135. Marolda and Fitzgerald, *From Military Assistance to Combat*, 294; *Bulletin of Ordnance Information*, 30 Sep 1958, 42–45; Commander, Operational Evaluation Organization, "Operational Evaluation of the 3″/70 Mk 6 Twin AA Gun Mount and GFCS Mk 69 Mod 4 Fitted in the *Restigouche* Class DDE's," 2 Nov 1959, File #60837, CNA; K. C. Malley, "A Descriptive Comparison of Gun Fire Control Systems Mk 86 and Mk 87," *Naval Ordnance Bulletin*, Sep 1967, 1; Turner interview, 4 May 1988; and *Bulletin of Ordnance Information*, 31 Dec 1958, 48.

136. McHugh, "Gaming at the Naval War College," 54; Iiams lecture, "Introduction to Surface Force Operations," 17 Oct 1958; William K. Yates, "Tactics Revival at the Naval War College," *Naval War College Review* (Nov–Dec 1973): 11; and OPNAV, NWIP 21–2 (A), "Naval Weapons Selection—Ships," c.1960, OA.

137. J. F. McNulty, "Naval Destroyer School," *Proceedings* 92 (Apr 1966): 157; and Harold H. Sacks, "Shoreside Checkout for Seagoing Destroyer Officers," *Proceedings* 88 (Feb 1962): 58–59.

138. W. D. Brinckloe, "Is the Versatile Line Officer Obsolete?" *Proceedings* 85 (Jun 1959): 27.

139. Ibid., 27–28; Alexander to author, 7 Jul 1992; and James H. Doyle and Wayne E. Meyer, "Management and Support of Aegis Cruisers and Destroyers," unpublished paper, 21 Apr 1991, 2–3.

140. *Destroyerman*; Norman Polmar, remarks at the American Military Institute, NHC, 9 Apr 1988; and Hone, *Power and Change*, 44.

141. Hone, 36, 38–39, 46; Crenshaw to author, 19 Jun 1992; Allison, "U.S. Navy Research and Development since World War II," 300; Joseph P. Smaldone, *History of the White Oak Laboratory, 1945–1975* (Silver Spring, MD, 1977), 173; *Bulletin of Ordnance Information*, 30 Sep 1959, 15–16; and Sylvia G. Humphrey, ed., *Meeting the Challenge: A 1986 History of the Naval Surface Weapons Center* (Washington, 1987), 3.

142. *DANFS* 3:552; 6:567; Elward F. Baldridge, "Lebanon and Quemoy—The Navy's Role," *Proceedings* 87 (Feb 1961): 95; Floyd D. Kennedy, Jr., "The Creation of the Cold War Navy, 1953–1962," in *In Peace and War: Interpretations of American Naval History, 1775–1984*, 2d ed., ed. Kenneth J. Hagan (Westport, CT, 1984), 316–17; Ryan, *First Line of Defense*, 20–21; and Hooper, Allard, and Fitzgerald, *Setting of the Stage*, 341.

143. *DANFS* 2:431; 3:225, 558; Calhoun, "The Destroyer—Key Ship of the Fleet," 48; and "I Wish I Had More Time to Give," *Surface Warfare* 18 (Jul–Aug 1993): 23. That particular boatswain, Robert S. Rawls, ended his career in 1993 at the rank of commander.

144. Burke as quoted in Brinckloe, "Missile Navy," 23; and Rosenberg, "Burke, Arleigh Albert," 132.

## 4. Caught in the Doldrums

1. Horacio Rivero to author, 27 Jun 1992; Henry C. Mustin interview, 27 May 1992; Amme, "Naval Strategy and the New Frontier," 23–24; and Polmar, ed., *Ships and Aircraft of the U.S. Fleet*, 11th ed., 1.

2. Sokolsky, "Seapower in the Nuclear Age," 141.

3. Ibid., 138, 151; and Kaufmann, Planning Conventional Forces, 1950–80, 11.

4. Amme, "Naval Strategy and the New Frontier," 23–24; and Moulton, "NATO and the Atlantic," 151.

5. Moulton, "NATO and the Atlantic," 150; Rohwer, "The Confrontation of the Superpowers at Sea," 179; *Brassey's Annual, 1967*, 78–79; and Davis, *Admirals Lobby*, 230–32.

6. Commander Cruiser-Destroyer Force, Atlantic Fleet to CINCLANT, 15 Dec 1962, "Documentation of Cuban Operations," 1–3, 4–2, Cruiser-Destroyer Force, Atlantic Fleet File, Post 1 Jan 1946 Report Files, OA.

7. Ibid., 1–3, 4–4; *DANFS* 5:79; 4:71; *Cruiser-Destroyerman*, Dec 1962, 2–3, NDL; Kennedy, "Creation of the Cold War Navy," 323–24; Kaufmann, *McNamara Strategy*, 271; and Love, *History of the U.S. Navy* 2:456–63

8. Elmo R. Zumwalt, Jr., "Remarks at the Annual Banquet of the SNAME, 12 Nov 1970," *Transactions of The Society of Naval Architects and Marine Engineers* 78 (1970): 46; David Fairhall, *Russian Sea Power* (Boston, 1971), 184–85; and James J. Tritten, *Declaratory Policy for the Strategic Employment of the Soviet Navy* (Santa Monica, 1984), 120–21, 140.

9. Burke oral history, 92.

10. Kenneth R. McGruther, *The Evolving Soviet Navy* (Newport, RI, 1978), 21; Fairhall, *Russian Sea Power*, 227; and Norman Friedman, *The Naval Institute Guide to World Naval Weapons Systems* (Annapolis, 1989), 89–90.

11. Doyle interview, 28 Mar 1988; Ruhe, "Cruise Missile," 48; D. W. Alderton and E. Lighter, "Light Attack Aircraft Versus PT Boat, *Combat Readiness*, Oct–Dec 1965, 19–20, OA; and Polmar, *Guide to the Soviet Navy*, 4th ed., 243–44.

12. Jordan, *Soviet Warships*, 15.

13. Polmar, *Guide to the Soviet Navy*, 4th ed., 188; *Brassey's Defence Yearbook, 1987*, 468; Breemer, *Soviet Submarines*, 92, 116–18; Huisken, *Strategic Cruise Missile*, 98; Richard M. Basoco and Richard H. Webber, "*Kynda*-Class Missile Frigates," *Proceedings* 90 (Sep 1964): 140–41; Rohwer, "The Confrontation of the Superpowers at Sea," 171–72; Polmar, *Soviet Naval Developments*, 29; and Friedman, *World Naval Weapons Systems*, 90–91.

14. J. F. Parker, interview with author, 10 Jun 1988 (hereafter Parker interview).

15. "Non-Nuclear Ordnance Study," 3d ed., vol. 5, "Surface-to-Surface Warfare," 1966, 24–25, File #129723, CNA; Turner interview, 4 May 1988; C. P. Ekas, Jr. to author, 30 Aug 1988; Adamson interview, 10 Mar 1988; Woods interview, 19 Apr 1988; Frank H. Price, Jr. to author, Jul 1988; Thomas J. Christman, "Naval Ordnance Today and Tomorrow," *Naval Ordnance Bulletin*, Sep 1972, 16, OA; and Jürgen Rohwer, *Superpower Confrontation on the Seas: Naval Development and Strategy Since 1945* (Beverly Hills, 1975), 50.

16. McGwire, "The Background to Russian Naval Policy," 151–52; Friedman, *World Naval Weapons Systems*, 69–70; Polmar, *Guide to the Soviet Navy*, 4th ed., 57; Polmar and Noot, *Submarines of the Russian and Soviet Navies*, 166, 333–34; and Moore and Compton-Hall, *Submarine Warfare*, 72.

17. Breemer, *Soviet Submarines*, 103, 105–6; Polmar and Noot, *Submarines of the Russian and Soviet Navies*, 165; and Rohwer, "The Confrontation of the Superpowers at Sea," 178.

18. C. P. Ekas, Jr. to author, 30 Aug 1988; Woods interview, 19 Apr 1988; and Polmar, *Guide to the Soviet Navy*, 4th ed., 420.

19. Lloyd M. Mustin interview, 24 Jun 1992; Russell S. Crenshaw, Jr. to author, 19 Jun 1992; William R. St. George to author, 18 Jan 1993; David F. Emerson to author, 20 Aug 1992; and Foreman interview, 28 Aug 1992.

20. Sacks, "Shoreside Checkout for Seagoing Destroyer Officers," 58–59.

21. Shepherd, "The Black Shoe," 40.

22. Adamson interview, 10 Mar 1988.

23. Ibid.; and Shepherd, "The Black Shoe," 39.

24. Zumwalt, *On Watch*, 44–45.

25. Keith Stewart, interview with author, 28 Oct 1987 (hereafter Stewart interview); Turner interview, 4 May 1988; and Arthur R. Gralla, interview with author, 22 Jun 1992 (hereafter Gralla interview).

26. Gralla interview, 22 Jun 1992.

27. William P. Mack, "The Exercise of Broad Command: Still the Navy's Top Specialty," *Proceedings* 83 (Apr 1957): 375; and Peet oral history, 166–67.

28. Richard G. Alexander to author, 7 Jul 1992.

29. Mack, "The Exercise of Broad Command," 371; W. A. Matson, "Seven Year Itch," *Proceedings* 84 (Apr 1958): 77; Jack E. Mansfield to author, 29 Sep 1992; and Roger W. Paine, Jr. to author, 29 Oct 1992

30. Smith, "Wanted: A Surface Line School for Junior Officers," 130; and "Surface Weapon Control," 1 Jan 1963, 1, Technical Area Plan # RM–15, Missile Development Office, Research, Development, Test and Evaluation Group, Bureau of Naval Weapons, CNO Command File, OA.

31. Elmo R. Zumwalt, Jr., "A Course for Destroyers," *Proceedings* 88 (Nov 1962): 39.

32. T. C. Grzymala, Comment on "The Surface Line Officer," *Proceedings* 98 (Jan 1973): 88; Gralla interview, 22 Jun 1992; Hart, "Surface Warfare Officers," 40; D. R. Larson, "The Surface Line Officer: Some Conn, Some Can't," *Proceedings* 98 (Jul 1972): 43; and H. C. George, Comment on "Surface Warfare Officers," *Proceedings* 102 (Nov 1976): 75.

33. CO *Long Beach* (CG(N) 9) to Commander Cruiser-Destroyer Force, Atlantic Fleet, 10 Jun 1966, "Report of Overhaul of USS *Long Beach* (CG(N) 9)," A–5, *Long Beach* File, Post 1 Jan 1946 Report Files; and Richard L. Madouse, "Surface Ship Overhauls," *Proceedings* 92 (Feb 1966): 30.

34. CO USS *Davis* (DD 937) to Chief of Naval Operations, 23 Dec 1962, "Unsatisfactory Personnel Situation," 7, Personal Files of Allan P. Slaff, Naples, FL.

35. William R. Smedberg III, "Manning the Future Fleets," *Proceedings* 89 (Jan 1963): 123–24.

36. Robert H. Smith, "Vital Goal—A Workable Navy," *Proceedings* 91 (Jun 1965): 62.

37. Gralla interview, 22 Jun 1992.

38. Madouse, "Surface Ship Overhauls," 31.

39. Ibid.; Russell S. Crenshaw, "Why We Are Losing Our Junior Officers," *Proceedings* 83 (Feb 1957): 132; and Sacks, "Shoreside Checkout for Seagoing Destroyer Officers," 59.

40. Manning interview, 2 Apr 1993.

41. *Surface SITREP* 7, no. 2 (May 1991): 2.

42. Adamson interview, 10 Mar 1988; Parker interview, 10 Jun 1988; and Smedberg, "Manning the Future Fleets," 123–24.

43. CO USS *Davis* (DD 937) to Chief of Naval Operations, 23 Dec 1962, "Unsatisfactory Personnel Situation," 2, 9, 11; Sacks, "Shoreside Checkout for Seagoing Destroyer Officers," 58; McNulty, "Naval Destroyer School," 157; and Smith, "Wanted: A Surface Line School for Junior Officers," 130.

44. *Destroyerman*, Jan 1962, 4, NDL.

45. Raymond J. Hart, "Surface Warfare Officers: The Need for Professionalism," *Proceedings* 102 (Jun 1976): 40; Sacks, "Shoreside Checkout for Seagoing Destroyer Officers," 62, 63; McNulty, "Naval Destroyer School," 160; and *Destroyerman*, Jan 1962, 2–5, 8–12.

46. McNulty, "Naval Destroyer School," 156–58, 161; and Shepherd, "The Black Shoe," 39–40.

47. Smith, "Wanted: A Surface Line School for Junior Officers," 131.

48. *Destroyerman*, Jan 1962, 19; *Cruiser-Destroyerman*, Apr 1962, 2–3; Ibid., Jan 1970, 6; and Ibid., Dec 1965, 20.

49. CDR Allen of Code 70, COMOPTEVFOR, "White Paper," 7 Jan 1963, File #85876, CNA; Naval Education and Training Program, Surface Ship Operations, 263; and Turner interview, 4 May 1988.

50. CO *Lawrence* (DDG 4) to Commander Middle East Force, 5 Jul 1963, Personal Files of T. W. Walsh, Fairfax, VA; CO USS *Luce* (DLG 7) to Commander Cruiser-Destroyer Force, Atlantic Fleet, 11 Apr 1964, "Terrier Systems Reliability and Firing," 2, Personal Files of Allan P. Slaff, Naples, FL; and Charles K. Duncan, 1981, 2: 881–82, USNI Oral History Collection, OA (hereafter Duncan oral history).

51. Duncan oral history, 2:890.

52. Seltzer interview, 12 Jun 1991; and Duncan oral history, 2: 890–93.

53. *Cruiser-Destroyerman*, Jan 1964, 16.

54. Ibid., 14–17; and *Surface*, Oct 1975, 10, NDL.

55. Oliver and Slifer, "Evaluating the DDG," 86; *Cruiser-Destroyerman*, Jan 1964, 15; Weschler interview, 24 Mar 1988; and Bustard: "USS *King* (DLG–10)," 165.

56. Robert C. Peniston to author, 25 Jun 1992.

57. Oliver and Slifer, "Evaluating the DDG," 78–85; Hughes, "The Split-Level Bridge," 72, 74; St. George to author, 6 Jul 1992; L. D. Carey, "USS *Henry B. Wilson* (DDG–7)," *Proceedings* 87 (Jul 1961): 152; *DANFS* 3:533; and James H. Doyle and Wayne E. Meyer, "Destroyers," Unpublished paper, 29 Aug 1991, 2.

58. T. W. Walsh to author, 10 Jul 1992.

59. Peniston to author, 25 Jun 1992; *DANFS* 6:279; and Friedman, *Naval Radar*, 164.

60. Peniston to author, 25 Jun 1992.

61. Alexander to author, 7 Jul 1992.

62. Walsh to author, 10 Jul 1992.

63. Peniston to author, 25 Jun 1992.

64. Lawrence D. Cummins to author, 4 Aug 1992.

65. Emerson to author, 20 Aug 1992.

66. Alexander to author, 7 Jul 1992; *DANFS* 6:280; and Oliver and Slifer, "Evaluating the DDG," 78, 80.

67. Bustard: "USS King (DLG-10)," 161–63, 166; and Dean C. Allard, "Zumwalt, Elmo Russell, Jr.," in *Dictionary of American Military Biography*, ed. Spiller, 3:1228.

68. H. H. Ries to author, 23 Jun 1992; *DANFS* 4:177, 196; and David F. Emerson to author, 20 Aug 1992.

69. Robert L. Baughan, Jr., to author, 18 Jul 1992.

70. Ibid.; Douglas C. Plate to author, 13 Aug 1992; and Robert L. Brandenburg, "USS *Bainbridge* Is Not the Answer," *Proceedings* 90 (Jan 1964): 41.

71. R. S. Wentworth, Jr. to author, 28 Jun 1992.

72. Ibid.; Baughan to author, 18 Jul 1992; and *Conway's* 1:214.

73. *Brassey's Annual, 1967*, 78; Peet oral history, 162, 214, 216; and J. H. Bell, "USS *Bainbridge* (DLGN–25)," *Proceedings* 88 (Nov 1962): 168. Reportedly, *Bainbridge* was to be named *New York City*, but Congress was reluctant to fund ships with cruiser names. See Peet oral history, 161.

74. Polmar & Allen, *Rickover*, 260–61; Memo, Eli T. Reich, Asst Chief for Surface Missile Systems, 20 Feb 1963, 1, Surface Missile Systems, NSSC Command File, OA; Robert J. Massey, "The First Hundred Days of the New Frontier," *Proceedings* 87 (Aug 1961): 31; Wilhelm Donko, "The USS *Long Beach* after Her 'Mid Life Conversion,'" in *Warship*, ed. Lambert, 10:25; and Ronald T. Kelly to author, 16 Feb 1993. During the ship's first major overhaul five years later, her missile systems were saddled with an incompetent contractor. See CO *Long Beach* to Commander Cruiser-Destroyer Force, Atlantic Fleet, 10 Jun 1966, "Report of Overhaul of USS *Long Beach* (CG(N)9)," A–1, A–4, A–5, IV–1.

75. Peet oral history, 208–9.

76. Morris L. Hayes, "Nuclear Propulsion: We Dare Not Delay," *Proceedings* 91 (Jan 1965): 31–32; Bell, "USS *Bainbridge* (DLGN–25)," 170; Peet oral history, 227; Raymond E. Peet, "Comments on the *Bainbridge*," *Proceedings* 89 (Jul 1963): 100; Bernard M. Strean to author, 30 Jan 1993; and Charles J. Smith to author, 15 Aug 1992.

77. Peet oral history, 198–99; and Kelly to author, 16 Feb 1993.

78. Peet oral history, 201–2, 236.

79. Ibid., 212.

80. Peet, "Comments on the *Bainbridge*," 97, 102.

81. Strean to author, 30 Jan 1993; *Cruiser-Destroyerman*, Jan 1965, 4–5; and *DANFS* 4:138.

82. William F. Raborn, "New Horizons of Naval Research and Development," *Proceedings* 89 (Jan 1963): 44; and Peet, "Comments on the *Bainbridge*," 96. For pronouncements similar to Raborn's, see Frederic G. Withington, "The Outcome of the Electronic Revolution in the Navy," *Proceedings* 89 (Nov 1963): 74; and Hayes, "Nuclear Propulsion: We Dare Not Delay," 31–32.

83. Ralph K. James, "The Ships of '73," *Proceedings* 89 (Jan 1963): 101.

84. Brandenburg, "USS *Bainbridge* Is Not the Answer," 37–38; Hannon, "Destroyers in Their Sixtieth Year," 139; *Brassey's Annual, 1967*, 72–73; Smith to author, 15 Aug 1992; and Robert H. Smith, "Vital Goal—A Workable Navy," 63.

85. "Surface Weapon Control," 1 Jan 1963, 1, Technical Area Plan #RM–15.

86. Ibid.; "Procedures for Selecting Configuration of Frigates, Destroyers and Destroyer Escorts," *Combat Readiness*, Jan–Mar 1965, 2–4; Nitze, remarks at the Joint Session of the National War College and Industrial College of the Armed Forces, 16 Mar 1964, 163; and Commander Cruiser Force Atlantic Fleet to CINCLANT, 29 Oct 1960, "Conclusions and recommendations based upon consecutive operating periods in the Second, First, Seventh and Sixth Fleets," 5–6, Cruiser Force Atlantic Fleet File, Post 1 Jan 1946 Report Files.

87. Friedman, *U.S. Cruisers*, 414, 418; Friedman, *U.S. Destroyers*, 223; Christopher C. Wright, "*Albany* (CG–10) and *Chicago* (CG–11) Leave the Active Fleet," *Warship International* 20, no. 1 (1983): 80.

88. Polmar, *Ships and Aircraft of the U.S. Fleet*, 14th ed., 124–26; *Army-Navy-Air Force Journal and Register* 100 (3 Aug 1963): 5; CDR Allen of Code 70, COMOPTEVFOR, "White Paper," 7 Jan 1963; and Carl D. Corse, Jr., *Introduction to Shipboard Weapons* (Annapolis, 1975), 13.

89. *Brassey's Annual, 1967*, 78–79; Polmar, *Ships and Aircraft of the U.S. Fleet*, 14th ed., 122–24; and *Cruiser-Destroyerman*, Jan 1964, 16–17.

90. Henry C. Mustin interview, 27 May 1992.

91. Wright quoted in William J. Flynn, "Comment on 'The Unfaced Challenge, Submarine Versus Free World,'" *Proceedings* 90 (Aug 1964): 113.

92. Nitze, remarks at the Joint Session of the National War College and Industrial College of the Armed Forces, 16 Mar 1964, 163; Moulton, "NATO and the Atlantic," 153; North Atlantic Assembly, *NATO Anti-Submarine Warfare: Strategy, Requirements and the Need for Co-operation* (North Atlantic Assembly, 1982), 29–30.

93. Polmar, *Ships and Aircraft of the U.S. Fleet*, 11th ed., 1; Lautenschläger, *Technology and the Evolution of Naval Warfare*, 53; and Hackmann, *Seek & Strike*, 355.

94. Nitze, remarks at the Joint Session of the National War College and Industrial College of the Armed Forces, 16 Mar 1964, 16; and Jensen, "Helicopters in Antisubmarine Warfare," 37.

95. Charles K. Duncan to author, 22 Aug 1992.

96. Rivero to author, 27 Jun 1992; *Brassey's Annual, 1967*, 79; and Kaufmann, *Planning Conventional Forces*, 13–14.

97. Joseph Metcalf III to author, 11 Aug 1992.

98. Ibid.; James, "The Ships of '73," 97, 100; Kelly to author, 7 Jan 1993; Donald A. Smith, "USS *Garcia* (DE–1040)," *Proceedings* 91 (Sep 1965): 161–62; and Hannon, "Destroyers in Their Sixtieth Year," 139.

99. Kaufmann, *McNamara Strategy*, 185; Smith, "USS *Garcia* (DE–1040)," 161; and Massey, "The First Hundred Days of the New Frontier," 31. The FRAM program underwent several changes under the Kennedy administration. For details, see Friedman, *U.S. Destroyers*, 285–87; *DANFS* 3:264, 357; and *Conway's* 1:224.

100. Friedman, *US Naval Weapons*, 264; Robert B. Cavanaugh, "The ASW Effort," *Proceedings* 90 (Feb 1964): 144; and Tom Stefanick, *Strategic Antisubmarine Warfare and Naval Strategy* (Lexington, MA, 1987), 171.

101. *Brassey's Defence Yearbook, 1987*, 472; John Jordan, "USS *California*," in *Warship*, ed. Anthony Preston (Annapolis, 1978) 2:85–86; *DANFS* 1 (rev.):91; and Cavanaugh, "The ASW Effort," 141, 143.

102. *DANFS* 8:319; Friedman, *US Naval Weapons*, 128–29; and Morgan, "The DASH Weapons System," 150–51.

103. Thomas D. McGrath, "Submarine Defense," *Proceedings* 87 (Jul 1961): 42; *Brassey's Annual, 1967*, 79; and Cavanaugh, "The ASW Effort," 145.

104. Cavanaugh, "The ASW Effort," 140–41.

105. Commander Cruiser-Destroyer Force, Atlantic Fleet to CINCLANT, 15 Dec 1962, "Documentation of Cuban Operations," 4–2.

106. Kaufmann, *McNamara Strategy*, 271.

107. CTG 81.0 to Commander Antisubmarine Warfare Force, Atlantic Fleet, 3 Mar 1965, "Report of CONVEX 1–65," A–1, Antisubmarine Warfare Force, Atlantic Fleet, Post 1 Jan 1946 Report Files.

108. Commander Cruiser-Destroyer Flotilla Nine to Commander First Fleet, 13 Nov 1964, "Exercise Union Square Final Report," 5–6, Cruiser-Destroyer Flotilla Nine File, Post 1 Jan 1946 Report Files.

109. Commander Cruiser-Destroyer Flotilla Three to Distribution List, 19 Aug 1966, "'Highlights' of Final Report of Fleet Exercise 'BELAYING PIN,'" 7, Cruiser-Destroyer Flotilla Three File, Post 1 Jan 1946 Report Files.

110. Brandenburg, "Destroyer Command," 38.

111. S. Dombroff, "Don't Misuse New Destroyers," *Proceedings* 88 (Nov 1962): 145.

112. Brandenburg, "Destroyer Command," 37–38, 40; Dombroff, "Don't Misuse New Destroyers," 143–45; and Flynn, "Comment on 'The Unfaced Challenge,'" 112.

113. Glennon, "An Approach to ASW," 49.

114. Dombroff, "Don't Misuse New Destroyers," 143–44.

115. COMDESRON 9 to COM7THFLT, "Chief Observer's Report of Evaluated AAWEX Conducted 4 May 1962," 22 May 1962, 2, File #80711, CNA.

116. Ibid., 2–3; Woods interview, 19 Apr 1988; Weschler interview, 24 Mar 1988; and Price to author, Jul 1988.

117. Paine to author, 29 Oct 1992; and Moorer interview, 26 May 1992.

118. Commander Cruiser-Destroyer Flotilla Nine to Commander First Fleet, 13 Nov 1964, "Exercise Union Square Final Report," 3–4.

119. CO USS *Luce* (DLG 7) to Commander Cruiser-Destroyer Force, Atlantic Fleet, 11 Apr 1964, "Terrier Systems Reliability and Firing," 1; and Robert H. Smith, "Vital Goal—A Workable Navy," 62–63.

120. Edward A. Christofferson, Jr. to author, 1 Jul 1992.

121. Friedman, *Postwar Naval Revolution*, 70; Duncan, *Rickover and the Nuclear Navy*, 129; Blades, "The Bumblebee Can Fly," 51–52; Friedman, *U.S. Destroyers*, 223; CDR Allen of Code 70, COMOPTEVFOR, "White Paper," 7 Jan 1963; Weschler interview, 24 Mar 1988; Memo, Eli T. Reich, Asst Chief for Surface Missile Systems, 20 Feb 1963, 3–4; and Timothy J. Keen to author, 3 Oct 1992.

122. Wayne E. Meyer interview with author, 12 Jun 1992 (hereafter Meyer interview).

123. Alexander to author, 7 Jul 1992.

124. Memo, Eli T. Reich, Asst Chief for Surface Missile Systems, 31 Oct 1962, 1, Surface Missile Systems, NSSC Command File.

125. Robert H. Smith, "Vital Goal—A Workable Navy," 64.

126. Blades, "The Bumblebee Can Fly," 51–52; and Meyer interview, 12 Jun 1992.

127. Memo, Eli T. Reich, Asst Chief for Surface Missile Systems, 23 Jul 1962, Surface Missile Systems, NSSC Command File; and Reich memo, 31 Oct 1962, 2.

128. Adelaide M. Madsen, "Three-T Effectiveness," *Naval Ordnance Bulletin*, Sep 1966, 25–27; and Emch, "Air Defense for the Fleet," 44.

129. Reich memo, 20 Feb 1963, 4.

130. Doyle and Meyer, "Management and Support of Aegis...," 3–4; and Emch, "Air Defense for the Fleet," 45.

131. Doyle and Meyer, 1, 3–4; Reich memo, 31 Oct 1962; Madsen, "Three-T Effectiveness," 27; Garten and Dean, "Evolution of the Talos Missile," 120; *Cruiser-Destroyerman*, Jan 1964, 12; Friedman, "The '3–T' Programme," 165; and Hyatt, "Fleet Air Defense: Countermeasures," 104, 106.

132. G. G. Beall, "Standard Missile," *Naval Ordnance Bulletin*, Jun 1973, 29; Reich memo, 23 Jul 1962; "Anti-Air Warhead Technology (Non-Nuclear), 1 Jan 1963, 1–2, Technical Area Plan #RM–2; and Gussow and Prettyman, "Typhon," 82–88; and Keirsey, "Airbreathing Propulsion for...the Surface Fleet," 62.

133. Meyer quoted in Gussow and Prettyman, "Typhon," 82; "Today's Missile Fleet," *Combat Readiness*, Apr–Jun 1963, 28–29; Friedman, "The '3–T' Programme," 181; R. J. Tamulevicz,

"Standard Missile: A Brief History," *Naval Ordnance Bulletin*, Jun 1969, 33; "Advanced Multi-Function Array Radar," *Naval Ordnance Bulletin*, Jun 1970, 2–3.

134. Dobbins and Luke, "From Kamikaze to Aegis," 234; Flanagan and Sweet, "Aegis: Advanced Surface Missile System," 243–44; Emch, "Air Defense for the Fleet," 48–49; Doyle and Meyer, "Management and Support of Aegis," 4–5; Beall, "Standard Missile," 29; and Tamulevicz, "Standard Missile: A Brief History," 33.

135. Svendsen and Ream, "Hardware in Tactical Military Systems," 797; Mahinske, Stoutenburgh, and Swenson, "NTDS," 9; and Robert E. May, "Digital Computers in Weapons Control," *Proceedings* 90 (Jan 1964): 126–28.

136. Commander Cruiser-Destroyer Flotilla Eleven to Commander Carrier Division One, 3 Jun 1962, "Chief Observer's Report on AAWEX 1, 2, 3, and 4 Conducted During exercise 'PORK BARREL,'" 4, Cruiser-Destroyer Flotilla Eleven File, Post 1 Jan 1946 Report Files; Naval Education and Training Command, *The Weapons Officer*, 182; M. Eckhart, Jr., "'The Wit to See,'" *Proceedings* 90 (Aug 1964): 39; Friedman, *U.S. Destroyers*, 318, 329; *Conway's* 1:211; and Isaac C. Kidd, Jr., "The Surface Fleet," in J. L. George, ed., *The U.S. Navy: The View from the Mid-1980s* (Boulder, CO, 1985), 86–87.

137. Ferris, Frey, and Mills, "The Ship Launched Projectile," 100; James, "The Ships of '73," 99; and Smedberg, "Manning the Future Fleets," 123–24. Macks appeared in the *Albany, Leahy, Belknap, Bronstein*, and *Knox* designs. See Friedman, "The '3–T' Programme," 184.

138. Highberg oral history, 8; H. W. Miller, Jr., "Weapon Firing Zones," *Naval Ordnance Bulletin*, Mar 1971, 38–39; "Surface Weapon Control," 1 Jan 1963, 2, 3, Technical Area Plan #RM–15. Norman Friedman has pointed out that the Aegis system of the 1980s "achieves substantially higher performance in a destroyer hull than the much more expensive Typhon system ... would have achieved in a large cruiser hull." See Friedman, *Postwar Naval Revolution*, 217.

139. CDR Allen of Code 70, COMOPTEVFOR, "White Paper," 7 Jan 1963.

140. Emch, "Air Defense for the Fleet," 45.

141. "Surface Weapon Control," 1 Jan 1963, p. 3, Technical Area Plan #RM–15; Commander Cruiser-Destroyer Flotilla Nine to Commander First Fleet, 13 Nov 1964, "Exercise Union Square Final Report," 8–9; and Withington, "The Electronic Revolution in the Navy," 68.

142. Friedman, *Postwar Naval Revolution*, 70.

143. COMCRUDIV 2 to Commander Amphibious Group Two, 20 Jun 1961, "Report of LANTFLEX 4–16," 5, Cruiser Division Two File, Post 1 Jan 1946 Report Files.

144. Proposal quoted in Stull, John O., "Guns Have Not Gone Yet!" 82.

145. Heinl, "The Gun Gap," 28.

146. Ibid., 85; *DANFS* 3:291; 4:145; and Marolda and Fitzgerald, *From Military Assistance to Combat*, 294.

147. Heinl, "The Gun Gap," 34–36; and Friedman, "Amphibious Fire Support," 234.

148. LeRoy Taylor, "Naval Operations in Confined Waters and Narrow Seas," *Proceedings* 86 (Jun 1960): 55–56, 60; Miles H. Hubbard, "The Design of Naval Weapons," *Proceedings* 91 (Oct 1965): 40; Stull, "Guns Have Not Gone Yet!" 80, 85; "Anti-Surface Warhead Technology (Non-Nuclear)," 1 Jan 1963, 1, Technical Area Plan #RM–3 and Friedman, *U.S. Battleships*, 392.

149. CDR Allen of Code 70, COMOPTEVFOR, "White Paper," 7 Jan 1963.

150. "Surface Weapon Control," 1 Jan 1963, 2, 3, Technical Area Plan #RM–15; and Friedman, *U.S. Cruisers*, 380.

151. K. C. Malley, "A Descriptive Comparison of Gun Fire Control Systems Mk 86 and Mk 87," *Naval Ordnance Bulletin*, Sep 1967.

152. Emerson interview, 26 Apr 1988; Weschler interview, 24 Mar 1988; "Assessment of Latest *Jane's Fighting Ships* Report in Regard to U.S. and Soviet Naval Forces," n.d. [1967], 2, CAPT James F. McNulty Papers, NWC.

153. "The Effective Use of a 5″/54 as a Surface Weapon," *Combat Readiness*, Oct–Dec 1962, 4–5.

154. Stull, "Guns Have Not Gone Yet!," 84; Gary L. Pickens, "5-Inch, 54 Gun Reliability Improvement Program," *Naval Ordnance Bulletin*, Jun 1973, 45; "Assessment of Latest *Jane's Fighting Ships* Report in Regard to U.S. and Soviet Naval Forces," n.d. [1967], 1; McCollum, *Dahlgren*, 140; Jordan, "USS *California*," 85; CDR Allen of Code 70, COMOPTEVFOR, "White Paper," 7 Jan 1963; and Highberg oral history, 13.

155. K. C. Malley, "A Descriptive Comparison of Gun Fire Control Systems Mk 86 and Mk 87," 1–2, 6; and Navy Department, Office of Information, *Weapon Systems of the United States Navy, 1977* (Washington, 1977), 40.

156. CDR Allen of Code 70, COMOPTEVFOR, "White Paper," 7 Jan 1963; Huisken, *Strategic Cruise Missile*, 29; Walters interview, 17 Dec 1987; and "Airborne Weapons Control," 1 Jan 1963, 7, 8, Technical Area Plan #RM-–16.

157. Peniston to author, 25 Jun 1992; Reich memo, 23 Jul 1962; Commander Cruiser-Destroyer Flotilla Eleven to Commander First Fleet, 22 Oct 1965, "Exercise RAG WEED Final Report," 4, Cruiser-Destroyer Flotilla Eleven File; Donald D. A. Gray, "The Talos Shipboard Test Program," *Johns Hopkins APL Technical Digest* 3 (Apr–Jun 1982): 168–69; and Frank A. Dean, "The Unified Talos," *Johns Hopkins APL Technical Digest* 3 (Apr–Jun 1982): 124.

158. Reich memo, 20 Feb 1963, 2; Memo, D. E. Willhite, OPEVAL Group, "Performance of Terrier Missile System in Surface-to-Surface Firings," 31 Jul 1968, File #(OEG) 0438–68, CNA; CDR Allen of Code 70, COMOPTEVFOR, "White Paper," 7 Jan 1963; and Zumwalt interview, 20 Apr 1988.

159. CDR Allen of Code 70, COMOPTEVFOR, "White Paper," 7 Jan 1963; Friedman, *US Naval Weapons*, 229–30; Woods interview, 19 Apr 1988; Jay Hurlbut, interview with author, 28 Oct 1987 (hereafter Hurlbut interview); Henry C. Mustin interview, 2 May 1988; and Walters interview, 17 Dec 1987.

160. "Anti-Air Warhead Technology (Non-Nuclear)," 1 Jan 1963, p. 7, Technical Area Plan #RM–2; Henry C. Mustin interview, 2 May 1988; Woods interview, 19 Apr 1988; Weschler interview, 24 Mar 1988; Walters interview, 17 Dec 1987; Parker interview, 10 Jun 1988; CDR Allen of Code 70, COMOPTEVFOR, "White Paper," 7 Jan 1963; and Hurlbut interview, 28 Oct 1987.

161. CDR Allen of Code 70, COMOPTEVFOR, "White Paper," 7 Jan 1963.

162. "Standard Missile Anti-Ship Capability," *Naval Ordnance Bulletin*, Jun 1974, 23–24.

163. G. L. Apted to Commander FMSAEG, Corona, 5 Feb 1968, "Report of Annual Training FLTEX-BEADSTRINGER-STRIKEX 1–68," n.p., *Long Beach* File, Post 1 Jan 1946 Report Files.

164. CDR Allen of Code 70, COMOPTEVFOR, "White Paper," 7 Jan 1963; Huisken, *Strategic Cruise Missile*, 29; "Standard Missile Anti-Ship Capability," *Naval Ordnance Bulletin*, Jun 1974, 23–24.

165. Reich memo, 23 Jul 1962; "Nuclear Weapons Components," 1 Jan 1963, 1, 5–6, Technical Area Plan #RM–4.

166. Hansen, *US Nuclear Weapons*, 186–88.

167. Montgomery to author, 28 Sep 1992.

168. Memo, D. E. Willhite, OPEVAL Group, "Performance of Terrier Missile System in Surface-to-Surface Firings," 31 Jul 1968; Emerson interview, 26 Apr 1988; Henry C. Mustin interview, 2 May 1988; and Price to author, Jul 1988.

169. Marolda and Fitzgerald, *From Military Assistance to Combat*, 488; and Robert D. Colvin, "Aftermath of the *Elath*," *Proceedings* 95 (Oct 1969): 61–62.

170. Ira W. Bonnett, Staff Commander Cruiser-Destroyer Force, PACFLT, "Countering the PT/*Swatow* Boat Threat," *Combat Readiness*, Jan–Mar 1965, 13.

171. Ibid., 12–13; Commanders First and Seventh Fleets to Distribution List, 27 Nov 1964, "Procedures for Combating Small High-Speed Surface Craft," 1–2; Commander Cruiser-Destroyer Force, Pacific Fleet to CNO, 24 Dec 1964, "Final Report on Project F/O 177 FY 65 'Conduct a Fleet Operational Investigation in Connection with Countering Small, High-speed Surface Craft with Conventional Armament,'" 1, both in Cruiser-Destroyer Force File, Post 1 Jan 1946 Report Files; Commander Cruiser-Destroyer Flotilla Eleven to Commander First Fleet, 3 May 1965, "Exercise TEE SHOT Final Report," 1–2, encl. 1, 2, Cruiser-Destroyer Flotilla Eleven File; and *Cruiser-Destroyerman*, Jan 1964, 14–15.

172. D. S. Appleton, "Inflatable Surface Gunnery Target," *Combat Readiness*, Jul–Sep 1965, 13.

173. Commander Cruiser-Destroyer Flotilla Nine to Commander First Fleet, 13 Nov 1964, "Exercise Union Square Final Report," 6–7; and "Firefish Operations with USS *Boston*, CAG–1," *Combat Readiness*, Jan–Mar 1966, 18–20.

174. Bonnett, "Countering the PT/*Swatow* Boat Threat," Jan–Mar 1965, 14.

175. Ibid., 15.

## 5. Shocks to the System

1. Hone, *Power and Change*, 62, 68–75. This was not exactly a new problem, as a look at the great imbroglio over the *Iowa*-class armament of 1938 will show. See Muir, *Iowa* Class Battleships, 12.

2. Allison, "U.S. Navy Research and Development Since World War II," 302–3.

3. Emerson interview, 26 Apr 1988.

4. Ekas oral history, 14–15, 24–26.

5. Alpers oral history, 79–80; and Rosenberg, "Burke, Arleigh Albert," 132.

6. Frank L. Pinney, Jr. to author, 10 Sep 1992.

7. Weschler interview, 24 Mar 1988; and Alpers oral history, 79–80. Not all officers were so critical of McNamara's reforms. Richard G. Alexander wrote the author, 7 Jul 1992: "We progressed from what Churchill called 'the romance of design' to the 'logic of design.'"

8. Highberg oral history, 13; Carlisle, *Powder and Propellants*, 163; and Isaac C. Kidd, Jr., interview with author, 3 May 1988 (hereafter Kidd interview).

9. Andrew G. Nelson, "A Black-Shoe in a Brown-Shoe World," *Proceedings* 96 (Jul 1970): 56.

10. Zumwalt, *On Watch*, 41, 63; Walters interview, 17 Dec 1987; and Kennedy, "David Lamar McDonald," in *Chiefs of Naval Operations*, ed. Love, 349.

11. Patrick Tyler, *Running Critical: The Silent War, Rickover, and General Dynamics* (New York, 1986), 24; and Kennedy, "David Lamar McDonald," 349.

12. Hart, "Surface Warfare Officers," 40–41.

13. Moulton, "NATO and the Atlantic," 152; and Sokolsky, "Seapower in the Nuclear Age," 185–86, 221.

14. Commander Cruiser-Destroyer Flotilla Seven, 3 Oct 1965, "Exercise HOT STOVE Final Report," 1, Cruiser-Destroyer Flotilla Seven File, Post 1 Jan 1946 Report Files, OA.

15. *DANFS* 6:13; and Ronald T. Kelly to author, 7 Jan 1993.

16. *DANFS* 3:648; 8:400; CINCPAC, "Pacific Area Naval Operations Review," Feb 1966, II-9 to II–10, OA; Ibid., Dec 1966, 101; and Commander Cruiser-Destroyer Flotilla Seven to Commander Cruiser-Destroyer Force, Pacific Fleet, 19 Jan 1967, "COMCRUDESFLOT SEVEN Cruise Report," 8, Cruiser-Destroyer Flotilla Seven File.

17. *DANFS* 3:565.

18. CINCPAC, "Pacific Area Naval Operations Review," Aug 1966, B–1; and Commander Cruiser-Destroyer Flotilla Seven to Commander Cruiser-Destroyer Force, Pacific Fleet, 19 Jan 1967, "COMCRUDESFLOT SEVEN Cruise Report," 9.

19. "USS *Albany* Recommissioned," *Naval Ordnance Bulletin*, Mar 1969, 63–64, OA; Friedman, *U.S. Cruisers*, 398, 400; Shepherd, "The Black Shoe," 40; and Metcalf interview, 1 Oct 1987; H. E. Reichert (CO of *Sterett*) to COM7FLT, 2 May 1972, File #164972, CNA.

20. CINCPAC, "Pacific Area Naval Operations Review," May 1968, 24–25.

21. CINCPAC, "Pacific Area Naval Operations Review," Aug 1966, B–1, B–2; U.S. Grant Sharp, interview by Etta-Belle Kitchen, 1976, 2:440, 457, USNI Oral History Collection, OA (hereafter Sharp oral history); U.S. Seventh Fleet, "Monthly Historical Summary," Jun 1967, 24, OA; CO *Long Beach* (CGN 9), "Firing Report, 11 May 1968," File Index, Post 1 Jan 1946 Report Files; and U.S. Seventh Fleet, "Monthly Historical Summary," Sep 1968, 26.

22. U.S. Seventh Fleet, "Monthly Historical Summary," Jun 1968, 26.

23. Sharp oral history, 2:440–41.

24. Gerald E. Miller interview, 1 Jun 1988; Goss, "Talos in Retrospect," 116; and Friedman, *U.S. Cruisers*, 398.

25. U.S. Seventh Fleet, "Monthly Historical Summary," Jul 1967, 66; Ibid., Nov 1967, 54–55; Commander Cruiser-Destroyer Flotilla Eleven to Commander Cruiser-Destroyer Force, Pacific Fleet, 30 Apr 1968, "Cruise Report," VII–3, Cruiser-Destroyer Flotilla Eleven File, Post 1 Jan 1946 Report Files; Garten and Dean, "Evolution of the Talos Missile," 121; Dean, "The Unified Talos," 125; and Emch, "Air Defense for the Fleet," 42.

26. K. C. Wallace to H. G. Rickover, 5 Sep 1967, 1–5, *Long Beach* File, Post 1 Jan 1946 Report Files; and *DANFS* 4:656.

27. *DANFS* 8:310; Marolda, "By Sea, Air, and Land" (MS), 47–51; *DANFS* 3:676; and U.S. Seventh Fleet, "Monthly Report," Mar 1965, 1; and "Enemy Trawler Captured," *Naval Ordnance Bulletin*, Dec 1967, 96.

28. U.S. Seventh Fleet, "Monthly Report," May 1965, 4–5; Ibid., Dec 1965, 3; and *DANFS* 4:306.

29. CINCPAC, "Pacific Area Naval Operations Review," Feb 1966, II–8.

30. CINCPAC, "Pacific Area Naval Operations Review," Jan 1966, 23; Ibid., Apr 1966, II–8, II–12; Ibid., May 1966, II–8; Ibid., Sep 1966, 21–23; Ibid., Nov 1966, 18; Ibid., Dec 1966, 28; Buell interview, 7 Oct 1992; *DANFS* 7:250; Commander Cruiser-Destroyer Flotilla Eleven, "Cruise Report, 31 March–18 August 1966," 14, Cruiser-Destroyer Flotilla Eleven File; and Commander Cruiser-Destroyer Flotilla Seven to Commander Cruiser-Destroyer Force, Pacific Fleet, 19 Jan 1967, "COMCRUDESFLOT SEVEN Cruise Report," 11.

31. CINCPAC, "Pacific Area Naval Operations Review," Mar 1967, 33; and U.S. Seventh Fleet, "Monthly Historical Summary," Mar 1967, 39, 43.

32. U.S. Seventh Fleet, "Monthly Historical Summary," Apr 1967, 39, 41; Ibid., May 1967, 48; Ibid., Dec 1968, 20–21; CINCPAC, "Pacific Area Naval Operations Review," Feb 1968, 28, 30, 32; Ibid., May 1968, 38; Commander Cruiser-Destroyer Flotilla Seven to Commander Cruiser-Destroyer Force, Pacific Fleet, 19 Jan 1967, "Cruise Report," 5; and Commander Cruiser-Destroyer Flotilla Eleven to Commander Cruiser-Destroyer Force, Pacific Fleet, 30 Apr 1968, "Cruise Report," I–1.

33. CINCPAC, "Pacific Area Naval Operations Review," Oct 1966, 24; Ibid., Oct 1967, 29; Ibid., Jun 1968, 27; Ibid., Aug 1967, 31; U.S. Seventh Fleet, "Monthly Historical Summary," May 1967, 43; Commander Cruiser-Destroyer Flotilla Three to Commander Cruiser-Destroyer Force, Pacific Fleet, 16 Nov 1967, "Cruise Report," 5–6, Cruiser-Destroyer Force, Pacific Fleet File, Post 1 Jan 1946 Report Files.

34. U.S. Seventh Fleet, "Monthly Historical Summary," Oct 1967, 41–42; Ibid., Sep 1967, 49–50; CINCPAC, "Pacific Area Naval Operations Review," Jul 1967, 40; Ibid., Nov 1967, 29; and Ibid., Aug 1967, 34.

35. "Six-Inch Guns on the Line," *Naval Ordnance Bulletin*, Dec 1967, 89; Edward J. Marolda to author, 29 Oct 1991; and Weschler interview, 24 Mar 1988.

36. Commander Cruiser-Destroyer Flotilla Eleven to Commander Cruiser-Destroyer Force, Pacific Fleet, 30 Apr 1968, "Cruise Report," VII–1 to VII–2.

37. U.S. Seventh Fleet, "Monthly Historical Summary," Jun 1968, 52–53; and Emch, "Air Defense for the Fleet," 47–48.

38. *DANFS* 6:13, 252–54.

39. "Admiral Woods," *Naval Ordnance Bulletin*, Jun 1968, 93; R. H. Small, "Naval Gunfire Support," *Combat Readiness*, Jul–Sep 1968, 10, OA; and Marolda, "By Sea, Air, and Land" (MS), 44–45.

40. Small, "Naval Gunfire Support," 10.

41. Ibid.; *Cruiser-Destroyerman*, Nov 1967, 8, NDL; U.S. Seventh Fleet, "Monthly Historical Summary," Nov 1967, 30; James B. Soper, "Naval Gunfire: Today and Tomorrow," *Proceedings* 92 (Sep 1966): 54; Marolda, "By Sea, Air, and Land" (MS), 46; U.S. Seventh Fleet, "Monthly Historical Summary," May 1967, 49; Commander Cruiser-Destroyer Flotilla Three to Distribution List, 19 Aug 1966, "'Highlights' of Final Report of Fleet Exercise 'BELAYING PIN,'" 1, 4–5, Cruiser-Destroyer Flotilla Three File, Post 1 Jan 1946 Report Files; and Edward A. Christofferson, Jr. to author, 1 Jul 1992.

42. G. S. Mustin, "Ammunition Handling for the USS *New Jersey*," *Naval Ordnance Bulletin*, Sep 1968, 13.

43. Robert C. Peniston to author, 25 Jun 1992.

44. Walters interview, 17 Dec 1987. For details of her deployment, see Muir, *Iowa Class Battleships*, 105–116; Alfred Fernandes, "Moving the Big One," *Naval Ordnance Bulletin*, Dec 1968, 71, 76; U.S. Seventh Fleet, "Monthly Historical Summary," Apr 1968, 24; CINCPAC, "Pacific Area Naval Operations Review," Sep 1968, 36; and Ibid., Nov 1968, 33.

45. U.S. Seventh Fleet, "Monthly Historical Summary," Jan 1969, 17.

46. Ibid., Nov 1968, 24; Ibid., Apr 1969, 21; CINCPAC, "Pacific Area Naval Operations Review," Feb 1969, 32, 35; and CINCPAC, "Fleet Operations Review," Mar 1969, 31.

47. U.S. Seventh Fleet, "Monthly Historical Summary," Aug 1969, 41.

48. Robert L. Baughan, Jr., to author, 18 Jul 1992.

49. CINCPAC, "Fleet Operations Review," Dec 1969, 25; Ibid., May 1970, 24; Ibid., Sep 1970, 24–25; CINCPAC, "Fleet Operations Review for April 1970," 19 Jun 1970, 24; and CINCPAC, "Quarterly Fleet Operations Review," 14 Dec 1970, 44–45, OA.

50. *DANFS* 7:62; U.S. Seventh Fleet, "Monthly Historical Summary," Feb 1968, 22, 27; and Commander Cruiser-Destroyer Flotilla Eleven to Commander Cruiser-Destroyer Force, Pacific Fleet, 30 Apr 1968, "Cruise Report."

51. U.S. Seventh Fleet, "Monthly Historical Summary," Apr 1969, 52, 53, 75–76; and *DANFS* 8:17.

52. Soper, "Naval Gunfire," 53.

53. McCollum, *Dahlgren*, 140; and "Assessment of Latest *Jane's Fighting Ships* Report in Regard to U.S. and Soviet Naval Forces," n.d. [1967], 1, CAPT James F. McNulty Papers, NWC.

54. McCollum, *Dalgren*, 58.

55. Naval Education and Training Command, *The Weapons Officer*, 128; *DANFS* 4:221; CINC-PAC, "Pacific Area Naval Operations Review," Dec 1966, 37; Ibid., Apr 1967, 33–34; U.S. Seventh Fleet, "Monthly Historical Summary," May 1965, 4–5; Ibid., Oct 1965, 3; Ibid., Mar 1967, 39; Ibid., Jul 1969, 20–21; and Ibid., Nov 1969, 1, 13, 14.

56. John W. Gay, "In-Bore Explosions in Five Inch Guns," *Naval Ordnance Bulletin*, Sep 1970, 75–77.

57. K. C. Malley, "A Descriptive Comparison of Gun Fire Control Systems Mk 86 and Mk 87," *Naval Ordnance Bulletin*, Sep 1967, 1; Corse, *Introduction to Shipboard Weapons*, 5; William Rowden, interview with author, 14 Dec 1987 (hereafter Rowden interview); and Department of the Navy, Secretary of the Navy, *Annual Report to the Secretary of Defense*, FY 1969, 43 (hereafter *SECNAV Annual Report*).

58. J. H. Wain, "Modern Lightweight 175-mm/60 Cal. Gun Mount Mark 1 Mod 0—Development for Landing Force Support Ship," *Naval Ordnance Bulletin*, Sep 1966, 11–13; Friedman, "Amphibious Fire Support," 240; J. T. Cianfrani and Ned Donaldson, "Major Caliber Lightweight Gun Mk 71 Mod 0 8-Inch 55 Caliber," *Naval Ordnance Bulletin*, Jun 1974, 27–29; and Weschler interview, 24 Mar 1988.

59. S. L. Maxwell and M. A. Henderson, "Long Range Bombardment Ammunition (Project Gunfighter)," *Naval Ordnance Bulletin*, Mar 1969, 33–35.

60. Ibid., 33–35; "Naval Ordnance Station, Indian Head, Maryland," *Naval Ordnance Bulletin*, Dec 1967, 9; and Carlisle, *Powder and Propellants*, 162.

61. Maxwell and Henderson, "Long Range Bombardment Ammunition (Project Gunfighter)," 34.

62. Ibid., 33–35; Carlisle, *Powder and Propellants*, 176–77; Doyle and Meyer, "Cruisers," 6; and CINCPAC, "Fleet Operations Review," Feb 1970, 23.

63. McCollum, *Dahlgren*, 143–44, 147; and Maxwell and Henderson, "Long Range Bombardment Ammunition (Project Gunfighter)," 35.

64. "Gun Propellant Program," *Naval Ordnance Bulletin*, Sep 1967, 11; Ibid., "Naval Ordnance Station, Indian Head, Maryland," Dec 1967, 9–10; U.S. Seventh Fleet, "Monthly Historical Summary," Oct 1967, 63; and Carlisle, *Powder and Propellants*, 176.

65. McCollum, *Dahlgren*, 144; and Maxwell and Henderson, "Long Range Bombardment Ammunition (Project Gunfighter)," 35.

66. Fairhall, *Russian Sea Power*, 229; Patrick Wall, "The Missile in Sea Warfare," in *Brassey's Annual: The Armed Forces Yearbook 1968* (New York, 1969): 162; Eller, *Soviet Sea Challenge*, 198; and Colvin, "Aftermath of the *Elath*," 61–62.

67. Emerson interview, 26 Apr 1988.

68. Frank H. Price, Jr. to author, Jul 1988.

69. Woods interview, 19 Apr 1988.

70. Colvin, "Aftermath of the *Elath*," 61–72; and Parker interview, 10 Jun 1988.

71. CDR E. C. Whelan, Jr., USN and ENS G.W. Fritz, USN, USS *Rich* (DD 820), "Reaction to the *Elath* Incident," *Combat Readiness*, Spring/Summer 1969, 12.

72. *SECNAV Annual Report*, FY 1969, 18 Mar 1970; and Colvin, "Aftermath of the *Elath*," 67.

73. Howard Bucknell, Comment on "Aftermath of the *Elath*," *Proceedings* 96 (Mar 1970): 87.

74. Hurlbut interview, 28 October 1987.

75. Zumwalt interview, 20 Apr 1988.

76. Weschler interview, 24 Mar 1988; Henry C. Mustin interview, 2 May 1988; Woods interview, 19 Apr 1988; U.S. Congress, Joint Senate-House Armed Services Subcommittee of the Senate and House Armed Services Committees, *CVAN–70 Aircraft Carrier*, 91st Cong., 2d sess., 1970, 282; and Turner interview, 4 May 1988.

77. Polmar, *Guide to the Soviet Navy*, 4th ed., 420, 428–29; Rohwer, "The Confrontation of the Superpowers at Sea," 182; *Brassey's Defence Yearbook, 1987*, 468; Polmar and Noot, *Submarines of the Russian and Soviet Navies*, 334; McGruther, *The Evolving Soviet Navy*, 28; Woods interview, 19 Apr 1988; and Terry R. Betzer, "Terrier/Tartar: New Threat Upgrade Program," Johns Hopkins APL Technical Digest 2 (Oct–Dec 1981): 276–77.

78. Walters interview, 17 Dec 1987.

79. Gerald E. Miller interview, 1 Jun 1988.

80. Armed Services Subcommittee, *CVAN–70*, 14.

81. Ibid., 14–15, 212, 283; Emerson interview, 26 Apr 1988; Albert H. Dell, OEG, "The Soviet Naval Threat to the U.S. CVA Task Force," 21 Sep 1972, 3, 14, File #72–1386, CNA.

82. Tritten, *Strategic Employment of the Soviet Navy*, 120.

83. William J. Ruhe, "Cruise Missile: The Ship Killer," *Proceedings* 102 (Jun 1976): 46; and Thomas J. Christman, "Naval Ordnance Today and Tomorrow," *Naval Ordnance Bulletin*, Sep 1972, 14.

84. Quoted in Polmar and Noot, *Submarines of the Russian and Soviet Navies,* 187.

85. Gerald E. Miller interview, 1 Jun 1988.

86. Jordan, *Soviet Warships*, 35–39, 41; Polmar, *Guide to the Soviet Navy*, 4th ed., 121; Christman, "Naval Ordnance Today and Tomorrow," 16; and James Reckner to author, 29 Oct 1991.

87. U.S. Seventh Fleet, "Monthly Historical Summary," Oct 1969, 25; *DANFS* 3:442; Polmar, *Guide to the Soviet Navy*, 4th ed., 50; Ryan, *First Line of Defense*, 76–77, 141; *SECNAV Annual Report*, FY 1970, 165; and Christman, "Naval Ordnance Today and Tomorrow," 14.

88. Ronald T. Kelly to author, 7 Jan 1993.

89. Commander Cruiser-Destroyer Flotilla Eight to Commander Second Fleet, 27 Dec 1968, "Report of Multi-Ship RIMEX," 5–3, Cruiser-Destroyer Flotilla Eight File, Post 1 Jan 1946 Report Files.

90. Commander Cruiser-Destroyer Flotilla Two to Commander Second Fleet, 6 Jan 1967, "Report of Exercise LANTFLEX 66," 2–4; Commander Cruiser-Destroyer Flotilla Two to Commander Amphibious Group Two, 22 Jan 1966, "Letter Report of PHIBASWEX 1–65," 1, 3–4, both in Cruiser-Destroyer Flotilla Two File, Post 1 Jan 1946 Report Files; Commander Cruiser-Destroyer Flotilla Three to Commander First Fleet, 1 Dec 1966, "Report of Exercise Eager Angler," 8, Cruiser-Destroyer Flotilla Three File.

91. Commander Cruiser-Destroyer Flotilla Two to Commander Amphibious Group Two, 22 Jan 1966, "Letter Report of PHIBASWEX 1–65," 4, Cruiser-Destroyer Flotilla Two File; *Brassey's Annual, 1974*, 283; Commander Cruiser-Destroyer Flotilla Six to Commander Cruiser-Destroyer Force, Atlantic Fleet, 21 Apr 1967, "Report of VDS Exercise," Cruiser-Destroyer Force, Atlantic Fleet File, Post 1 Jan 1946 Report Files; and *DANFS* 7:454.

92. *Conway's* 1:226; *DANFS* 1 (rev.):146–47; Ibid. 6:277, 378; Ibid. 7:554; U.S. Seventh Fleet, "Monthly Historical Summary," Jul 1967, 71; and Ronald T. Kelly to author, 7 Jan 1993.

93. Metcalf interview, 1 Oct 1987; Kennedy, "David Lamar McDonald," in Love, *The Chiefs of Naval Operations*, 344; *DANFS* 7:251; and Polmar, *Ships and Aircraft of the U.S. Fleet*, 11th ed., 154.

94. *Conway's* 1:226–27.

95. Fairhall, *Russian Sea Power*, 219; Felt oral history 1:307; Turner interview, 4 May 1988; Zumwalt interview, 20 Apr 1988; Henry C. Mustin interview, 2 May 1988; Rohwer, "The Confrontation of the Superpowers at Sea," 182; Commander Cruiser-Destroyer Flotilla Ten to Distribution List, 26 Aug 1969, "RIMEX 1–70 Final Report," 2–6, Cruiser-Destroyer Flotilla Ten File, Post 1 Jan 1946 Report Files; Albert H. Dell, OEG, "The Soviet Naval Threat to the U.S. CVA Task Force," 21 Sep 1972, 31–32, File #72–1386, CNA.

96. Emerson interview, 26 Apr 1988; O'Neil, "Gun Systems? For Air Defense?," 46; Hatch, Luber, and Walker, "Fifty Years of Strike Warfare Research at the Applied Physics Laboratory," 115; Richard W. Illgen, "Notional Conical Scan and Monopulse Missile Guidance Model. Progress Report No. 1 for Counter-Antiship-Missile Study," 30 Aug 1968, File OEG #182–69 Type 13, CNA. One officer intimately connected with this effort, Rear Admiral Claude Ekas, Jr., suspected that defense received halting attention because of the Navy's historic preference for offensive over defensive measures. C. Ekas, Jr. to author, 30 Aug 1988.

97. R. A. Bowling, "Naval Warfare Specialists," *Proceedings* 96 (Aug 1970): 54; W. M. Harnish, Director, Office of Program Appraisal, USN to SECNAV with copy from Elmo R. Zumwalt, Jr., Director Systems Analysis Division to President, CNA, "Anti-Ship Missile Threat," 11 Jul 1968, File #140082, CNA.

98. Naval Ordnance Systems Command, "Technical Development Plan 17–6DX: Close-In Weapon System," 1 Aug 1969, 4.1, File #171079, CNA.

99. H. W. Freeman, "Relationship of Target Vulnerability to Guided Missile Warheads," *Naval Ordnance Bulletin*, Dec 1970, 40–41.

100. Commander Cruiser-Destroyer Flotilla Seven, 3 Oct 1965, "Exercise HOT STOVE Final Report," 1–6; Commander Cruiser-Destroyer Flotilla Eleven to Commander First Fleet, 22 Oct 1965, "Exercise RAG WEED Final Report," 2–3; and Commander Cruiser-Destroyer Flotilla Eleven to Commander First Fleet, 7 Jan 1966, "Exercise RANGE BUSH Final Report," 4–4, both in Cruiser-Destroyer Flotilla Eleven File.

101. Commander Cruiser-Destroyer Flotilla Three to Commander First Fleet, 1 Dec 1966, "Report of Exercise Eager Angler," 14, 17.

102. Commander Cruiser-Destroyer Flotilla Eleven, "Final Report: Anti-Shipping Cruise Missile Project, June–August 1967," I–1 to I–4, Cruiser-Destroyer Flotilla Eleven File

103. Commander Cruiser-Destroyer Flotilla Eight to Commander Second Fleet, 27 Dec 1968, "Report of Multi-Ship RIMEX," 1–2.

104. Rowden interview, 14 Dec 1987; Friedman, *Naval Radar*, 167; and William G. Bath, "Terrier/Tartar: Integration and Automation of Navy Shipboard Surveillance Sensors," *Johns Hopkins APL Technical Digest* 2 (Oct–Dec 1981): 263.

105. Zumwalt interview, 20 Apr 1988; Gerald E. Miller interview, 1 Jun 1988; Moore and Compton-Hall, *Submarine Warfare*, 73; Breemer, *Soviet Submarines*, 113; and Fred L. Lewis, remarks at the Surface Navy Convention, Arlington, VA, 22 Apr 1988.

106. Adelaide M. Madsen, "Three-T Effectiveness," *Naval Ordnance Bulletin*, Sep 1966, 24–25; Commander Cruiser-Destroyer Flotilla Eleven to Commander First Fleet, 22 Oct 1965, "Exercise RAG WEED Final Report," 2–3; Commander Cruiser-Destroyer Flotilla Eleven to

Commander Cruiser-Destroyer Force, Pacific Fleet, 30 Apr 1968, "Cruise Report," II–21; and Commander Cruiser-Destroyer Flotilla Three to Commander First Fleet, 1 Dec 1966, "Report of Exercise Eager Angler," 24; Emch, "Air Defense for the Fleet," 51; Goss, "Talos in Retrospect," 116; Keirsey, "Airbreathing Propulsion for...the Surface Fleet," 60; "Talos Propulsion Performance," *Naval Ordnance Bulletin*, Dec 1970, 27; and Dobbins and Luke, "From Kamikaze to Aegis," 234.

107. Doyle interview, 28 Mar 1988.

108. Albert H. Dell, OEG, "The Soviet Naval Threat to the U.S. CVA Task Force," 21 Sep 1972, 31–32, File #72–1386, CNA; Adelaide M. Madsen, "Three-T Effectiveness," *Naval Ordnance Bulletin*, Sep 1966, 24–25; "Talos Propulsion Performance," *Naval Ordnance Bulletin*, Dec 1970, 27; and Oliver, "Terrier/Tartar," 258.

109. R. J. Tamulevicz, "Standard Missile: A Brief History," *Naval Ordnance Bulletin*, Jun 1969, 33–35; G. G. Beall, "Standard Missile," *Naval Ordnance Bulletin*, Jun 1973, 29; Emch, "Air Defense for the Fleet," 47; Jordan, USS *California*," 85; and Oliver and Sweet, "Standard Missile," 284–85.

110. "Point Defense Surface Missile System," *Naval Ordnance Bulletin*, Jun 1969, 37, 39; Ardyce Rogers, "Improved Point Defense Surface Missile System (IPDSMS)," *Naval Ordnance Bulletin*, Jun 1973, 23; Emch, "Air Defense for the Fleet," 48; and Woods interview, 19 Apr 1988.

111. *SECNAV Annual Report*, FY 1970, 53; "Point Defense Surface Missile System," *Naval Ordnance Bulletin*, Jun 1969, 37, 39; Author's observations on USS *Stump* (DD 978), Jan 1988; and Polmar, "Shooting at the Arrow," 175–76.

112. Commander Cruiser-Destroyer Flotilla Three to Commander First Fleet, 1 Dec 1966, "Report of Exercise Eager Angler," 2; Commander Cruiser-Destroyer Flotilla Six (CTU 28.3.2) to Commander Second Fleet, 5 Jan 1967, "Report of LANTFLEX-66 AFWR RIMEX," 1, 14, Cruiser-Destroyer Flotilla Six File, Post 1 Jan 1946 Report Files; Commander Cruiser-Destroyer Flotilla Eight to Commander Second Fleet, 28 Apr 1969, "Report of WHITE Task Group GUNEX (Z–9–AA (MOD)) and Small Scale AAWEX," 1, 2, 5–1; Commander Cruiser-Destroyer Flotilla Eight to Commander Second Fleet, Apr 1969, "White Task Groups Operations (TG 27.2) from 9 March through 4 April 1969," II–1 & II–2, both in Cruiser-Destroyer Flotilla Eight File; Rowden interview, 14 Dec 1987; Woods interview, 19 Apr 1988; Doyle interview, 28 Mar 1988; Naval Education and Training Command, *The Weapons Officer*, 194; and CNA memo, "A Sample Model of the Effectiveness of Gun Fire Against Cruise Missiles," 27 Mar 1970, File #(SEG) 50–70, Type 43, CNA.

113. "Assessment of Latest *Jane's Fighting Ships* Report in Regard to U.S. and Soviet Naval Forces," 1–2; and O'Neil, "Gun Systems? For Air Defense?," 49–50.

114. Weschler interview, 24 Mar 1988; Naval Ordnance Systems Command (ORD-08), "Proposed Technical Approach for the Close-In Gun Weapon System," 5 Mar 1969, 1.2, 1.4, File #145416, CNA; and Naval Ordnance Systems Command, "Technical Development Plan 17–6DX: Close-In Weapon System," 1 Aug 1969, 4.5, File #171079, CNA.

115. Naval Ordnance Systems Command (ORD-08), "Proposed Technical Approach for the Close-In Gun Weapon System," 5 Mar 1969, 1.2, 1.4; Weschler interview, 24 Mar 1988; Frank H. Price, Jr. to author, c. Jul 1988; and Friedman, *US Naval Weapons*, 162.

116. Jordan, *Soviet Warships*, 39; Bath, "Terrier/Tartar: Navy Shipboard Surveillance Sensors," 263; O'Neil, "Gun Systems? For Air Defense?," 47; Commander Cruiser-Destroyer Flotilla Eleven to Commander Cruiser-Destroyer Force, Pacific Fleet, 30 Apr 1968, "Cruise Report," VII–1 to VII–2; and Christian J. Eliot, "Ship-to-Ship Missiles," *Proceedings* 98 (Nov 1972): 109. According to James Reckner, 29 Oct 1991, one anti-IR missile device tested in the 1968 period was a tumbling shell called "Great Balls of Fire."

117. Walters interview, 17 Dec 1987; and Turner interview, 4 May 1988.

118. Emerson interview, 26 Apr 1988.

119. Friedman, *U.S. Cruisers*, 364; and James Reckner to author, 29 Oct 1991.

120. Commander Cruiser-Destroyer Flotilla Three to Commander First Fleet, 1 Dec 1966, "Report of Exercise Eager Angler," 1; Commander Cruiser-Destroyer Flotilla Seven, 3 Oct 1965, "Exercise HOT STOVE Final Report," 1–11; Commander Cruiser-Destroyer Flotilla Eleven to Commander First Fleet, 7 Jan 1966, "Exercise RANGE BUSH Final Report," 4–8; and Bath, "Terrier/Tartar: Navy Shipboard Surveillance Sensors," 261, 262.

121. Commander Cruiser-Destroyer Flotilla Six (CTU 28.3.2) to Commander Second Fleet, 5 Jan 1967, "Report of LANTFLEX-66 AFWR RIMEX," 15; "USS *Albany* Recommissioned," 63–64; and Allison, "U.S. Navy Research and Development since World War II," 324–25.

122. Robert C. Peniston to author, 25 Jun 1992.

123. W. M. Montgomery to author, 28 Sep 1992.

124. Friedman, *Naval Radar*, 166; Emch, "Air Defense for the Fleet," 50; and Emch and Kirkland, "Search Radar Automation," 90.

125. "Advanced Multi-Function Array Radar," *Naval Ordnance Bulletin*, Jun 1970, 3, 35; Oliver and Sweet, "Standard Missile," 284–85; *SECNAV Annual Report*, FY 1970, 52; Doyle and Meyer, "Management and Support of Aegis...," 12; and "AEGIS Missile System," *Naval Ordnance Bulletin*, Jun 1970, 1.

126. Peniston to author, 25 Jun 1992; and Thomas R. Weschler, "DX/DXG Program," *Naval Engineers Journal* 79 (Dec 1967): 932.

127. Constantine Xefteris, interview with author, 22 Jan 1988.

128. Armed Services Subcommittee, *CVAN–70*, 161.

129. Bucknell, Comment on "Aftermath of the *Elath*," 88; and Walters interview, 17 Dec 1987.

130. Zumwalt, *On Watch*, 82; Kidd interview, 3 May 1988; Ryan Aeronautical Co., "Firebee Low Altitude Ship-to-Ship Homing Missile: FLASH," 15 Nov 1968, File #154724, CNA; and Friedman, *US Naval Weapons*, 230–31.

131. "Free World Frigate," 1971, 91, Loeser Papers, NWC.

132. Ibid.

133. O'Neil, "Gun Systems? For Air Defense?," 46; CNA to CNO, "Exocet," 21 Dec 1970, 3–4, File #01700329, CNA; Zumwalt interview, 20 Apr 1988; Woods interview, 19 Apr 1988; and Frank H. Price, Jr. to author, c. Jul 1988.

134. Bucknell, Comment on "Aftermath of the *Elath*," 87.

135. Henry C. Mustin interview, 2 May 1988.

136. Moorer interview, 26 May 1992; Friedman, US Naval Weapons, 211; Friedman's view is supported by others: Gralla interview, 22 Jun 1992; Casey Croy, "Harpoon Celebrates Its First 20 Years as MDMSC's Premier Missile," *Vision: McDonnell Douglas Missile Systems Company* 3 (24 Jun 1991): 1; and David A. Rosenberg and Harlan K. Ullman, "Project 'Sixty:' Landmark or Landmine—An Evaluation," Unpublished paper, c. 1982. 23.

137. Zumwalt interview, 20 Apr 1988.

138. Ibid.; Norman Friedman, "Elmo Russell Zumwalt, Jr.," in Love, *The Chiefs of Naval Operations*, 367; and Zumwalt, *On Watch*, 81. Supporting Zumwalt's version are a number of officers including J. F. Parker, Mark Woods, Claude Ekas, Jr., and Henry C. Mustin, Jr. Certain authorities have also singled out other key individuals in the drive to provide the surface navy with a cruise missile: Allan Slaff (Weschler interview, 24 Mar 1988); John E. Dacey

(Emerson interview, 26 Apr 1988); and Lloyd M. Mustin and Kleber Masterson (Isaac C. Kidd, Jr. interview, 3 May 1988).

139. Ekas oral history, 4; C. Ekas, Jr. to author, 30 Aug 1988; Hatch, Luber, and Walker, "Fifty Years of Strike Warfare Research at the Applied Physics Laboratory," 115; Croy, "Harpoon Celebrates Its First 20 Years ...," 1; and R. Meller, "The Harpoon Missile System," *International Defense Review* 8 (Feb 1975): 60.

140. Oliver, "Terrier/Tartar," 257; *DANFS* 8:320; Friedman, U.S. Cruisers, 380; *Cruiser-Destroyerman*, Jan 1970, 22; and Frederick H. Hartmann, *Naval Renaissance: The U.S. Navy in the 1980s* (Annapolis, 1990), 11.

141. *Conway's* 1:215; Foreman interview, 28 Aug 1992; Edward A. Christofferson, Jr. to author, 1 Jul 1992; William R. St. George to author, 6 Jul 1992; and *DANFS* 8:39.

142. Moorer interview, 26 May 1992; and McDonald, "Thomas Hinman Moorer," in Love, *The Chiefs of Naval Operations*, 359–60.

143. Polmar, *Ships and Aircraft of the U.S. Fleet*, 14th ed., 120–22; Jordan, "USS *California*," 84–87; and Charles J. Smith to author, 15 Aug 1992.

144. Jordan, "USS *California*," 83.

145. Zumwalt, *On Watch*, 81.

146. Ibid.; Oliver, "Terrier/Tartar," 259; Weschler interview, 24 Mar 1988; Doyle and Meyer, "Management and Support of Aegis ...," 5–6; and Polmar, *Ships and Aircraft of the U.S. Fleet*, 14th ed., 118.

147. Doyle and Meyer, "Management and Support of Aegis ...," 6–7.

148. F. Jonasz, "NAVORD Participation in the New Ship Procurement Process," *Naval Ordnance Bulletin*, Sep 1968, 5, 7.

149. Weschler interview, 24 Mar 1988.

150. Ibid.

151. Ibid.; Dean A. Rains and Ronald J. d'Arcy, "Considerations in the DD 963 Propulsion System Design," *Naval Engineers Journal* 84 (Aug 1972): 76; Peet oral history, 307–310; and Leopold, "Surface Warships for the Early Twenty-First Century," 284.

152. Jonasz, "NAVORD Participation in the New Ship Procurement Process," 5, 7; and Henry C. Mustin interview, 2 May 1988.

153. Weschler interview, 24 Mar 1988; William L. Duke, "DD 963 Class Combat System Installation and Testing," *Naval Engineers Journal*, 91 (Feb 1979): 34; Doyle and Meyer, "Management and Support of Aegis ...," 7–8; and Doyle interview, 10 Jun 1992.

154. Weschler interview, 24 Mar 1988.

155. Ibid.

156. Ibid.

157. Ibid.; Polmar, *Ships and Aircraft of the U.S. Fleet*, 14th ed., 432–40; *Cruiser-Destroyerman*, Jan–Feb 1972, n.p.; and H. E. Reichert (CO of *Sterett*) to COM7FLT, 2 May 1972, File #164972, CNA.

158. W. A. Brockett, et al., "U. S. Navy's Marine Gas Turbines," *Naval Engineers Journal*, 78 (Apr 1966): 217; Maido Saarlas, *Steam and Gas Turbines for Marine Propulsion*, 2d ed. (Annapolis, 1987), 223–24; W. M. N. Fowden, Jr., R. R. Peterson, and J. W. Sawyer, "The Gas Turbine as a Prime Mover on U.S. Naval Ships," *Naval Engineers Journal* 66 (Feb 1954): 109–110, 122–23; Leopold, "Surface Warships for the Early Twenty-First Century," 279; Rains and d'Arcy, "DD 963 Propulsion System Design," 66; James, "The Ships of '73," 100; George E. Ponton, "Fuel Oil System Design for the Gas Turbine Powered DD963 Class Destroyers,"

*Naval Engineers Journal* 86 (Feb 1974): 71, 76; and author's observations during FLTX–1–88 while on board *Stump* (DD 978), Jan 1988.

159. Christian K. Neilsen, Jr., "A Summary of Controllable Pitch Propeller Systems Employed by the U.S. Navy," *Naval Engineers Journal* 86 (Apr 1974): 82–83, 88–89.

160. Weschler interview, 24 Mar 1988; Metcalf interview, 1 Oct 1987; Kehoe and Brower, "Warship Design in the Future," 141–42; and Charles K. Duncan to author, 22 Aug 1992. When Rear Admiral Duncan was Assistant Chief of NAVPERS for Plans and Programs (1962–1964) he personally carried a proposal for slightly increased sea pay "all the way to the top [to] Mr. McNamara's office. He asked how much it would cost—one years—5 years—etc. When I told him, depending on the size of the Navy, he said— 'If you take that money and buy airplanes, you will have them ten years from now—with your plan you will have nothing to show for it ten years from now!' He even displayed resentment about the numbers of men it took to man a ship. It cost too much!"

161. H. H. Ries to author, 23 Jun 1992.

162. Polmar, *Ships and Aircraft of the U.S. Fleet*, 11th ed., 2; Doyle and Meyer, "Destroyers," 2–5; Kidd, "The Surface Fleet," 84; and Henry C. Mustin interview, 27 May 1992.

163. Henry C. Mustin interview, 2 May 1988.

164. Metcalf interview, 1 Oct 1987; Seltzer interview, 19 Jun 1991; and Duke, "DD 963 Class Combat System Installation and Testing," 33.

165. Weschler interview, 24 Mar 1988.

166. Friedman, *U.S. Destroyers*, 371; Hone, *Power and Change*, 79; Duke, "DD 963 Class Combat System Installation and Testing," 33; *Cruiser-Destroyerman*, Jan 1974, 7–8; and Doyle and Meyer, "Management and Support of Aegis," 10.

167. Peet oral history, 300, 303–4; Hubbard, "The Design of Naval Weapons," 42; and Doyle and Meyer, "Management and Support of Aegis," 9–10.

168. Weschler interview, 24 Mar 1988; Duke, "DD 963 Class Combat System Installation and Testing," 35–41; and "DXGN—A New Class Frigate," *Naval Ordnance Bulletin*, Sep 1968, 11.

169. Doyle and Meyer, "Management and Support of Aegis," 11–12.

170. Ibid., 5–6; and Duke, "DD 963 Class Combat System Installation and Testing," 40.

## 6. The Zumwalt Years and Their Immediate Aftermath

1. Zumwalt, *On Watch*, 46; and Friedman, "Elmo Russell Zumwalt, Jr.," in *Chiefs of Naval Operations*, ed. Love, 367.

2. Allard, "Elmo Russell Zumwalt, Jr.," 1227–29.

3. Zumwalt, *On Watch*, 66.

4. Rosenberg and Ullman, "Project 'Sixty,'" 6–8. Turner had been selected for rear admiral at this point.

5. Stansfield Turner, "Missions of the U.S. Navy," *Naval War College Review* 26, no. 5 (Mar–Apr 1974): 2; Rosenberg and Ullman, "Project 'Sixty,'" 17; Zumwalt, "Remarks at the Annual Banquet of the SNAME," 45; and Shepherd, "The Black Shoe," 40. Many officers hated the personnel changes wrought by the "Z-grams." See Peet oral history, 362–63. Also Allan Slaff to author, 25 Jun 1992.

6. Zumwalt, *On Watch*, 63; Tyler, *Running Critical*, 69, 102; David F. Emerson to author, 20 Aug 1992; and Henry C. Mustin interview, 27 May 1992.

7. Gerald E. Miller interview, 1 Jun 1988; and Hone, *Power and Change*, 99.

8. Gerald E. Miller interview, 1 Jun 1988; and Henry C. Mustin interview, 27 May 1992.

9. Rosenberg and Ullman, "Project 'Sixty,'" 9; Henry C. Mustin interview, 27 May 1992; Zumwalt interview, 20 Apr 1988; and Zumwalt, *On Watch*, 84.

10. J. William Middendorf, remarks, Science and the Future Navy Symposium, National Academy of Sciences, Washington, 1977; and Ruhe, "Cruise Missile," 46–49.

11. *Cruiser-Destroyerman*, Sep 1972, 12, NDL; Jordan, *Soviet Warships*, 32; and McGruther, *Evolving Soviet Navy*, 57.

12. James Reckner to author, 29 Oct 1991.

13. Huisken, *Strategic Cruise Missile*, 129; Zumwalt, "Remarks at the Annual Banquet of the SNAME," 47; Polmar, *Guide to the Soviet Navy*, 4th ed., 430; and Commander Attack Carrier Air Wing Three, "ASW Protection of the Carrier Task Force," 9 Jul 1974, File #182435, CNA.

14. Weschler interview, 24 Mar 1988.

15. Ibid.; Ruhe, "Cruise Missile," 49; and Friedman, "Elmo Russell Zumwalt, Jr.," 368.

16. *Brassey's Defence Yearbook, 1975/76*, 346; Ruhe, "Cruise Missile," 46; Mark Hewish, "Weapon Systems: Gabriel," *Proceedings* 102 (Jul 1976): 101; Gunther Rothenberg, *The Anatomy of the Israeli Army* (New York, 1979), 199–200; and Friedman, *World Naval Weapons Systems*, 89–90.

17. Zumwalt, *On Watch*, 361, 368; and Ryan, *First Line of Defense*, 81.

18. Norman Friedman, *U.S. Small Combatants: Including PT-Boats, Subchasers, and the Brown-Water Navy* (Annapolis, 1987), 271.

19. Zumwalt, *On Watch*, 301.

20. Walters interview, 17 Dec 1987.

21. Albert H. Dell, OEG, "The Soviet Naval Threat to the U.S. CVA Task Force," 21 Sep 1972, 31–32, File #72–1386, CNA; Desmond Wilson and Nicholas Brown, "Warfare at Sea: Threat of the Seventies," CNA Professional Paper No. 79, 4 Nov 1971, 10; and Gerald E. Miller interview, 1 Jun 1988.

22. Walters interview, 17 Dec 1987.

23. Zumwalt, *On Watch*, 446.

24. Lawrence J. Korb, "The Erosion of American Naval Preeminence, 1962–1978," in *Peace and War: Interpretations of American Naval History, 1775–1984*, 2d ed., ed. Kenneth J. Hagan (Westport, CT, 1984), 328; Polmar, *Guide to the Soviet Navy*, 4th ed., 45; Reckner to author, 29 Oct 1991; Walters interview, 17 Dec 1987; and Seltzer interview, 19 Jun 1991.

25. Zumwalt's 1974 Senate testimony quoted in Sokolsky, "Seapower in the Nuclear Age," 335.

26. Henry C. Mustin interview, 27 May 1992; and Zumwalt, *On Watch*, 338, 386–87. Zumwalt later maintained that the United States would have lost such a war through 1982 at least. See Hartmann, *Naval Renaissance*, 14. But other analysts, such as James Reckner, disagreed. Reckner spent "all day of every day concentrating on the Soviet Navy during the period 1972 to 1978." Reckner to author, 29 Oct 1991.

27. Turner interview, 4 May 1988.

28. Gerald E. Miller interview, 1 Jun 1988.

29. Turner interview, 4 May 1988.

30. Ibid.

31. Robert S. Salzer, "The Surface Forces," *Proceedings* 102 (Nov 1976): 33.

32. Ibid.; Gary L. Pickens, "5-Inch, 54 Gun Reliability Improvement Program," *Naval Ordnance Bulletin*, Jun 1973, 45–46, OA; and Zumwalt, *On Watch*, 381.

33. Commander Cruiser Destroyer Group 12, "Final Report of LANTREADEX 3–73, 7 May–7 June 1973," I–3, Cruiser Destroyer Group 12 File, Post 1 Jan 1946 Report Files, OA; Commander Cruiser-Destroyer Group Eight to Commander Sixth Fleet, 5 Mar 1974, "End of Deployment Report," 1–2, 6, 9, Cruiser-Destroyer Group Eight File, Post 1 Jan 1946 Report Files; CINCPAC, "Command History, 1 October 1973–31 December 1974," IV–29, OA; and Duncan, *Rickover and the Nuclear Navy*, 166.

34. U.S. Seventh Fleet, "Monthly Historical Summary," Aug 1970, 23, OA; and CINCPAC, "Command History, 1 October 1973–31 December 1974," IV–30.

35. *DANFS* 7:251; 8:19; and Ronald T. Kelly to author, 16 Feb 1993.

36. *DANFS* 8:472; *Cruiser-Destroyerman*, Apr 1973, 11; Metcalf interview, 1 October 1987; and Marolda, "By Sea, Air, and Land" (MS), 89, 93–95.

37. *DANFS* 7:251, 318; Blades, "USS *Galveston*," 233; and *Conway's*, 1:211, 215.

38. Naval Ships Systems Command, *Technical News*, Dec 1972, 40–41, OA; *DANFS* 6:622; and H. E. Reichert (CO of *Sterett*) to COM7FLT, 2 May 1972, File #164972, CNA.

39. Reichert to COM7FLT, 2 May 1972; Walters interview, 17 Dec 1987; Charles J. Smith interview, 10 Dec 1987; Henry C. Mustin interview, 2 May 1988; Emerson interview, 26 Apr 1988; and Christman, "Naval Ordnance Today and Tomorrow," *Naval Ordnance Bulletin*, Sep 1972, 17. When Stansfield Turner commanded a frigate on PIRAZ patrol, he kept armed missiles on the rails around the clock. Turner interview, 4 May 1988.

40. Rosenberg and Ullman, "Project 'Sixty,'" 9; *Conway's* 1:223; and Polmar, ed., *Ships and Aircraft of the U.S. Fleet*, 11th ed., 2. The *Gearing*-class destroyer *Southerland* (DD 743) earned one battle star in WWII, eight in Korea, and ten in Vietnam. See *DANFS* 6:568.

41. Zumwalt, "Remarks at the Annual Banquet of the SNAME," 48; Terzibaschitsch, "Mothball Fleet," 99; and Frederick H. Schneider, Jr. to author, 17 Feb 1993; and "USS *Saint Paul* (CA–73)", 159.

42. Zumwalt interview, 20 Apr 1988.

43. Ibid., 18–19.; U.S. Congress, Congressional Budget Office, *Naval Surface Combatants in the 1990s: Prospects and Possibilities* (Washington, 1981), 3; and *Surface Warfare*, Sep 1975, 14, NDL.

44. Doyle and Meyer, "Management and Support of Aegis," 8–9; Jordan, "USS *California*," 84–85; Polmar, *Ships and Aircraft of the U.S. Fleet*, 14th ed., 118; and Weschler interview, 24 Mar 1988.

45. Doyle and Meyer, "Cruisers," 8–9; Doyle and Meyer, "Management and Support of Aegis," 13; Michaelis, Remarks at the 83d Annual Banquet of The Society of Naval Architects and Marine Engineers, 14 Nov 1975; Friedman, *U.S. Destroyers*, 343–46; Friedman, *U.S. Cruisers*, 419–20; CNO Executive Board Memo, "CEB [CNO Executive Board] Prebriefing Material on Strike Cruiser," 13 Nov 1974, 6, File #180163, CNA; and Donko, "The USS *Long Beach* after Her 'Mid Life' Conversion," 25, 31–32.

46. Friedman, *U.S. Destroyers*, 321–22, 343; and Friedman, "Elmo Russell Zumwalt, Jr.," 373.

47. Zumwalt, *On Watch*, 74–75.

48. Doyle and Meyer, "Management and Support of Aegis," 6–7; and Leopold, "Surface Warships for the Early Twenty-First Century," 284.

49. Robert J. Shade, "Marriage of Necessity," *Proceedings* 116 (Aug 1990): 31; Weschler interview, 24 Mar 1988; Polmar, *Ships and Aircraft of the U.S. Fleet*, 14th ed., 162–64; Kidd, "The Surface Fleet," 87; Henry C. Mustin interview, 27 May 1992; and *Conway's* 1:228.

50. Zumwalt interview, 20 Apr 1988.

51. Polmar, *Ships and Aircraft of the U.S. Fleet*, 14th ed., 224; "Harpoon Missile Test Vehicles Fired From *High Point* (PCH–1)," *Naval Ordnance Bulletin*, Mar 1974, 32.

52. Rodney Carlisle, *Where the Fleet Begins: A History of the David Taylor Research Center, 1899–1987* (Rockville, MD, 1987), 482.

53. Ibid., 481–85.

54. Polmar, *Ships and Aircraft of the U.S. Fleet*, 11th ed., 300.

55. McCollum, *Dahlgren*, 147–48; R. O. Schlegelmilch, "A Systems Approach to Gun Weapon Systems: The Gunnery Improvement Program," *NAVSEA Journal*, Oct 1975, 44–45, 53, OA.

56. Christman, "Naval Ordnance Today and Tomorrow," 18; F. Garza, Jr., "Mk 45 Mod 0 5-inch 54 Lightweight Gun Mount," *Naval Ordnance Bulletin*, Jun 1973, 47–49; and F. D. Vogel, "Gun Fire Control System Mark 86," *Naval Ordnance Bulletin*, Jun 1973, 39–40.

57. J. T. Cianfrani and Ned Donaldson, "Major Caliber Lightweight Gun Mk 71 Mod 0 8-Inch 55 Caliber," *Naval Ordnance Bulletin*, Jun 1974, 27–29; Herbert M. Effron, "8"/55 Major Caliber Lightweight Gun: Big Punch for Small Ships," *Proceedings* 101 (Dec 1975): 91–93; J. T. Cianfrani and H. M. Effron, "Navy Tests Biggest Gun in the West," *NAVSEA Journal*, Jul 1975, 20–23; Friedman, *US Naval Weapons*, 24; and Navy Department, Office of Information, *Weapon Systems of the United States Navy 1977*, 39.

58. Weschler interview, 24 Mar 1988.

59. F. N. Ryan, "A New Weapons System for the Fleet," *NAVSEA Journal*, Sep 1975, 26–27; Navy Department, Office of Information, *Weapon Systems of the United States Navy 1977*, 43; and Jon Sweigart, "Mk 75 76–mm OTO-Melara Gun Mount," *Naval Ordnance Bulletin*, Jun 1973, 50–51.

60. NWL, Dahlgren, "Considerations on the Design of a 5-Inch Guided Projectile for Air and Shipping Targets," Oct 1971, 1, File #163346, CNA.

61. Zumwalt interview, 20 Apr 1988.

62. Rosenberg and Ullman, "Project 'Sixty,'" 10; Emerson interview, 26 Apr 1988; CNA, Information Processing Section, "Anti-Ship Missile Defense—A Bibliography," 22 Sep 1975, File #751378, CNA; and CNA Memo, R. R. Liguori to Phil DePoy, "Summary of New Directions in ASMD," 30 Jun 1971, File #43 710119, CNA.

63. Godfrey Geller, "The Aegis Weapon System," *Naval Ordnance Bulletin*, Jun 1973, 3; R. J. Zabriski, "Aegis Weapon Direction System Mk 12," *Naval Ordnance Bulletin*, Mar 1974, 35–37; and Hartmann, *Naval Renaissance*, 140.

64. Gralla interview, 22 Jun 1992.

65. Stansfield Turner to author, 23 Jul 1992.

66. Henry C. Mustin interview, 27 May 1992.

67. Stephen Skelley to author, 7 Sep 1992; and Emerson to author, 20 Aug 1992.

68. Flanagan and Luke, "Aegis: Newest Line of Navy Defense," 239; Doyle and Meyer, "Management and Support of Aegis," 12–13; Emch, "Air Defense for the Fleet," 49; and *Surface Warfare*, Sep 1975, 19.

69. Henry C. Mustin interview, 27 May 1992.

70. Geller, "The Aegis Weapon System," 5, 9.

71. Henry C. Mustin interview, 27 May 1992; Holloway interview, 28 Sep 1992; and Hone, *Power and Change*, 101–2. The radar was the fixed array SPS–32/33; *Long Beach* was the only other ship equipped with it.

72. W. E. Meyer, comment on "Cruise Missile: The Ship Killer," *Proceedings* 102 (Oct 1976): 94.

73. Doyle interview, 28 Mar 1988.

74. Flanagan and Luke, "Aegis: Newest Line of Navy Defense," 240–41; and Doyle and Meyer, "Cruisers," 9.

75. Kidd, "The Surface Fleet," 95.

76. Chester C. Phillips, "Battle Group Operations: War at Sea," *Johns Hopkins University APL Technical Digest* 2 (Oct–Dec 1981): 300–301; Rowden interview, 14 Dec 1987; Gerald E. Miller interview, 1 Jun 1988; and Weschler interview, 24 Mar 1988.

77. *Cruiser-Destroyerman*, Jan–Feb 1972, n.p.; and Zumwalt, *On Watch*, 80.

78. Seltzer interview, 12 Jun 1991.

79. Flanagan and Sweet, "Aegis: Advanced Surface Missile System," 245; "The 3 'T' Escorts of the Surface Fleet," *Naval Ordnance Bulletin*, Jun 1973, 13–14; Walters interview, 17 Dec 1987; Terzibaschitsch, *Cruisers of the US Navy*, 262; Garten and Dean, "Evolution of the Talos Missile," 122; Dean, "The Unified Talos," 125; D. E. Madsen, "Talos: Low Altitude Supersonic Target (LAST) Missile: New Target from an Old Missile," *Naval Ordnance Bulletin*, Jun 1973, 41, 43; and Keirsey, "Airbreathing Propulsion for the Surface Fleet," 57.

80. Oliver, "Terrier/Tartar," 259–60; Betzer, "Terrier/Tartar: New Threat Upgrade Program," 276–77; and Dobbins and Luke, "From Kamikaze to Aegis," 235.

81. "The 3 'T' Escorts of the Surface Fleet," 15–16; G. G. Beall, "Standard Missile," *Naval Ordnance Bulletin*, Jun 1973, 29, 31; Eaton, "Bumblebee Missile Aerodynamic Design," 80; and Oliver, "Terrier/Tartar," 259. The nuclear version of the Terrier remained in the fleet's magazines simply because there was no corresponding Standard.

82. R. Galpeer, "AAW/ASW Guided Missile Launching System Mark 26," *Naval Ordnance Bulletin*, Jun 1973, 33–35.

83. Ibid.

84. Doyle interview, 28 Mar 1988.

85. Frieden, *Principles of Naval Weapons Systems*, 511–15; and Henry C. Mustin interview, 2 May 1988.

86. Friedman, "Elmo Russell Zumwalt, Jr.," 371; Ardyce Rogers, "Improved Point Defense Surface Missile System (IPDSMS)," *Naval Ordnance Bulletin*, Jun 1973, 23; "Experimental Missile Launcher/Canister Successfully Completes Tests," *Naval Ordnance Bulletin*, Jun 1973, 52, 55; and Seltzer interview, 12 Jun 1991.

87. J. E. Paulk, "CIWS: Close In Weapon System," *Naval Ordnance Bulletin*, Dec 1972, 27–29; Walters interview, 17 Dec 1987; Rowden interview, 14 Dec 1987; Emerson interview, 26 Apr 1988; and Woods interview, 19 Apr 1988.

88. Zumwalt, *On Watch*, 81.

89. Metcalf interview, 1 October 1987; Rosenberg and Ullman, "Project 'Sixty,'" 9; Melissa J. Allen, "Naval Ordnance Systems Command Headquarters Reorganization," *Naval Ordnance Bulletin*, Mar 1971, 63.

90. James R. Whalen, "Standard Active Missile: A New Dimension in Anti-Ship Weapon Systems," *Naval Ordnance Bulletin*, Jun 1974, 19–21; "Standard Missile Anti-Ship Capability," *Naval Ordnance Bulletin*, Jun 1974, 23–24; Claude Ekas, Jr. to author, 30 Aug 1988; and CNA to CNO, "Exocet," 21 Dec 1970, 3–4, File #01700329, CNA.

91. Beall, "Standard Missile," 30; *Cruiser-Destroyerman*, Aug 1972, 16–17; and Friedman, *U.S. Small Combatants, 271–72*.

92. Christman, "Naval Ordnance Today and Tomorrow," 17; Steven J. Bannat, Comment on "Ship-to-Ship Missiles," *Proceedings* 99 (Nov 1973): 88; and "Standard Missile Anti-Ship Capability," 23–24.

93. Friedman, *World Naval Weapons Systems*, 241; Werrell, *Evolution of the Cruise Missile*, 150; Hatch, Luber, and Walker, "Fifty Years of Strike Warfare Research at the Applied Physics Laboratory," 116; Huisken, *Strategic Cruise Missile*, 29; Croy, "Harpoon Celebrates Its First 20 Years," 2; and Ekas oral history, 4–6, 20–22, 24.

94. Walker, "Air-to-Surface Weapons," 38; General Dynamics, *The World's Missile Systems*, 7th ed. (Pomona, CA, 1982), n.p; *Brassey's Defence Yearbook, 1975/76*, 345; and Mark Hewish, "Weapon Systems: Harpoon," *Proceedings* 103 (Feb 1977): 104.

95. Claude Ekas to author, 30 Aug 1988.

96. Rowden interview, 14 Dec 1987; and General Dynamics, *The World's Missile Systems*, 7th ed., n.p.

97. Emerson interview, 26 Apr 1988.

98. Thomas S. Amlie, 24 Aug 1976, 8, USNI Oral History; and GAO Staff Study, "Harpoon Weapon System," Feb 1973, 2, File #170490, CNA.

99. Ekas oral history, 19, 22–23; Werrell, *Evolution of the Cruise Missile*, 150; GAO Staff Study, "Harpoon Weapon System," Feb 1973, 1, 5; Croy, "Harpoon Celebrates Its First 20 Years," 3; Naval Air Systems Command, "Harpoon Weapon System: NTE Test Plan," Aug 1974, File #180218, CNA; "Harpoon Missile Test Vehicles Fired From *High Point* (PCH–1)," 32; Meller, "The Harpoon Missile System," 60, 66; Emerson interview, 26 Apr 1988; Claude Ekas to author, 30 Aug 1988; Stewart interview, 28 Oct 1987; Woods interview, 19 Apr 1988; and Commander Naval Surface Force, Pacific Fleet to Director of Naval History, 18 Jun 1975, "Commander Cruiser-Destroyer Force, U.S. Pacific Fleet Command History 1974 and to 'Secure the Watch,' March 31, 1975," 1, Naval Surface Force, Pacific Fleet File, Post 1 Jan 1946 Report Files.

100. Claude Ekas to author, 30 Aug 1988; Metcalf interview, 1 Oct 1987; Werrell, *Evolution of the Cruise Missile*, 150; and Naval Air Systems Command, "Harpoon Weapon System Validation Phase Report," v. 7 "Ship Interface," 31 Jul 70, 3–5, File #156793, CNA.

101. Naval Air Systems Command, "Harpoon Weapon System: NTE Test Plan," Aug 1974, 3–4, File #180218, CNA; Friedman, *U.S. Small Combatants*, 386; Walters interview, 17 Dec 1987; and Croy, "Harpoon Celebrates Its First 20 Years," 2.

102. Polmar, *Ships and Aircraft of the U.S. Fleet*, 14th ed., 405–9; Beshany oral history, 2: 852; and Zumwalt, *On Watch*, 70.

103. Polmar, *Ships and Aircraft of the U.S. Fleet*, 11th ed., 1; General Dynamics, *The World's Missile Systems*, 7th ed., n.p; Claude Ekas to author, 30 Aug 1988; and Doyle interview, 28 Mar 1988.

104. James Stevens, interview with author, 27 January 1988; Zumwalt interview, 20 Apr 1988; Walters interview, 17 Dec 1987; Emerson interview, 26 Apr 1988; Parker interview, 10 Jun 1988; and Kidd, "The Surface Fleet," 88.

105. Friedman, "Elmo Russell Zumwalt, Jr.," 375.

106. Huisken, *Strategic Cruise Missile*, 30; Hatch, Luber, and Walker, "Fifty Years of Strike Warfare Research at the Applied Physics Laboratory," 117; Friedman, *World Naval Weapons Systems*, 43; and Werrell, *Evolution of the Cruise Missile*, 144.

107. General Dynamics, *The World's Missile Systems*, 7th ed., n.p.; Walker, "Air-to-Surface Weapons," 39–40; JHU/APL, "Anti–Ship Missile Targeting with Surveillance Satellite Data," 22 Aug 1973, 1–3, File #182256, CNA; Hatch, Luber, and Walker, "Fifty Years of Strike War-

fare Research at the Applied Physics Laboratory," 119; Fred G. Berghoefer, "Over-the-Horizon Targeting Alternatives," CNA paper prepared for the Office of Naval Research, Center for Naval Analyses, Sep 1977, 13–16; Walters interview, 17 Dec 1987; Rowden interview, 14 Dec 1987; Woods interview, 19 Apr 1988; Emerson interview, 26 Apr 1988; Ekas to author, 30 Aug 1988; and Zumwalt interview, 20 Apr 1988.

108. Henry C. Mustin interview, 2 May 1988; and Gerald E. Miller interview, 1 Jun 1988.

109. Gerald E. Miller interview, 1 Jun 1988; and CNO Executive Board Memo, "CEB Prebriefing Material on Air-to-Ground Weapons Review," 29 Sep 1972, 7, File #169036, CNA.

110. Rosenberg and Ullman, "Project 'Sixty,'" alternate draft, 7.

111. CNO Executive Board Memo, "CEB Prebriefing Material on Air-to-Ground Weapons Review," 29 Sep 1972, 1.

112. Adamson interview, 10 Mar 1988.

113. Hart, "Surface Warfare Officers," 38; and Hone, *Power and Change*, 74–75.

114. Adamson interview, 10 Mar 1988; and Hone, *Power and Change*, 91.

115. Turner interview, 4 May 1988.

116. Frederick H. Schneider interview with author, 23 Jun 1992.

117. Salzer, "The Surface Forces," 34; and Larson, "The Surface Line Officer," 44.

118. *Cruiser-Destroyerman*, Jun 1972, 20–22; and Shepherd, "The Black Shoe," 40.

119. *Cruiser-Destroyerman*, Jun 1972, 20–22.

120. Hart, "Surface Warfare Officers," 40–41.

121. Shepherd, "The Black Shoe," 41.

122. *Surface*, Feb 1975, 29, NDL; Salzer, "The Surface Forces," 31; Frederick K. Smallwood, Comment on "The Surface Line Officer," *Proceedings* 98 (Jan 1973): 89; and Larson, "The Surface Line Officer," 44.

123. Yates, "Tactics Revival," 11–13; and Hone, *Power and Change*, 90.

124. *Surface Warfare*, Jan 1976, 3; and Peet oral history, 362–63.

125. Weschler interview, 24 Mar 1988; and Salzer, "The Surface Forces," 27–30. Salzer recalls being advised in 1966 by a chief to "go into minesweepers because they never do anything." The Mine Force was unusual in accepting amalgamation without much argument, "on the pragmatic basis that they had nothing more to lose," Salzer believed.

126. CINCPAC, "Command History, 1 October 1973–31 December 1974," IV–50; Salzer, "The Surface Forces," 27–29; and Emerson interview, 26 Apr 1988.

127. Commander Naval Surface Force, Pacific Fleet to Director of Naval History, 18 Jun 1975, "Commander Cruiser-Destroyer Force, U.S. Pacific Fleet Command History 1974 and to 'Secure the Watch', March 31, 1975," 5–6; *Surface*, Feb 1975, 4–8; and *Surface Warfare*, Sep 1975, 14.

128. Humphrey, *Meeting the Challenge*, 3, 5.

129. Hart, "Surface Warfare Officers," 38; *Surface*, Feb 1975, 1; and Shepherd, "The Black Shoe," 41.

130. *Surface Warfare*, Sep 1975, 16.

131. Charles J. Smith interview, 10 Dec 1987; Salzer, "The Surface Forces," 32; and author's observations during RIMPAC–88 while on board *Cleveland* (LPD 7), temporary flagship of Third Fleet, July 1988.

132. Larson, "The Surface Line Officer," 47.

133. Charles J. Smith interview, 10 Dec 1987; Grzymala, Comment on "The Surface Line Officer," 89; Gerald E. Miller interview, 1 Jun 1988; Henry C. Mustin interview, 2 May 1988; and Frank H. Price, Jr. to author, Jul 1988.

134. Hart, "Surface Warfare Officers," 44; and Charles J. Smith interview, 10 Dec 1987.

135. *Cruiser-Destroyerman*, Dec 1974, 1, 32; and *Surface Warfare*, Sep 1975, n.p.

136. Naval Education and Training Program Development Center, *Surface Ship Operations*.

137. John C. Reilly to author, 29 Oct 1991.

138. *Surface*, Feb 1975, 29; Polmar, *Ships and Aircraft of the U.S. Fleet*, 14th ed., 145; and Congressional Budget Office, *Naval Surface Combatants*, 4.

139. Zumwalt, *On Watch*, 462–66.

140. Shepherd, "The Black Shoe," 41.

141. Rosenberg and Ullman, "Project 'Sixty,'" 14–15; and Salzer, "The Surface Forces," 30.

## Postscript

1. Congressional Budget Office, *Naval Surface Combatants*, 15.

2. Salzer, "The Surface Forces," 33.

3. Polmar, *Ships and Aircraft of the U.S. Fleet*, 11th ed., 1.

4. Weschler interview, 24 Mar 1988.

5. Hurlbut Interview, 28 Oct 1987; Ray W. Walsh, remarks at the Surface Navy Convention, Arlington, VA, 22 Apr 1988; and author's observations during RIMPAC–88 while in *Antietam* (CG 54), 11 Jul 1988.

6. Norman Friedman, *The US Maritime Strategy* (Annapolis, 1988), 105; and Gallotta, "Navy EW and C3CM," 215.

7. Hurlbut interview, 28 Oct 1987; Henry C. Mustin, remarks at the Surface Navy Convention, Arlington, VA, 22 Apr 1988; Stewart Interview, 28 Oct 1987; CNO Memo, "CNO Lessons Learned," 13 Feb 1975, 2, WARG 1–74, File #181773, CNA; Walters interview, 17 Dec 1987; and George Galdorisi, "Déjà Vu All Over Again," *Proceedings* 114 (Jan 1988): 107.

8. Richard F. Pittenger, remarks at the Surface Navy Convention, Arlington, VA, 22 Apr 1988.

9. Hurlbut interview, 28 Oct 1987; and Weschler interview, 24 Mar 1988.

10. Parker interview, 9 Jun 1988.

11. Pat Shepherd, Comment on "The Surface Forces," *Proceedings* 103 (Mar 1977): 77.

12. Adamson interview, 10 Mar 1988.

13. Woods interview, 19 Apr 1988; Walters interview, 17 Dec 1987; and Frank H. Price, Jr. to author, Jul 1988.

14. Walters interview, 17 Dec 1987; Frank C. Seitz, Jr. and Theodore F. Davis, "From Cockpit to Bridge," *Proceedings* 114 (Jan 1988): 53; and Robert L. Walters, "Letter to Members," *Surface SITREP* 4 (Mar 1988): 1.

15. Author's observations during RIMPAC-88 while in *Cleveland* (LPD 7); Charles J. Smith interview, 10 Dec 1987; and Parker interview, 9 Jun 1988.

16. Leopold, "Surface Warships for the Early Twenty-First Century," 267; and Congressional Budget Office, *Naval Surface Combatants*, 19.

17. Doyle and Meyer, "Cruisers," 11; Doyle and Meyer, "Management and Support of Aegis . . . ," 16; and Price to author, Jul 1988.

18. Hans S. Pawlisch, "Operation Praying Mantis, The Revenge of the *Samuel B. Roberts* Incident," *Pull Together* 28, no. 1 (Spring/Summer 1989): 8; John W. Nyquist, remarks at the Surface Navy Association convention, Arlington, VA, 22 Apr 1988; and Henry C. Mustin, remarks at the Surface Navy Convention, Arlington, VA, 22 Apr 1988.

19. Doyle and Meyer, "Cruisers," 12.

20. Congressional Budget Office, *Naval Surface Combatants*, 17.

21. Kidd, "The Surface Fleet," 84; and Paul H. Nitze et al., *Securing the Seas: The Soviet Naval Challenge and Western Alliance Options* (Boulder, CO, 1979), 154.

22. Turner, "Missions of the U.S. Navy," 2.

23. For a recent doomsday pronouncement, see John Keegan, *The Price of Admiralty: The Evolution of Naval Warfare* (New York, 1989), 274–75.

# Bibliography

## Primary Sources

### *Archival Records*

Two of the three principal repositories for the records on which this work is based are located in the Washington, D.C. area: the Naval Historical Center and the Center for Naval Analyses. The Naval Historical Center in the Washington Navy Yard maintains many of the primary materials relevant to the U.S. Navy's past. Of special importance to this study of surface warfare are the holdings of the Operational Archives Branch, particularly the records in the following broad areas: Bureau Files, Command Files of the Chief of Naval Operations, Command Files of the Naval Sea Systems Command, and Post 1 January 1946 Report Files, which include exercise and action reports and the complete run of Commander in Chief, Pacific reviews and Seventh Fleet summaries relating to the Vietnam War. A number of accounts in the oral history collections of the Operational Archives are also valuable. The Naval Aviation History Branch holds significant missile files and the Ships Histories Branch maintains records pertinent to individual ships in the U.S. Navy.

The Center for Naval Analyses in Alexandria, Virginia, harbors a wealth of largely untapped material, mostly on the development and employment of ordnance and warships.

Another archive, too little investigated by historians, is the records collection of the Naval War College, Newport, Rhode Island. Among its materials that are especially useful are certain papers in the following files: RG 4 (Operations Problems), RG 8 (Intelligence and Technical Archives), RG 14 (Faculty and Staff Presentations), and RG 15 (Guest Lectures).

Other significant materials on missile development are held in the David Taylor Research Center, Carderock, Maryland. The President's Secretary's File at the Harry S. Truman Library, Independence, Missouri, contains documents on early postwar naval policymaking at the highest levels. The National Archives and Records Administration in Washington, D.C., holds some pertinent papers in RG 72 (Records of the Bureau of Aeronautics).

Two officers kindly furnished documents from their personal files: Allan P. Slaff, Naples, Florida, and T. W. Walsh, Fairfax, Virginia.

### *Oral History Collections*

Naval Historical Center, Operational Archives, Washington, DC.

Carney, Robert B. Interview by Michael A. Palmer. 2 July 1987.

*Bibliography*

Naval Weapons Center, China Lake, CA *(Copies in Operational Archives)*.

Alpers, Frederick C. (with Robert C. Fletcher). Interview by Leroy L. Doig III. 27–28 January 1981.

Hardy, John I. Interview by Albert B. Christman. 13 February 1967.

Highberg, Ivar E. Interview by Leroy L. Doig III. 1 April 1981.

Naval Weapons Center, China Lake, CA *(Copies in Navy Laboratory/Coordinating Group, Naval Surface Warfare Center, White Oak, MD)*.

Amlie, Thomas S. Interview by Michelle Ballenger. 24 August 1976.

Ekas, Claude P. Interview by Robert L. Hansen. c. 1975.

U.S. Naval Institute, Annapolis, MD *(Copies in Operational Archives)*.

Beshany, Philip A. Interview by John T. Mason, Jr. Vol. 2, 1983.

Burke, Arleigh A. Interview by John T. Mason, Jr. 1973.

Duncan, Charles K. Interview by John T. Mason, Jr. Vol. 2, 1981.

Felt, Harry D. Interview by John T. Mason, Jr. Vol. 1, 1972.

Masterson, Kleber S. Interview by John T. Mason, Jr. 1973.

Miller, George H. Interview by John T. Mason, Jr. 1975.

Peet, Raymond E. Interview by Etta-Belle Kitchen. 1984.

Reich, Eli T. Interview by John T. Mason, Jr. 1982.

Ruckner, Edward A. Interview by John T. Mason, Jr. 1977.

Sharp, U. S. Grant. Interview by Etta-Belle Kitchen. Vol. 2, 1976.

Wertheim, Robert H. Interview by John T. Mason, Jr. 1981.

Withington, Frederic S. Interview by John T. Mason, Jr. 1972.

Interviews by author.

Adamson, Robert E., Jr. 10 March 1988.

Buell, Thomas C. 7 October 1992.

Cloward, Richard. 6 July 1988.

Doyle, James H. 28 March 1988 and 10 June 1992.

Emerson, David F. 26 April 1988.

Foreman, Robert P. 28 August 1992.

Gralla, Arthur R. 22 June 1992.

Guilbault, R. G. 9 January 1988.

Hernandez, Diego E. 6 July 1988.

Holloway, James L., III. 26 May 1992 and 28 September 1992.

Hurlbut, Jay. 28 October 1987.

Kidd, Isaac C., Jr. 3 May 1988.

Manning, William J. 2 April 1993.

Metcalf, Joseph, III. 1 October 1987.

Meyer, Wayne E. 12 June 1992.

Miller, Gerald E. 1 June 1988.

Moorer, Thomas H. 26 May 1992.

Mustin, Henry C. 2 May 1988 and 27 May 1992.

Mustin, Lloyd M. 24 June 1992.

Parker, J. F. 10 June 1988.

Rodgers, Michael. 13 June 1988.

Rowden, William. 14 December 1987.

Schneider, Frederick H. 23 June 1992.

Seltzer, William. 12 and 19 June 1991.

Smith, Charles J. 10 December 1987.

Stevens, James. 27 January 1988.

Stewart, Keith. 28 October 1987.

Turner, Stansfield. 4 May 1988 and 22 January 1990.

Walters, Robert L. 17 December 1987.

Weschler, Thomas R. 24 March 1988.

Woods, Mark W. 19 April 1988.

Xefteris, Constantine. 22 January 1988.

Zumwalt, Elmo R., Jr. 20 April 1988.

### Correspondence with Author

Alexander, Richard G. 7 July 1992.

Bagley, Worth H. 27 May 1992.

Baughan, Robert L. Jr. 18 July 1992.

Beshany, Philip A. 31 October 1991.

*Bibliography*

Castle, Hal C. 22 August 1992.

Christofferson, Edward A., Jr. 16 June 1992.

Colwell, John B. 16 July 1992.

Crandall, C. N., Jr. 21 July 1992.

Crenshaw, Russell S., Jr. 19 June 1992.

Cummings, Edward J., Jr. 5 July 1992.

Cummins, Lawrence D. 4 August 1992.

Doak, Joseph J., Jr. 3 July 1992.

Duncan, Charles K. 22 August 1992.

Ekas, Claude P., Jr. 30 August 1988.

Emerson, David F. 20 August 1992.

Gayler, Noel. 22 September 1992.

Hayward, Thomas B. 2 July 1992.

Holmes, Ephraim P. 5 August 1992.

Hyland, John J. 29 June 1992.

Janney, Frederick E. 28 September 1992.

Keen, Timothy J. 3 October 1992.

Kelly, Ronald T. 7 January 1993 and 16 February 1993.

Mansfield, Jack E. 29 September 1992.

Marolda, Edward J. 29 October 1991.

Metcalf, Joseph, III. 11 August 1992.

Montgomery, William M. 28 September 1992.

Paine, Roger W., Jr. 29 October 1992.

Peniston, Robert C. 25 June 1992.

Phillips, Jewett O., Jr. 24 June 1992.

Pinney, Frank L., Jr. 10 Sep 1992.

Plate, Douglas C. 13 August 1992.

Price, Frank H., Jr. c. July 1988.

Reckner, James. 29 October 1991.

Reilly, John C. 29 October 1991.

Ries, Herbert H. 23 June 1992 and 22 October 1992.

Rivero, Horacio. 27 June 1992.

Rohwer, Jürgen. 3 March 1990.

Rossell, Robert H. 15 July 1992.

St. George, William R. 6 July 1992 and 18 January 1993.

Schneider, Frederick H., Jr. 31 July 1992, 29 December 1992, 17 February 1993, and 5 April 1993.

Semmes, Benedict J., Jr. 14 July 1992.

Shamer, Preston N. 27 September 1992.

Sharp, U. S. Grant. 22 June 1992.

Skelley, Stephen. 7 September 1992.

Slaff, Allan P. 25 June 1992.

Smith, Charles J. 15 August 1992.

Smith, Harold Page. 23 July 1992.

Strean, Bernard M. 30 January 1993.

Turner, Stansfield. 23 July 1992.

Walsh, Thomas W. 10 July 1992.

Wentworth, R. S., Jr. 28 June 1992.

Zenni, Martin M. 31 July 1992.

### *Printed Primary Sources*

Bowen, Harold G. *Ships Machinery and Mossbacks: The Autobiography of a Naval Engineer*. Princeton: Princeton University Press, 1954.

Millis, Walter, ed. *The Forrestal Diaries*. New York: Viking, 1951.

Radford, Arthur W. *From Pearl Harbor to Vietnam: The Memoirs of Admiral Arthur W. Radford*. Edited by Stephen Jurika, Jr. Stanford University: Hoover Institution Press, 1980.

U.S. Congress. Congressional Budget Office. *Naval Surface Combatants in the 1990s: Prospects and Possibilities*. Washington: GPO, 1981.

U.S. Congress. Joint Senate-House Armed Services Subcommittee of the Senate and House Armed Services Committees. *CVAN–70 Aircraft Carrier*. 91st Cong., 2d sess., 1970.

U.S. Department of the Navy. *Secretary of the Navy, Annual Report to the Secretary of Defense*. Various years.

Zumwalt, Elmo R., Jr. *On Watch: A Memoir*. New York: Quadrangle, 1976.

*Bibliography*

**Official Publications**

Operational Archives Branch, Naval Historical Center, maintains runs of the following Navy publications:

*Bulletin of Ordnance Information*

*Combat Readiness*

*Naval Ordnance Bulletin*

*NAVSEA Journal*

*ONI Review*

## Secondary Sources

**Books**

Adams, Henry H. *Witness to Power: The Life of Fleet Admiral William D. Leahy.* Annapolis: Naval Institute Press, 1985.

Albion, Robert G., and Robert H. Connery. *Forrestal and the Navy.* New York: Columbia University Press, 1962.

*Brassey's Annual, 1947, 1966, 1968, 1972, 1973, 1974.* New York: Macmillan, 1947; Praeger, 1967, 1969, 1973, 1974, 1975.

*Brassey's Defence Yearbook, 1974, 1975/76, 1987.* New York: Praeger, 1975, 1976, 1988.

Breemer, Jan. *Soviet Submarines: Design, Development and Tactics.* Coulsdon, Surrey: Jane's Information Group, 1989.

Buell, Thomas B. *The Quiet Warrior: A Biography of Admiral Raymond A. Spruance.* Annapolis: Naval Institute Press, 1987.

Cagle, Malcolm W., and Frank A. Manson. *The Sea War in Korea.* Annapolis: U.S. Naval Institute, 1957.

Carlisle, Rodney. *Powder and Propellants: Energetic Materials at Indian Head, Maryland, 1890–1990.* Washington: Naval Ordnance Station, 1990.

———. *Where the Fleet Begins: A History of the David Taylor Research Center, 1899–1987.* Rockville, MD: History Associates, 1987.

Coletta, Paolo E., ed. *American Secretaries of the Navy.* Vol. 2. Annapolis: Naval Institute Press, 1980.

———. *The United States Navy and Defense Unification, 1947–1953.* Newark: University of Delaware Press, 1981.

Condit, Doris M. *History of the Office of the Secretary of Defense.* Vol. 2, *The Test of War, 1950–1953.* Washington: Historical Office, Office of the Secretary of Defense, 1988.

Corse, Carl D., Jr. *Introduction to Shipboard Weapons*. Annapolis: Naval Institute Press, 1975.

Davis, Vincent. *The Admirals Lobby*. Chapel Hill: University of North Carolina Press, 1967.

*Dictionary of American Naval Fighting Ships*. 8 vols. Washington: Naval History Division, Naval Historical Center, 1959–1991.

Duncan, Francis. *Rickover and the Nuclear Navy: The Discipline of Technology*. Annapolis: Naval Institute Press, 1990.

Eller, Ernest M. *The Soviet Sea Challenge*. New York: Cowles, 1971.

Eskew, Garnett Laidlaw. *Cradle of Ships*. New York: G. P. Putnam's Sons, 1958.

Fairhall, David. *Russian Sea Power*. Boston: Gambit, 1971.

Frieden, David R. *Principles of Naval Weapons Systems*. Annapolis: Naval Institute Press, 1985.

Friedman, Norman. *The Naval Institute Guide to World Naval Weapons Systems*. Annapolis: Naval Institute Press, 1989.

———. *Naval Radar*. Greenwich: Conway, 1981.

———. *The Postwar Naval Revolution*. Annapolis, Naval Institute Press, 1986.

———. *U.S. Battleships: An Illustrated Design History*. Annapolis: Naval Institute Press, 1985.

———. *U.S. Cruisers: An Illustrated Design History*. Annapolis: Naval Institute Press, 1984.

———. *U.S. Destroyers: An Illustrated Design History*. Annapolis: Naval Institute Press, 1982.

———. *The US Maritime Strategy*. Annapolis: Naval Institute Press, 1988.

———. *US Naval Weapons*. London: Conway, 1983.

———. *U.S. Small Combatants: Including PT-Boats, Subchasers, and the Brown-Water Navy*. Annapolis: Naval Institute Press, 1987.

Gebhard, Louis A. *Evolution of Naval Radio-Electronics and Contributions of the Naval Research Laboratory*. NRL Report 8300. Washington: Naval Research Laboratory, 1979.

General Dynamics. *The World's Missile Systems*. 7th ed. Pomona, CA: General Dynamics, Pomona Division, 1982.

George, James L., ed. *The U.S. Navy: The View from the Mid-1980s*. Boulder, CO: Westview Press, 1985.

Gerrard-Gough, J. D., and Albert B. Christman. *History of the Naval Weapons Center, China Lake, California.* Vol. 2, *The Grand Experiment at Inyokern.* Washington: Naval History Division, 1978.

Hackmann, Willem. *Seek & Strike: Sonar, Anti-Submarine Warfare and the Royal Navy, 1914–54.* London: Her Majesty's Stationery Office, 1984.

Hallion, Richard P. *The Naval Air War in Korea.* Baltimore: The Nautical & Aviation Publishing Co. of America, 1986.

Hansen, Chuck. *US Nuclear Weapons: The Secret History.* New York: Orion, 1988.

Hartmann, Frederick H. *Naval Renaissance: The U.S. Navy in the 1980s.* Annapolis: Naval Institute Press, 1990.

Hone, Thomas C. *Power and Change: The Administrative History of the Office of the Chief of Naval Operations, 1946–1986.* Contributions to Naval History No. 2. Washington: Naval Historical Center, 1989.

Hooper, Edwin B., Dean C. Allard, and Oscar P. Fitzgerald. *The United States Navy and the Vietnam Conflict.* Vol. 1, *The Setting of the Stage to 1959.* Washington: Naval History Division, 1976.

Huisken, Ronald. *The Origin of the Strategic Cruise Missile.* New York: Praeger, 1981.

Humphrey, Sylvia G., ed. *Meeting the Challenge: A 1986 History of the Naval Surface Weapons Center.* Washington: GPO, 1987.

*Jane's All the World's Aircraft 1975–76.* New York: Jane's Publishing, 1975.

Jordan, John. *Soviet Warships: The Soviet Surface Fleet, 1960 to the Present.* Annapolis: Naval Institute Press, 1983.

Kaufmann, William W. *The McNamara Strategy.* New York: Harper & Row, 1964.

———. *Planning Conventional Forces, 1950–80.* Washington: The Brookings Institution, 1982.

Keegan, John. *The Price of Admiralty: The Evolution of Naval Warfare.* New York: Viking, 1989.

King, Randolph W., ed. *Naval Engineering and American Seapower.* Baltimore: The Nautical & Aviation Publishing Co., 1989.

Lautenschläger, Karl. *Technology and the Evolution of Naval Warfare, 1851–2001.* Lecture No. 9 of the Charles H. Davis Lecture Series. Washington: National Academy Press, 1984.

Love, Robert W., Jr., ed. *The Chiefs of Naval Operations.* Annapolis: Naval Institute Press, 1980.

———. *History of the U.S. Navy.* Vol. 2, *1942–1991.* Harrisburg, PA: Stackpole Books, 1992.

McCollum, Kenneth G., ed. *Dahlgren*. Dahlgren, VA: Naval Surface Weapons Center, 1977.

McGruther, Kenneth R. *The Evolving Soviet Navy*. Newport, RI: Naval War College Press, 1978.

Marolda, Edward J. *By Sea, Air, and Land: An Illustrated History of the U.S. Navy and the War in Southeast Asia*. Washington: Naval Historical Center, 1994.

Marolda, Edward J., and Oscar P. Fitzgerald. *The United States Navy and the Vietnam Conflict*. Vol. 2, *From Military Assistance to Combat, 1959–1965*. Washington: Naval Historical Center, 1986.

Melia, Tamara Moser. *"Damn the Torpedoes": A Short History of U.S. Naval Mine Countermeasures, 1777–1991*. Contributions to Naval History No. 4. Washington: Naval Historical Center, 1991.

Moore, John E., and Richard Compton-Hall. *Submarine Warfare: Today and Tomorrow*. Bethesda, MD: Adler & Adler, 1987.

Muir, Malcolm, Jr. *The Iowa Class Battleships: Iowa, New Jersey, Missouri & Wisconsin*. Poole, Dorset: Blandford Press, 1987.

Naval Education and Training Command. *The Weapons Officer*. NAVEDTRA 10867–C1. Washington: Naval Education and Training Program Development Center, 1982.

Naval Education and Training Program Development Center, Pensacola, FL. *Surface Ship Operations*. Washington: Naval Education and Training Support Command, 1978.

Naval Ordnance Laboratory, Corona. *From Sky to Sea: Twenty Years of Guided Missile Development at NBS and NOLC*. NOLC Report 471. Corona, CA: Naval Ordnance Laboratory, 1959.

Navy Department, Office of Information. *Weapon Systems of the United States Navy 1977*. Washington: Office of Information, 1977.

Neufeld, Jacob. *The Development of Ballistic Missiles in the United States Air Force, 1945–1960*. Washington: Office of Air Force History, 1990.

Nitze, Paul H., et al. *Securing the Seas: The Soviet Naval Challenge and Western Alliance Options*. Atlantic Council Policy Study. Boulder, CO: Westview Press, 1979.

North Atlantic Assembly. *NATO Anti-Submarine Warfare: Strategy, Requirements and the Need for Co-operation*. NP: North Atlantic Assembly, 1982.

Palmer, Michael A. *Origins of the Maritime Strategy: American Naval Strategy in the First Postwar Decade*. Contributions to Naval History No. 1. Washington: Naval Historical Center, 1988.

Polmar, Norman. *Guide to the Soviet Navy*. 3d and 4th eds. Annapolis: Naval Institute Press, 1983 and 1986.

## Bibliography

————. *The Ships and Aircraft of the U.S. Fleet.* 11th and 14th eds. Annapolis: Naval Institute Press, 1978 and 1987.

———— (ed.). *Soviet Naval Developments.* Annapolis: Nautical & Aviation Publishing Co., 1979.

Polmar, Norman, and Thomas B. Allen. *Rickover.* New York: Simon & Schuster, 1982.

Polmar, Norman, and Jurrien Noot. *Submarines of the Russian and Soviet Navies, 1718–1990.* Annapolis: Naval Institute Press, 1990.

Potter, E. B. *Admiral Arleigh Burke.* New York: Random House, 1990.

Rearden, Steven L. *History of the Office of the Secretary of Defense.* Vol. 1, *The Formative Years, 1947–1950.* Washington: Historical Office, Office of the Secretary of Defense, 1984.

Reynolds, Clark G. *Admiral John H. Towers: The Struggle for Naval Air Supremacy.* Annapolis: Naval Institute Press, 1991.

————. *Command of the Sea: The History and Strategy of Maritime Empires.* New York: William Morrow, 1974.

————. *The Fast Carriers: The Forging of an Air Navy.* New York: McGraw-Hill, 1968.

Rohwer, Jürgen. *Superpower Confrontation on the Seas: Naval Development and Strategy since 1945.* The Washington Papers, Vol. 3, No. 26. Beverly Hills: Sage Publications, 1975.

Rothenberg, Gunther. *The Anatomy of the Israeli Army.* New York: Hippocrene, 1979.

Rowland, Buford, and William B. Boyd. *U.S. Navy Bureau of Ordnance in World War II.* Washington: GPO, 1953.

Ryan, Paul B. *First Line of Defense: The U.S. Navy Since 1945.* Stanford, CA: Hoover Institute Press, 1981.

Saarlas, Maido. *Steam and Gas Turbines for Marine Propulsion.* 2d ed. Annapolis: Naval Institute Press, 1987.

Smaldone, Joseph P. *History of the White Oak Laboratory, 1945–1975.* Silver Spring, MD: Naval Surface Weapons Center, 1977.

Smith, Merritt Roe, ed. *Military Enterprise and Technological Change: Perspectives on the American Experience.* Cambridge, MA: The MIT Press, 1985.

Stefanick, Tom. *Strategic Antisubmarine Warfare and Naval Strategy.* Lexington, MA: Lexington Books, 1987.

Stockholm International Peace Research Institute. *Tactical and Strategic Antisubmarine Warfare.* Cambridge, MA: The MIT Press, 1974.

Terzibaschitsch, Stefan. *Cruisers of the US Navy, 1922–1962*. Translated by Harold Erenberg. Annapolis: Naval Institute Press, 1984.

Tritten, James J. *Declaratory Policy for the Strategic Employment of the Soviet Navy*. Santa Monica: Rand Corp., 1984.

Tyler, Patrick. *Running Critical: The Silent War, Rickover, and General Dynamics*. New York: Perennial, 1986.

Werrell, Kenneth P. *The Evolution of the Cruise Missile*. Maxwell Air Force Base, AL: Air University Press, 1985.

### *Articles*

Allard, Dean C. "An Era of Transition, 1945–1953" In *In Peace and War: Interpretations of American Naval History, 1775–1984*, 2d ed., edited by Kenneth J. Hagan. Westport, CT: Greenwood Press, 1984.

———. "Zumwalt, Elmo Russell, Jr." In *Dictionary of American Military Biography*, vol. 3, *Q–Z*, edited by Roger J. Spiller. Westport, CT: Greenwood Press, 1984.

Allison, David K. "U.S. Navy Research and Development since World War II." In *Military Enterprise and Technological Change: Perspectives on the American Experience*, edited by Merritt Roe Smith. Cambridge, MA: The MIT Press, 1985.

Amme, Carl H. "Naval Strategy and the New Frontier," U.S. Naval Institute *Proceedings* 88 (March 1962): 22–33.

*Army-Navy-Air Force Journal and Register* 100 (3 August 1963): 5.

Baker, A. D., III. "Historic Fleets." *Naval History* 7 (September/October 1993): 61.

Baldridge, Elward F. "Lebanon and Quemoy—The Navy's Role." U.S. Naval Institute *Proceedings* 87 (February 1961): 94–100.

Bannat, Steven J. Comment on "Ship-to-Ship Missiles." U.S. Naval Institute *Proceedings* 99 (November 1973): 89.

Basoco, Richard M. and Richard H. Webber. "*Kynda*-Class Missile Frigates." U.S. Naval Institute *Proceedings* 90 (September 1964): 140–42.

Bath, William G. "Terrier/Tartar: Integration and Automation of Navy Shipboard Surveillance Sensors." *Johns Hopkins APL Technical Digest* 2, no. 4 (October–December 1981): 261–65.

Bell, J. H. "USS *Bainbridge* (DLGN–25)." U.S. Naval Institute *Proceedings* 88 (November 1962): 168–70.

Benson, Roy S. "Fleet Air Defense—Vital New Role of the Cruiser." U.S. Naval Institute *Proceedings* 84 (June 1958): 46–49.

Betzer, Terry R. "Terrier/Tartar: New Threat Upgrade Program." *Johns Hopkins APL Technical Digest* 2, no. 4 (October–December 1981): 276–82.

*Bibliography*

Blades, Todd. "The Bumblebee Can Fly." *Naval History* 2 (Fall 1988): 48–52.

———. "USS *Galveston*: The First Talos Guided Missile Cruiser." In *Warship*, vol. 4, edited by John Roberts. Annapolis: Naval Institute Press, 1980.

Blandy, W.H.P. "The Future Value of Sea Power." *Transactions of The Society of Naval Architects and Marine Engineers* 55 (1947): 495–98.

Boehe, Rolf. "Modern Warships for Combat in Coastal Waters." In *R.U.S.I. and Brassey's Defence Yearbook, 1975/75*, edited by The Royal United Services Institute for Defence Studies. Boulder, CO: Westview Press, 1975.

Bowling, R. A. "Naval Warfare Specialists." U.S. Naval Institute *Proceedings* 96 (August 1970): 53–59.

Boyd, Carl. "Radford, Arthur William." In *Dictionary of American Military Biography*, vol. 3, *Q–Z*, edited by Roger J. Spiller. Westport, CT: Greenwood Press, 1984.

Brandenburg, Robert L. "Destroyer Command: Critical ASW Subsystem." U.S. Naval Institute *Proceedings* 90 (July 1964): 36–43.

———. "USS *Bainbridge* Is Not the Answer." U.S. Naval Institute *Proceedings* 90 (January 1964): 36–43.

Brinckloe, W. D. "Is the Versatile Line Officer Obsolete?" U.S. Naval Institute *Proceedings* 85 (June 1959): 26–33.

———. "Missile Navy." U.S. Naval Institute *Proceedings* 84 (February 1958): 23–29.

Brockett, W. A., G. L. Graves, M. R. Hauschildt, and J. W. Sawyer. "U.S. Navy's Marine Gas Turbines." *Naval Engineers Journal* 78, no. 2 (April 1966): 217–23.

Brown, Charles R., and Charles F. Meyer. "The Talos Continuous-Rod Warhead." *Johns Hopkins APL Technical Digest* 3, no. 2 (April–June 1982): 157–59.

Buchan, Alastair. "The United States and the 'New Look.'" In *Brassey's Annual: The Armed Forces Year-Book 1954*, edited by H. G. Thursfield. New York: Macmillan, 1954.

Bucknell, Howard. Comment on "Aftermath of the *Elath*." U.S. Naval Institute *Proceedings* 96 (March 1970): 87–88.

Burke, Kip. "Farewell to the Backbone of the Fleet: DDG 2." *Surface Warfare* 18 (May/June 1993): 18–21.

Bustard, M. E. "USS *King* (DLG–10)." U.S. Naval Institute *Proceedings* 87 (March 1961): 161–66.

Cagle, Malcolm W. "Sea Power and Limited War." U.S. Naval Institute *Proceedings* 84 (July 1958): 22–27.

Calhoun, C. R. "The Destroyer—Key Ship of the Fleet." U.S. Naval Institute *Proceedings* 85 (February 1959): 46–51.

Carey, L. D. "USS *Henry B. Wilson* (DDG–7)." U.S. Naval Institute *Proceedings* 87 (July 1961): 152–54.

Carney, Robert B. "Always the Sea." U.S. Naval Institute *Proceedings* 81 (May 1955): 497–503.

Carrison, Daniel J. "Defense Against Nuclear Attack at Sea." U.S. Naval Institute *Proceedings* 90 (May 1964): 35–43.

———. "Reserves—What Kind?" U.S. Naval Institute *Proceedings* 81 (May 1955): 528–33.

Cavanaugh, Robert B. "The ASW Effort." U.S. Naval Institute *Proceedings* 90 (February 1964): 140–145.

Coletta, Paolo E. "Francis P. Matthews." In *American Secretaries of the Navy*, vol. 2, *1913–1972*, edited by Paolo E. Coletta. Annapolis: Naval Institute Press, 1980.

———. "John Lawrence Sullivan." In *American Secretaries of the Navy*, vol. 2, *1913–1972*, edited by Paolo E. Coletta. Annapolis: Naval Institute Press, 1980.

Colvin, Robert D. "Aftermath of the *Elath*." U.S. Naval Institute *Proceedings* 95 (October 1969): 60–67.

Craig, J. Laurence. "USS *Northampton* (CLC–1)." U.S. Naval Institute *Proceedings* 86 (July 1960): 154–58.

Crenshaw, Russell S., Jr. "Why We Are Losing Our Junior Officers." U.S. Naval Institute *Proceedings* 83 (February 1957): 127–32.

Croy, Casey. "Harpoon Celebrates Its First 20 Years as MDMSC's Premier Missile." *Vision: McDonnell Douglas Missile Systems Company* 3 (24 June 1991): 1–5.

Danis, A. L. "Offensive ASW: Fundamental to Defense." U.S. Naval Institute *Proceedings* 83 (June 1957): 583–89.

Dean, Frank A. "The Unified Talos." *Johns Hopkins APL Technical Digest* 3, no. 2 (April–June 1982): 123–25.

Dobbins, Billy D., and George W. Luke. "From Kamikaze to Aegis: An Introduction." *Johns Hopkins APL Technical Digest* 2, no. 4 (October–December 1981): 233–37.

Dombroff, S. "Don't Misuse New Destroyers." U.S. Naval Institute *Proceedings* 88 (November 1962): 143–45.

Donko, Wilhelm. "The USS *Long Beach* after Her 'Mid Life' Conversion." In *Warship*, vol. 10, edited by Andrew Lambert. Annapolis: Naval Institute Press, 1986.

Duke, William L. "DD 963 Class Combat System Installation and Testing." *Naval Engineers Journal* 91, no. 1 (February 1979): 33–41.

Eaton, Alvin R. "Bumblebee Missile Aerodynamic Design: A Constant in a Changing World." *Johns Hopkins APL Technical Digest* 13, no. 1 (January–March 1992): 69–81.

*Bibliography*

Eckhart, M., Jr., "'The Wit to See.'" U.S. Naval Institute *Proceedings* 90 (August 1964): 34–41.

Effron, Herbert M. "8"/55 Major Caliber Lightweight Gun: Big Punch for Small Ships." U.S. Naval Institute *Proceedings* 101 (December 1975): 91–93.

Eliot, Christian J. "Ship-to-Ship Missiles." U.S. Naval Institute *Proceedings* 98 (November 1972): 108–114.

Emch, George F. "Air Defense for the Fleet." *Johns Hopkins APL Technical Digest* 13, no. 1 (January–March 1992): 39–56.

Emch, George F., and Glenn I. Kirkland. "Search Radar Automation: AN/SYS–1 and Beyond." *Johns Hopkins APL Technical Digest* 13, no. 1 (January–March 1992): 90–100.

Fahy, Edward J. "Pushbuttons Need Men." U.S. Naval Institute *Proceedings* 75 (February 1949): 148–53.

Featherston, Frank H. "P. G. School." U.S. Naval Institute *Proceedings* 89 (December 1963): 62–71.

Ferris, Laurence, W., Richard A. Frey, and James L. Mills, Jr. "The Ship Launched Projectile." *Naval Engineers Journal* 75, no. 1 (February 1963): 93–102.

Flanagan, James D., and George W. Luke. "Aegis: Newest Line of Navy Defense." *Johns Hopkins APL Technical Digest* 2, no. 4 (October–December 1981): 237–42.

Flanagan, James D., and William N. Sweet. "Aegis: Advanced Surface Missile System." *Johns Hopkins APL Technical Digest* 2, no. 4 (October–December 1981): 243–45.

Flynn, William J. "Comment on 'The Unfaced Challenge, Submarine Versus Free World'" U.S. Naval Institute *Proceedings* 90 (August 1964): 112–16.

Foster, W. F. "The Naval Aviator Speaks." U.S. Naval Institute *Proceedings* 90 (May 1964): 140–43.

Fowden, W.M.M., Jr., R. R. Peterson, and J. W. Sawyer. "The Gas Turbine as a Prime Mover on U.S. Naval Ships." *Naval Engineers Journal* 66, no. 1 (February 1954): 109–124.

Friedman, Norman. "Amphibious Fire Support: Post War Development." In *Warship*, vol. 4, edited by John Roberts. Annapolis: Naval Institute Press, 1980.

———. "Elmo Russell Zumwalt, Jr." In *The Chiefs of Naval Operations*, edited by Robert W. Love, Jr. Annapolis: Naval Institute Press, 1980.

———. "The '3–T' Programme." In *Warship*, vol. 4, edited by John Roberts. Annapolis: Naval Institute Press, 1982.

———. "The US Command Cruiser." In *Warship*, vol. 5, edited by John Roberts. Annapolis: Naval Institute Press, 1981.

———. "USS *Worcester*." In *Warship*, vol. 4, edited by John Roberts. Annapolis: Naval Institute Press, 1980.

Galdorisi, George. "Déjà Vu All Over Again." U.S. Naval Institute *Proceedings* 114 (January 1988): 106–7.

Gallery, Philip D. "A Few Ideas of a Cruiser Skipper." U.S. Naval Institute *Proceedings* 81 (July 1955): 784–87.

Gallotta, Albert A. Jr. "Navy EW and C3CM." In *Naval Tactical Command and Control*, edited by Gordon R. Nagler. Washington: AFCEA International Press, c. 1985.

Garten, William, Jr. and Frank A. Dean. "Evolution of the Talos Missile." *Johns Hopkins APL Technical Digest* 3, no. 2 (April–June 1982): 116–22.

George, H. C. Comment on "Surface Warfare Officers." U.S. Naval Institute *Proceedings* 102 (November 1976): 75–76.

Gerber, Ralph. "The Choice of a Career within the Navy." U.S. Naval Institute *Proceedings* 79 (June 1953): 620–27.

Glennon, Allan N. "An Approach to ASW." U.S. Naval Institute *Proceedings* 90 (September 1964): 48–55.

Goss, Wilbur H. "Talos in Retrospect." *Johns Hopkins APL Technical Digest* 3, no. 2 (April–June 1982): 116.

Gray, Donald D. A. "The Talos Shipboard Test Program." *Johns Hopkins APL Technical Digest* 3, no. 2 (April–June 1982): 167–69.

Graybar, Lloyd J. "The Buck Rogers of the Navy: Admiral William H. P. Blandy." *New Interpretations in Naval History: Selected Papers from the Ninth Naval History Symposium Held at the United States Naval Academy, 18–20 October 1989*, edited by William R. Roberts and Jack Sweetman. Annapolis: Naval Institute Press, 1991.

Green, Laurence B., and John H. Burt. "Massive Retaliation: Salvation or—?" U.S. Naval Institute *Proceedings* 84 (October 1958): 23–28.

Grzymala, T. C. Comment on "The Surface Line Officer." U.S. Naval Institute *Proceedings* 98 (January 1973): 87–89.

Gussow, Milton, and Edward C. Prettyman. "Typhon—A Weapon System Ahead of Its Time." *Johns Hopkins APL Technical Digest* 13, no. 1 (January–March 1992): 82–89.

Hannon, E. J., Jr., "Destroyers in Their Sixtieth Year." U.S. Naval Institute *Proceedings* 88 (November 1962): 138–42.

Hart, Raymond J. "Surface Warfare Officers: The Need for Professionalism." U.S. Naval Institute *Proceedings* 102 (June 1976): 38–44.

*Bibliography*

Hatch, Ross R., Joseph L. Luber, and James H. Walker. "Fifty Years of Strike Warfare Research at the Applied Physics Laboratory." *Johns Hopkins APL Technical Digest* 13, no. 1 (January–March 1992): 113–23.

Hay, James C. "The Attack Submarine." In *The U.S. Navy: The View from the Mid-1980s*, edited by J. L. George. Boulder, CO: Westview Press, 1985.

Hayes, Morris L. "Nuclear Propulsion: We Dare Not Delay." U.S. Naval Institute *Proceedings* 91 (January 1965): 26–36.

Heinl, Robert D., Jr. "The Gun Gap and How to Close It." U.S. Naval Institute *Proceedings* 91 (September 1965): 26–36.

Hertel, Frank M. "The Naval Academy and Naval Aviation." U.S. Naval Institute *Proceedings* 74 (January 1948): 37–41.

Hessler, William H. "The Battleship Paid Dividends." U.S. Naval Institute *Proceedings* 72 (September 1946): 1143–54.

Hewish, Mark. "Weapon Systems: Gabriel." U.S. Naval Institute *Proceedings* 102 (July 1976): 101.

———. "Weapon Systems: Harpoon." U.S. Naval Institute *Proceedings* 103 (February 1977): 102.

Hitchcock, John H. "Discrimination in Selections: Fact or Fancy?" U.S. Naval Institute *Proceedings* 86 (September 1960): 72–75.

Holloway, James L., Jr. "The Holloway Plan—A Summary View and Commentary." U.S. Naval Institute *Proceedings* 73 (November 1947): 1293–1303.

Hubbard, Miles H. "The Design of Naval Weapons." U.S. Naval Institute *Proceedings* 91 (October 1965): 38–45.

Hughes, W. P. "The Split-Level Bridge." U.S. Naval Institute *Proceedings* 88 (May 1962): 68–77.

Hyatt, W. Coleman. "Fleet Air Defense: Countermeasures." *Johns Hopkins APL Technical Digest* 13, no. 1 (January-March 1992): 101–9.

"I Wish I Had More Time to Give." *Surface Warfare* 18 (July/August 1993): 23.

James, Ralph K. "The Ships of '73." U.S. Naval Institute *Proceedings* 89 (January 1963): 95–103.

Jensen, Wayne L. "Helicopters in Antisubmarine Warfare." U.S. Naval Institute *Proceedings* 89 (July 1963): 36–41.

Jordan, John. "USS *California*." In *Warship*, vol. 2, edited by Anthony Preston. Annapolis: Naval Institute Press, 1978.

Katzenbach, Edward L., Jr. "The Demotion of Professionalism: The War Colleges." U.S. Naval Institute *Proceedings* 91 (March 1965): 34–41.

Kehoe, James W., and Kenneth S. Brower. "Warship Design in the Future." In *The U.S. Navy: The View from the Mid-1980s*, edited by J. L. George. Boulder, CO: Westview Press, 1985.

Keirsey, James L. "Airbreathing Propulsion for Defense of the Surface Fleet." *Johns Hopkins APL Technical Digest* 13, no. 1 (January–March 1992): 57–67.

Kelly, Robert B. "The Education of the Line." U.S. Naval Institute *Proceedings* 85 (December 1959): 48–52.

Kennedy, Floyd D., Jr. "The Creation of the Cold War Navy, 1953–1962." In *In Peace and War: Interpretations of American Naval History, 1775–1984*, 2d ed., edited by Kenneth J. Hagan. Westport, CT: Greenwood Press, 1984.

———. "David Lamar McDonald." In *The Chiefs of Naval Operations*, edited by Robert W. Love, Jr. Annapolis: Naval Institute Press, 1980.

Kennedy, Gerald. "William Morrow Fechteler." In *The Chiefs of Naval Operations*, edited by Robert W. Love, Jr. Annapolis: Naval Institute Press, 1980.

Kidd, Isaac C., Jr. "The Surface Fleet." In *The U.S. Navy: The View from the Mid-1980s*, edited by J. L. George. Boulder, CO: Westview Press, 1985.

Knox, Robert J. "The Twentieth Century Clermont." *Journal of the American Society of Naval Engineers* 66, no. 1 (February 1954): 42–47.

———. "Twentieth Century Clermont's First Cruise." *Journal of the American Society of Naval Engineers* 68, no. 2 (May 1956): 245–54.

Korb, Lawrence J. "The Erosion of American Naval Preeminence, 1962–1978." In *In Peace and War: Interpretations of American Naval History, 1775–1984*, 2d ed., edited by Kenneth J. Hagan. Westport, CT: Greenwood Press, 1984.

Kossiakoff, Alexander. "APL—Expanding the Limits." *Johns Hopkins APL Technical Digest* 13, no. 1 (January–March 1992): 8–14.

Laning, R. B. "The *Seawolf*: Going to Sea." *Naval History* 6 (Summer 1992): 55–58.

Larson, D. R. "The Surface Line Officer: Some Conn, Some Can't." U.S. Naval Institute *Proceedings* 98 (July 1972): 42–49.

Le Bailly, Louis. "The Need for NATO Maritime Forces." In *R.U.S.I. and Brassey's Defence Yearbook 1976/77*, edited by The Royal United Services Institute for Defence Studies. Boulder, CO: Westview Press, 1976.

Leopold, Reuven. "Surface Warships for the Early Twenty-First Century." In *Problems of Sea Power as We Approach the Twenty-First Century: A Conference Sponsored by the American Enterprise Institute for Public Policy Research*, edited by James L. George. Washington: American Enterprise Institute for Public Policy Research, 1978.

Lewis, D. D. "The Problems of Obsolescence." U.S. Naval Institute *Proceedings* 85 (October 1959): 26–31.

*Bibliography*

Lofton, Edgar K. "A Modern Navy for Modern Defense." U.S. Naval Institute *Proceedings* 86 (November 1960): 56–61.

McCain, John S., Jr. "Where Do We Go from Here?" U.S. Naval Institute *Proceedings* 75 (January 1949): 46–51.

McDonald, J. Kenneth. "Thomas Hinman Moorer." In *The Chiefs of Naval Operations*, edited by Robert W. Love, Jr. Annapolis: Naval Institute Press, 1980.

McGoldrick, R. T. "Rudder-Excited Hull Vibration on USS *Forrest Sherman* (DD 931). . . (A Problem in Hydroelasticity)." *Transactions of The Society of Naval Architects and Marine Engineers* 67 (1959): 341–53.

McGrath, Thomas D. "Antisubmarine Defense Group ALFA." U.S. Naval Institute *Proceedings* 85 (August 1959): 49–55.

———. "Submarine Defense." U.S. Naval Institute *Proceedings* 87 (July 1961): 36–45.

MccGwire, Michael K. "The Background to Russian Naval Policy." In *Brassey's Annual: The Armed Forces Yearbook 1968*, edited by J. L. Moulton, et al. New York: Praeger, 1969.

———. "Comparative Warship Building Programs." In *Soviet Naval Developments: Capability and Context: Papers Relating to Russia's Maritime Interests*, edited by Michael MccGwire. Halifax, NS: Centre for Foreign Policy Studies, 1973.

McHugh, Francis J. "Gaming at the Naval War College." U.S. Naval Institute *Proceedings* 90 (March 1964): 48–55.

Mack, William P. "The Exercise of Broad Command: Still the Navy's Top Specialty." U.S. Naval Institute *Proceedings* 83 (April 1957): 370–75.

McNulty, J. F. "Naval Destroyer School." U.S. Naval Institute *Proceedings* 92 (April 1966): 156–62.

Madouse, Richard L. "Surface Ship Overhauls." U.S. Naval Institute *Proceedings* 92 (February 1966): 26–33.

Massey, Robert J. "The First Hundred Days of the New Frontier." U.S. Naval Institute *Proceedings* 87 (August 1961): 26–39.

Matson, W. A. "Seven Year Itch." U.S. Naval Institute *Proceedings* 84 (April 1958): 75–79.

May, Robert E. "Digital Computers in Weapons Control." U.S. Naval Institute *Proceedings* 90 (January 1964): 126–28.

Meller, R. "The Harpoon Missile System." *International Defense Review* 8, no. 1 (February 1975): 60–66.

Meyer, W. E. Comment on "Cruise Missile: The Ship Killer." U.S. Naval Institute *Proceedings* 102 (October 1976): 94.

Misa, Thomas J. "Military Needs, Commercial Realities, and the Development of the Transistor, 1948–1958." In *Military Enterprise and Technological Change: Perspectives on the American Experience*, edited by Merritt Roe Smith. Cambridge, MA: The MIT Press, 1985.

Moore, Granville A. "The Naval War College Takes a New Look at Its Courses." U.S. Naval Institute *Proceedings* 81 (January 1955): 68–73.

Morgan, Edward A. "The DASH Weapons System." U.S. Naval Institute *Proceedings* 89 (January 1963): 150–52.

Moulton, J. L. "NATO and the Atlantic." In *Brassey's Annual, 1973*. New York: Praeger, 1974.

Muir, Malcolm, Jr. "The United States Navy in World War II: An Assessment." In *Reevaluating Major Naval Combatants of World War II*, edited by James J. Sadkovich. Contributions in Military Studies No. 92. New York: Greenwood Press, 1990.

Neilsen, Christian K., Jr. "A Summary of Controllable Pitch Propeller Systems Employed by the U. S. Navy." *Naval Engineers Journal* 86, no. 2 (April 1974): 81–90.

Nelson, Andrew G. "A Black-Shoe in a Brown-Shoe World." U.S. Naval Institute *Proceedings* 96 (July 1970): 57–59.

Nimitz, Chester W. "The Future Employment of Naval Forces." In *Ironclad to Trident: 100 Years of Defence Commentary: Brassey's 1886–1986*, edited by Bryan Ranft. London: Brassey's Defence Publications, 1986.

Oliver, J. D., and A. W. Slifer. "Evaluating the DDG." U.S. Naval Institute *Proceedings* 91 (July 1965): 78–86.

Oliver, Marion E. "Terrier/Tartar: Pacing the Threat." *Johns Hopkins APL Technical Digest* 2, no. 4 (October–December 1981): 256–60.

Oliver, Marion E., and William N. Sweet. "Standard Missile: The Common Denominator." *Johns Hopkins APL Technical Digest* 2, no. 4 (October–December 1981): 283–88.

O'Neil, William D., III. "Gun Systems? For Air Defense?" U.S. Naval Institute *Proceedings* 97 (March 1971): 44–55.

Parke, Everett A. "The Unique and Vital DER." U.S. Naval Institute *Proceedings* 86 (February 1960): 88–93.

Pawlisch, Hans S. "Operation Praying Mantis: The Revenge of the *Samuel B. Roberts* Incident." *Pull Together* 28, no. 1 (Spring/Summer 1989): 5–9.

Peet, Raymond E. "Comments on the *Bainbridge*." U.S. Naval Institute *Proceedings* 89 (July 1963): 90–103.

Phillips, Chester C. "Battle Group Operations: War at Sea." *Johns Hopkins APL Technical Digest* 2, no. 4 (October–December 1981): 299–301.

331

Ponton, George E. "Fuel Oil System Design for the Gas Turbine Powered DD 963 Class Destroyers." *Naval Engineers Journal* 86, no. 1 (February 1974): 71–76.

Raborn, William F. "New Horizons of Naval Research and Development." U.S. Naval Institute *Proceedings* 89 (January 1963): 41–47.

Rahill, Gerald W. "Destroyer Duty." U.S. Naval Institute *Proceedings* 78 (October 1952): 1080–89.

Rains, Dean A., and Ronald J. d'Arcy. "Considerations in the DD 963 Propulsion System Design." *Naval Engineers Journal* 84, no. 4 (August 1972): 65–77.

Rairden, P. W. "What Is a Line Officer?" U.S. Naval Institute *Proceedings* 80 (January 1954): 53–55.

Reynolds, Clark G. "Forrest Percival Sherman." In *The Chiefs of Naval Operations*, edited by Robert W. Love, Jr. Annapolis: Naval Institute Press, 1980.

Robinson, Elmer D. "The Talos Ship System." *Johns Hopkins APL Technical Digest* 3, no. 2 (April–June 1982): 162–66.

Rohwer, Jürgen. "The Confrontation of the Superpowers at Sea." In *R.U.S.I. and Brassey's Defence Yearbook, 1974*. New York: Praeger, 1975.

Rosenberg, David A. "Arleigh Albert Burke." In *The Chiefs of Naval Operations*, edited by Robert W. Love, Jr. Annapolis: Naval Institute Press, 1980.

———. "Burke, Arleigh Albert." In *Dictionary of American Military Biography*, vol. 1, *A–G*, edited by Roger J. Spiller. Westport, CT: Greenwood Press, 1984.

Ruhe, William J. "Cruise Missile: The Ship Killer." U.S. Naval Institute *Proceedings* 102 (June 1976): 45–52.

Sacks, Harold H. "Shoreside Checkout for Seagoing Destroyer Officers." U.S. Naval Institute *Proceedings* 88 (February 1962): 58–67.

Salzer, Robert S. "The Surface Forces." U.S. Naval Institute *Proceedings* 102 (November 1976): 26–35.

Scheina, Robert L. "Search for a Mission." In *Naval Engineering and American Seapower*, edited by Randolph W. King. Baltimore: The Nautical & Aviation Publishing Co., 1989.

Schofield, Brian B. "The Role of the NATO Navies in War." U.S. Naval Institute *Proceedings* 87 (April 1961): 65–69.

Schratz, Paul R. "Robert Bostwick Carney." In *The Chiefs of Naval Operations*, edited by Robert W. Love, Jr. Annapolis: Naval Institute Press, 1980.

Seitz, Frank C., Jr. and Theodore F. Davis. "From Cockpit to Bridge." U.S. Naval Institute *Proceedings* 114 (January 1988): 53–56.

Shade, Robert J. "Marriage of Necessity." U.S. Naval Institute *Proceedings* 116 (August 1990): 31–35.

Shepherd, P. M. "The Black Shoe: Back in Fashion." U.S. Naval Institute *Proceedings*, 100 (December 1974): 38–41.

Shepherd, Pat. Comment on "The Surface Forces." U.S. Naval Institute *Proceedings*, 103 (March 1977): 77–78.

Slaff, Allan P. "Time for Decision." U.S. Naval Institute *Proceedings* 82 (August 1956): 809–13.

Smallwood, Frederick K. Comment on "The Surface Line Officer." U.S. Naval Institute *Proceedings* 98 (January 1973): 89–90.

Smedberg, William R., III, "Manning the Future Fleets." U.S. Naval Institute *Proceedings* 89 (January 1963): 121–29.

Smith, Donald A. "USS *Garcia* (DE–1040)." U.S. Naval Institute *Proceedings* 91 (September 1965): 160–62.

Smith, Robert H. "Vital Goal—A Workable Navy." U.S. Naval Institute *Proceedings* 91 (June 1965): 60–67.

Smith, Roy C., IV. "Wanted: A Surface Line School for Junior Officers." U.S. Naval Institute *Proceedings* 89 (November 1963): 129–31.

Soper, James B. "Naval Gunfire: Today and Tomorrow." U.S. Naval Institute *Proceedings* 92 (September 1966): 52–59.

Stillwell, Paul. "Battleships for the 1980s: Symbol and Substance." In *The U.S. Navy: The View from the Mid-1980s*, edited by J. L. George. Boulder, CO: Westview Press, 1985.

Stone, Norman L. "Naval Electronic Combat." In *Naval Tactical Command and Control*, edited by Gordon R. Nagler. Washington: AFCEA International Press, c. 1985.

Stryker, J. W. "The Battleship as an Auxiliary Supply Ship." U.S. Naval Institute *Proceedings* 73 (October 1947): 1181–84.

Stull, John O. "Guns Have Not Gone Yet!" U.S. Naval Institute *Proceedings* 90 (April 1964): 81–85.

Stumpf, David K. "Blasts from the Past." U.S. Naval Institute *Proceedings* 119 (April 1993): 60–64.

*Surface SITREP* 7, no. 2 (May 1991): 2.

Taylor, LeRoy. "Naval Operations in Confined Waters and Narrow Seas." U.S. Naval Institute *Proceedings* 86 (June 1960): 55–60.

Terzibaschitsch, Stefan, "Mothball Fleet: The United States 'Naval Inactive Ships Maintenance Facilities.'" In *Warship*, vol. 11, edited by Andrew Lambert. Annapolis: Naval Institute Press, 1987.

Turner, Stansfield. "Missions of the U.S. Navy." *Naval War College Review* 26, no. 5 (March–April 1974), 2–17.

## Bibliography

"USS *Saint Paul* (CA–73)," U.S. Naval Institute *Proceedings* 86 (May 1960): 159–61.

Walker, J. R. "Air-to-Surface Weapons." In *Weapons and Warfare: Conventional Weapons and Their Roles in Battle*, edited by K. Perkins. London: Brassey's, 1987.

Wall, Patrick. "The Missile in Sea Warfare." In *Brassey's Annual: The Armed Forces Yearbook 1968*, edited by J. L. Moulton, et al. New York: Praeger, 1969.

Walters, R. L. "Letter to Members." *Surface SITREP* 4, no. 2 (March 1988): 1–4.

Weschler, Thomas R. "DX/DXG Program." *Naval Engineers Journal* 79, no. 6 (December 1967): 930–35.

Wheeler, Rexford V., and Sheldon H. Kinney. "The Promotion of Career Officers." U.S. Naval Institute *Proceedings* 80 (June 1954): 637–46.

Withington, Frederic G. "The Outcome of the Electronic Revolution in the Navy." U.S. Naval Institute *Proceedings* 89 (November 1963): 66–75.

Wright, Christopher C. "*Albany* (CG–10) and *Chicago* (CG–11) Leave the Active Fleet." *Warship International* 20, no. 1 (1983): 75–81.

———. "The Tall Ladies: *Columbus, Albany* & *Chicago*." *Warship International* 14, no. 2 (1977): 104–32.

Xydis, Stephen G. "The Genesis of the Sixth Fleet, U.S. Naval Institute *Proceedings* 84 (August 1958): 40–50.

Yates, William K. "Tactics Revival at the Naval War College." *Naval War College Review* (November–December 1973): 11–15.

Young, Harold L. "Techniques and Practices in Recent Naval Steam Turbine Construction." *Journal of the American Society of Naval Engineers* 71, no. 4 (November 1959): 711–17.

Zikmund, Joseph. "James V. Forrestal 19 May 1944–17 September 1947." In *American Secretaries of the Navy*, vol. 2, *1913–1972*, edited by Paolo E. Coletta. Annapolis: Naval Institute Press, 1980.

Zumwalt, Elmo R., Jr. "A Course for Destroyers." U.S. Naval Institute *Proceedings* 88 (November 1962): 26–39.

### Unpublished Papers and Dissertations

Berghoefer, Fred G. "Over-the-Horizon Targeting Alternatives." CNA paper prepared for the Office of Naval Research, Center for Naval Analyses, September 1977.

Bruins, Berend Derk. "U.S. Naval Bombardment Missiles, 1940–1958: A Study of the Weapons Innovation Process." Ph.D. dissertation, Columbia University, 1981.

Doyle, James H., and Wayne E. Meyer. "Cruisers." Draft paper, 9 March 1992.

———. "Destroyers." Draft paper, 29 August 1991.

————. "Management and Support of Aegis Cruisers and Destroyers." Draft paper, 21 April 1991.

Mahinske, Edmund B., Joseph S. Stoutenburgh, and Erick N. Swenson. "NTDS: A Chapter in Naval History." ASNE Day Papers, 1988.

Rosenberg, David A., and Harlan K. Ullman. "Project 'Sixty': Landmark or Land-mine—An Evaluation." Draft paper, c. 1982.

Sokolsky, Joel Jeffrey. "Seapower in the Nuclear Age: NATO as a Maritime Alliance." Ph.D. dissertation, Harvard University, 1986.

Wilson, Desmond P., and Nicholas Brown. "Warfare at Sea: Threat of the Seventies." CNA Professional Paper No. 79, Center for Naval Analyses, 4 November 1971.

## Conference Addresses

Lewis, Fred L. Remarks at the Surface Navy Convention, Arlington, VA, 22 April 1988.

Michaelis, Frederick H. Remarks at the 83d Annual Banquet of The Society of Naval Architects and Marine Engineers, 14 November 1975. Published in *Transactions of The Society of Naval Architects and Marine Engineers* 83 (1975): 20–21.

Middendorf, J. William. Remarks at the Science and the Future Navy Symposium, National Academy of Sciences, Washington, 1977.

Mustin, Henry C. Remarks at the Surface Navy Convention, Arlington, VA, 22 April 1988.

Nitze, Paul H. Remarks at the Joint Session of the National War College and Industrial College of the Armed Forces, 16 March 1964. Published in the U.S. Naval Institute *Proceedings* 90 (July 1964): 160–66.

Nyquist, John W. Remarks at the Surface Navy Convention, Arlington, VA, 22 April 1988.

Pittenger, Richard F. Remarks at the Surface Navy Convention, Arlington, VA, 22 April 1988.

Polmar, Norman. Remarks at the American Military Institute, Naval Historical Center, Washington, 9 April 1988.

Rosenberg, David. Remarks at the U.S. Military Academy Symposium, West Point, NY, 14 April 1988.

Svendsen, Edward C., and Donald L. Ream. "Design of a Real-Time Data Processing System." Paper presented at International Federation for Information Processing, IFIP Congress 65, New York City, 29 May 1965.

————. "What's Different about the Hardware in Tactical Military Systems." Paper presented at the National Computer Conference, 1973.

*Bibliography*

Walsh, Ray W. Remarks at the Surface Navy Convention, Arlington, VA, 22 April 1988.

Zumwalt, Elmo R., Jr., "Remarks at the Annual Banquet of the SNAME; 12 November 1970." Published in *Transactions of The Society of Naval Architects and Marine Engineers* 78 (1970): 45–48.

336

# Index